CROSSING HORIZONS

Crossing Horizons

WORLD, SELF, AND LANGUAGE
IN INDIAN AND WESTERN THOUGHT

Shlomo Biderman

TRANSLATED BY ORNAN ROTEM

COLUMBIA UNIVERSITY PRESS   NEW YORK

Columbia University Press
Publishers Since 1893
New York Chichester, West Sussex
Copyright © 2008 Columbia University Press

Library of Congress Cataloging-in-Publication Data
Biderman, Shlomo.
Crossing horizons : world, self, and language in Indian and Western
thought / Shlomo Biderman; translated by Ornan Rotem.
p. cm.
Includes bibliographical references and index.
ISBN 978-0-231-14024-9 (cloth : alk. paper)
ISBN 978-0-231-51159-9 (e-book)
1. Philosophy, Comparative. 2. Philosophy, Indic. 3. Self (Philosophy)
4. Transcendence (Philosophy) 5. Language and languages—Philosophy.
I. Title.
B799.B53   2008
181'.4—dc22   2007029930

∞
Casebound editions of Columbia University Press books
are printed on permanent and durable acid-free paper.

Printed in the United States of America
Designed by Audrey Smith

c 10 9 8 7 6 5 4 3 2 1

To Israela, Shai, Uri, Tamar, Yaron, and Yael

CONTENTS

Acknowledgments   *ix*

Introduction   1

1. Far and Beyond: Transcendence in Two Cultures   13

2. One Language, Many Things: On the Origins of Language   75

3. My-Self: Descartes and Early Upaniṣads on the Self   119

4. No-Self: Kant, Kafka, and Nāgārjuna on the Disappearing Self   175

5. "It's All in the Mind": Berkeley, Vasubandhu, and the World
   Out There   241

Notes   *313*
Bibliographical Notes   *329*
Index   *347*

ACKNOWLEDGMENTS

I have spent many years contemplating, teaching, and researching comparative philosophy and philosophy in general, and during this period I have never ceased conversing with two colleagues at Tel Aviv University, Yoav Ariel and Ben-Ami Scharfstein: teachers, friends, and confidants. Not only did Ben-Ami Scharfstein found Tel Aviv University's Department of Philosophy, he also established, single-handedly, the department's engagement with the philosophical cultures of India, China, and Japan and, significantly, he managed to place this activity at the center of international academic notice. Yoav Ariel has always been a bountiful source of philosophical inspiration, forever overflowing with original ideas, novel points of view, and challenging responses. No words can adequately express my gratitude for these qualities and for his friendship too.

Ornan Rotem is present in nearly every possible way in this book. His rare combining of Buddhological scholarship, Western philosophical training, and inimitable originality as a philosopher and an artist has made him a unique interlocutor, which has considerably influenced the development and formation of this book. He has closely followed the Hebrew manuscript from its inception to publication. He then undertook the job of its rendering to English, and his exceptional linguistic capabilities make the translation surpass the original. Without his constant intellectual involvement during the writing of the original as well as the translation, it is doubtful whether this book would have matured as it has. I thank him for this.

Sue Hamilton meticulously went through the final version of the book and made many helpful and important suggestions. Her input has often steered me away from error. Zvi Tauber has been for me a constant source of philosophical knowledge and wisdom. Shaul Mishal has given helpful advice and vigorous encouragement. The three anonymous readers of Columbia University Press made many useful comments, most of which I have incorporated. Wendy Lochner, editor at Columbia University Press, has been supportive all along, a source of encouragement and motivation. Susan Pensak edited the book with great wisdom and skill, sensitive to both argument and structure and, equally, to nuances and detail. I am grateful to them all.

I would like to dedicate this book, with boundless love, to my family: Israela, Shai, Uri, Tamar, Yaron, and Yael.

CROSSING HORIZONS

Introduction

This book sets itself the task of examining and comparing the views, outlooks, and attitudes of two distinct cultures. However, its purpose is neither to offer a bird's-eye view of these cultures nor to gaze at them from the privileged point of view of some disinterested ideal spectator. On the contrary, the book as a whole is imbued by the author's philosophical outlook and intellectual convictions, which are, in this case, distinctly Western (as they are commonly—and perhaps inaccurately— referred to). In adopting the comparative method to examine Indian and Western philosophical views it is not my intention to cast myself into an apparent or hidden "extracultural wasteland." Instead, the comparative gaze functions as an aid enabling Western readers to gain a better understanding of the sources of their culture. I regard the comparative method as the arena where the perpetual struggle between certain questions and certain answers is played out or the place where divergent formulations of certain problems meet their respective solutions.

The comparative method adopted by this book will be, for the main part, philosophical. Admitting this does not divulge much; philosophy and its philosophers, as is well known, is a colorful family with many descendents in its fold, some similar, others different, some at peace with one another and some openly hostile toward others. It is therefore better to avoid the pitfalls of strict definitions of and brazen characterizations on the nature of philosophy and philosophical thinking. Rather, let the different schools speak for themselves in the relevant chapters of the book. The ensuing cross-cultural comparisons will be conducted, for the most part, between some of the most fundamental issues of Western philosophy and the corresponding outlooks that developed in the course of philosophical reasoning in India. Having said that, in what follows I will merely offer a fragmented picture of Indian civilization since, as mentioned previously, the discussion of India will, quite intentionally, center only on the intellectual-philosophical dimensions of this rich civilization, which is but a segment of the culture that developed there during the course of more than three millennia. Perhaps this fragmented picture is the only possible course, since, as those exposed to and occasionally tantalized by Indian culture know well, it is so diverse and multifarious that it can sometimes seem one is merely finding there what one was initially seeking. Even sober academics who try to write impartially about India are not completely lacking in some degree of personal involvement. It appears that lurking behind the shoulder of whoever writes about India there lies an autobiographical demon occasionally guiding the author's hand. Writing about India, just as encountering India itself, is usually influenced by the primary motivations and hidden agendas one is harboring. To exorcise the autobiographical demon I should say right away in this introduction, as a kind of personal declaration, that India's allure for me is primarily a philosophical allure. India affords me an encounter with philosophies whose consequences are so far-reaching I am compelled to redefine some of the most pertinent philosophical problems that have occupied me for many years. I find in Indian philosophy a combination of daring and audaciousness that does not dampen even in the face of systematization or the espousal of critical procedures.

Let me be more specific. What I find so fascinating about reading Indian philosophy is discovering the many ways in which its philosophers have grappled with the question of human nature, its abilities and its limitations. The question of human nature in India is a question about the *boundaries* of the human: what are the limits of the mind? How do human beings construct their futures as a projection of their aspirations and fears? Is liberation a viable option? Classical Indian thought offers unique answers to these questions. This uniqueness, as we shall see, lies mainly in the specificity of the conceptual framework through which Indian thought articulated itself as well as in the questions themselves. In other words, the uniqueness of philosophical India lies in the specific conceptual framework on which basis these questions as well as the attempts at resolving them are established. Such a philosophical enterprise is therefore anything but simple—it hinges on the very foundations of this civilization, the melting pot where both the philosophical impulse and its outcome were forged. This melting pot is scorching, much more so than any theoretical platform from which answers are offered.

This book will not present a comprehensive treatment of Indian thought. Thus, for example, I shall deal with the doctrines of two key Buddhist philosophers—Nāgārjuna and Vasubandhu. Each developed a fascinating, intricate, and complex philosophy, and each of their doctrines served as the foundation of rich and long-lasting philosophical traditions. But the discussion of their philosophical doctrines here will have to be very limited, and I shall consider their ideas only inasmuch as they contribute to our understanding of the nature of the human mind as compared and contrasted with ontological assumptions about the existence of external reality and of a transcendent being. Furthermore, on the whole, I shall steer away from any direct references to one prominent and well-attested dimension of Indian thought: the soteriological dimension. Perhaps it is this aspect that has made Indian thought familiar to the West, especially through the nonphilosophical use of such terms as *nirvāṇa, meditation,* or *yoga.* Disregarding soteriology (the very use of this typical Christian term is problematic in the Indian context) will limit matters furthermore. In this book I will examine questions relating to the mind and the world, sidestepping one major concern: the possibility of the liberating mind's actualization and realization. The absence of a discussion of nirvāṇa should not be seen as attempt to marginalize its importance in Indian philosophy or as an attempt to devalue the import of the therapeutic dimension of Indian thought. There is little doubt that Indian philosophy saw itself as harnessed to the possibility of liberation and was engaged in the attempt to enunciate the conditions making liberation possible. Accordingly, I shall refer here to this possibility only in passing, mainly because the therapeutic goals of Indian philosophy merit a discussion of their own.

Contemporary postmodern Western culture glorifies India as a cultural icon and gladly displays it in its colorful shopwindow. Despite a degree of conservatism, mostly within the confines of certain academic circles, it seems that the West is quite liberal in its approach to India and is less prone now to displays of arrogant exclusivity that used to plague it. These days it is rare to come across the sort of condescending attitude that was prevalent mainly among monotheists who would talk derisively about "India's nontheistic religions." Though this attitude has not been eradicated completely, it is rare among contemporary Western philosophers and academics. However, in this age of relativism, some sort of subtle orientalism still trickles down the corridors of academic pluralism. It is most apparent in the duplicitous dichotomy of seeing the West as active and the East as passive. People of the West are portrayed as those who seek to take control of their fate (and through this control to attain life goals, both personal and communal). Our Indian counterparts are seen as those who succumb to fate submissively and lack the basic drive to change it. Needless to say, any fruitful comparison of Indian and Western philosophy should resist any form of orientalism.

But removing prejudices is not enough. Moreover, it might well be the case that the very openness to other cultures and the willingness to open up, to appreciate the other and the different, might turn out to be something of a stumbling block standing in the way of a true understanding of another culture. The heavy mists of relativism that cloud contemporary Western culture necessarily bring about a certain inevitable blurring of essential, conceptual differences, and this might turn every basic difference into a distinction of context, conditioned by circumstances of taste, will, power, and preference. India's accessibility to the West, especially to its younger generations, is often—perhaps all too often—the product of that obscuring mist.

In the prologue to V. S. Naipaul's *An Area of Darkness* is an illuminating example of the cross-cultural shortcut brought about through the mistaken understanding of Indian culture by a Westerner. Naipaul is the son of Hindu parents whose ancestors emigrated from India to Trinidad. He grew up outside of India but was raised in the traditional Hindu way of life. India was for him always a kind of idea, a promised land whose actuality was very far away, but spiritually and emotionally it seemed almost inseparable from his being. He lived India without ever having actually seen her. The book begins when, as an adult, he arrives, for the first time in his life, for a visit to the subcontinent that until now was for him "an area of darkness." It is an artist's rendition of a twelve-month trip to India. Naipaul starts his literary tour de force by relating his first encounter with that dark "homeland." This encounter dwells on his attempts to retrieve two liquor bottles that were confiscated from him by the port of Bombay's custom officials. At the time Bombay was subject to a particular kind of prohibition in which it was illegal to buy or sell any alcoholic beverages; their import was permitted only to tourists under severe restrictions. Naipaul describes in minute detail the many stages of his journey to redeem the confiscated bottles—endless wanderings from one office to another in different parts of the city, filling in forms, being misdirected from one official to another, from building to building, until in the end, to his horror, it transpires that besides the endless forms that he has already managed to obtain, he also needs a "transport permit," without which he cannot physically move the above bottles from their storage place to his person. Naipaul admits that, wandering to yet another office that was supposed to issue him the aforementioned permit, he was on the verge of tears. In this office he faces another obstacle. A serious difference of opinion exists among the clerks: there are those who vehemently deny the very existence of such a permit, as opposed to others who seem to vaguely remember a regulation of this kind. In the end he is referred to yet one more government building, located in the center of town. With failing feet, he returns to his waiting taxi. The driver does not need to be informed of the new address—apparently, he knows its location from fares with previous tourists. Naipaul arrives at the appropriate building and finds himself in a large and spacious room peopled by many clerks. The head clerk deals with his matter and asks him to write a letter in which he requests the receipt of a transport permit. Naipaul admits that he found it difficult to write this letter; words simply did not add up to sentences. While he was composing the request letter, his companion, who was sitting next to him, fainted and fell to the ground. "Water," Naipaul yells, but no one stirs—none of the many clerks even budge. "Water," he pleads to the clerks, until finally one of them rises to leave the room. The head clerk shows compassion and tenderly addresses him, saying, "Not feeling well?" In the meantime, the clerk that had left the room returns, albeit empty-handed. Since he did not bring water, Naipaul loses his temper and begins to shout, "Where is the water?"

> [The head clerk's] eyes distastefully acknowledged my impatience. He neither shrugged nor spoke; he went on with his papers. . . . Presently, sporting his uniform as proudly as any officer, a messenger appeared. He carried a tray and on the tray stood a glass of water. I should have known better. A clerk was a clerk; a messenger was a messenger.

This tale has an epilogue from which there is an interesting moral to be gleaned. The same evening Naipaul and his companion dine with an Indian friend. Naipaul begins to recount the saga of the two confiscated liquor bottles. "We went to get a transport permit," he says, "and she fainted." Not wishing to sound critical, he adds, "Perhaps it's the heat." His Indian friend replies acridly: "It isn't the heat at all. Always the heat or the water with you people from outside. There's nothing wrong with her. You make up your minds about India before coming to the country. You've been reading the wrong books."

Undoubtedly this is a real hazard: to read the wrong books about India, especially since what they mostly tell us, given the prevailing atmosphere of pluralism, is that in fact "the East is not the East" and "the West is not the West" and consequently there really are no "wrong books" about India because there are no "right books" either. In fact, this is the same complaint Naipaul's Indian friend makes when he criticizes the complacent attitude of supposing that one can simply attribute the differences between cultures to differences in drinking water or the weather. If we take into account the colorful effulgence associated with India, her wide palate and her many scents, her plentiful shrines and places of worship, the incredible variety of astonishing tales and no less astonishing array of eccentrics—we have something similar to a gigantic supermarket of ideas, outlooks, and practices that allows one to grab at one's heart's delight from these abundant shelves. But these Western images (not to say imaginings) of India seriously distort the picture. In truth, the cultural rift is far greater than seems at first, particularly since it is infused with conceptual differences. Any mists attempting to obscure this rift will compel us to light a warning beacon.

Yet how is it possible to appreciate Indian civilization, given the presence of this inevitable rift? Ostensibly, comparative philosophy might seem like a promising approach. By submitting the basic philosophical suppositions of Indian civilization to a careful comparison with the basic philosophical suppositions of a civilization close and familiar to us, we might obtain a more lucid and reliable picture of the civilization we are trying to unravel. Obviously, too exhaustive a comparison might induce tedium and weary the reader. Still, it seems that in such a case the benefits outweigh the drawbacks. Discovering that among the dense boughs of dissimilarity there lurks an intercultural similarity will probably gladden the heart of anyone who feels ill at ease with cultural and tribal parochialism. This is in fact one of the discreet charms of a successful comparison. Unfortunately, this charm could be tarnished the moment the comparison gets snarled in a vicious trap, which takes the form of a question lurking beneath many comparisons: the infamous "so what?" What does it matter whether two views from two different cultures are similar in this, but different in that? One should not treat this seemingly crude question too lightheartedly. If it is not possible to come up with a satisfactory reply, this infamous "so what?" will trivialize the comparison and inevitably deal it a deadly blow. Infecting a comparison by asking "so what?" can cause the comparison to disintegrate or, at best, to be dependent on the specific vantage point from which the comparison is being made. From afar, from a bird's-eye point of view, distinguishing marks become obliterated, yet, when an intrusive point of view is adopted, even that which appears similar might seem different. The threat posited by "so what?" lies in that it can unduly contextualize the position from which the comparison is being made, and thus any insights gleaned merely reflect the comparer's specific vantage point rather than provide any true knowledge about the phenomena that are supposed to be similar or different.

One way out of this predicament is to employ the comparative method not in order to counterpose theories, philosophical schemes, viewpoints, and predispositions, but rather to uncover and impart cultural presuppositions that are otherwise difficult to expose when this is attempted from within the presuppositions of the culture in question. Accordingly, in the different chapters of this book I will compare the West and India, employing the comparative method for a specific goal: to enable us to recognize the presuppositions and identify conceptual frameworks that underlie each culture. To put it somewhat crudely, what I intend to offer is an X-ray picture of a culture's hidden and "internal" philosophical elements, which is notably different from (to expand this medical analogy) a surgeon's view of these elements, since it does not touch them—neither for better or worse. A comparison of this kind will enable us not only to understand Indian civilization but also, and mainly, to understand our own. Its purpose is not only to throw light on the obscure (that is, to understand) but also to attempt an ostensible backward journey into the melting pot of Western thought to reassess it in light of the Indian perspective. This comparative exercise need not be symmetrical. Thus, for instance, a reader deeply entrenched in Western culture, whose main interest lies in grasping the development and practices of this culture, can make use of these comparisons with Indian culture as a lucid mirror capable of reflecting his or her hidden cultural presuppositions. Perhaps this comparison will penetrate even deeper strata, in the manner of a Rorschach test that reveals the deepest recesses of our minds by asking us to report what we see in formless inkblots. Naturally, the asymmetry can go in other directions too.

A few words are in order regarding the character of the arguments employed in this book. Western philosophers who try to understand Indian philosophy are often bewildered by one of its most notable characteristics, namely, the ubiquitous and pervasive presence of examples and the place they occupy in the inferential process. For philosophers in India, a certain conclusion can be said to be derived from certain premises if, and only if, it is possible to furnish convincing examples corroborating the transition from premise to conclusion. For an argument to be valid, it has to cite a confirming example, an excluding example, or both. The example plays a crucial role in the Indian inferential process, even though, formally speaking, an example is a redundant member of the argument (at least from a Western point of view): if the conclusion is implied from the premises, this formal relationship of implication will be valid regardless of whether a corroborating example exists or not. But in classical Indian logic an argument will be immediately invalidated if it is not corroborated by applicable examples (which are, in any case, informal by Western standards, since they are conditioned by factual circumstances). The significance of examples is no passing matter, and it is not confined solely to the realm of Indian logic. It seems that Indian philosophers considered the example not only a rhetorical device, but, more important, an argumentative device. Not only are examples necessary in order to corroborate the formal aspect of an argument, they are also a means of guaranteeing its adequacy. Thus, an example is not something that is supposed to prove a rule, but it is used in order to demonstrate or apply a statement. In other words, examples serve the pragmatic function of demonstrating the conclusion's plausibility or acceptability in concrete relevant situations. If I were asked to supply a metaphor with which to describe the relations between the abstract process of inference and the example as it is employed in Indian argumentation, I would suggest the relation between the score of a musical composition and its actual performance. In this book I will adopt this form of Indian argumentation. The example offered are not meant to "prove" my arguments but merely to demonstrate one possible use of them.

I have chosen various sources to demonstrate my arguments and will include, among others, philosophical writings (both Western and Indian), the Bible, the Upaniṣads, modern Western literature. My reliance on works of literature needs some elaboration. It arises from the way I perceive the limits—and, moreover, limitations—of philosophy. It is not uncommon to encounter the kind of metaphilosophy that strives to unravel the interrelationship (if it exists) between philosophy and the arts—more specifically between philosophy and literature. Philosophers tend to think of these affinities in asymmetrical terms: philosophy is "recruited" to reveal the deeper, and more general, meaning of a certain literary work. In this, for all intents and purpose, philosophy functions as an additional "literary critic" (whether overt or covert) whose duty it is to unveil some general meaning out of, say, a novel, a philosophical sense that in most cases is superimposed on the more contextual meanings of the work itself. I have to admit that I find little point in this practice; I have yet to be convinced that philosophy can make a worthwhile contribution to the understanding of a work of literature. My interest in the affinity between philosophy and literature is somewhat different: it seems to me that the underlying structure of philosophical claims—and moreover the presuppositions from which they are derived—can sometimes become clarified and made more explicit by the use of works of literature as explanatory devices. Occasionally, a poem, a story, a novel, or a myth may help us by disclosing the intellectual foundation upon which a philosophy has arisen, expose its implied presuppositions, sweeping aside the dust accumulated on the philosophical floor, thus assisting us to penetrate those hidden recesses that a philosophical scheme cannot deal with since this scheme constitutes part of the very foundations upon which it is formed. Generally speaking, I would suggest that one should regard the ways in which philosophy turns to literature as a process through which it can reassess some of its most pressing problems. The philosophical question under investigation is subjugated to a series of literary operations in the course of which philosophy is being "performed" by literature. By these "performances" or operations a philosophical problem may gain a unique perspective it could not have obtained by means of pure philosophical discourse. True, not every literary text is capable of functioning as an explanatory device for philosophy, and there are no clear guidelines on how to choose the right text for the task; it may well depend on the author's literary skill and the reader's sensibilities. From the philosophical side, it is equally true that not any philosophical question can—or should, indeed—be subjected to literary operation. There are cases in which a philosophical argument can take care of itself perfectly well. But literature can be of assistance to other philosophical arguments—those calling for analogical thinking to clarify them or for some additional reflective light to be shed on their basic premises. If Indian reasoning teaches us anything, it is that we should be very attentive not only to linear arguments but also to analogical elaborations. Turning to literature is, in a certain sense, of therapeutic value: it can cure us of being all too philosophical in the sense in which philosophy inhibits us from relying on the analogical gaze to enrich our understanding.

The last of my general remarks concerns the use of generalizations. Needless to say, every generalization on Indian thought or on Western civilization can be undermined by constantly appealing to exceptions. Furthermore, "Indian thought" is anything but uniform and "Western civilization" is, in a sense, merely a convenient expedient. But even this qualification is a generalization that has its own exceptions. Instead of joining the relativistic campaign against the general, and especially the universal, I shall not refrain from using generalizations, cautiously, employing them only when they make sense and when their explanatory force is evident. To be more specific, the generalizations offered in this book will in most cases refer to the conceptual and foundational level, and as such they will draw their force not from a sharp exclusion of exceptions, but rather from their plausibility and their ability to shed new light on the issues under consideration.

Last, a few stylistic remarks. I am aware that the use of the twin terms *West* and *East* reeks of patronization. Accordingly, I shall use them as little as possible, but sometimes it is unavoidable. The comparisons I shall undertake will be between ideas that evolved in the Indian subcontinent and that of Europe (to which, for convenience, I will mostly refer as Western civilization or culture). The second stylistic remark has a more personal touch: I find it difficult to express philosophical arguments in the absence of a dialogue. I am referring to that all too common philosophical fashion in which a text is purged of any kind of dialogic expression, cleansed of any mention of the writer discoursing with his or her reader. Philosophical reflection is, for me, one of the most deeply rooted expressions of dialogue and thus I have not tried to exorcise it from the present text since I feel the indispensability of engaging the reader in a conversational style.

ONE

Far and Beyond

TRANSCENDENCE IN TWO CULTURES

"He is the Rock, his work is perfect":
His work is perfect with all mortals
And let us not cast even the slightest doubt over His actions.
And none of his acts will look around and say:
Would that I had three eyes
And would that I had three hands
And would that I had three legs
And would that I were to walk on my head
And would that my front be my behind,
How fine it would be for me.
                    —*Seferei Dvarim*, chapter 32, v. 4

The following verse, whose beauty is suffused by its simplicity, is the first line of an ancient Hebrew liturgical poem (*piyyut*) describing the high priest's rites on the Day of Atonement. Before the actual description itself, the poet turns to what he sees as the absolute beginning of all beginnings, namely, God:

Then, with all naught   you were all
And with all being   you were filled by all

It would seem that this verse needs no explanation: a poet can take as much license as he wants and choose to reveal while concealing, shedding light only to then obscure his words with a thick shadow.

After all, ambiguity may well be the essence of his artistic expression. Yet how are we to understand the following words, admittedly not in verse, which one would expect to be the epitome of clarity, as they are the opening sentences of a tract on prosaic legal matters: "The foundation of foundations and the pillar of wisdom is to know that there is a first Being. And He brings into existence everything there is. And all existent things in heaven, on earth and in between exist only through the truth of His Being." These words are taken from the preface to *Mishneh Torah*, Maimonides' monumental compendium on Jewish religious law (halacha). Yet these opening sentences are not concerned with legal intricacies, but rather with the very foundations of belief on which the halacha is based. While the text itself is written in Hebrew that is both lucid and stirring, the meaning of this opening assertion, like the opening verse of the aforementioned *piyyut*, is shrouded in ambiguity. Nearly every term begs to be interpreted, yet any such attempt to interpret them burdens us with heaps upon heaps of further explanations, counterexamples, proofs, refutations, and ever more hermeneutical devices. What, for instance, is the meaning of "foundation of foundations"? And what distinguishes it from "the pillar of wisdom"? Still pondering over this question, the perplexed reader immediately stumbles over the next phrase: "is to know that there is a first Being." Why knowledge? Why not the customary "belief"? What does "to know" mean when applied to the "first Being"? Is it on a par with knowledge, as in knowing the laws of physics? Or perhaps it is more like the knowledge of mathematical truths? Or perhaps it is a knowing-how claim, meant to instruct one in life rather than changing one's cognitive horizons? Perhaps it is a different kind of knowledge altogether? Surely, these questions will be resolved once we understand the true nature of this transcendent Being—the object of knowledge set forth by Maimonides. But this Being is so encompassing and illimitable, so rich with varied meanings, that any attempt to understand His true nature will probably fail and induce utter despair in the perplexed.

Whether we opt for the poet's confidence or the philosopher's rational perplexity, it is easy to see that these two points of view—the poem and the philosophical tract—share common ground. They share, as it were, a vast horizon of beliefs, opinions, expectations, and aspirations. Often we call this common ground, somewhat parochially, "Western culture." In other words, a common conceptual framework is shared by both the poetic rendering and the philosophical reflection.

Exposing the underlying frameworks that make up a worldview is a tricky business. As any art collector will admit, the ideal picture frame is one that is somehow transparent, framing the painting, yet never drawing too much attention to itself. When we move from art to pictures of the world, the difficulty of recognizing the frame is most conspicuous. All the more so when what we are attempting to uncover is a *conceptual* framework. Here, besides the intricacy of discerning the frame, there is the additional problem of recognizing the picture itself. The reason for this difficulty is that the very vocabulary we employ in this quest is inseparable from the picture we are trying to recognize. Different philosophers (such as Wittgenstein) have drawn our attention to the inherent difficulties in justifying cultural frameworks. Yet these difficulties manifest themselves even before one offers justifications; it appears the moment we seek to describe these frameworks, since it is evident that any description inevitably relies on the terms and conceptual schemes that condition this framework, thus making description impossible. It would seem that we are confronted with another instance of bootstrapping.

One way to disengage ourselves from this problem is to take a step in the direction of cross-cultural comparison. To begin with, a small stride will suffice; a slight nudge aimed at highlighting some interesting differences of opinion over two distinct cultural positions regarding the attribution of knowledge to a divine Being. Recall Maimonides' formative words: "The foundation of foundations and the pillar of wisdom is to know that there is a first Being. And He brings into existence everything there is. And all existent things in heaven, on earth and in between exist only through the truth of His Being." We might commence our comparative journey by wondering whether such a claim is conceivable within the framework of Indian thought? Given that any culture can put forward any claim, perhaps we should reformulate this question: are we likely to find a claim such as this at the bedrock of Indian thought? Can the conceptual framework of this culture sustain such a claim? As a prelude, we could examine an apparently similar Indian expression of the search for an omniscient First Being. What was there in the beginning, then, with all naught, before any creature had taken form? To counter Maimonides' reply, we could posit the reply to this question as it appears in the Ṛg Veda, the oldest surviving collection of Indian texts available to us.[1]

The hymn I am alluding to forms part of the tenth section of the Ṛg Veda and is surely one of the better known Vedic hymns, probably familiar even to those not well versed in the philosophy and religion of ancient India. This hymn begins with an absorbing characterization of "beginning":

> Then, there was neither existence nor non-existence;
> There was neither air nor the ether which is beyond.
> What did it conceal? Where? In whose protection?
> Was there water, unfathomably deep?
>
> There was neither death nor the deathless then.
> There was no sign of night nor of day.
> That one breathed, windless, by its own impulse.
> Other than that there was nothing at all.

The hymn belongs to the later stratum of the Ṛg Veda and would probably have been composed around the ninth or eighth centuries BCE. Most scholars agree that this stratum heralds a break from the pervading polytheism of the earlier hymns. This specific hymn is seen to be advocating an unmistakable monistic outlook whereby the plurality of existence is subsumed by one all-embracing and boundless being. The source of plurality is unity, since "that one *(tad ekam)* breathed, windless, by its own impulse" and, moreover, "other than that there was nothing at all." Until quite recently, orientalists waxed lyrical over these verses, seeing in them a vindication of their romantic depiction of India. In fact, all too often, in the West this hymn was brought forward as evidence of India's espousal of monism. It is not that difficult to envisage Western scholars in the not-too-distant past expressing a restrained appreciation and even admiration: imagine, they might have said to themselves, even in India, abstract thought occasionally developed! Seen from this angle, one cannot deny the similarity between Maimonides' claim and the Vedic outlook—the similarities seem to outweigh the dissimilarities. Despite the yawning gulf that exists between Maimonides' philosophical language and the loose, mythic language of the Vedic hymn, it would seem that prima facie the frameworks within which both ideas operate are similar. The beginning, so claim both the Vedic poet and Maimonides, is the "One," the "first Being," that which exists even when "there was nothing at all."

And yet, the Vedic hymn quoted above has more to say about the attributes of the One. Further along, the poet outlines the stages by which the universe was formed from that primary being (mostly through evolution or birth rather than creation). Culminating the description of this evolutionary process, a reflective afterthought is presented that is not only incongruent with the kind of presuppositions that may have begun to take root in the Western reader's mind but also deviates from them sharply. This is how the hymn ends:

> Who really knows? Who here will proclaim it?
> Whence has it come? Whence is this creation?
> The gods came later with its emanation.
> Who then knows whence it has come?
>
> Whence this creation has come—
> Whether he formed it or did not—
> The one who surveys it in the highest heaven—
> Only he knows, or maybe he does not.
>
> (Ṛg Veda, 10.129)

The contrast between what Maimonides is claiming and the position of the Vedic hymn is immediately clear. As a foundation of all foundations, Maimonides installs man's paramount requirement to know the existence of the first present. And it is clear that this requirement arises from his unfaltering conviction that the "first present" not only constitutes the content of man's knowledge, but, moreover, is what *enables* it, by virtue of "the First Being," such that "all existent things in heaven, on earth and in between exist only through the truth of His Being." Stated somewhat differently, the possibility of knowing the First Being is thoroughly grounded by the ontological assumption that Being and Truth are identical. Human knowledge may "reveal" to the knower the truth of the first Being, and, from his or her psychological viewpoint, it precedes divine truth. But this is only psychological precedence; it has no ontological significance whatsoever. It is clear ontologically that the necessity of the first Being's existence precedes any human attempt to attain truth. Moreover, "human" truth is unattainable without presuming the independent status of a divinity in which Being and knowledge are identical.

On the other hand, the Vedic hymn, also describing a supposedly unique supreme being (that windless "One" breathing by his own impulse), does not grant his self-knowledge any ontological precedence over human knowledge. The very possibility of this knowledge is seriously questioned by the Vedic poet, who doubts if "that One" (*tad ekam*) knows at all. Maybe he does not know? Moreover, the final section of the hymn clearly seems to draw certain epistemological conclusions about the possibility of human knowledge: knowledge, if possible at all, is not bound by any predetermined ontological assumptions according to which divine knowledge is assumed as being necessarily true. On the contrary, divine knowledge is shrouded by a thick cloud of doubt, and even the supposed omnipotence of the windless One cannot vouch for his veracity. Consequently, the very act of doubting the primary Being's "knowledge" shows that the concluding verses of the Vedic hymn assume a different conceptual scheme from that of Maimonides.

What then is this conceptual scheme? What lies at the foundation of knowledge in the West, and to what extent is it different from India? As a possible solution I would like to consider what might be succinctly termed the presupposition of transcendence (where *presupposition* means an assumption, a notion, preceding and underlying any conceptual framework). This presupposition is rooted in the conceptual bedrock sustaining the West's philosophical and religious framework, and its origins can be traced back to ancient Greece.

A prominent appearance of the presupposition of transcendence in Western philosophy occurs with Plato's theory of Forms (also known by the less adequate term *theory of Ideas*).[2] Among other things, this theory may be characterized as an all-embracing and far-reaching claim for the ontological precedence of the outward over the inward, exteriority over interiority, the universal over the particular, the transcendent over the immanent, and structure over content. The underlying supposition of the theory of Forms is that, apart from their existence in the visible world, things also exist as pure form, invisible to the eye and inaccessible to the other organs of sense. In other words, Plato establishes a palpable hierarchy between phenomena that are particular and contingent and belong to the visible world and universal and eternal truths belonging to the world of Forms. For him, the "right track" to know reality is by means of the "unaided intellect," disavowing the senses and instead allowing knowledge to appear to "pure and unadulterated thought." Whatever we perceive by means of the senses is subject to change and permutation. Forms, on the other hand, "never admit to change" and always remain "constant and invariable."

For Plato, it is perfectly natural to assume that things are independent and unrelated to us: "[All things] must be supposed to have their own proper and permanent essence; they are not in relation to us, or influenced by us, fluctuating according to our fancy, but they are independent, and maintain to their own essence the relation prescribed by nature." This independent existence of things shifts us from the sensual world to the abstraction of Forms, which do not rely on any specific content in order to exist: Forms are immaterial, atemporal, and unchanging. They are inaccessible to bodily senses and can be known solely by the intellect. The existence of the transcendent world of Forms is a necessary condition for the existence of the varying and changing objects of the sensible world. Indeed, particulars can exist only as manifestations of universals and can therefore be understood only by relying on the existence of nonsensible universals. Moreover, the very process of comprehension would be impossible without the existence of an objective and independent criterion through which understanding grasps its objects. This is also true with regard to the evidence our senses draw from the phenomenal world. Evidence needs to be subjugated to universal principles that in themselves are not sensual. Arithmetic provides a good example for this: the distinction between a set comprised of five members and a set comprised of seven members is only possible because of the existence of the Form "number" as an entity that is itself abstract, self-reliant, and completely severed from its (sensual) appearances. An even better known example is geometrical Form; the Form "triangle" is not conditioned in any way by its empirical manifestations. When considering Plato's attitude to geometry, it is possible to understand his preference of essences over particulars and his predilection for essentialist definitions over demonstrative definitions. Geometry allows one to obtain knowledge of the eternal, "that which always is," as opposed to the knowledge of "something which at some time comes into being and passes away." Consequently, these Forms exist irrespective of appearances and are quite independent of any mind perceiving them. At the same time, Forms enable the existence of the manifold appearances of our world. For example, red poppies are only possible by virtue of the transcendent existence of the Form "red." The appearance of red in a poppy's petal, according to Plato, "partakes" of, or "imitates" the Form "red."

Plato's adherence to the theory of Forms leads him to assign the utmost importance to the distinction between knowledge and mere opinion. Knowledge is determined by virtue of the fact that things exist independently of being known. Knowledge is no more than bringing to light that which exists in itself. By contrast, opinion arises from the subjective mental state of the knower. Therefore, knowledge is possible if, and only if, one relies on one's intellect instead of succumbing to the tempting power of imagination. Bodily senses will be of no use in this goal of attaining knowledge, since the picture of reality they offer is always conditioned in one way or another. On the other hand, knowledge has no context. Since knowledge is based on the intellect, the preferred life—life worth living—is a spiritual life governed solely by reason. Life governed by reason is a life in which the intellect restrains the subordinate echelons of the soul, which are predominantly geared toward the satisfaction of baser desires.

This is how Plato's theory of Forms explicates not only the primacy given to the universal and the abstract over the particular and the concrete but also the primacy of the intellect over the senses as a means of knowing the truth. That is to say, this theory is not only a metaphysical outlook but also a model of rationality. Indeed, the theory of Forms clearly demonstrates the customary Western paradigm of rationality: if Being does not reside in the phenomenal but in its abstraction, and if Form precedes any of its concrete appearances, one should conduct one's life according to the rule of reason rather than follow one's senses and imagination, which are both saturated in the ephemeral. Plato's counsel is unmistakable: wherever desire pervades, let wisdom rule; ideal human life should not be controlled by the blind power of instinct, but by nondesirous, detached, and contemplative intellect.

No wonder Plato places the Form of the Good at the top of the hierarchical scale of Forms. The Platonic Good is abstraction in its most abstract sense, lying beyond any categorical distinction (in this Plato follows in the footsteps of his great predecessor Parmenides). About six hundred years after Plato, the Neoplatonist philosopher Plotinus characterized this abstraction in a metaphysical language that is likely to strum a few mystical chords in certain readers. Plotinus referred to the Being that exists absolutely and independently as the "One" and characterized it as completely transcendent: "Since the nature of the 'One' is generative of all things it is not any one of them. It is not therefore something or qualified or quantative or intellect or soul; it is not in movement or at rest, not in place, not in time, but 'itself by itself of single form' [Plato, *Symposium* 211B]." The Platonic Form of Good and Plotinus's "One," despite the differences between them, share the same transcendent conceptual framework. As we shall see, the same framework underlies the dominant forms of Western religiosity (except that in religion it mostly takes a personal form, whereas the Platonic Forms are totally impersonal).

Aristotle, Plato's renowned pupil and adversary, came up with the most extensive critique of Plato's theory. For reasons that need not concern us here, Aristotle rejected the *metaphysical* assumptions that sustained the Platonic theory of Forms. In the present context we need only stress that Aristotle's repudiation of Plato's theory of Forms does not displace the *conceptual* presupposition of transcendence. On the contrary, Aristotle seems to have absorbed this presupposition from Plato, despite the fact that its expression is not as explicit as it is in Plato's. Indeed, it is not difficult to find in Aristotelian metaphysics claims that rely, in one way or another, on the foundational presupposition of transcendence. Consider, for example, the way in which Aristotle understands the nature of God. He argues for the existence of a divine substance ("unmoved first mover"), this being a perfect actuality: eternal, infinite, immovable, and unchanging being. There is no material element to God (since matter does not preclude the possibility of change, while God, as an eternal being, is above change). Moreover, the dichotomy between subjectivity and objectivity cannot be attributed to him. The way he "moves" the world is unique to him; he is the cause of the world but he did not create it, since the world is primordial, nor does he meddle in the affairs of the world. As pure intellect, he thinks only in his own thinking. Yet, his existence as a thinking intellect attracts to him those existing in the world, first and foremost human beings. Everything that exists, especially man, aspires to God and is thus drawn to him. Between man and God there is a clear unilateral relationship: man's thoughts desire God, while God has no desire whatsoever. As pure thought, God transcends the world. In this respect, Aristotle can be seen to be Plato's loyal disciple.

An illuminating corollary of the role that transcendence plays in Plato and Aristotle's philosophy is, I think, the limited significance that both thinkers grant to the notion of reflexivity. It clearly follows from Plato's understanding of transcendence that any form of reflexivity is inevitably restricted and bound up, since reflexivity has to align itself with the universal and abstract order of Form, and this order does not divulge itself through introspection, but rather through the mind's observation of the exteriority of the Forms. As we shall see, the apparent similarity between the Delphic inscription "Know thyself" (in the sense that Plato awards it) and the Indian demand for self-knowledge is superficial and perhaps even misleading. That "self" whom Plato wants us to know can only be obtained at the price of radically divorcing man from his subjective interiority, while at the same time pushing forward in the metaphysical province of Forms. Every human appeal to the concrete "self" that purportedly lies inside the soul of every person is a move in the wrong direction, a withdrawal from the intellectual search for an understanding of the true nature of reality, allowing oneself to be immersed in everyday phenomena as they are experienced by the mind of a particular person. That is to say, "Know thyself" is not a psychological recommendation. Plato identifies it with man's visual faculty—he describes the pupil of the eye as the part where vision occurs and accordingly suggests an analogy in which self-knowledge is likened to the case of the eye, when "if the eye is to see itself, it must look at the eye, and at that part of the eye [the pupil] where sight, which is the virtue of the eye, resides." Further on, Plato explains what he means by the eye into whose pupil the onlooking eye needs to gaze in order to distinguish itself, but we shall not enter this discussion here. For our purposes, it will suffice to note that self-knowledge is conditioned by the presence of something external to it. In later chapters we shall return to the role of reflexivity both in the West and India respectively.

That Platonism has been a very dominant factor in the course of the West's development warrants no proof. Different outlooks, at different times and different places, have all shared Plato's view that objectivity is not determined by cultural or normative considerations; neither is it established by means of a subjectivity that dwells in a particular soul. Not only did this form of Platonism come to the fore in the embryonic days of Christianity, but even before that, in the first half of the first century CE, we find the Jewish philosopher Philo suggesting a novel approach on how to combine Plato's Forms and the Jewish Godhead. According to Philo, the two converge through their shared reliance on a presupposition of transcendence. Different Christian thinkers—Saint Augustine is certainly the most prominent—adopted the hierarchical structure of Plato's theory of Forms, substituting Plato's Form of good, which occupied the highest rung, with the absolute and necessary existence of God. This is one of the meeting points between the Platonic-philosophical version of the presupposition of transcendence and its religious counterpart. Though Plato's theory of Forms and Aristotle's metaphysics of the unmoved mover are philosophical versions of the presupposition of transcendence, they are not exclusive. Alongside these abstract philosophical principles, other manifestations, as religious belief, developed in the West. Here the presupposition of God's inevitable outwardness assumed a key position. Heinrich Heine conceived that the prominence allocated to the presupposition of transcendence in the West arose out of the fusion of the Platonic-Aristotelian metaphysical assumption and Judeo-Christian religious belief in a transcendent personal God. Heine drew attention to the inherent irony of this fusion. According to him, Plato and Aristotle's philosophy overcame "ancient Greek merriment," namely, the paganism of the Olympian gods and their escapades. Greek philosophers (especially Plato and Aristotle) made no attempt to disown the intricate tangle of stories in which the gods actively participated. Their solution was to claim that these myths were irrelevant to their philosophy. By positing the hidden world of Forms, or a divine substance that has no ontological precedence over any kind of thing or event, any prospect of harmonizing philosophy with myth was doomed to failure. Indeed, it was only Judeo-Christian philosophers who took it upon themselves to curb the scope of the mythical world, and they did this by positing a transcendent being as something existing above us, while, at the same time, obstructing our mythological worldview. Heine could not withhold his critical scorn from those Greek philosophers who failed miserably in doing what he thought it was their duty to do, namely, "To defend Hellenism itself, or the Greek way of feeling and thinking." With astuteness and profound understanding, Heine realized that it was Christianity (following Judaism) that installed the presupposition of transcendence as the foundation of culture and induced, to his mind, a worldview that is "dismal, emaciated, ascetic, over-spiritual.[3]

It is more difficult to make general claims about religion than it is about philosophical doctrines. Mostly, the term *religion* is used as an umbrella, safely sheltering a large array of beliefs and opinions, a variegated set of lifestyles, customs, and traditions. This plurality of beliefs and practices may thwart any attempt to make a sweeping, general claim about a specific religion. It is not my intention here to make such generalizations about the nature of this or that religion, the objects of their belief or the forms of their worship, but merely to make a few general remarks solely on the *conceptual framework* of the three major religions of the West: Judaism, Christianity, and Islam.[4] Much like any other general statement, this is not an incontrovertible claim; moreover, since this generalization traverses much cultural terrain, there can be little doubt that exceptions abound at its extremities too. However, the presence of ample exceptions should not prevent us from noting the general conceptual framework that underlies the rich and varied phenomena of religion in the West. And, if many exceptions have the tendency to obfuscate the broader picture, then a comparison with other, non-Western religions will come to the aid and disperse these obscuring clouds.

It is common knowledge that the three forms of Western monotheism share between them the belief in the existence of a divine being. But it is less commonly observed that this belief is deeply rooted in a common conceptual bedrock, and that through this shared foundation these religions relate to God or to the Godhead. As I mentioned previously, I suggest referring to this conceptual bedrock as the "presupposition of transcendence." This is a presupposition about God's exteriority, His outwardness, His being different, the total "Other," unlike any other being. God's transcendence expresses his otherness and this otherness is especially emphasized by His complete contrariness to both nature and human beings. As Amit has rightly emphasized, when dealing with the Bible, "the set of beliefs and opinions that make up the biblical worldview is keen to highlight the gulf existing between the divine and the human. Man as such has weaknesses and he should not be placed on the side of the divine." A well-known characterization of God is clearly expressed by one of Isaiah's declarations: "For my thoughts are not your thoughts, neither are your ways my ways. . . . For as the heavens are higher than the earth, so are my ways higher than your ways, and my thoughts than your thoughts" (Isaiah 55:8–9). Saint Paul makes a similar declaration: "O man, who art thou that repliest against God? Shall the thing formed say to him that formed it, Why hast thou made me thus?" (Romans 9:20), and further on: "O the depth of the riches both of the wisdom and knowledge of God! how unsearchable are his judgments, and his ways past finding out!" (11:33). These declarations are not only self-revealing, they also signify a rich and complex culture at the center of which lies the presupposition of God's transcendence, that is, the view that God exists beyond the world, so identifying a yawning gap between Him and humans, since His motives and objectives lie far beyond comprehension. Job's question expresses this chasm poignantly: "Canst thou by searching find out God? canst thou find out the Almighty unto perfection? It is as high as heaven; what canst thou do? deeper than hell; what canst thou know?" (Job 11:7–8). These are but a few select examples; neither the means of expression nor the modes of interpretation are ever exhausted in demonstrating God's exteriority. The demarcation between the inward and the outward is, for the most, a rigid boundary. There are, of course, exceptions to the rule, even at the very core of Western culture—suffice it to recall, for example, the Stoics or Neoplatonism—but these exceptions do not obliterate the boundaries, they simply make the rule more malleable. Later on we shall see that even when the Godhead was depicted in immanent terms, in many cases this depiction still centered on a transcendence.

God, then, is deemed a being whose existence is not dependent in any way whatsoever upon either man or anything else in the world. Having said that, one must stress that this claim should not be taken as a statement of fact, but rather as a conceptual clarification. To put it crudely, it is not my intention to regard the presupposition of transcendence as something that necessarily manifests itself in the beliefs and practices of the believer's everyday life. Nor do I intend to point to the presupposition of transcendence as a characteristic of a (Western) believer's frame of mind or mental state. Religious feelings and sentiments are seldom limited to a strict feeling of awe or "otherness." André Neher manages to lucidly convey this complexity of religious feelings, and, though he is in fact describing Judaism, I think this description perfectly captures the situation in the other Western religions too:

> The Hebrew man was well aware that he stood opposite a divine dimension utterly different from himself. And yet, the explanation he gave himself for this feeling was quite unique: he did not see this as an accidental confrontation that repeats itself at given intervals, but as a veritable condition stemming from man's position in the world. The Hebrews did not see the encounter with God as a split, but rather as the realization of their existence.

Although man's encounter with God is not to be understood in terms of a split, Neher rightly acknowledges that the most significant feature of the believer's religious experience is her or his place *opposite* the "divine dimension." Of course, the omniscience and omnipotence of God means that He has it in his power to instigate a direct line of communication with man. This communion between God and man is often portrayed as the ultimate ideal to which the believer should aspire. Moreover, in monotheism, the relationship between God and man is conveyed by means of a rich assortment of images that, on the whole, describe actual propinquity: the relationship between a father and his son, or between a shepherd and his flock, or between a king and his loving subjects, or, at times, even between a man and his wife. These are merely a few typical examples; they show that, more often than not, humans relate to God anthropomorphically. However, the existence of imagery fails to undermine the conceptual framework of the presupposition of transcendence; on the contrary, these images are both appealing and potent to most believers, precisely because they offer a metaphoric way to bridge, in a certain limited sense, the unfathomable abyss that exists between God and the world. In other words, for there to be a direct communion between God and man, it is necessary to bridge a gulf, to cross over an abyss dividing "my thoughts" from "your thoughts," "my ways" from "your ways." The communion between God and man is portrayed in terms of a connection of two separate planes, two strata clearly partitioned so that, even if it is possible to cross over from one to the other, the barrier itself will always remain intact; that is to say, whoever attempts to approach God has to overcome impediments, traverse vast expanses and immense spiritual stages, but overcoming these obstacles does not detract from or remove the barrier itself. Still, the yearning to take refuge in God is not unique to religions that entertain the presupposition of transcendence; perhaps it expresses a primary and universal human need. But in the worldview endorsed by Western religions this need articulates itself in the form of a conceptual conflict: God's presence in the world or in man's soul, given His transcendence, is not only fundamentally necessary, but at the same time essentially impossible.

Stated succinctly, the presupposition of transcendence cannot to be reduced to anything one believes in; rather, it reflects certain thought patterns, a way of understanding, a mode of expression. To put it more precisely, it is not one of God's attributes or qualities; it is neither based on speculative theology nor sustained by certain belief systems. It is the very existence of an ever perfect God; that is, by diminishing God's transcendence you thereby reduce His perfection. As a concept, transcendence has served, and still serves, a constitutive role within Western religious languages. It is the crack through which nature is grasped and without which both the world and humankind would become meaningless. In this sense, transcendence *precedes* both belief and practice by virtue of being a "mental paradigm," a conceptual framework that draws a clear-cut demarcation between interiority and exteriority and sees this demarcation as being essentially asymmetrical—positing a clear precedence of exteriority over interiority, of the objective over the subjective.

A characteristic feature of the presupposition of transcendence in its religious manifestations is the idea of ascribing sanctity to the divine being. Indeed, starting with the Bible, sacredness in Western religions has been a typical and unmistakable attribute of transcendence. This began to take form with the attempts to establish the extrahuman status of transcendence when a barrier was erected between God and that which is not God (let us not forget the word *sacred* is derived from the Latin *sacrare*, meaning to set apart as holy, to consecrate). The injunction "Ye shall be holy: for I the Lord your God am holy" (Leviticus 19:2) is not, after all, some kind of didactic battle cry bawled out by an energetic leader spurring the multitude to follow his example. The attribution of sacredness to divinity has clear ontological repercussions: it separates the pure from the impure. Thus, the injunction calling upon humans "to be holy" serves only as a sort of unattainable regulative idea. It is more like a beacon showing humans the way to follow when searching for a holiness they will never fully attain. After all, it does not make sense to expect humans to arrive at divine sacredness given the place they occupy on the line suspended between purity and impurity. A typical response to the transcendent manifestation of sacredness can be seen in the prophet Isaiah's reaction: not only does it arouse in him a strong feeling of insignificance and incompetence, but, moreover, a strong sense of impurity (Isaiah, 6:5).

The presupposition of transcendence is not logically dependent on monotheism, nor does this presupposition necessarily entail monotheism. It is not entirely clear whether the Bible, for example, upholds a monotheistic vision of the godhead. Perhaps, rather than monotheism, the term *henotheism*, a term coined by Max Müller roughly a century ago, denoting the belief in a plurality of gods, of which one is the central and overruling god, is more appropriate. It may well be that biblical claims such as "Who is like unto thee, O Lord, among the gods?" (Exodus 15:11) were written with a henotheistic mindset since they celebrate God's supremacy among all other gods. The exact deployment of the different strata of monotheism in the Hebrew Bible is an open question that has been, is, and will be the subject of extensive debating among biblical and literary scholars. Even in postbiblical times it is not quite clear to what extent monotheism was upheld by the different forms of Judaism and Christianity.

Discussions on the nature of divinity in Western religions bear witness to the influence of philosophical reasoning. These have not only determined that God must be a singular unity, but have also sought to conceive of Him as being, in essence, an abstract entity. Indeed, philosophers and theologians in the West are preoccupied by their attempt to eradicate from God any signs of materiality or corporeality. There is nothing objectionable in this; however, the same does not hold true of the attempt to see these views as characterizing the principal beliefs of Western religions as they were actually expressed through the religious life of believers throughout the ages.

Clearly, the monotheistic thinkers that were deeply inspired by the beauty of philosophical reasoning found in philosophy a useful tool in their attempt to corroborate their monotheistic vision of God. Here, the transcendent otherness of God was emphasized by means of philosophical abstractions on the nature of His uniqueness. However, it would be wrong to conclude that anyone adhering to the conceptual framework of transcendence is necessarily a philosophical monotheist. To do this would be to place God on the Procrustean bed of abstraction, a bed far too short to fit the variegated expressions used to characterize Him. It's not difficult to find explicit depictions of God in bodily form, endowed with a countenance and corporeal in a manner that is not metaphorical.

In a fascinating article discussing the changing concepts of God in Jewish thought, Ithamar Gruenwald has shown unequivocally that there is no point in seeking a unified monotheistic view of God in Judaism (and, one is tempted to add, in other Western religions as well). On the contrary, the basic terms by which God is predicated—including those that portray him as a singular unity—have undergone many transformations in the course of history. Besides conceiving God in abstract terms and thus seeing Him as an entirely immaterial being, beyond sentient perception and at complete odds with any likelihood of being fully understood, there were other perceptions of God endowing Him with many attributes and qualities (even corporeal form) and, in certain conditions, within the grasp of man's direct sentient perception. But these anthropomorphic depictions of God—which, as I mentioned before, frequently appear at the heart of monotheism—do not in any way challenge the belief that God is apart, concealed, and categorically different from the world. The religious texts of monotheism often amalgamate anthropomorphism with transcendence. It is thus possible to envisage God as being both transcendent and, at the same time, endowed with form. Transcendence is an inseparable component in the fabric of belief in the existence of God, while his anthropomorphic attributes constitute part of his behavior and his actions. In other words, religious anthropomorphism is, in the main, something that represents divine semantics, the variety of meanings that a believer's mind tries to cast into this complex concept. On the other hand, the presupposition of transcendence is primarily a formal-syntactic presupposition that draws the boundary line separating God from the world. Even when a particular anthropomorphic depiction presents us with a picture of divinity that is intimate with the human, and even when this depiction tries to undermine the barrier engendered by the presupposition of transcendence, or at least to make it more pliant, it still accepts, ex post facto, the presence of the barrier. The same holds true of the attempts to overcome or to subjugate God by means of magic: the presupposition of a barrier that needs to be traversed remains intact (the Indian outlook, as we shall see, considers the distance that the magician attempts to reduce in terms of a kind of rectifiable mental error).

To sum up, the fascinating variance evident in those religions we loosely define as monotheistic does not encroach on the presupposition of transcendence. This presupposition is present at the very inception of Western religions, whether they portray God as an abstract being, formless and incorporeal, or, alternatively, when they conceive Him as a personal God with identifiable qualities, manifesting Himself, in varying degrees, in form and in vision. Monotheism seeks to present a picture of divinity—its nature, qualities, and other attributes. To attribute monotheism to God is to make a "biographical" claim about Him. On the other hand, to assume that God is transcendent is not to determine anything about His biography but rather to recognize the backbone, the conceptual skeleton, upholding His existence by which Jews, Christians, and Muslims relate to God, to the world He created, and to the role allotted to humans in His creation. This backbone is, however, not immediately visible, since it is covered with a rich variety of beliefs and practices. Nonetheless, it is present within a number of religious expressions: in shared stories, in learned treatises, and in ritual practices. I would like to briefly consider one typical instance of a religious story that instigates transcendence. I refer to the biblical story considered by Western religions to deal with the first (and perhaps formative) act of ritual, namely, the murderous conflict between Cain and Abel—a conflict that incisively demonstrates God's otherness and the disaster inevitably following from it.

The story recounts the first murder, the outcome of contact between two brothers, the first humans, in the full sense of the word—unlike their parents (who both were created by God and thus not born of a womb) Cain and Abel were born to a mortal woman from the seed of a human father. Since, at this point, there were no other descendents of Adam and Eve, the two brothers embody, perhaps even symbolize, the very possibility of social contact between humans. Nevertheless, a third party is involved; the reality in which Cain and Abel dwell is, of course, a reality governed by the outward, other God who transcends these earthlings. And so, within the bounds of this reality (about which God said, upon its recent completion, that it was "very good"), the first alliance between two human beings ends in an act of extreme violence. It has at times been suggested that this murder has all the hallmarks of the archetypal best-seller story—inflamed familial tensions that drive Cain to a horrendous homicide that completely, yet predictably, shatters the family unit. Needless to say, this is a somewhat superficial account. The story of Cain and Abel is neither a family saga nor a dissection of the latent destructive forces within a family. As a matter of fact, there is no proper family to speak of; the divine presence and intervention obstructs its formation. It would seem that the real difficulty here is not the collapse of the family unit, but, alas, grave misgivings about its actual viability.

Cain's fratricide is presented as a response to the act of sacrifice. That is to say, it arises as a result of man's attempt to draw nearer (the literal meaning of "sacrifice" in Hebrew) to God, and it might even be possible to see it as a paradigmatic expression of the human aspiration to build a bridge above the transcendent abyss. The text describes man's attempt to communicate with God in a few simple, laconic, and restrained verses, leaving the more intricate matters unresolved. For instance, how did the two brothers know that a sacrifice was expected of them? This question is left unanswered. It would seem that sacrificing to God is conceived as a natural occurrence, requiring neither justification nor explanation. Consider some other unresolved questions: what, in Abel's sacrifice, made it efficacious? What, on the other hand, was lacking in Cain's sacrifice that made it unwelcome? Various commentators have offered many different explanations. The more traditional commentators felt compelled to justify God's partiality. Among them were those who assumed that Abel's offering was accepted since he brought the finest of his flock, while Cain's offering was rejected since it was comprised of the abject part of his agricultural produce.

Among the more critical commentators are those who saw God's preference as a demonstration of the text's predilection for nomadic shepherds over agricultural settlers. Others saw a preference for Abel's livestock offering, "the firstlings of his flock and of the fat thereof" (a blood sacrifice) as opposed to Cain's vegetative offering (the fruit of the ground). Yet all these explanations are a posteriori interpretations. They offer replies to questions never asked in the text and thereby miss the point. The biblical author, it would seem, is not interested in these questions; he does not care why Abel's offering was preferable to Cain's; perhaps he never even considered it, since his perception of God's transcendence is immersed in the idea of God's otherness. The replies offered to these questions by traditional and critical commentators alike fail to note that their absence in the text is not accidental: far from making the story incomplete, this incompleteness is precisely what gives it meaning.

God rejects the offering brought by the "tiller of the ground" and takes to the sacrifice of the "keeper of sheep." No explanation is awarded, no reason advanced. The transcendent being operates in accordance with rules incomprehensible to those performing the sacrifice. In all likelihood, they do not even seek to understand these rules. Perhaps Cain's fallen countenance after his offering was rejected was not caused by the fact that the rejection of his offering was not explained and seemed arbitrary; rather Cain suddenly understood that God's rejection of his offering would forever remain meaningless since God's actions, by virtue of His transcendence, are necessarily inexplicable to humans. Let us recall that this fratricide was the direct outcome of Cain's "fallen countenance." If we consider this instance of violence as a paradigm of the inner tensions that prevent the formation of a harmonious family unit, then we have no choice but to conclude that the cause of this disharmony is God himself. This horrific violence erupts from the tension that God's exteriority generates in Cain's soul. In this respect, we should note that the motive behind the world's first murder is the failure of a sacrificial act. Roberto Calasso has drawn our attention to the presence of a tragic tension existing between murder and sacrifice and has used this tension to characterize the essence of Greek tragedy. It seems to me that in the story of Cain and Abel this same element of tragedy is demonstrable, even though it fails to ripen into a full-fledged tragedy. Indeed, tragedy is quite a rarity in the Bible, since the presence of God fetters the development of a genuine tragic conflict. George Steiner has rightly noted that the transcendent God of Western religions is equated with the principle of absolute justice, and wherever absolute justice resides tragedy cannot take root. Having a complete hold on the principles of justice guarantees the exercise of strict retribution. This, in turn, hinders the development of tragedy, whose articulation draws on the kind of heroism available only if it is, in principle, impossible to determine absolute justice. Yet this absence of tragedy does not open the portals of understanding, enabling man to grasp the meaning of divine conduct. The conflict between Cain and Abel is a poignant expression of the consequences arising from the basic lack of understanding and resentment that exists between man and God.

Not only do nonreligious commentators of the text see the motive behind Abel's murder as arising from God's otherness. Interestingly enough, one can evidence a similar attitude even within the folds of certain traditional hermeneutists. Take, for example, the commentary advanced by the nineteenth-century orthodox Jewish commentator Rabbi Meir Simcha Cohen of Dvinsk, author of *Meshech Chochma* (The duration of wisdom). He agrees with the contention that this murder had a religious motive behind it, the devastating result of man's attempt to petition God, who is different from all else. Yet the rabbi does not only allocate God a passive role (the object of incomprehensibility), but confers upon Him a much more active role (the reason for this incomprehensibility). The rabbi says the murder resulted from Cain's failure to comprehend the exact meaning of God's speech. After Cain's offering fails to reach its destination, God turns to Cain and addresses him, uttering something quite incoherent: "sin lieth at the door. And unto thee shall be his desire, and thou shalt rule over him" (Genesis 4:7). In his gloss, the rabbi suggests that Cain understood these words thus: "sin" is Abel who "lieth at the door." That is to say: Abel is lying in ambush somewhere near. "And unto thee shall be his desire"—the desire is Abel's and its object is Cain. As Cain understood it, God is warning him that Abel desires to kill him (or, to use the commentator's exact words, "to destroy him and eliminate him from the world"). And God, so at least Cain understands him, concludes that "thou shalt rule over him"—Abel's plot will fail and you shall thwart it. The rabbi's gloss remains consistent throughout, not straying from his reading even in face of the next dramatic verse: "And Cain talked with Abel his brother: and it came to pass, when they were in the field, that Cain rose up against Abel his brother, and slew him" (Genesis 4:8). The rabbi notices what one cannot fail to notice, that the verse is truncated; it is not quite clear what Cain said to Abel his brother. This abbreviation allows him to suggest the following sophisticated reading: "And Cain said[:] 'to my brother Abel . . . ' [is what God meant when he told me "sin lieth at the door. And unto thee shall be his desire, and thou shalt rule over him," and thus:] Cain rose up against Abel his brother, and slew him."

This far-fetched commentary uproots the text from the topography of simple meaning and allows the commentator to wander beyond the horizons of any reasonably literal interpretation. This is precisely what makes it such a fascinating interpretation. Rabbi Meir Simcha Cohen of Dvinsk had no qualms whatsoever about twisting the text to meet his own needs and arrive at his chosen conclusion: that Abel's murder is patently the result of a misapprehension of divine speech. According to him, Cain murders his brother believing that he is in fact complying with God's will and, moreover, that he is obeying God's *command*. God turns to Cain, Cain listens attentively, and what Cain hears is God commanding him to commit a murder. It is unlikely that a traditional commentator of this sort, who offered such a startling interpretation, did not have, in the back of his mind, the memory of a descendent of Cain to whom God revealed Himself and who also heard God commanding him to kill the next of all possible kin—who then, without hesitation, also nearly did what he too understood God to be commanding him. In a subtle way, murderous Cain is portrayed by the rabbi of Dvinsk as an ancient uncle of Abraham. Be that as it may, Abel's murder is presented as a vehement expression of the unbearable gulf induced by the framework of transcendence. For no apparent reason, God does not pay heed to Cain's offering, and, in the same motiveless and gratuitous manner, Cain understands the order to commit a murder. The rabbi's interpretation is audacious enough to allow room for an element of tragedy to seep into the story (as noted, the occurrence of tragedy in the Bible is quite rare). This element comes to the fore in the rabbi's concluding remarks, the moment he considers God's response to Cain following the murder: "the voice of thy brother's blood crieth unto me from the ground." His succinct and piercing comment on this verse runs thus: "because he [God] supposedly caused Cain to be angry over Abel." That is to say, the dead brother's blood does not cry *unto* the Lord, but rather cries *at* him. Abel's blood demands an explanation not from the murderer but from the one who supplied the motive for this murder, the creator of incomprehensibility whose consequences now lie motionless on the ground.

God's transcendence finds expression not only in the unbridgeable ontological rift but also in an epistemic failure of understanding. Epistemologically speaking, the presupposition of transcendence posits an impassable boundary on what man can grasp and what he can understand. From the same epistemological point of view, turning to transcendence signals a (partial or complete) reconciliation of the knower with his or her limitations, recognition of the irrevocability of understanding, a kind of admission that "some things are beyond comprehension." Needless to say, this epistemological breakdown is apparent not only in cultures that entertain the presupposition of transcendence; it is a universal feature of the limitations of man qua man. However, within the realm of Western religions this understanding of man's limitations assumes another dimension. Human limitations are seen as not only determined by the human condition but are apparent, in another sense, beyond man too: God's transcendence turns any act of understanding into something that is, in essence, imperfect. It is one thing to claim that human understanding is limited and incapable of breaking down its own boundaries, it's something else to commit oneself to the idea of spheres of being transcending the phenomenal world. The presupposition of transcendence does not merely endorse the former linguistic-epistemological claim; it also expands it by making a claim about God's ontological precedence over creation and assumes that understanding is quite apart from whoever understands. What we are witnessing here is not simply an effort to reveal man's epistemological and linguistic capabilities, but rather an attempt to unravel his stance on the nature of being, pointing to what exists in its own right, that which is beyond perception and verbalization. This kind of ontology is clearly subsumed by Platonism and also underlies Judaism, Christianity, and Islam (as we shall see in later chapters, the presupposition of transcendence is also present in modern Western philosophy, primarily in Cartesian thought, where it comes to the fore mainly in Descartes's obsessive quest for objectivity.)

Platonism and Neoplatonism posed the idea of transcendence as an abstraction and thus did not encounter *concrete* expressions of the above-mentioned epistemological problem, at least not in the sense that found its morbid expression in the story of Cain and Abel. Moreover, Plato's theory of Forms was founded on the supposition that the ontological precedence of the Forms concomitantly endows man's intellect with epistemological privilege. Even Aristotle, who vehemently rejected Plato's theory of Forms and replaced it with a predominantly realistic philosophical outlook, nevertheless shared with Plato the belief that the intellect is capable of unraveling reality "as it is," unhampered by the sensibility that exposes it. In contradistinction to the prominence of reason in Greek thought, the presupposition of transcendence in Western religions awards human reason, at most, a secondary role. On many occasions religious thinkers even urged their believers to abandon reason, deeming it injurious, delusive, and even subversive, seductive, and seditious for the very reason that it might, in their view, harm or damage that otherwise obvious preference for the outward over the inward.

This rejection of reason often gives rise to a taxing dilemma: the gulf between God and man is endless and, as such, unbridgeable; nevertheless, man and God must connect. To express this in Kafkaesque terms, what is impossible is at the same time necessary. Logically speaking, this is an intolerable situation because it necessitates a radical movement from the inside to the outside, but only within an enclosure that in fact precludes such a movement. So here is a dilemma: on the one hand, renouncing the very attempt to advance toward God is usually taken by Western religions to be a horrendous heresy. On the other hand, moving forward, seeking direct revelation, demanding of transcendence that it maintain a direct link with creation, most often involves a terrifying risk; "meeting" transcendence might turn out to be a perilous, even fatal, encounter. The pronouncement "No man see me, and live" (Exodus 33:20) is not just a rhetorical expression of boundaries, but it expresses a genuine threat. Divine revelation in the Hebrew Bible is a precarious affair. The danger arises from the fact that this is not just a revelation but also an attempt to reduce an irreducible gulf. Any revelation has the potential to become a catastrophe since God, as an "other," has precedence over man, and any attempt to mix between the other and the known, between exteriority and in-

teriority, ignites the fuse that can bring about its destruction. Whosoever sees God must die; this is transcendence in its full force—absolute
outwardness cannot be comprehended (that is, internally perceived).
Consider, for example, Moses. Here is a man dispatched on a great
mission: to form the nation of Israel, to act as its leader and its helms-
man. But Moses, let us recall, violently (and almost rudely) rejected
his designated role. Having finally acceded to its inevitability, having
allocated a place for it in his vision of the future, we find him reposing
with his wife and son in a certain inn. And then, for no apparent reason, God "falls upon him" and seeks to kill him (Exodus 4:24). If God
had managed to slay Moses, his imminent future would have disappeared, consumed by God, the eternal present. Only his wife's frenzied
intervention averts the slaughter. Perhaps it is no coincidence that the
three biblical characters to whom God did reveal his face share a common fate: Enoch, who "walked with God," Moses, who saw God face
to face (or, according to a different biblical account, his rear side), and
Elijah, who obtained through his explicit request a sort of "reconstruction" of the revelation on Mount Sinai. Enoch, Moses, and Elijah all
vanish without leaving a trace, the most radical and complete disappearance. Enoch did not die: he "was not; for God took him" (Genesis
5:24). The same holds for Elijah, who "went up by a whirlwind into
heaven" (2 Kings 2:11). Moses did die, but his place of burial is never
revealed (having been buried by God himself). These three men who
had communicated with God directly—perhaps even too directly—finally either disappeared or were consumed.

There are of course different stories: the Bible is not a philosophical system that places consistency on a pedestal; it contains a plurality
of different ideas and beliefs. There is the story of Abraham playing
host to God in his tent and then conversing with Him about Sodom
and Gomorrah, not to mention his audacity in challenging God on
moral issues. If we take this story out of context (as did Jewish apolo-
gists throughout the ages), it is easy to use it as a demonstration that
the barrier between God and man is, in fact, quite supple. But to consider this story out of context would prevent us from realizing that
Abraham's haggling with God is but the exception that proves the
rule. Were it not so, one doubts whether it would be so attractive to so
many of its readers. It is important, primarily, because it is an anomaly.
Abraham does what, in principle, he cannot do and, moreover, what

is inconceivable. It thus comes as no surprise that his bargaining with God is a complete failure and ends as abruptly as it began. Direct appeals to a transcendent being—such as those of Abraham's or Moses's importunate attempts to appease God's wrath and thus prevent the annihilation of the sinning Israelites—are merely extreme cases of non-mystical attempts to close up, whether temporarily or momentarily, the gulf dividing the divine and the human. Even when these attempts do turn out to be successful, they only highlight their rarity, while the essential gulf dividing God and the world of man remains intact.

It is not surprising then that this gulf also comes to the fore in the divine status of moral standards: God is the law, as ultimate justice and supreme moral ruler. For this reason God, and only God, is seen by Western religions as the absolute arbiter and sole standard in any judicial system or moral scheme. It is no coincidence that in the texts of Western religions God and justice are equated, and this equation is forever emphasized. This is of utmost importance, since not only does it install God as the ultimate form of righteousness, it also endows Him with the role of the exclusive and supreme creator of justice. The transcendent nature of such an ethical scheme is demonstrated in two interrelated ways. To begin with, it is objective, that is, its assumptions are wholly universal. Next, its exteriority is expressed by the fact that it is not subject to the vicissitudes of human affairs or adulterated by man's accessibility to them. With this as a background, the well-attested distinction in the West between the priest and the king—or, stated more generally, the distinction between God's theocratic rule and worldly governments (mostly kingdoms)—is not merely a contextual distinction, but deeply rooted in the attitude to God as the supreme manifestation of law, justice, and morality. In a fascinating book the anthropologist Mary Douglas has suggested a new reading of Leviticus. At the core of her reading lies the idea that the authors and redactors of Leviticus tried to promulgate a purified religion based solely on the uniqueness and separateness of God; the rituals and religious practices of everyday life were integrated into this religious outlook. According to Douglas, this explains the conspicuous absence of any kind of reference in Leviticus to the different forms of political rule—most notably, that of kingship. The religion of Leviticus is transcendent, and thus, in its political perspective, it embraces republicanism. The authors do not feel a need for a king or a kingdom since the idea of justice resides within one God and one God only. Attributing justice in its entirety to God makes Him the sole addressee for any complaint humans have against gross distortions of justice, harrowing cases of inequality, violent strikes of excessive evil, and blatantly unfair dispensations of moral retribution. These grievances are quite often aimed at finding the hidden motive behind apparent injustice or, occasionally, as a demand for God to account for His ways of dispensing justice. At times these claims even revolt against what appear to be a horrendous wrongdoing on the part of God, whose righteousness is deemed to be an inseparable part of Him. In times of crisis supplications such as these reveal a dramatic and, at times, even critical dimension. Crisis gives these questions a unique sense of urgency, endowing them with formidable depth and vitality. But why the urgency? Why, in a certain sense, is Job's cry against God paradigmatic of a whole religious culture? Is it possible to entertain the thought of a religious outlook that will not lend itself to this cry against the heavens by a man smitten with sore boils and afflicted by bereavement? It would seem that the only way to diminish the effect of such a rebuke (or make it completely meaningless) is to redefine the nature of God's transcendence, whether doing it moderately (such as in the cases of deistic outlooks that see God as totally uninvolved in His creation, once He has created it) or more excessive redefinitions (such as atheistic outlooks that deny the existence of a transcendent God altogether). There is, of course, another possibility: to assume the existence of a God that *to begin with* has no independent stance on moral issues and matter of justice since God, if He exists, is as much subject to the fundamental moral principle as anyone else. This, in effect, is the stance taken by Śaṅkara (an Indian philosopher of the seventh or eighth century CE). Job's rebuke would not be perceived as a paradigmatic question in the religious culture to which Śaṅkara subscribes. The agonizing presence of suffering may induce the sufferer to seek someone to take the "blame" or someone to be held "responsible," but for Śaṅkara this is no more than a symptomatic expression of one's intolerable pain. Beyond that, I think that Śaṅkara would have considered Job's trenchant rebukes as a pointless exercise in crude self-deception. Taking on God merely because one has deemed that He is the sole arbiter of justice—and then to insist that God reveal Himself as the only way of restoring cosmic order—to Śaṅkara this would seem like deceitful religious narcissism afflicting whoever refuses to admit that there is nothing personal in his suffering, and plainly nothing intentional, that his affliction is but one expression of the universal human condition. But in the province of Western religions, once Job's rebuke is voiced, all other thoughts are quelled. The reason is quite plain. The urgency and predominance of the paradigm epitomized in the West by Job arises from a conceptual framework that gives precedence to exteriority over interiority, to objectivity over subjectivity, to the transcendent over the psychological. The presence of this framework enables Western religions to see a hierarchy of values as established on a Being completely separated from the sphere of human activity. As we shall see later on, Indian thought does not comply with this framework, and thus Śaṅkara can effortlessly reject any view claiming that the creator God is responsible for the inequality apparent in the world. If you come across inequality and injustice, says Śaṅkara, look for its causes within yourself.

As we have seen, Western transcendence, manifested in the form a personal God, severely inhibits the development of any theory of ethics that sees humans as autonomous moral agents.[5] Moreover, not only are humans deprived of full-fledged moral autonomy, they are also utterly denied the ability to see themselves as individuals. In other words, the presupposition of transcendence impedes or at least hampers the emergence of an autonomous self. Needless to say, this last claim should be taken in a very particular sense. One is not trying to deny the obvious, namely, that each human can view herself or himself as a distinct person, replete with preferences, mental inclinations, personality traits, volitions. But this ability is not identical with the urge to become an autonomous self, a subject whose traits, preferences, and plans belong solely to itself—residing within itself, derived from itself, and defined by itself. This urge can easily infringe the presupposition of transcendence; as long as the presupposition of transcendence is present within culture, there can, in fact, be only one autonomous subject, in the full sense of the word. This is, of course, God. As a divine "subject," God is often depicted in terms expressing possession—He is considered "the possessor of heaven and earth" (Genesis 14:19), owner of the land, of nature, of history, indeed, owner of the body and soul of anything ever created. This form of capitalistic transcendence makes everything that is not God contingent. Only divine Being is necessary. We should take note that there is an intriguing closeness between necessity and autonomy. Whatever is contingent cannot be taken to be wholly autonomous since its existence is, in one way or another, dependent on factors external to it.

The gulf between God and that which is not God is clearly manifested in the view that regards nature as being *created* by God (rather than, say, springing out of Him). Western religions share the same cosmology according to which God is the sole creator of everything, and there was nothing before creation. Creation is therefore perceived as a singularly divine act in which nothing becomes something. Many consider this ex nihilo view of creation the most significant feature of Western religions. Subscribing to this ex nihilo view of creation is yet another expression of the conceptual framework that stresses the ultimate discontinuity between God and his works. One might say the notion of creation ex nihilo is merely a specific instance of this much broader picture of disparity between God and creation. The presupposition of transcendence in itself does not necessitate subscription to an ex nihilo view of creation (since one may, like Aristotle, assume that God is totally uninterested in the world), but it does enable it. The idea that everything arose out of nothing is not congruent with common sense, let alone critical thinking. The presupposition of transcendence supplies the conceptual underpinning enabling the development of this particular, not to say baffling, cosmogony. Be that as it may, there is a gulf between God and nature. The autonomy expunged from man is, metaphorically speaking, expunged from the totality of creation too. This perennial view of nature sowed, in a certain sense, the seeds of the scientific revolution since, in this context, science shares with religion the same approach to the contingency of the very existence of the natural world, understanding it as lacking necessity (evidently, with regard to the *manner* in which the world exists, the scientific outlook sees the world as subject to the immutable laws of nature).

The otherness and exteriority of a transcendent God facing His creation appears in the Bible the very moment creation is brought to a close with the creation of Man. When Paul Ricoeur considers the biblical creation stories, he rightly notes that the process of man's creation is a process of progressive disassociation. According to Ricoeur, this disassociation already appears in the very act of creation, an act that symbolizes, above all else, the disparity between the creator and his creation. It would seem that, alongside the creation of the world, God's impassable exteriority was created opposite it. Then came the original sin that exposed the disassociation between God and the world, transposing it into the disparity between God and humans, the latter reaching its peak with the expulsion of man and woman from the Garden of Eden. Ricoeur sees the disassociation between God and man expressed, for example, in the inexplicable (and therefore also senseless) injunction forbidding man to eat from the fruit of the tree of knowledge. The ontological cleft between He who orders and they who comply generates in the human a sense of disassociation with God. Ricoeur says the serpent, as the archetype of seduction, knew well how to exploit this lack of understanding and thus triggered off his seduction of woman with what seems like an irrelevant question: "Hath God said, Ye shall not eat of every tree of the garden" (Genesis 3:1). The purpose of this question is to undermine her confidence in the existence of the divine injunction. Thus, according to Ricoeur, this question sets off the human epoch as an epoch of suspicion: a line of deceit is stretched around the most basic condition of language—the existence of trust, the supposition of sincerity on behalf of the speaker (what linguists refer to as the "sincerity clause").

Suspicion does not just typify the relationships between God and man, but also, at the same time, the relationship between God and anything else that might jeopardize the nature of His absolute exteriority. Religions (and also certain philosophical schools) are suspicious of—not to mention hostile—to anything that is likely to impinge on the separation between the outward and inward, between the noumenal and phenomenal. This explains the hostility encountered by any attempt to eradicate or reduce the gap between the absolute and the human. Mostly, this kind of activity is derided and labeled, derogatively, *heresy* or *idolatry*. Rejecting idolatry means seeing God as the exclusive source of everything that exists. The vehement and often violent rejection of the different forms of idolatry becomes the basic foundation of Western religions operating under the umbrella of the presupposition of transcendence. Jan Assmann has quite rightly termed this family of religions (which he called the family of Mosaic religions) *counter-religion*, since these religions reject anything opposing them, derisively labeling any such alternatives *paganism*, *heresy*, or *idolatry*.

Idolatrous practices are often described in terms of seduction, even in instinctual terms at times. Idolatry is seen as a powerful uncontrollable impulse.[6] The many different forms of idolatrous worship tend to be portrayed in great detail, employing much flare and nuance. This is markedly different from the elusive descriptions of that transcendent "other" being residing somewhere beyond the realm of any possible rendition. Having said that, the interrelationship between the worship of a transcendent God and the multifarious worship of "false" gods is anything but simple. Nowhere is this dialectical complexity more dramatically evidenced than in one of the most highly celebrated instances of idolatrous worship described in the Hebrew Bible: the investiture and worship of the Golden Calf. This event occurs merely forty days after God spectacularly reveals Himself on Mount Sinai to His chosen people. The whole episode is described in six succinct verses. The opening phrases convey the dread of anticipation. This is achieved through a description of the multitude's sense of incapacitating passivity: "And the people saw that Moses delayed to come down out of the mount" (Exodus 32:1). The episode ends in ecstatic merriment, in a tumultuous flow of activity, in a flourish of verbs rapidly chasing each another: "And they rose up early on the morrow, and offered burnt offerings, and brought peace offerings; and the people sat down to eat and to drink, and rose up to play" (Exodus 32:6). Between these two verses, we see how languid passivity is exchanged for exuberant activity. Moses's unexplained disappearance is fully compensated for. Yet this is more than a simple substitution: it "overflows"—the Golden Calf is more than just a substitute Moses, it is considered the very God that "brought us up out of the land of Egypt."

This tale takes up a central role in Judaism's collective memory, and for many generations it was one of the primary stories forming the core of Jewish historical awareness. There can be no doubt that this episode was of prime importance for the original storyteller too. The story of the Golden Calf is recounted under the onerous shadow of Mount Sinai, and this shadow is, among other things, the shadow of the first commandment given to the people of Israel—the commandment stipulating God's exclusivity before His people: "Thou shalt have no other gods before me" (Exodus 20:3); second, the commandment that explicitly prohibits the use of any iconic images in His worship: "Thou shalt not make unto thee any graven image, or any likeness of any thing that is in heaven above, or that is in the earth beneath, or that is in the water under the earth" (Exodus 20:4). The worship of the Golden Calf is a malicious violation of these two commandments. It unequivocally defies God's exclusivity and rebuffs His declared war on graven images, likenesses, and other iconic representations. This brazen idol worship is performed, at the foot of Mount Sinai, only thirty-nine days after God reveals Himself on the same mount, explicitly forbidding any form of idolatry. The proximity of this event, both in time and place, is very curious. Curious, but certainly not coincidental.

Idolatry is not worlds apart from worshipping the one true God, and this proximity is, I think, a key issue in the evolution of Judaism as much as in other religions that function within the framework of the presupposition of transcendence. Worshipping the Golden Calf is a gravely subversive act because it undermines the very foundations of worshipping God. And yet, given that this sedition takes place so soon after God's commandment on iconoclasm, one finds it difficult to place them apart (despite vigorous commentarial attempts to do so). Mount Sinai is smoking as God "descends upon it on fire"; then this fire heralds the "false" fire of the molten calf. Similarly, "Thou shalt not make unto thee any graven image" heralds the very making of the calf, but we should not read any psychological insights into this propinquity. It is not the author's intention here to suggest that human nature is such that, when they encounter God Himself, humans nevertheless want an idol; that when you provide them with celestial fire, they, for obscure reasons, prefer "to play" with fire. This propinquity defines something much more essential: worshipping an idol is the worship of a different and "other" kind of element, mainly because God Himself, the God of absolute truth, is "otherness," is exteriority, severance, and disassociation. His absolute otherness is what necessitates His exclusivity; that is to say, the believer is forced to consider other religious practices not as *different* religious practices but as *false* religious practices. The fact that God is an absolute other is what makes other, idolatrous worship possible. To put it more carefully, one might say that God's otherness and distinctiveness are what draw false worship to His midst. For so long as God's otherness is an integral part of what defines Him, it will give rise to the possibility of idolatry and keep it a viable, vibrant, and explosive option. Eradicating the proximity between the worship of God and idolatry will exact a clear price: an obvious diminution of God's otherness (the Jewish midrashic, kabbalistic, and Hasidic literature attests to such attempts as do the mystical speculations of Meister Eckhart and certain forms of Sufism). So long as transcendence is divinity's conceptual frame of reference, the concept of idolatry will remain some sort of mirror image. The story of the Golden Calf plainly demonstrates such a condition: the connection between divinity and its antithesis. This requisite exclusivity in the worship of God necessarily brings about, sooner than later, devotion to the Golden Calf. The idolaters who made the calf will for many years continue to wander the wilderness and, on more than one occasion, will recall and yearn for the delights of Egypt. Yet this is not the yearning of a liberated man suddenly recalling his days of captivity and asking to return there, but rather the yearning of someone who is enslaved by an exterior, different, and foreign God and remembers a different form of slavery that was dominated by pluralism, not monism. So the Israelites will nostalgically recall their heyday, when their palate was not governed by the same interminable dish, that insipid manna dribbling from the sky, but rather by a profusion of flavors, colors, and smells: meat, fish, cucumbers, melons, leeks, onions, and garlic.

This significant propinquity between the worship of God and the Golden Calf comes into the limelight even before Moses pulverizes the idol and then scattering the powder upon the water, which he then forced the children of Israel to drink. Before this Moses shatters the tablets of stone that he brought down from the mountain, tablets inscribed on both sides and written by the finger of God. It would seem that the presence of an idol turns the tablets (which emphatically prohibit the worship of idols) into an idol. The exclusivity and uniqueness that defines the worship of God instigates an apocalyptic war against any other kind of worship. This war brings the two forms of worship together and risks obliterating the differences between them. When does proper worship become idolatrous? Perhaps the tablets of stone, the Tables of the Covenant, are themselves a form of idolatry?

The presupposition of transcendence imparts a sense of remoteness, of severance and loss, but one receives something in return. If the religious cost of presupposing transcendence is a growing sense of alienation and threat coupled with a feeling of estrangement, in exchange one receives the security of knowing that there are boundaries (ontological as well as psychological) for which one needs to be held accountable. This sense of security enables the formation of a limited, yet relatively secure, self-awareness and self-identity whose strength is its very weakness. The primacy of outward objectivity over inward subjectivity guarantees, at least in principle, the stability of the line demarcating the outward and the inward. It sustains the existence of a limited independent self-awareness, since its existence is warranted, supposedly, from without, by an external guarantor preceding awareness, and independent of it. Thus the presupposition of transcendence can diligently and successfully uphold its duty as a stable and solid bar against any attempt to give precedence to interiority. If the presupposition of transcendence incorporates a clear boundary between in and out, between the subjective and the objective, it means that one's mental states play no constitutive part in determining this boundary. Even in the case when believers are called upon to worship their God in the deepest recesses of their soul, or to love him boundlessly in their hearts (and, moreover, even when this God is equated with love), the state of mind of these believers is still seen as entirely dependent on the omnipotent presence of an outward God. The autonomy of this state of mind has been "impounded," so to speak. In addition, it is ultimately aimed outward, since "inner" revelations of God are possible only by virtue of the fact that He exists "out there." It is for this reason that autonomous mental acts of internalization—introspection, the search for identity, self-realization, and so on—are viewed with suspicion by the institutions of Western religions. This suspicion is a grave matter; it is not merely a priestly clerical issue. So long as we are "basking" in the light of transcendence, it is deemed appropriate that one's personal identity be determined without any due psychologization; preferring the inner to the outer is blatantly inadvisable. Fenced in by the presupposition of transcendence, the mind is expected to make do with whatever it finds within this enclosure. Interiority's full sense of self-expression is inhibited by these limits. This is an intriguing situation since, as mentioned previously, these limitations are perceived as an advantageous reward rather than an unwanted restriction. A mind delimited by transcendence is a "secure" mind, protected from any kind of serious internal disturbances or an unconscious mental downfall. The presupposition of transcendence—while posited at the foundation of a culture—forbids you to psychologize reality; you are required to prefer exteriority to any kind of internalization. If the price you pay in accepting the precedence of exteriority over interiority is an inevitable sense of alienation, then what you receive in return is a certain objectivization of consciousness itself, since this consciousness has determinable boundaries that do not depend on its mental operations.

Advancing the claim that the presupposition of transcendence acts as the conceptual framework of Western religions might seem incredible. Is it really possible to think of a religious culture grounded in one basic conceptual scheme? Prima facie, this reductionism seems unwarranted. For instance, scholars of religion and philosophers of religion acknowledge that in the different theological discourses of Western religions there is notable tension (whether conspicuous or latent) between God's transcendence and His immanence. One of the verses describing the prophet Isaiah's revelation clearly demonstrates this tension: "Holy, holy, holy, is the Lord of hosts: the whole earth is full of His glory" (Isaiah 6:3). If the first part of the verse thrice emphasizes that holiness is the main attribute of God's transcendence, then the second part is notable for its opposite, describing God's presence *in* the world (God Himself, or at least a certain aspect of Him, referred to as the "glory" of God). At first glance, it would therefore seem that the presupposition of transcendence is but one component (albeit a crucial one) in the depiction of God in Western religions; denying His immanent side may create a distorted and one-sided picture of the complex and intricate scheme by which God is portrayed in Western religions. Indeed, accounts of an all-pervading, ever present divinity are not that difficult to come by. Such accounts clearly seem to reduce the gap between God and creation in general, between Him and humans in particular. Thus, while God's sanctity drives Him away from man, His omnipresence draws Him nearer to His creation. Moreover, Isaiah shows God's immanence as being somehow contradictory to His transcendent character. On the other hand, certain mystical doctrines have attempted to grant His immanence precedence by portraying a vision of divinity whose presence in the world is all-inclusive, both in the furthest reaches of the heavenly realms and in the deepest recesses of man's soul. The predominant mystical worldview of immanence sees God's presence in the world as part of the divine essence itself and thus as inevitable. Any barrier supposedly erected between divinity and man is imaginary, one that a passionate believer or practiced mystic can overcome. An air of egalitarianism engulfs this view: the divine omnipresence means that at least some elected or sensitive humans can actively engage it. Occasionally, the claim about God's immanence takes another, more extreme, turn: some mystics went further, claiming that God is in some way dependent on man. As it is well known, some mystical trends within Western religions incorporate into the idea of the divine being a kind of imperfection. According to such a view, man was allocated an active role: he has to find a remedy (a tikkun, in kabbalistic terms) for God's deficiency, a way of restoring divinity's misaligned harmony. Either way, it would seem that one can find in Western religions a kind of presupposition of immanence that establishes proximity between the divine and the human, while at the same time it tends to blur the boundaries and eradicate the unfathomable gap that exists between the divine and the human. Quite often, this proximity is described in terms of intimacy, and its vocabulary is crammed with erotic and sexual allusions.

Against this background, it is imperative to readdress the question: in emphasizing the presupposition of transcendence, am I not presenting too biased a view of Western religions? This question, if it does arise, is founded, in my mind, on a categorical mistake. More precisely, we might say that the error lies in a lack of proper discrimination between, on the one hand, the conceptual dimension and, on the other hand, the theological and mystical dimension of Western religious phenomenology. I contend that, when we look at the actual contents of immanence in Western religions, we shall see that they are, for the most part, still determined by the presupposition of transcendence's conceptual structure. The upshot of this is that there is no symmetry between transcendence and immanence—exteriority precedes interiority, both logically and ontologically. The tension that exists between transcendence and immanence arises only when one attempts to see immanence as bridging, even if only to a degree, the gap created by transcendence. This is precisely what the different mystical doctrines that have managed to infiltrate the foundations of institutionalized Western religions have aimed to do. They attempt to somehow bring together the interior and exterior, whether by uplifting the interior, raising it to its absolute true sources (as is the case, for example, in Neoplatonic mysticism) or else by bringing transcendence down, so that the intrepid mystic can make contact. But even when this intrepid Western mystic excels himself, and attempts to bridge the gap between transcendence and immanence, he is still functioning within the conceptual linguistic framework that recognizes that there is an "original" gap to begin with. Obviously, there is no point in trying to reduce or bridge a gap unless you assume it to exist prior to your attempts at reducing it. This means that the mystic, in aspiring to bride the gap, is implicitly acknowledging its presence and at the same time giving precedence to transcendence. Take, for example, the various gnostic schools that evolved alongside early Christianity. The gnostic thinkers tried to create a mystic unity between the spirit of man and the sublime God (doing this by overcoming the rigid and onerous barrier of evil that manifests itself in the very existence of the world, a barrier begot by a malicious creator of the world). Their goal was therefore to reach a transcendent being residing beyond any universe. It was in this manner that the sublime God was considered an absolute "other" who is, in essence, alien to the world. Saint Augustine too, who more than any other early Christian philosopher is identified with the quest for man's inwardness, saw this inwardness as the most appropriate setting for divulging the transcendent nature of God, since for him what man finds in the depths of his inwardness is the divine light that enables him to know transcendent truth, which means for Augustine, notwithstanding the fact that one finds God in the immanent depths of one's mind, this immanent occurrence highlights the logical and ontological precedence of God's outwardness. Jean Luc Marion rightly notes that what enables intimate relations between God and man in Christian theology is the essential distance separating them. The connection between God and man, so concludes Marion, is only possible by virtue of the fact that the two share no common ground. As we shall see in chapter 3, even Descartes—who apparently tried to undermine the Platonic notion of transcendence by replacing it with a subjective inwardness—could not disassociate himself from the framework of transcendence, despite the emphasis he put on the inward.

Of course, one should bear in mind that even more radical positions were advanced, positions that completely ignored the presupposition of transcendence. Here one should distinguish between two kinds of challenges to the precedence of transcendence: the first philosophical and the second mystical. As an example of the former one could mention the Stoics of ancient Greece or Spinoza's pantheistic philosophy, which sought to completely undermine the status of God's transcendence.

Spinoza, as is well known, repudiated not only the Jewish idea of a personal God but even the abstract, philosophical idea of a transcendent God. Besides his denial of divine providence and reward and punishment, he even sought to challenge, once and for all, the basic assumption of transcendence itself. Thus, for example, in *Ethics* he says that God's immanence is necessarily derived from the proposition that "God is the immanent and not the transitive cause of all things: All things which are, are in God, and must be conceived through God; therefore God is the cause of those things which are in him. . . ." For Spinoza, this proves the impossibility of God's transcendence. Even from the few sentences quoted above, it can be seen that this understanding of immanence is conscious of what it is rebelling against and aware of the conceptual underpinning that it challenges. Indeed, most appearances of God's immanence in Western philosophy and religious ideas until the nineteenth century relied to some extent or other on the presupposition of transcendence as a primary conceptual vantage point. Mostly, the notion of immanence was employed to undermine the foundations of the presupposition of transcendence and, in radical cases, to bring about its complete demolition. Either way, these Western notions of immanence are completely different from Indian notions of immanence that evolved within a framework that did not *presume* this precedence of transcendence.

The same holds true when we briefly turn to consider those immanent perceptions of God that abound in accounts of mystical experiences and mystical reflections. These too are, on the whole, counterresponses to overriding transcendence. In his monumental work on Jewish mysticism, Gershom Scholem described institutionalized Western religions' primary point of view as being based on the gap existing between an infinite creator God and man, His finite creation. Scholem has called this gap a "yawning abyss" and said that it can be bridged solely by means of the voice—on the one hand, the voice of a revealing, commanding, legislating God and, on the other hand, the voice of a man in prayer. Monotheistic religions, claimed Scholem, exist and evolve within this notion of a polarity, of an eternal abyss.[7] The account of mysticism in these religions is therefore the chronicle of the attempts to bridge an unbridgeable abyss. In one of Scholem's more speculative articles on the Kabbalah (which this prudent historian called "Ten Unhistorical Aphorisms on Kabbalah"), he pursues this line of thought. When considering the character of kabbalistic pantheism, he first draws attention to the transcendent quality of divinity in its epistemic aspects and then moves on to consider its ontological aspects: divine being, in its full essence, is totally transcendent. According to Scholem, among the first kabbalists this essence underwent a process of "annihilization" (expressed, among other things, in the act of creation), and this finally brought about the blurring of transcendence—superseding it with a pantheistic account in which the barrier between divinity and the world of men disappeared. This "pantheistic turn," as Scholem calls it, is a direct and evident counterresponse to the presupposition of transcendence. Neoplatonic influences are evident here.[8] Another Jewish example is the Hasidic concept of God's immanence. The principal element in Hasidic understanding of immanence is the idea that God is omnipresent and is accessible to any devotee's soul. In addition, God's immanence makes it possible for man to discover that the most profound encounter between God and man occurs within his heart and soul. But this idea too is not divorced from the presupposition of God's transcendence. On the contrary, this is precisely the assumption that, to a certain extent, the Hasidic movement tried to challenge. The fact that the tzaddik was given the opportunity to "bring down the heavens" testifies to the existence of a vantage point in which there is a clear demarcation between above and below as two separate and distinguishable entities. The tzaddik's virtues enable him to annihilate this difference and thus expose God's ever present immanence. As mentioned previously, immanence is here a counterresponse, at times even seditious, and contests the conceptual structure: it raises intellectual issues, recommends modes of behavior, nourishes acts of religious (even ecstatic) devotion—all in order to partially undermine the barrier imposed by the idea of transcendence. This mystic endeavour has an obvious ontological dimension to it. The kabbalist or the tzaddik need to perform a "rectification" (a tikkun), that is, to restore harmony within the Divine Being. In this context the presupposition of transcendence is perceived as the cause of disharmony, which can be rectified only by experiencing God as immanence. Accordingly, this form of mysticism is fundamentally different from its Indian counterpart. Indian mysticism that endorses a vision of immanence is different because it bears no trace whatsoever of subversion. If the presupposition of transcendence does not exist in the Indian conceptual bedrock, needless to say there can also be no revolt or subversion against such a presupposition. Thus, all the comparisons between, for example, Hasidism and Indian devotionalism (bhakti)[9] are grossly mistaken (Martin Buber was among those who committed this error by trying to portray Hasidic mysticism in an "Oriental" light). Bhakti is an attempt to draw closer to the deity's immanence, hoping to fuse with her or him by means of complex, sometimes radical forms of personal devotion. But there is nothing subversive in this devotionalism, since there is no real barrier between the outward and the inward. Any existing barrier is only the product of the devotee's false imaginings. That is to say, this form of mysticism is not subject to an unequivocal ontology.

There is then a palpable difference between Western ideas of immanence that undermine the presupposition of transcendence and the ideas of immanence that tend to flourish in philosophical and religious milieus that do not put the presupposition of transcendence at the center. This, in my mind, is the case with Indian thought over a period of at least two millennia. Indeed, it is very difficult to find the presupposition of transcendence in the fabric of Indian thought and religious practices, neither in its abstract Platonic philosophical form, nor in the more tangible religious shape it took in the West. Whether India accepts a plurality of gods or, alternately, whether for India this plurality is a manifestation of the many faces of one God, divinity is nevertheless not considered as something *essentially* different from the world and as something that has ontological precedence over man and the world. I am not claiming that transcendence is completely absent from India's vast religious literature, but I do sense that it rarely occupies a key position in the conceptual framework of Indian culture. I believe that this can explain one of the primary reasons why the West misconstrues Indian civilization. We gaze at India and see ample references to gods, divinities, and even a solitary God. This immediately gives us the impression that we "understand" what we see since we assume that the conceptual framework underpinning the language of Indian religion is not categorically different from the conceptual framework with which we are familiar. And, truly, why should we be at fault? The Indians themselves seem to talk about "God" while constantly worshiping a plethora of "divinities." They delight in recounting Śiva's omnipotence, or wax about Kṛṣṇa's allure, or ruminate on the metaphysical aspects of that divine impersonal principle that they refer to as *Brahman*.

Is it not plain that there is a striking similarity between a brahmin's talk about the "One" and, for example, Plotinus's Neoplatonist "One"?

Still, there is something mistaken about this approach since it ignores the conceptual dissimilarities that exist between the two cultures.[10] We read the Indian religious texts without noticing that in their conceptual framework the presupposition of transcendence is completely lacking. Despite that plurality of gods, goddesses, demigods, and many other divine beings, one should be on guard and avoid mistaking quantity for quality. When looking carefully at the many Indian gods, at least as they were perceived in ancient and classical India (until the arrival of Western religions—Islam to begin with and then Christianity), we see that none are attributed with the notion of transcendence in the Western sense of the term; quite the contrary. As we shall see in the following pages, it appears that even when it is assumed that one or another god is transcendent, it is but one factor in a complex set of reciprocal relationships between human and divine realms. That is to say, those who nurtured the Indian pantheon, and performed the ritual practices ordained to serve this pantheon (mostly referred to by means of the inclusive terms *Brahmanism* or *Hinduism*), worked with a much more restricted view of their gods compared to the prevailing religious outlooks in the West. Moreover, one has to take into account that the Indian subcontinent witnessed the emergence of professedly atheist religious and philosophical outlooks. Buddhism is often portrayed as a paradigmatic instance of a religion in which divinity does not play any substantial role. God, or gods, are irrelevant to anyone following the Buddhist path to enlightenment, and they are unlikely to assist man in his quest for liberation. The Buddha vehemently denied the practicability of seeking answers to man's fundamental existential problems in realms transcending him. Such answers must be sought within the same realm where the problem arises to begin with, namely, the realm of human existence, the here and now. It is therefore very difficult to imagine the Buddha rising to meet the challenge of transcendence that Plato put before Western civilization. The famous image of cave dwellers poised in front of a philosopher who shows them how to liberate themselves from their forlorn condition would have probably appealed to the Buddha, but there is little doubt that he would reject Plato's assumption that true reality is "out there," beyond the cave (that is, beyond phenomenal life), and he would definitely refuse to accept that

liberation from the phenomenal realm is determined by the unconditioned existence of such an external reality. It is true that over the ages
folkloristic Buddhism adopted no small part of the Indian pantheon, but
divine beings were not considered essentially different from humans:
they live longer (though they are not immortal) and they are more potent—but even these gods, like humans, are an inseparable part of the
endless cycle of birth and death and thus subject to its governing rules.
It is worth noting that in the more psychological strands of Buddhism
every human could, in theory and in practice, become a divine being.
Thus, even if one does accede to the idea of a divinity in Buddhism, it
is a very different form of divinity from its Western counterpart.

If we concentrate on the more argumentative-philosophical side of
Indian Buddhism, we shall see that it raises some pertinent questions
about the likelihood of a creator God—most notably as a creator of the
world or worlds. Stated differently, it might be said that most forms of
Indian philosophical Buddhism upheld a view that, in the West, would
be labeled *atheism*. Atheism in Buddhist philosophy stems from an uncompromising severity in the application of speculative thought and its
use to counter the cultivation of irrational states of mind based merely
on faith. Turning from Indian Buddhism to Hindu philosophy, we find
that certain schools of orthodox Hinduism rejected the existence of
God or divinity for more religious reasons. It was seen as jeopardizing
the unique, absolute, and independent status of the religious structure
itself. Other Indian outlooks were more concerned with establishing
valid means of knowledge and unraveling the status of the perceived
world, so they were less interested in ontology as such.

One could easily expand on the absence of the presupposition of transcendence from the conceptual framework of religious and metaphysical discourse of Indian civilization. In this chapter it will suffice to examine three examples that illustrate this absence. Each of them looks at
this issue vis-à-vis the mutual relations of men and God or gods—and
each example offers a somewhat different angle on this relationship.
These differing viewpoints nevertheless all share between them the
same conceptual grounding: the denial of an ontological precedence
of God or gods over the world or over man. As mentioned earlier, one

can easily find many illuminating examples of such disregard for transcendence in India's rich *philosophical* heritage. But, in this instance, I have preferred to draw my examples straight from its *religious* texts—especially from texts that deal explicitly with the nature of divinity.

To begin with, let us consider an example that is steeped in a ritualistic context. It is drawn from the world of Vedic hymns.[11] To be more specific, it is part of the Nirukta, a commentary written on the Veda around the seventh or sixth century BCE by a legendary author called Yāska. The following short excerpt considers the ṛsis, the "seers," those magnificent seven sages of yore endowed with many exceptional qualities (to which we shall return in the next chapter). This excerpt describes the ṛsis' final departure from the face of the earth and the response of the gods to this act of withdrawal:

> When the ṛsis rose above
> The gods asked the ṛsis:
> Who will now be our seers?
> And they answered: would that reasoning (*tarka*) be your seer.[12]

A more tempting translation for the word *tarka* would perhaps be "wisdom," "understanding," or even "reason," which would evoke, above all else, the modern notion of rationality. But these ancient ṛsis use the term *tarka*, which in the Indian context has a very specific meaning. It is limited in its range of application and refers, in the main, to "argumentative inferential procedure." The author of this excerpt was not interested in elevating the status of reason, making it an autonomous activity, but rather in juxtaposing the procedural process of reasoning with Vedic ritual activity.

This amazing passage from the Nirukta illustrates the unique role ritual has in ancient Vedic religion. It also demonstrates the interesting relationship between man's ritualistic activity and the status of the gods for whom these rituals were performed.

We should note that this relationship is diametrically opposed to the paradigmatic act of sacrifice evidenced in Cain and Abel's sacrifice. Vedic rituals are directed, of course, at the gods with the intent of obtaining favors from them. Nevertheless, underlying this activity are not the gods, but rather man's ritualistic tendencies. Indeed, at that time ritualistic activity was often considered the most sublime expression of being human, since it was a force with which the sacrificer could define himself. "If the heavens are thy wish—sacrifice!" is one well-known injunction of the period. The idea of heaven here does not imply proximity to a certain god but, in more general terms, the attainment of immortality or, better said, immortalization. Through the act of sacrifice, man posits himself as a permanent or ineradicable being. It is no coincidence that immortality acquired by means of sacrifice is compared to the immortality a man obtains through his (male) offspring. On more than one occasion Vedic sacrificial activities are compared to sexual activities: the male and female reproductive organs are allegorized as the different parts of the sacrificial alter, while penetrating and uniting with a woman's body is compared to the symbolic penetration of the sacrificial body and the sacrificer's discovery of himself by means of the sacrificial act.

We could sum up by saying that in the Vedic world the most important aspect of sacrificial activity is that it distinguishes man from all that is not man—beasts, on the one hand, and gods, on the other. The gods formed part of a grand cosmic scheme, but still there was a place for them beneath the foreboding shadow of ritual activities. Moreover, the gods, much like sacrificial activity, were also subject to this general cosmic order. Since sacrifice was endowed with an efficacious internal force, it meant that any proper sacrifice would necessarily fulfill the sacrificer's goals. This efficaciousness stems from the existence of universal causal laws regulating the causal connections between an act of sacrifice and its outcome. A sacrifice will succeed in reaching its preordained goals since it is neither dependent upon the will or grace of a god, nor on any other element external to it. The efficacy of a sacrificial act was reliant only on its proper execution. The act of sacrifice is therefore a certain kind of performance, but this performance was clearly considered in epistemological terms too. The idea, that religious knowledge is equivalent to obtaining control of worldly life, is familiar from other religions as well, and it will also recur in the developments of Indian culture.

The Indian version of the idea may seem strange to an ear habituated to a religious language necessitating that there be a chasm between man and god. What then are we to make of it? As long as our main concern is the respective differences between the two cultures, our task is not that difficult—after all, the role played by the transcendent God in that horrid affair between Cain and Abel is noticeably different from the role of the gods in Vedic ritualism. But if we are seeking a deeper understanding of the Vedic world, then we should be more wary. Let there be no doubt: the Vedic seers imagined gods that commanded great awe and boundless respect, and these sentiments are expressed through the presence of a genuine difference between the divine and the human. Gods were considered much more virile and powerful than humans; the Vedic hymns wax profusely on their courage and their valor. Given this, and given that the gods are somewhat capricious, they should be approached carefully; they need to be appeased and their clemency should be sought. Moreover, their most salient feature (unlike their Buddhist counterparts) is their immortality. Regrettably, humans are mortal and this makes the difference between them and the gods all the more striking. Yet this is only part of the story. As broad, terrifying and daunting as this difference between gods and mortals may be, it is *not* grounded in a necessary conceptual framework. When one examines Vedic ritualism, one sees a striking example of how this difference functions, of how it separates the immediacy of the here and now as opposed to remoteness of the beyond, without at the same time suggesting that this rift is conceptually unbridgeable. Although the gods are mightier than humans, when man's immortalization is at stake the gods occupy only a secondary role. It is interesting to note that one of the prevailing accounts, in the Vedas themselves, of how the gods attained their own immortality suggests that it was not part of their innate nature but rather something they had to acquire, somewhat ironically, by faultlessly performing a kind of primordial ritual. The idea that rituals are self-contained and totally independent of the capricious whims of the gods finds its expression not only in the poetic language of the Vedic hymns but also in the more abstract language of Indian religious thought. To mention but one instance of the major role that Indian religious thinkers give to the autonomy of the ritual act, one should consider their insistence that the Vedas, which are the source and inspiration of every sacrificial activity, are independent of the gods in every conceivable manner. The Vedas were neither composed by the gods, nor did the gods magnanimously grant them to humans; the Vedas are totally self-sufficient and their validity is derived from within.

Given all this, it is clear why the relationship between the seers and gods in the excerpt quoted above is of a very different order from the one we know in the West. Although, as I have just said, in a certain sense the gods are superior to the seers; nonetheless, the imminent departure of the seers creates a genuine sense of unease among the gods. It would seem that notwithstanding the gods' immense prowess, the seers still have an edge over them, an advantage that arises from their nature as "seers": the gods cannot contain the nature of the seers. The gods are thus dependent on the seers, not merely in the manner that a creator might be in need of the services of those he has created. This dependence is clearly expressed by the assumption that the seers' non-divine nature is independent of the whims of the gods and is not subject to their control or judgment. Moreover, it is beyond their reach. As we shall see in the next chapter, it was the ṛṣis who were responsible for the worldly realization of the sublime language, and also that this language was revealed from within their interiority (that is to say, they did not obtain it either from without or from the gods). In this sense too the gods are dependent upon them—their query "Who will now be our seers?" also expresses the independent linguistic status that the ṛṣis have—but this will be dealt with further on. For the time being, suffice to say that it is possible to pose the question "Who will now be our seers?" only within a conceptual grounding in which divinity has no ontological precedence over the seers. The seers' reply is indeed congruent with that conceptual framework in which transcendence lacks ontological precedence: "would that reasoning be your seer."

This precedence is evident in the course of the evolution of Vedic religion. Rituals are performed, and increasingly their purpose becomes completely absorbed by the ritual itself. Rituals cease to be performed as a means to something beyond them; they are performed for their own sake. It is but one short step to seeing the whole of man's ritualistic activity in cosmic terms, seeing it as an act of creation and preservation of the whole cosmos. This cosmic role of ritual was described by a profusion of metaphors: ritual creates the world, preserves it, prevents the heavens from clashing with the earth; it establishes the immutability of day and night and other such cosmic sureties intended to safeguard the world as we know it. That is to say, ritual is the source of creative energies as well as the source of eternal life. Cosmology and a subtle form of magic are fused together: through ritual one attains immortality, the very existence of the world is preserved, and its destruction is thwarted. There came a time (most scholars refer to this as the late Vedic period, i.e., the ninth to seventh centuries BCE) when Indian culture came up with what to my mind is one of its most fascinating innovations: the possibility of the internalization of ritualistic activity.

The idea of internalization arose out of the process of individualization of the person performing the ritual. The sacrificer himself began to take an increasingly more significant role in the ritual. Correspondingly, the material and more concrete aspects of the ritual act became redundant. If the meaning of sacrifice lies within man and man alone, there is no reason not to "place" inside him the actual sacrificial act itself and thus, plainly, ritual is transformed from a physical occurrence to mental event. As in S. Y. Agnon's wonderful tale of an architect who enters the drawing he made of the king's palace only to disappear inside it without a trace, it seems that the Indian sacrificer discovered the hidden structure and governing laws of ritual, so that he could "enter" them instead of performing them externally, outwardly. If a ritual takes place according to a set of rules that have no external source, and if in effect this set of rules actually exists inside man, then one cannot help but think of this ritual as something that transpires invisibly, in some inward and intimate stratum of mental activity in which it is truly possible to imagine the exact and precise particulars of the ritual.[13]

This is the sense in which the ṛṣis, those ancient seers, are superior to the gods and epitomize the gods' unobtainable desideratum. The seers manifest the inescapable human side of ritual activity, and their departure from the scene signifies the possibility of internalization—the seers may indeed have departed for the heavens, but "reasoning" is left behind as a blueprint, as an interior forecast the gods have no choice but to accept. Such an understanding would not have been possible if the concept of god in Indian culture were entrenched in the presupposition of transcendence. On the contrary, this clearly demonstrates its absence from the relationships existing between man and gods in the world of Indian ritualism. One contemporary Vedic scholar has crowned an important article on this dimension of the Vedic worldview with a very fitting title: "Man—the Creator." The ritualistic act is perceived as a unique act of creation: man upholds the cosmos through his ritualistic activity (and, alongside that, by means of his linguistic activity, he preserves the Vedas, the framework of the cosmos, by performing them). This is not the same sense of cosmic creation envisaged by Western religions when they think of God's creation of the world, and it is not even "creation" in certain modern and postmodern senses. Man's active role here is not akin to that of a painter creating a world in his painting; it is more akin to the role a musician has in performing music: by playing a musical piece over and over again he is not only preserving it but also preventing its destruction.

The second instance of the absence of the presupposition of transcendence from the conceptual bedrock of Indian culture that I want to examine does not concern ritual, but a more philosophical idea of the gods and their role in the world. It is drawn from the Upaniṣads.[14] The passage I want to consider is from the Bṛhadāraṇyaka Upaniṣad and deals with an idea to which we will return, the homology between *brahman* (as a universal reality principle) and *ātman* (the kernel of subjective selfhood). Here, knowing *brahman* is contrasted with the might of the gods, indeed even with their very divine status:

In the beginning, this world was only *brahman*, and it knew only itself (*ātman*), thinking: "I am *brahman*." As a result, it became the Whole. Among the gods, likewise, whosoever realized this, only they became the Whole.[15] It was the same also among the seers and among humans. Upon seeing this very point, the seer Vāmadeva proclaimed: "I was Manu, and I was the sun." This is true even now. If a man knows "I am *brahman*" in this way, he becomes this whole world. Not even the gods are able to prevent it, for he becomes their very self (*ātman*). So when a man venerates another deity, thinking, "He is one, and I am another," he does not understand. As livestock is for men, so is he for the gods. As having a lot of livestock is useful to a man, so each man proves useful to the gods. The loss of even a single head of livestock is painful; how much more if many are lost. The gods, therefore, are not pleased at the prospect of men coming to understand this.

This is a typical Upaniṣadic excerpt, endowed with that characteristic Upaniṣadic vision whose most salient feature is the presence of a certain kind of vagueness that hovers around the text: who is dependent on whom? Men on gods, or vice versa? The Upaniṣadic author seems to be far from certain: on the one hand, mortals are dependent on the gods, but on the other hand, gods are dependent on mortals. Mostly, men's dependence on the gods is brought about by virtue of the fact that they are mortal, unlike the immortal gods. And yet, the gods are dependent on men because humans entertain a uniqueness of which the gods cannot partake. Carefully scrutinizing this passage will reveal two distinct depictions of humanity, two pictures superimposed upon each other (one picture on top of another—supposedly traced on transparency paper—such that their combination, the "spatial" merger of the two, offers the complete picture of man). In this pictorial simile the top layer represents the dimension of man that is subject to the gods in the same manner that the beasts are subject to man, for he does not fully comprehend the meaning of what it is to be human. Yet, underneath this layer, there lies another picture that depicts man as fully comprehending the meaning of his position as a spiritual being. This realization releases man from his unilateral dependence on the gods. Indeed, inner knowledge such as "I am *brahman*" turns the tables around in the relationships between man and gods, making the gods dependent on the subject, i.e., the knowing self. It is for this reason that the gods are so keen to conceal the "lower" picture. A complete appreciation of what it is to be human is instilled in a unique and complex attainment of self-knowledge (which we shall consider in the following chapters), and this self-knowledge, which is in fact "everything," makes the gods necessarily dependent on humans, since their existence is conditioned by a kernel of selfhood lacked by the former. Just imagine! A god who relinquishes all celestial responsibilities and takes up a life devoted to introspective speculation, intently seeking his interiority. And what does he find in his profound inwardness if not his favorite animal—man? In the words of the Upaniṣad, man constitutes gods' selfhood and what the gods find in their inwardness is, therefore, a selfhood that is beyond their control. A brilliant idea if there ever was one: fundamental alienation, a sense of "otherness," is grounded in the paradigm of a foreign body (or, better, a foreign soul) the god finds within himself! A god's innermost being contains a foreign element, an element of otherness, residing beyond his divine control, and this turns out to be the pivot of selfhood motivating this divinity. "Not even the gods are able to prevent it," the Upaniṣadic author notes wryly, "for he becomes their very self" (*ātman*).

The Upaniṣadic claim with regard to the interrelationship between gods and humans is yet another example of those underlying conceptual discrepancies that exist between the West and India in matters pertaining to God or divinity. Yet it also sheds light on another unique feature of Indian thought clearly prominent in the Upaniṣads: the self's perception of its selfhood is inexplicably identified with "everything." This needs to be thoroughly elaborated, and it will be—further on, in later chapters. At this stage, we turn to this Upaniṣadic passage mainly for one reason: to draw attention to the dialectics underlying the relationships between the gods and men. It would seem that both men and gods tread a circular path in which there is no identifiable starting point that offers the gods an essential advantage over man.

_____

The third example exploring the absence of the presupposition of transcendence from the conceptual bedrock of Indian culture is drawn neither from the world of ritual nor from the realm of meditative contemplation. Rather, it is derived from the opulent corpus of Indian mythic literature. The story I want to examine is oft told and frequently cited in the various explorations of Indian thought, most notably in attempts to demonstrate Hinduism's response and counterargument to Buddhism. This controversy between Buddhism and Brahmanism bears no immediate relation to the issue at hand, and I will use this story here merely as part of our attempt to demonstrate the absence of the presupposition of transcendence in Indian culture. The story itself is taken from relatively late Purāṇas (a form of Hindu folk literature), and the main character of the story is the god Śiva, one of the most prominent of India's many divine beings. Śiva's deeds are well attested in the many different forms of Indian literature, invariably recounted with much flair and many contradictions. For example, Śiva is seen as the arch-destroyer, annihilating the universe, yet at the same time, he is a god whose virility and erotic prowess (notably as Lord of the dance) express fertility and vitality. Another well known element in Śiva's contradictory nature is that he is, on the one hand, the most accomplished of all ascetics, capable of completely detaching himself from the totality of the sensual world, while at the same time he is notoriously interested in the foibles of the temporal world (it is said that he chases mortal women, brandishing his colossal member and, similarly, that he is an irrepressible and compulsive gambler). Perhaps more than anything else, Śiva is associated with that Golden City, that place like no other in the whole universe, namely, Varanasi (Benares or Kashi), which is not only where he resides but also the source of his divinity and the source of everything derived from his sublime divinity.

The story I would like to consider tells us about the ties between Śiva and Varanasi or, more precisely, the strange circumstances that brought him back to the city after he had been forced to abandon it. This Purāṇic tale claims that long ago, Śiva had to leave his beloved city since the gods (and Śiva among them) were incapable of overcoming the effects of a horrific drought that was ravaging the city, destroying everything good about it (not only in the fields but among men too). It became apparent to the gods that only a human could bring this drought to an end and so they elected the great ascetic Divodāsa, who had made Varanasi into his place of retreat, to rule over the city. At first Divodāsa declined, but finally he acceded, saying he would accept it on one irrevocable condition: that the gods, with Śiva at their head, would leave the city and return to their celestial dwelling. The gods, including Śiva, agreed to this condition and duly departed from the city. After they had left, they had certain misgivings and tried to trick Divodāsa into renouncing his rule over Varanasi. Different gods all tried to overcome Divodāsa. To begin with, Agni withdrew fire from Varanasi, then Vayu withdrew the wind, followed by Indra who held back the rain. But still, fire burned, the wind did not cease to blow, and the heavens rained. Divodāsa, an ascetic and moreover a human, had enough power within him to generate these elements. Divodāsa's enormous powers came from his being a *dharmarāja*, a king of Dharma. Everything he did, he did with the utmost care and in complete accord with Dharma.[16] Thus his rule was blessed by perfect harmony: everything he did was executed in the best possible manner. Whatever he refrained from doing was unmeritorious and doing it would have been a disgrace. Divodāsa's Varanasi, the city of supreme justice, was beyond the reach of the gods. But Śiva coveted Varanasi. His consort, Pārvatī, refused to dwell anywhere else. Varanasi's beauty, she said, whispering in Śiva's ear, is second to none; it is like a lotus flower: though planted in the soil, its beauty is of another world. Pārvatī poignantly harps on the pain of their separation, their exile, from this coveted city. Śiva himself was overcome with longing, yet he knew that any attempt to strike Divodāsa would fail; the only way to remove him from the city would be by creating a breach in his Dharma and thus foundering his rule, which, as we shall recall, was based on the absoluteness of his harmonious Dharma. And so, relying the aid of his divine accomplices, Śiva tried to inflict transgressions upon the city. To begin with he sent to Varanasi a host of goddesses armed with powerful magic spells. For the duration of a whole year, these goddesses tried to disrupt the Dharma in many different ways, after the fashion of goddesses-enchantresses, but all to no avail. Divodāsa's Dharma remained unharmed and unruffled, and his hold on Varanasi was as strong as ever. Just to make things worse, the goddesses (who were sixty-four in number) decided to remain in Varanasi permanently, since, so they said, only a fool would leave such a splendid city. Śiva did not give up and sent another envoy: Sūrya, the sun god. He too tried to breach the Dharma for the duration of a whole year and he too failed, also choosing in the end to remain in the city. After him, Brahmā, the creator-god, was sent, and the outcome of his mission was not much different from that of his predecessors. Finally, Śiva sent the god Viṣṇu who took on the form of a Buddhist monk. Viṣṇu was escorted by his consort Śrī, who took the form of a Buddhist nun, and the giant bird Garuda, his celestial vehicle, who took the form of a Buddhist novice. These three began teaching Buddhist doctrine throughout Varanasi. Among other things, they claimed that the world has no source, that existence is pointless, that it is indecent to perform rituals and make animal sacrifices, and even that the division of society into four classes should be denounced. This teaching created an upheaval in the city and Dharma was ridden by vile immorality (men took to their neighbors' wives and the different classes intermingled). The people of Varanasi lost their sense of order and stability. As a result, Divodāsa's power was weakened and he lost his interest in ruling the city. In the end, Divodāsa departed from Varanasi and Śiva returned to take his place in his beloved city

As I mentioned previously, the point of this tale is, most likely, to emphasize and highlight the differences between Hindu Dharma as opposed to its vastly inferior Buddhist adversary. Yet this moral embraces a fascinating hidden message: Śiva, who is an exemplary representative of the Hindu way of life, can take his place (and here the expression *take his place* should be taken quite literally) at the helm only by resorting to an aggressive (even violent) espousal of its exact opposite (i.e., Buddhism). I shall not take issue with this since my interest here does not lie with morals and hidden messages, but rather with what the story explicitly assumes. The story presupposes that gods are in a certain sense dependent on men. We have already seen that this in itself is not unique to India and can be evidenced, to some extent or other, in other religious traditions too. The uniqueness of the conceptual framework that enables the story of Śiva and Divodāsa is the lack of an impassable barrier between the world of gods and the world of men. The ascetic Divodāsa is not dependent upon the gods mainly due to the fact that his being, and his rule of the city, arises from an autonomous sense of harmony, order, law, and custom the gods are incapable of altering. The most they can aspire to is to bring man to betray his human nature, as expressed in that autonomous dharmic framework. Indeed, the only way for a god to impose his superiority over man, at least in this story, is by resorting to cunning, making man betray his true, dharmic, nature. If we briefly consider this story in a comparative light, juxtaposing it to the story of Adam and Eve, we shall see that there is little point in comparing Śiva to the biblical God (who insists on unconditional obedience and punishes whoever violates these commands), but rather to the murmuring serpent who claims that Dharma is not Dharma, that a command is not actually a command, that the worthy are despicable, and the despicable worthy. Some may want to claim that the serpent in the biblical story represents the other face of God. Yet, even if we endorse this reading, even if the serpent's face is similar to God's, this is merely a superficial similarity. The serpent is clearly not transcendent to man; on the contrary, the act of seduction was possible only by virtue of the serpent's intimate proximity to Adam and Eve. On the whole, it is difficult to conceive of an act of seduction when an impassable barrier separates the seducer from the seduced, the former transcending the latter. Seduction necessitates cooperation, and cooperation necessitates proximity, or at the very least, accessibility. My somewhat twisted and protracted words are succinctly summed up by Kafka in one pithy remark: "It simply goes without saying that the falling of a human hair must matter more to the devil than to God, since the devil really loses that hair and God does not." Apparently, the Indian storyteller would find it difficult to "transpose" Kafka's insight and apply it to a hypothetical Indian situation, in which, for example, Śiva plays the role of a god who does not care about the fate of one human hair, and this in contradistinction to a spirit or a demon (which abound in Indian mythology) that *is* concerned about the fate of one human hair. Such a "transposition" would miss the point, since in Indian culture there are no essential differences between Śiva and whoever isn't Śiva, at least not in respect to the fate of one human hair or, in more general terms, to the fate of humanity itself. From this point of view, gods and demons fare alike. If, on the other hand, we turn to consider how the author of the story of the Garden of Eden would, in theory, relate to the story of Śiva and Divodāsa, then, it seems to me, we cannot help but think that Śiva and Viṣṇu, his attendant in this case, are serpents seducing man to forsake his "objective" goal, the goal he has to pursue independently of them. That is to say, the biblical author would find it difficult to consider the Indian gods as fulfilling the role of the biblical God and would most likely cast them in the role of the serpent. Yet even here there is only a partial similarity, since the "serpent" in the story of Śiva and Divodāsa does not seduce man to disobey a divine injunction, but to deviate from a notion of general and universal order (Dharma) that is in no way subject to divine will. Obeisance to Dharma and abidance by dharmic laws determines one's self-identity and this allows no room for god (that is why Divodāsa, so long as he faithfully keeps the path ordained by Dharma, is impervious to divine incursions). Man, in this respect, is the custodian of Dharma, it is he who nourishes it and gives it form. Thus one should not be tempted to see Dharma as an Indian version of the Western presupposition of transcendence. Dharma is order, harmony, the true and equanimous unfolding of reality. It is like a perfect orchestral score, but this score needs to be performed, and the performers here are humans, whether in actual deeds or their "spiritual" performance or by internalizing them in their minds. Only a perfect performance—a performance motivated neither by personal aspirations nor the hope of attaining extra benefits—will express the perfection embedded in harmony and order. Thus Śiva and Divodāsa, man and god, entwine each other, neither having a logical or ontological precedence over the other.

These three examples tie in perfectly with the lines from the Ṛg Veda quoted at the beginning of this chapter: "The one who surveys it in the highest heaven—Only he knows, or maybe he does not." This question lies at the bedrock of Indian thought. I see it as indicative of the Indian approach to transcendence. After all, what is being questioned here is the very idea of transcendence itself. The possibility that the heavenly one may not know, the dependence of the gods on those they have created, their envy of humans and their powerlessness when facing dharmic order—this clearly illustrates that transcendence is not a necessary ingredient in India's idea of divinity.

For anyone relying on the commonly held notion that, despite appearances, religious beliefs in India are not much different from Western religious beliefs, and that, at the end of the day, both subsume one transcendent divinity as the bedrock of all existence, the above conclusion might come as a surprise. Those who endorse this idea claim that even though, at first glance, there are differences between the concept of God in the two cultures, in truth, these are mere variations in points of emphasis, quantity, style, and states of mind. In actual fact, so it is claimed, the enormous variety of divinities in India are but different ways of expressing, of presenting, the variegated manifestations of one divinity, and each community of believers is free to choose for itself the manner in which to worship this one unique divinity. Thus, for example, one Indologist has gone so far as to claim that it is a gross error to characterize Hinduism as polytheism; admittedly, he says, there is a plurality of gods, yet when one social group worships this or that god, for them this divinity is one and unique, much as for Jewish, Christian, and Muslim monotheists their God is one and unique.

Claiming that Indian religions are "monotheistic" is at times a value judgment and, as such, it is a matter for the heart and soul and surely stands beyond the pale of any value-free philosophical discussion. Sometimes, though, this suggestion does not describe a set of beliefs but rather raises a conceptual issue, that is, it is a sort of "diagnosis" of the intellectual and religious worldview of classical India. There is something deceptive about a diagnosis of this kind. The alleged monotheism of classical India is not based on transcendence's ontological precedence over immanence, on the outward's superiority over the inward. Needless to say, those who advocate a "Western" picture of Indian divinities claim they can corroborate their view with ample textual evidence. Now, admittedly, it is not too difficult to find descriptions of Indian divinities that, ab initio, do in fact make one think of the solitary divinity of Western transcendent monotheism. It is even possible to find in India "theistic" religious traditions that entertain the idea of a solitary God, a God who alone is the subject of deep contemplation and worship. Still, it would be erroneous to regard these theistic movements as an Indian version of the West's presupposition of transcendence. Monotheism it might be—but even here one will not find a rigid barrier separating man and god. On the contrary, man can devote himself to this solitary god precisely because of the supposition that despite the fact that there are obvious discrepancies between man and god, these discrepancies are inessential. In other words, the sort of monotheism extant in India is not exclusivist (it would be difficult to append the idea of idolatry, in its evident Western sense, to India), while Western monotheism is explicitly and decisively exclusivist. What we have here is a sort of conceptual acid test, differentiating between monotheism in the West and its alleged Indian counterpart. Idolatry is an essential component of Western monotheism (recall the above discussion of the Golden Calf), while Indian monotheism cannot even conceive of what idolatry might be.

———————

A full survey of divinity in India, much like delineating the many faces of divinity in this culture, is a huge and complex project that goes far beyond the confines of this book. However, it is possible to glean a few important insights even when considering a single instance of ancient Indian monotheism, as it is portrayed in the first four verses of one chapter of the later Upaniṣads. These remarkable verses, with their obvious theistic overtones, praise and glorify the one and only god:

> Who alone, himself without colour, wielding his power creates variously countless colours, and in whom the universe comes together at the beginning and dissolves in the end—may he furnish us with lucid intelligence.
>
> The fire is simply that; the sun is that; the wind is that; and the moon is also that! The bright one is simply that; *brahman* is that; the waters are that; and Prajāpati is that!
>
> You are a woman; you are a man; you are a boy or also a girl. As an old man, you totter along with a walking-stick. As you are born, you turn your face in every direction.

You are the dark blue bird, the green one with red eyes, the rain cloud, the seasons, and the oceans. You live as one without a beginning because of your pervasiveness, you, from whom all beings have been born.

These verses clearly reveal the poet's strong impulse to exalt and glorify the idea of a singular god. There is little doubt that this issue plays a crucial role here, especially given that it is set in a cultural milieu that makes room for a rich and varied pantheon of gods. Committing oneself to the divinity of one being, given this cultural setting, means that one needs to be able to establish this view in opposition to other religious views (and the poet was surely well aware of this). In other words, our "monotheistic" Upaniṣadic poet, in advocating his one God, had to confer upon him a rich catalogue of attributes and features that the poet's nonmonotheistically inclined adversaries and peers "stretched" over their plethora of gods. Accordingly, in the Upaniṣadic verses quoted above, the attempt to collect these attributes and features, and concentrating them in one divine being, can be seen as a representative trait of "Indian monotheism." This has less to do with ways in which the author refers to the divinity and more to do with what he refrains from saying about it: not the precise dose of qualities attributed to this god (since these descriptions are subject to the limitations of the poet's imagination and thus it is reasonable to encounter great stylistic variances in the different attitudes toward god), but rather drawing our attention to attitudes and images that are absent from these verses. The absence, so I suggest, is not arbitrary but paradigmatic; it is not confined to the idiosyncrasies of this or that specific author but is yet another instance of "meaningful silence."

What these verses lack is precisely what lies at the foundation of the Platonic worldview and Western monotheism. God is different from man, but this is not an essential difference! God is not an "other," and definitely not an absolute other. If there is a basic conceptual commitment, it is aligned with the idea of immanence: god is the source of everything that exists, but not as an external creator that has created ex nihilo through speech, and not even seen as a skillful maker molding raw clay in the fashion he deems fit. Since an ex nihilo picture of creation is conceivable only within the framework of the presupposition of transcendence, it should come as no surprise that this picture of creation does not exist in ancient and classical India. Thus, in the verses quoted above, God is not imagined as someone who actively creates the world, either manually or verbally (since creation through speech or manual action necessitates the supposition of a severance between the artisan and his art, between the speaker and his words). Instead, a world of organic metaphors is employed: the relationship between god and the world is that of birth, derivation, and pervasion. "In whom the universe comes together at the beginning and dissolves in the end." This interesting metaphorical preference (birth and derivation rather than creation and formation) is not unique only to this verse, but broadly reflects the general tendency of Indian religious literature. For instance, in another "monotheistic" Upaniṣad god is referred to as an eternal uprooted upside down banyan tree (aśvattha): its roots up above, its branches swaying below to form the phenomenal world. A prominent scholar of Indian philosophy mistook this for an insinuation of god's transcendence (though even he acknowledged that this appearance of an external god was greatly shadowed by the many Upaniṣadic appearances of a divinity that exists mysteriously within us). This mistake came about because he did not pay the necessary attention to the image of god as a tree: even when god is conceived as a supposedly "external" essence, the imagery employed still remains organic: the roots and branches are in fact the same tree—there is no essential difference between roots and branches! Moreover, when Upaniṣadic literature depicts god as giving birth and sprouting, what invariably is being described is not merely the birth or derivation of the universe from god, but, simultaneously, the birth of god himself. Through derivation, divinity defines its own identity. Accordingly, even when the question being addressed is patently metacosmological, the search for origins and beginnings is not exempt from the supposition of a strong mutual dependency between cause and effect. This mutual dependency will occupy us later on, when we shall review the special role that selfhood occupies in Indian philosophy.

The supposition of immanence in the Upaniṣadic verses is present not only as a reply to metacosmological questions that seek primary origins but also to cosmological questions that attempt to understand the actual nature of the world. Here too god resides in the interiority of natural phenomena—fire, sun, wind, seasons, etc. Yet, his immanence has another facet too, a psychophysical dimension that is, to my mind, its most interesting feature: "You are a woman; you are a man; you are a boy or also a girl. As an old man, you totter along with a walking-stick." Here immanence is identified with ideas that signify humanity (male and female and distinguishable bodily states) and different temporal states (birth to old age). God, even though he is singular entity, is still not separable from the different human expressions of spatial extension and temporal duration. Quite the opposite is true: the spatiotemporal dimensions of god are expressed in terms parallel to human life span, from birth to excessive old age. Thus, the essence of god is constructed in such a way that it is "all-pervading" in all those metacosmological, cosmological, and psychophysical senses just mentioned—and what is absent in all these senses is the specific viewpoint according to which exteriority is supposed to have ontological precedence over any kind of interiority. On the contrary, divinity in India—as any Westerner visiting India immediately notes with stupefaction—is splendidly multifarious, it is blessed with countless manifestations and infinite appearances—inside and outside, in body and soul, revealed and concealed, tangible and intangible. In India God's immanence is not begotten by a retracting transcendence; it is, in contradistinction, an explicit expression of the preference, the precedence, and the primacy allocated to man's human inwardness. Wendy Doniger has managed to lucidly convey this primacy by noting that for many Indians encountering god in a dream is worth seven times a meeting with him when awake.[17] While in the West the highest aspiration is to see God by means of a mystical trance, in India this would be considered a deficient encounter: connecting to the sublime while dreaming is beyond doubt preferable to any other kind of revelatory experience, since "both the dream and the god partake of an inner reality that is 'taken for granted' in India; each substantiates the reality of the other." Doniger quite rightly emphasizes the precedence of the assumption of interiority, which enables, in India, not only bestowing a dream with ontological status but, similarly, bestowing god with the same status conferred to a dream. Be that as it may, ontological assumptions are utterly dependent on psychological assumptions about human inwardness and its creative powers.

If the presupposition of transcendence is at all present in Indian civilization, it is there in a condition that I would call "inverse transcendence": God does not necessarily exist "above" man, but rather man can position himself "above" God. This condition is—almost by definition—inconceivable in Western monotheistic religions. In this sense the Indian concept of transcendence brings to mind the Stoics. This inverse movement is also present in the Upaniṣadic excerpt discussed earlier, since there the human imagery applied to divinity is not advanced from the anthropomorphic point of view of Western religions, where God is personified to show that He is present as an image inside man. The Upaniṣadic portrait suggests a diametrically opposite picture: man is present as an image in divine being: not man as created in God's image, but God as concretized in the image of man. This difference is attested by ubiquity of the claim, in Indian spiritualism, that God is but a projection of the human mind. In the Western context it is difficult to imagine that such a claim would be put forward within a religious framework; it is mostly voiced by Western theism's staunchest critics.

———————

The conceptual differences between India and the West concerning the presupposition of transcendence are evident in the different conceptual depictions of these two cultures. One (of many) fascinating illustrations of the structural differences between India and the West can be seen in the application of the presupposition of transcendence or exteriority and its presence or absence in building each respective notion of history. It would seem that the ubiquitous presence of the idea of history in the West is so common that it hardly needs mentioning. Its influence on how we think, how we talk, respond and act is well attested, regardless of whether what we have in mind are collective or personal histories. Rarely would one stop to consider on what we base our ubiquitous use of the notion of history and its many derivative concepts. What then will be our response when we find out that this notion is conspicuously absent from the core of classical Indian culture? A typical, all too typical, "Western" response is to deride these immature "Orientals" who fail to distinguish between myth and fact, between fiction and actual events. Since history proper can only be established the moment myth has been eradicated, it follows that whosoever has not yet erected the edifice of history exposes his inability or unwillingness to disengage from that ragbag collection of stories, legends, and fables that have nothing in common with proper history. But these condescending remarks merely reveal the deep-rooted ignorance of whoever voices them. There is, no doubt, an essential difference between the "historical" West and "ahistorical" ancient and classical India, yet the source of this difference lies in their respective attitudes to the very idea of history, i.e., of a linear narrative of facts and events that unfold sequentially.

The dominant Western approach—both its Greek version and its Judeo-Christian-Muslim version—sees history as an outcome of the outward's precedence over the inward, the objective's over the subjective and the transcendent over the immanent.[18] This precedence enables us to see external reality as events and processes whose occurrences can be described in a clear linear structure: i.e., to organize events sequentially so that any given event is preceded and followed by another event. That is to say, history is dependent upon the possibility of presenting a linear account of events, and this possibility is conditioned by the kind of conceptual precedence that I have presented in this chapter. The presupposition of transcendence is employed here as a criterion for the possibility of an idea of history as something that always marches along a straight and irrevocable line, flowing from the past into the future. (Figuratively speaking, one might be inclined to say that this criterion functions like a ruler, upholding linearity itself as well as the ability to draw a straight line without any curves, hollows, or twists.) This is true regardless whether the transcendent being is Platonic Form or an Aristotelian prime mover, both of which do not meddle in the affairs of the world and accordingly "enable" a historical account in which their presence will be merely conceptual (again, as a criterion that enables the very concept of linear progression) and will not be noticeable in the actual deployment of history. This claim is just as valid when applied to Western religions in which God reveals himself in human and cosmological history. God's intervention in history imparts on the presupposition of transcendence two honorary roles: it enables the very existence of history, as well as linear historical narratives, and endows this historical line with a clear content, operating as a force driving it forward along its temporal route. Punctuated along this linear historical route are points that Western religions choose to designate as starting points. In this respect, those persistent oracular pronouncements that history is coming to an end—whether coined by loin-clothed prophets of doom or by elegant diversion-seeking academics who try to abate the misery of their professional desolation by imagining a passionless, artificial end-of-history—these declarations are possible only on account of the prosaic, seemingly natural presence of the concept of linear history.

On the other hand, ancient and classical India gives an a posteriori negative reply to the possibility of history. In Indian culture it is difficult to find a supposition envisaging the possibility that historical temporality runs along an uninterrupted straight line. In India one will be hard-pressed to find a conceptual framework that guarantees, for instance, that historical events are, in a primary sense, unique and will remain so—the situation is completely different. Who can vouch that history cannot repeat itself? Where shall we find an external criterion that will allow us to imagine a linear description of history? In the absence of a conceptual pivot of exteriority, a circular depiction of events seems almost inevitable, and this circularity negates the meaning of history. Here we must be very precise. We are not hearing the wailing and bitter laments of someone, like Ecclesiastes, who, from the profoundest depths of his transcendent outlook, is decrying against a malignant circularity: "The thing that hath been, it is that which shall be" (Ecclesiastes 1:9) and "it hath been already of old time, which was before us" (Ecclesiastes 1:10). In India the exact opposite is true. There is a conciliatory attitude toward circularity, and repetition is viewed as the elemental condition of the world. Events go round and round in an endless cycle with no beginning and no end and thus perpetually repeat themselves. This "circularity" is quite natural and takes the place of "directionality." Any attempt to unpack the circle and turn it into a line will be perceived as a subtle or gross form of self-deception. Under these terms it will be impossible to conceive of the idea of history since history necessitates the recognition that exhausted opportunities will never reavail themselves. In at least one sense history is the rejection of repetition. A repetitive account of reality is inevitably an ahistorical account. Yet the concern India takes in the possibilities afforded by this cyclic repetitive motion is not centered on the status of history and the possibility of historiography. The main concern with repetition focuses on the psychological opportunities this allows in the definition of selfhood and the process of reflexive self-knowledge.

TWO

One Language, Many Things

ON THE ORIGINS OF LANGUAGE

> Words strain,
> Crack and sometimes break, under the burden,
> Under the tension, slip, slide, perish,
> Decay with imprecision, will not stay in place,
> Will not stay still.
>
> —T. S. Eliot, *Four Quartets*

In the West the presupposition of transcendence has made the idea of exteriority—whether in the guise of abstract Platonic Forms or of a personal deity—the underlying conceptual scheme by which the world is understood, described, and evaluated. Evidently, the presence of this presupposition served as a conceptual bulwark preventing the intrusion of chance into the inner core of the Platonic or monotheistic worldview. Both Plato and his disciples, and the Western promulgators of monotheism, rejected out of hand any outlook that allowed capricious chance to assume an important role. Indeed, chance has been viewed as the archenemy of meaning and significance. And yet, neither the adherents of Platonism nor the sages of monotheistic religions were prepared, or even able, to similarly reject the contrasting role, namely, connection between transcendence and necessity, the notion that every actual event was bound to have happened the way it actually did happen. Moreover, for them necessity was deeply embedded in the inner recesses of transcendence, since the rift or barrier between exteriority and interiority wasn't conceived as the product of any internal mental manipulations, but, on the contrary, as having been brought about before any such mental operations and independently of any conscious activity of the mind. The presupposition of transcendence is shrouded by the dark mists of necessity. If exteriority thwarts arbitrariness, then this bulwark seems to overextend itself since there is a price to pay for preventing chaos, namely, the imposition of necessity. As Joseph K., the hero of Kafka's *The Trial*, knew all too well, absolute necessity—no less than fleeting chance— is the bitter enemy of truth and, moreover, of the linguistic activity that is supposed to distinguish between truth and falsehood. If anything that happens was bound to happen the way it did, then, patently, any linguistic utterance that is in itself an event in the world is also necessary; that is to say, anything being said must have been said precisely as it was actually said, including, of course, this very utterance.

What remains for someone who seeks to understand and know the truth? If he were a Platonist, he would surely seek to release himself from the shackles imposed by the senses so that his intellect could freely partake in the immaterial world of Forms. For such a person, true understanding is located in the "beyond" and is conditioned by the possibility of crossing over from the transient, phenomenal here and now to the formal, substantial, and unchangeable beyond. If, on the other hand, he were a monotheist (Jewish, Christian, or Muslim), he would gladly endorse the words acquired through divine revelation, acknowledging these utterances as the way in which God chooses to make Himself known to the believers, despite, or perhaps because of, their obscurity (true meaning being forever concealed in the impenetrable depths of the Godhead). Either way, we see that truth is not to be found in the here and now and its residency in the beyond means that it is a sort of spirit, divinity, or idea, totally independent of anything save itself.

It comes as no wonder, then, that whosoever endorses the presupposition of transcendence is at the same time gravely suspicious of any attempt to depict truth in a manner that fails to recognize the primacy of the external and its precedence over the internal. This is the case both in the many guises of Platonism and in the legacy of Western religions. This suspicion was evidenced in many ways, among them in the rejection of the importance of introspection as a valid means of attaining truth. Indeed, it is difficult to imagine how the quest for truth could be founded on introspection, given the place allocated to the notion of transcendence in both Platonism and Western monotheism. There is an evident parity between the Platonist perception of things and the worldview espoused by monotheistic religions: namely, the discernible hostility evident in any attempt to internalize truth. The idea of an introspective mind focusing on itself is not only superfluous but also reprehensible on two accounts: besides failing to reach the truth, it deflects the truth seeker from his goal. Moreover, such introspection is, in fact, futile. After all, introspection, if it makes sense at all, should reveal to us the way things ultimately are; but if this transpires within the conceptual framework of transcendence, introspection will inevitably lead us from interiority back to exteriority, since it will only show us the primacy of the beyond over the here and now. Meditative-psychological efforts running along this vein will inevitably give rise to certain disturbances that are not only grotesque but also tinged with no little irony. That is, whoever seeks truth within himself is destined to discover, at the end of his search, the conceptual foundation of the transcendent, according to which externality precedes any interiority. Thus he will end up lending his ear to his mind, only to hear it gently whispering to him: why have you entered? The truth you seek is waiting for you outside, over there.

Indeed, what do general and abstract Platonic Forms have to look for in the particular state of mind of this or that individual? Partaking in the world of Forms means casting aside any meditative, subjective experiences, deeming them insignificant and distracting. Similarly, monotheistic religions require their followers not to dwell on matters of the flesh but rather on matters of the spirit—introspection is seen as a sensual hurdle, obstructing any significant spiritual development. If for Plato enwrapping oneself in the entrails of subjectivity is simply an unfortunate state of affairs, wholly unconducive to the one who seeks the truth, the prevailing view among Western religions is that this entwinement is not only unconducive but may also be perilous, sometimes constituting a threat of such magnitude that it necessitates aggressive countermeasures. The self's sense of uniqueness threatens to undermine the foundations of the transcendent; conceiving man as the sum of his mental activity was often seen as the gravest of heresies, since man's personal identity is established by the rejection of the precedence of the external over the internal.

Thus truth cannot be dependent on, or conditioned by, the beholder's interiority. It must, perforce, be conditioned by that which lies outside him—and, at the same time, this severance between the beholder and that which is beyond him is precisely what makes it the truth. From here it is but a short stride to the characterization of truth as a correspondence between our internal ideas and concepts and the external reality to which they refer. Indeed, this is the most common account of truth to be found in the annals of Western philosophy. When asked "What is Truth?" the ordinary response is to draw attention to the possibility of a correspondence between our thought and language and the external world of things and events outside us.

Characterizing truth by means of the correspondence between ideas and concepts and the objects and occurrences in the external world may seem entirely self-evident. What could be more commonsensical than to assume that truth resides in the correspondence between things and ideas? Of course, there have been philosophers who questioned this assumption, but their appeals have usually been considered problematic in one way or another. For any rebuttal of correspondence seems, at least at first glance, as a rebuttal of what in fact lies at the foundation of the search for truth, namely, the urge to find answers to questions such as "to what do my thoughts relate? what do my words refer to? how do my internal dream images differ from my wakeful images?" The apparently self-evident reply to these and similar questions is the same: drawing attention to the correspondence between thoughts, ideas, and concepts and to something external to them.

Mostly, when one points to a correspondence between the internal and the external, it is not only to define the nature of truth but also to offer a criterion by which to distinguish truth from falsehood. Here the correspondence between linguistic utterances and the world (or between words and things or between ideas and objects) as a criterion of truth is founded on the supposition that truth is dependent on the world, and thus a proposition will be true if the world is as the proposition claims it to be.[1] In this respect, truth hinges solely on reality, which is, in itself, totally independent of any perception of it. In the same manner, language is considered a means or a tool that generates correspondence of ideas and concepts to things and events; true propositions are expected to be as transparent as possible; that is, they should represent the external entities to which words refer.

Correspondence as a criterion of truth is based on the premise (which, in the annals of Western philosophy, is called realism) that the world—and all the objects that comprise it—is independent of anything mental. The world is neither subject to the various means by which we perceive it nor to the means of representation by which we qualify and describe it. This intrinsic independence lies at the very foundation of the process of knowing, opening thereby the ominous possibility that reality as such resides beyond all its possible representations. This is, of course, the philosophical realist's most fearful nightmare. Ultimately, it might not be possible to eradicate the impending failure of representation. Thus at the core of the realist worldview lies a gap between the external and the internal. Only on account of this chasm does it make sense to seek, if somewhat desperately, a correspondence between the two. In this strong sense, language is in opposition to reality even at the preliminary stage of "deployment" preceding the actual search for correspondence. Reality is standing aloof, facing language, while language, preparing for a supposed assault, will, at best, eventually find itself devoured by truth. At worst, language will be crushed by the impassable barrier imposed upon it by the reality that it unsuccessfully tried to represent.

This concept of truth as correspondence was held by Western philosophy from its earliest days, right from the time of the great Greek thinkers. Consider, for example, Plato. Things are important, he says, not the names with which we refer to them. Consequently, one should contemplate things in themselves rather than the words that represent them. As Plato puts it, "knowledge of things is not to be derived from names. No, they must be studied and investigated in themselves." In all events, the knowledge of the things in themselves precedes the possibility of verbalizing them. The origin is preferable to its tokens. This vision was also shared by Aristotle, who mentions (in *Metaphysics*) the theory of language entertained by Socrates' pupil Antistheses (4–5th century BCE) asserting that we expect language to portray and depict reality. Every element in reality has a verbal equivalent. Thus language in its most primary and basic form functions in the manner of proper names. In this respect language relates to a reality that is not only independent of it but also makes it possible. Aristotle's oft-quoted definition of truth comes then as no surprise: "It is impossible for anything at the same time to be and not to be" and "It is not possible to assert and deny the same thing truly at the same time." A similar ontological commitment is evident even before Aristotle's time. This can be gleaned from the few scattered remarks Plato found fit to contemplate on the nature of human language as opposed to the reality it supposedly represents. Plato's Theory of Forms is the theory of ultimate order, and this order inevitably projects itself onto anything and everything that participates in these Forms, including, of course, the conceptual framework through which human language operates. Our use of concepts is made possible because these concepts actually exist, irrespective of us. This is indeed an extreme form of realism. To sum up, language is derived from the external reality that precedes it. As such, language turns out to be no more than a tool, an accessory or prop: "a name is an instrument." Language thus plays only a secondary, not to say subsidiary, role in the kingdom of the Forms. The aptitude of words is derived solely from their capacity to index the things that they denote. As such, the correspondence of ideas and concepts to things and events is indifferent to the actual success the speaker demonstrates when referring (verbally) to the world outside. To put it more bluntly, according to this Platonic outlook, correspondence "belongs" to the external thing much more than it "belongs" to the epistemic process of knowledge and justification.

Interestingly, a similar vein of thought runs through the core teachings of major Western religious thought. Rather than the abstract Aristotelian contention about a correspondence between the claim about the given and the given itself, a more tangible suggestion about revelation takes hold. In the discussion of revelation, and ponderings over its deeper meanings, there is a tendency among theologians to focus on the contents of the variegated forms of revelation and their implications for the lives of its respective believers. So predominant is this line of investigation that there is a tendency to overlook the fact that the very act of revelation, regardless of its actual content, is that which is deemed by the Western religions to be an absolute truth both with regard to the nature of the Godhead, its relation to the world, and, needless to say, to humans. Yet the very presence of revelation implies that, in effect, a statement will be true if, and only if, it concurs with that revelation. Furthermore, the correspondence between thoughts and words, on the one hand, and objects and occurrences, on the other, is manifestly beyond epistemic considerations. The process by which truth is secured is of secondary importance and, more often than not, it is considered as merely an auxiliary to the presence of divine revelation. After all, truth is considered to be derived from the nature of God and of the reality of His manifest revelation. There are no other considerations to take into account—certainly not those that relate to one's motives for obtaining truth or the means by which it was procured. The divine pronouncement "Ye have seen that I have talked with you from heaven" (Exodus 20:22) not only demands complete acquiescence to divine law, it is also a clear affirmation of the fact that in no way is truth reliant on those who receive it. Obviously, what we find here is an incisive version of the truth-as-correspondence approach. Needles to say, it is deeply anchored in the presupposition of transcendence; the ontological and logical precedence of exteriority to interiority is such that it necessitates correspondence and furthermore allows only for correspondence.

Let me state this in more general terms: what is most striking in Plato's view of language—and that of the Western monotheistic traditions—is the claim that, since the meaning of language wholly depends on its ability to reflect or represent an independent external reality, language should mirror external reality and necessarily underlies any distinction between "true" and "false." Characterizing language in any other terms—for instance, emphasizing its reliance on internal-mental elements that do not explicitly refer to the external—was conceived as being philosophically problematic or religiously deplorable, not to mention subversive or even heretical.

Consider the act of name giving as an explicit instance of this relationship between words and the world; to understand this we might entertain the idea of a game in which a child is asked to place a card on a board so that the name printed on the card matches the drawing of the same object on the board. Apparently, this is not only a very common learning device but also the first game in history, at least according to how the biblical authors saw it. Let us recall Adam on the day he named the beasts. God presents before him "images" of many animals, and Adam "places" them with names: "[The Lord] brought them unto Adam to see what he would call them: and whatsoever Adam called every living creature, that was the name thereof" (Genesis 2:19). As we shall see, this act of name giving was considered by many thinkers as indicative of humanity, that is, as a distinctive manifestation of man's linguistic uniqueness, setting him apart from all the other "living creatures" surrounding him. Still, it is important to note that Adam was giving names to things that were *already* differentiated categories—i.e., the very animals that were placed before Adam so that he could append to them his verbal markers. In this respect, linguistic labeling is secondary to categorical divisions, the latter being entirely beyond the control of man, a mere provider of names.

We have already seen that Plato suggested a very similar a view of language: language as the mirror of reality or else as an image of it. Saint Augustine (who was undoubtedly greatly influenced in these matters both by Scripture and by Plato and his disciples) managed to express these ideas beautifully in his lucid prose. This declaration from his *Confessions* became the definitive account of the correspondence theory of truth as image of reality:

When people gave a name to an object and when, following the sound, they moved their body towards that object, I would see and retain the fact that that object received from them this sound which they pronounced when they intended to draw attention to it. Moreover, their intention was evident from the gestures which are, as it were, the natural vocabulary of all races, and are made with the face and the inclination of the eyes and the movements of other parts of the body, and by the tone of voice which indicates whether the mind's inward sentiments are to seek and possess or to reject and avoid. Accordingly, I gradually gathered the meaning of words, occurring in their places in different sentences and frequently heard; and already I learnt to articulate my wishes by training my mouth to use these signs. In this way I communicated the signs of my wishes to those around me, and entered more deeply into the stormy society of human life.

As is well known, in the twentieth century Wittgenstein remonstrated with this pictorial model of language (he quotes this very passage at the beginning of his *Philosophical Investigations*). However, modern developments are not the concern of this chapter.

At the core of Augustine's conception of language resides God, the eternal guarantor of the very adequacy of any and every verbal utterance. The fact that it is He who vouches for the very possibility of language implies a conclusion quite similar to the Platonic view: language—at least in its human, everyday form—is auxiliary, that is, it plays only a secondary role, depicting reality rather than shaping it. To put it somewhat blatantly, the presence of God cannot but narrow the boundaries of autonomous linguistic activity. There is some comfort to be gained from the knowledge that the guarantor of the veracity of our worldview does not lie within our sphere of responsibility. As we well know, shunning responsibility is a soothing balm. Therefore, it comes as no surprise to find that in the nineteenth century the awareness that we can no longer deflect responsibility from ourselves led to a deep sense of disillusionment, reaching its apogee, among other things, in the "linguistic turn," which made language into a necessary component in any philosophical attempt to understand the world. However, so long as man acknowledged the fact that the correspondence between language and reality lies beyond his responsibility, he could set apart the problem of meaning, seeing it as immune to any contextual upheavals. Consider, as a cursory example, the metaphorical implications of the story of Noah's ark. Every living thing, small and large, and first and foremost the human race, owes it existence to the ark that was destined to protect the world and secure its future. Following Hegel, it is even possible to argue that the metaphorical meaning of this ark (containing within it the different species of living beasts) represents Unity within Diversity. And yet, it is doubtful whether the biblical author would endorse such a Hegelian interpretation since he plainly indicates that the ark's existence does not come from within, namely, from what is found inside it, but from without. The ark could perform its arduous task only if it were totally impregnable to the waters of the deluge, that is, only if it could withstand the cataclysmic, inundating torrents. This kind of impregnability could not be obtained from within the ark, but, at the same time, no human is left to lock it from the outside. Thus the future of Noah's ark, on which the destiny of the whole of creation lies, can be secured only because it will be shut from the outside (and only from the outside!) by God himself. "And they went in unto Noah into the ark, two and two of all flesh, wherein is the breath of life. And they that went in, went in male and female of all flesh, as God had commanded him: *and the Lord shut him in*" (Genesis 7:15–16; my emphasis).

How can language function? On the one hand, it is supposed to be impeccable and transparent—reflecting reality—while, on the other hand, it is ontologically overshadowed by transcendence (philosophically abstract or religiously personal). The ontological precedence the external has over the internal implies that a complete correspondence between interiority and exteriority is possible, but, at the same time, it makes the actual act of affirming this correspondence as something utterly irrelevant in determining the real. Language is forlorn, abandoned in bleak terrain, cut off and severed from the world. This is a rather odd situation: one posits exteriority as a set of criteria for the possibility of understanding that will be free from error and doubt, but, concomitantly, this set creates a threshold well above the ability of human language. Accordingly, the conditions of understanding might turn out to be, somewhat ironically, the possibility of misunderstanding. In the previous chapter I illustrated this condition by considering how Cain positioned himself opposite the transcendent Godhead. Let us recall that according to one Jewish exegete Abel's murder arose out of Cain's inherent inability to comprehend divine speech. One could raise the following objection: if God speaks, and His are the heavens and all therein (including all possible linguistic permutations)—why did He not speak clearly, plainly, and unambiguously? Why did He subject Cain to that enigmatic phrase ("sin lieth at the door. And unto thee shall be his desire, and thou shalt rule over him") that completely confounds any sort understanding? But perhaps these questions are out of place. Perhaps an understanding that necessarily distorts meaning is symptomatic of a framework within which truth is seen through the finely polished lens of correspondence to exteriority. Let us reconsider that primary name-giving game. Evidently, this game is a clear case of correspondence, with Adam playing a passive role here. The actual existence of the components of reality (the animals presented before Adam), as well their existence as concepts, precedes the names they were given. This precedence is not accidental—it lies within the precedence divine creation has over anything and everything else. There is a thin thread of irony woven into this story: at first glance, it may seem as though Adam is being turned into the Creator's junior partner. But it would be a grievous error to think that there is any kind of partnership here, even between two unequal partners. That would verge on the ridiculous. Creation itself is over and the act of giving names is but an epilogue, void of any cosmological significance. This is plainly evident from the text itself as the author notifies us that this act of name giving is brought about for the sole purpose of alleviating Adam's dire condition of loneliness, to find him, as the text says, a "helpmeet [against him]."[2] That is to say, naming has no ontological or cosmological import and it has failed either to create or reveal something except, of course, man's profound loneliness. Through naming, God tried to offer Adam a "helpmeet." This term has become a trite and deplorable cliché used to describe woman and her role in man's life, so much so that we fail to notice the very claim that sets off the quest for a helpmeet ("It is not good that the man should be alone") reveals more about Adam's solitarily loneliness in the face of God rather than anything about his absent partner. Could it be that the word *against* in "a helpmeet against him" refers, in fact, to God? Either way, naming the beasts (which did not find Adam a helpmeet) and then woman (which managed to do so) was meant to assuage his loneliness, to enable him to live in the shadow of a hidden exteriority that would always remain so. The role language plays here is interesting. It articulates both the severance between inside and outside as well as the first attempt to bridge this gap by means of those acts of naming—and this even before the inevitable violent consequences of the presence of transcendence had had a chance to hatch: the fall, expulsion, perpetual exile, murder, and incessant wickedness. Perhaps this is one of the reasons for that acute sense of longing, of a yearning to return to the original, primordial language that was purportedly on intimate terms with God. This primary language was seen as a nonviolent expression of man's place in the face of a transcendent God. It might be that, in the West, this yearning for a primordial language was not a quest for some kind of lucid knowledge that was never really available to man (since this type of knowledge was never a fully realizable possibility), but rather a yearning for the primordial innocence associated with what the act of naming expresses.

At this point, it seems to me, it would be conducive to compare Indian and Western thought and their respective approach to language. A comparison of this sort might uncover some fascinating insights on the presuppositions of both cultures. Let us recall that the point of departure for such a comparison hinges on the notion of absence: how is one to understand the rarity of a correspondence theory of truth in the core of Indian philosophy? This question should perhaps be stated more precisely: how can we comprehend the rarity, in India, of a correspondence theory in its *strong sense*? In trying to supply an answer to this question we will inevitably find ourselves investigating the role of language in ancient India and also obtaining some kind of understanding of why it exerted such an influence on ancient Indian thinkers.

It is not uncommon to characterize cultural phenomena by drawing attention to the hidden forces that motivate them. All too often this kind of characterization is based on the hackneyed metaphor of a soul dwelling inside a body. If culture is a body of vast proportions, replete with internal and external organs, clothed and adorned—in order to properly understand this variety it is suggested that one should seek the soul of this culture, the spirit that animates the body. Seen thus, to understand a culture is to identify the inner forces that propel it forward. Yet this metaphor can be quite misleading. To understand a culture is not merely to comprehend what motivates it, since culture is not merely a forward movement but also, no less, the refusal to move. Alongside its driving force, a culture is defined by its gravitational forces—those situations in which it seems to act in a compulsive manner, when rather than move it is drawn as strongly to a center of attraction, such that, even when it does budge, the movement is determined by the weight of that locus of fascination.

If I were asked to identify one gravitational force residing at the core of Indian culture I would choose language, and I would elaborate on the immense fascination it has cast upon generations and generations of Indians, on the importance they lend to language and on the unfaltering passion with which they entwine themselves around it, seeing in it the paradigm of every kind of human activity (as well as many non-human occurrences). One scholar has aptly described this attraction by contrasting two "models of fascination": the dominant Western model of fascination is formed around the kind of certainty mathematics can offer, while the Indian model of fascination is primarily based on the type of certainty offered by natural language and its formalization, i.e., grammar. What the West found in the notion of certainty encapsulated by mathematics, ancient India embraced in the sense of order evident in natural languages.

The dawning of India's compulsive attraction to natural language is evident in ancient, Vedic, India. It will be recalled that this period placed a strong emphasis on man's role as a performer of rituals. But, interestingly, that which deems the ritual as efficacious (capable of actualizing the goals for which it was performed) is the sonic-vocal dimension of the ritual. In other words, ritual is a "sonic performance," the ritual creates hidden vibrations penetrating the deepest recesses of heaven and earth. This sonic process was generally described in harmonic terms: it safeguards the cosmos, it prevents the heavens from collapsing, it determines the pace of night and day, it steers the seasons and sets the course of rebirth. Language or, more precisely, speech, is located at the foundation of existence. The perfect formulation of this speech is to be found in the language of the Vedas. The Vedic tongue is perceived as the purest paradigm of language as such. There, deep inside Vedic speech, lies Indian culture's source of fascination, a source to which it was forever attracted.

The language of the Vedas was seen as being eternal, and this is vouched for by the fact that the Vedas are authorless: neither humans nor gods, nor any other external source, composed them.[3] Had they an author, they would have been temporal and would have thus inevitably lost their claim of being eternal. The orthodox Indian position is that the Vedas exist so long as time exists; their existence is absolutely congruent with the existence of the universe. Many Indian schools of thought held that the universe is subject to cyclic expansion and contraction, creation and annihilation. According to this cosmology, the Vedas too expand and contract, and they too are being formed and destroyed alongside the universe. On the other hand, the more orthodox schools felt it necessary to uphold the view that the Vedas are primordial and thus conceived of the universe as being primordial too. Either way, the role of a transcendent source validating Scriptures and authenticating them (of the kind that Western religions assigned to God) was absent from Indian thought; in India the Vedas' authority is self-validating; that is, their authority lies within them.

How is one to assess the claim that Vedic language is self-empowered and that this should be the paradigm of language as such? To come up with an exhaustive reply to this question is no simple matter. Given our limitations, I suggest a reply that hinges on the oral status of the Vedas in Indian culture. Different scholars researching the history of religious ideas have rightly drawn attention to the extreme importance that religions allocate to the oral dimension of their textual traditions, whereby many "Scriptures" that were not committed to writing were publicly performed and took an active part in social life. Such, evidently, is the case of ancient India. Notwithstanding the fact that the Vedas are often called Scriptures, this convenient appellation is also highly misleading. The word *scripture* is deceptive; it is derived from the Latin *scribere*, meaning "to write." By comparison, the corresponding Sanskrit term is *śabda*, derived from a root whose meaning is "to make a sound." For Indians, the Vedas in their most authoritative formation were transmitted orally. Thus, in the Indian context, one can speak of the texts as having a voice. Admittedly, at the end of a long period, the Vedas were finally committed to writing, but it was felt that this made them lose much of their vigor and impinged on their authority as an aural system. Generally speaking, Hinduism is not a scriptural religion, but rather one of the spoken word. An oft-quoted instruction (found in one of the later Vedic texts) deems the act of writing to be an act of defilement. In keeping with this, it is forbidden for someone studying the Vedas to recite them after he has eaten meat, seen blood or a corpse, had sexual intercourse, or been occupied in writing. Learning the Vedas requires a state of complete purity, and this purity is compromised when one comes in contact with one of three things that most religions see as creating impurity: death, blood, and sex. Except that here a fourth is added: the act of writing.

Writing contaminates! Why? Perhaps because it transforms something that is eternal and formless, and confines it in words or restrictive texts, something that is essentially finite since it is bound by its media (e.g., bark, parchment, paper, or even a computer). There are scholars who have suggested that the oral status of the Vedas should be ascribed to the fact that the majority of people in India at that period were illiterate. This argument is far from convincing—not only because it is very unlikely that the rate of illiteracy in India at that time would have been notably different from any other civilization but mainly because in no other culture do we witness so wholeheartedly and unequivocally an endorsement of the oral transmission of sacred texts as we do in ancient India.

This last claim should be elaborated by way of a comparison. One might think that at the end of Plato's dialogue *Phaedrus* there lurks similar idea. Plato seems to be saying there that direct speech is prior to writing and therefore preferable. Thus, for example, Plato draws a comparison between writing and painting: both make things come alive, appear before us, as if inviting us some way or other to turn to them directly. But this is an illusion; the moment we turn to the written words themselves, hoping to extract a reply to a question that might have arisen from our reading, we get no reply. The written word will "maintain a most majestic silence." Plato is snide about this silence:

> It is the same with written words: they seem to talk to you as though they were intelligent, but if you ask them anything about what they say, from a desire to be instructed, they go on telling you just the same thing forever. And once a thing is put in writing, the composition, whatever it may be, drifts all over the place, getting into the hands not only of those who understand it, but equally of those who have no business with it; it doesn't know how to address the right people and not address the wrong.

Thus written words are contrasted with speech which is direct, comprehensive and whose margin of vagueness is much narrower than that of writing. The contemporary French philosopher, Jacques Derrida, sensed that this particular Platonic idea was indicative of a general attitude that was, in his mind, prevalent throughout the history of Western philosophy. Writing is seen as a doomed attempt to return to the directness and animation of its oral source though, in fact, it only gives witness to the ever-increasing and everlasting disparity that exists between it and that oral source.

Yet, according to Derrida, Plato failed in his attempt to argue in favor of speech's precedence over writing, and, moreover, when he does deal with that primary direct speech, his description of it, ironically, makes use of the very terms and concepts so obviously drawn from the realm of written language. Thus, for instance, Plato describes speech in terms of something that "is *written* in the soul of the learner" (my emphasis). Thus the priority speech has over writing becomes illusory, as in fact speech is also a form of writing, albeit internal or mental writing. In this manner speech's precedence over writing was substituted by the more complex relationship of mutual dependency. I think that a similar case of dependency can be witnessed in the Bible, between the expression of divine law stated orally ("Moses spake, and God answered him by a voice," Exodus 19:19) and between the setting of the same law in writing ("tables of stone, written with the finger of God," Exodus 31:18). It is now obvious why the supposed similarity between the West's concept of oral precedence over writing and the seemingly similar Indian idea is both superficial and misleading. In India speech was perceived as having precedence over writing because it was evident that there is no reason to assume its dependence upon anything beyond it, definitely not a form of writing and especially not the existence of a transcendent, divine source from whose throat this speech issues.

In ancient India the precedence oral transmission had over written transmission was quite intentional and, moreover, it indicated a clear conceptual preference. Spoken language precedes writing and is superior to it. The language in question is Sanskrit, and even its name attests its status. A language's name usually signifies its geographic origin or some kind of ethnographic indicator about its speakers. Sanskrit is one of those few languages whose name reveals something about the role its speakers allocate it. Sanskrit epitomizes the height of all conceivable purity. The name *saṃskṛta* ("Sanskrit" in Sanskrit) means "well-formed" or, less literally, "refined," "pure," "perfect." The perfection that ancient India recognized in this language relates primarily to its tonal, rather then semantic, qualities. That is to say, this language is above all a perfected collection of sounds, a kind of sublime musical mold. The actual meanings of the words themselves were less important; semantics was perhaps ancillary to sound and negligible at times.[4] Merely hearing the language without comprehending it was enough to bring someone to what might be called a religious epiphany. Perhaps that is why, to this very day, any important Indian ceremony is accompanied by the recital of Sanskrit verses, even when the majority of those present fail to understand one word of it—and sometimes even when the verse is not directly linked to the ceremony's immediate intentions.

All this exposes the reciprocality underlying the relationships between man and sacred works. One scholar has referred to this characteristic Indian state of affairs as a condition in which form has precedence over content. Someone else has likened the role of the reciting Vedic "chanter" (orally preserving and transmitting the Vedas to subsequent generations) not to a sermonizing priest in his pulpit but rather to a medieval monk crouched in his dark cell, patiently copying Latin Scriptures without understanding a word of the text he is transcribing. The presence of this direct bond, in the Vedas, between man and sound comes to the fore in the decisive role awarded to the teacher (the guru) or the seer (the ṛṣi). Even though the sonic Veda is endowed with inherent validity, in theory (and in practice) it is the teacher who gives authority to the texts. Prima facie, this kind of relationship between teacher and pupil may recall similar patterns, extant in other conservative and traditional religious communities. It would, nevertheless, be an error to construe the guru's place in traditional Indian society as merely a particular case of the teacher's vital psychological and epistemological role extant in other traditional societies. Besides this, the guru in the Indian tradition also takes on an ontological role. The Vedic corpus's oral transmission is its only means of preservation and thus the teacher is perceived as both a material and spiritual embodiment of this preservation. The guru, we can see, functions not only pedagogically, he is also, in a sense, a "holy relic," since he contains within him the continuity of the Vedas' presence. Coburn has noted that, by ancient custom, if an aging teacher is unable to find a student worthy of inheriting the tradition he guards, he should throw the traditional sacred texts in his possession into the river, as if they were no more than ashes, since, in themselves, lacking the continuity of an oral passage from teacher to disciple, they lack both authority and value: "written documents, unvivified by personal relationship, are lifeless."

This notion that Vedic language has a self-authoritative status that is embodied in its perfect "execution," has interesting semantic corollaries. One of the most notable attributes of Scripture in Western religions is the assumption that the text holds within it infinite meanings that defy any one definitive interpretation. On the contrary: it is believed that despite the presence of blatant hermeneutic discrepancies—and, moreover, because of them—the text is blessed with divine inspiration and thus its richness cannot be gleaned within one interpretative tradition. These texts have boundless meanings. They can refer to everything and thus are in principle open to an infinite number of interpretations, each of which can, at most, convey only part of their assertions and values. Interpretational plurality attests to the permanent struggle the reader has in extracting an iota of meaning from the text, a struggle that ultimately serves to show the perplexed what he knew all along: Scripture is a vehicle for the transmission of absolute truth. The divine text is established by its indeterminacy, while its variegated meanings depend on the scope and ability of its interpreters. In this context many will be familiar with Augustine's oft-repeated claim at the end of the twelfth chapter of his *Confessions*, namely, that if he were Moses, endowed as he was with the divine spirit and fully aware of the many faces of the truth he was communicating, he would have formulated each of his claims in a such a manner that it would allow for the greatest scope of interpretation:

> Certainly, to make a bold declaration from my heart, if I myself were to be writing something at this supreme level of authority I would choose to write so that my words would sound out with whatever diverse truth in these matters each reader was able to grasp, rather than to give a quite explicit statement of a single true view of this question in such a way as to exclude other views—provided there was no false doctrine to offend me.

Augustine's claim is fascinating: divine language is portrayed as a language that each of us can understand in his or her own manner. Let us note that what we have here isn't yet another postmodernist propounding cultural relativism. Augustine is merely demarcating the boundaries of God's language—a language that expresses everything and in which everything is contained, and accordingly it contains within it a necessary component of incomprehensibility. Truth cannot be exhibited as something exuding harmony and wholeness because it is associated with a Being separated from man by a transcendent and unbridgeable abyss. One needs to be accurate here: the claim about the incomprehensibility of divine language is not a claim about man but a claim about language (when in India an apparently similar claim is made, it usually does not refer to language but to the degrees of understanding caused by the inevitable difference in man's intellectual and spiritual capabilities). It is not human diversity that endows divine language with its many different meanings, but rather the fact that it stems directly from God's transcendence. The presupposition of transcendence is thus manifestly present in Augustine's claim, as it is in many other claims that abound throughout the history of Judaism, Christianity, and Islam; permissiveness in interpreting divine speech is allowed since it is derived, with abounding irony, from the fundamental gulf that exists between God and creation.

In India too there is an interpretational permissiveness with regard to the Vedas, but its similarity with the corresponding Western attitude is rather limited: the plurality of interpretations in India is not the token of a struggle about the veracity of the professed explanations. Different interpretations are, in the main, concerned with the text's performance, much the same as any performance of a musical piece is also an interpretation of it. One could say that what we see here is an exceptional phenomenon; a serious "reading" of a text means marginalizing its semantic dimension and instead highlighting an alternative that is professedly performative, i.e., memorization, recitation, repetition, chanting, and compliance with grammatical rules. Embracing an understanding of the text is not a prerequisite of these activities. Since the Vedas do not derive their authority from an external source (they were neither uttered by gods nor delivered by an appointed messenger), the prime importance of the Vedas' accurate "performance" is the continuing confirmation of their inner authoritative status; they are sustained by their repeated performance. There is no need to elaborate on the profound difference, in this respect, between the West and India. One might want to liken it to the difference between what we experience when we ponder the expressive nature of certain movement in Beethoven's *Appassionata* sonata as opposed to the experience of accurately playing the interval of a diminished fourth between F sharp and B in this sonata. Not that Western religions are unfamiliar with or intolerant of such pedantic and localized attention in matters of Scripture. Consider Abraham Ibn Ezra when he proposes a classification of the different kinds of believers according to their attitude toward Scripture (in the first section of his book *Yesod Mora*). There he offers a succinct portrait of the Indian type of believer, i.e., those "learned men" whose only interest is in the text's musical structure: "[Such a man is concerned with] whatever is concealed and revealed, decipherable and indecipherable, alluded to and excluded from, with minor and major letters, either hanging above or interspersed." Ibn Ezra does not proscribe this approach, yet, since he is no Indian, he endorses it only as a preliminary step in a long journey whose ultimate goal is extracting from a text its hidden meanings. Ibn Ezra disparages those who fail to venture out and go beyond this initial stage, referring to them as those "whose efforts amount to naught and are like a man who has a book of medicinal prescriptions who wears himself out in the practice of counting the number of pages in this book, and the number of columns in every page, and the number of letters in every column; Such labour can heal no ailment." Such a believer is "like a camel wearing silk: neither will the silk benefit from him nor will he benefit from the silk." We need only guess how Ibn Ezra would have chosen to label an Indian diligently reciting the Vedas without in the least being bothered by the exact meaning of his utterances. Yet this same Indian, contrary to Ibn Ezra's portrait, considers exact recitation to be of utmost importance since by doing this, by taking on the role of a participant-performer of the Vedas, he is validating them. Needless to say, I am not suggesting that the original poets or the "performers" were completely uninterested in finding out the actual meaning of the verses. On the contrary, a sonic approach to Vedic language did not curb the evolution of interpretational procedures specifically aimed at extracting the proper meaning of these inspiring hymns. Interestingly enough, it even accelerated the process; the Vedas allow a large variety of interpretations, not only because the source was conceived as initially charged with countless meanings (like Augustine's approach to Scripture) but also, and mainly, because the eternal and absolute harmony of Vedas was perceived as being utterly independent of any interpretation whatsoever.

One of the better known Indian accounts relating to the origin and nature of language appears in those Ṛg Vedic hymns that were dedicated to Vāc, the goddess of speech, language, or "holy utterances." Vāc is a mysterious goddess, for to see her in all her glory one needs to be actively engaged in the process of uncovering her. One hymn describes the goddess as composed of four parts, only one of which is visible to humans and expressible in their language, the remaining three parts are concealed, wrapped in secrecy. Even among those performing the rituals, only an exceptional few have the capacity to reveal her hidden parts. Vāc presents herself as a queen—the first being worthy of sacrifice—and, because this is so, it is she who inspires the other gods. Other accounts portray Vāc as the mother of the universe, from whose womb (which is hidden beneath the waters) are derived all the creatures of the world. These descriptions also emphasize the feminine and erotic nature of language and the obvious sexual connotations surrounding ritual activity. Vāc is described as tensing Rudra's bow so that his arrow may strike at whoever loathes ritual. The hymn, whose first part is quoted below, begins by describing how language was discovered and then outlines the way in which it was passed on to mortals. I think that the first four verses of this hymn are especially important as they illustrate ancient India's attitude to language:

Bṛhaspati! When they set in motion the first beginning of speech, giving names, their most pure and perfectly guarded secret was revealed through love.

When the wise ones fashioned speech with their thought, sifting it as grain is sifted through a sieve, then friends recognized their friendships. A good sign was placed on their speech.

Through the sacrifice they traced the path of speech and found it inside the sages. They held it and portioned it out to many; together the seven singers praised it.

One who looked did not see speech, and another who listens does not hear it. It reveals itself to someone as a loving wife, beautifully dressed, reveals her body to her husband.

On the face of it, there seems to be a certain similarity between the biblical-Neoplatonic-Augustinian picture of language and the one presented by this hymn: the ancient Indian seers, the ṛsis, the originators of language, seem to be exposed to this ancient language through the act of giving names to objects (more or less like Adam), since they too "set in motion the first beginning of speech, [by] giving names." Furthermore, in this hymn it seems that language is being discovered or being formed by naming. This apparent similarity is misleading. Whereas in the West naming occurred as a conjunction between the existence of things in a world outside of language and the act of naming itself, there is nothing in this Vedic hymn to suggest that the process of naming implies a juxtaposition of a copy to an original. It is evident that this hymn does not support or even hint at Plato's idea that it is better to view things in themselves rather than the language that purportedly represents them. Moreover, the act of naming described in the hymn is not committed to a view of the precedence of exteriority over interiority. Contrary to the biblical and Augustinian points of view, there is nothing in the Vedic act of name giving that indicates an attempt to find a correspondence between one's verbal-conceptual apparatus and the external reality preceding it and independent of it. Nowhere does the hymn subsume any kind of correspondence between the world of things and language. Instead, it relies on something quite different: language originates from the names that the primordial seers gave to things "through love"! The profundity of this dramatic shift cannot be overemphasized: love—that innermost feeling, that uniquely personal experience of fullness—is thought of as containing within it the secret of how language is formed. This secret is impervious to things beyond, that is, the ontological status, order, or regularity of any object whatsoever. The formation of language springs from an internal process of connection, from the deep relation between existence and interiority. Vāc can be revealed by recognizing that in the minds of those exalted primordial seers there occurs a kind of primal linguistic communication. These seers are exalted precisely because they are capable of uninterrupted, inexorable, and unhindered inner communication. This is embodied by the word *love* and thus this is the force that "set in motion the first beginning of speech."

The other verses quoted from this striking hymn also tend to emphasize that language was extracted from the inner depths of man. It is somewhat surprising that many of those who have written about this hymn have failed to notice this. The second verse adds another dimension to this process of language revealing itself from the inner depths of its primordial seers. After giving names, the seers sift speech as "grain is sifted through a sieve" (much like the ritual purification of the soma juice often used during sacrifices at that period). I suggest that the meaning of this purification, or sieving, is similar to the moment language turns from a collection of names to a set of rules. What happens, to my mind, is that language's inner grammar is being revealed: the process of sieving grants language its deep structure, and it is difficult not to notice how this hymn stands in fascination of this structure. It is characterized as a "good sign" (similar to ritual activity). Here too, as in the previous verse, language is exposed by acts of intimacy, of interiority, without in any way making assumptions about an exteriority preceding it. The seers sieve speech in their minds, and the driving force behind this creative activity is intimate friendship. Among Vedic scholars, there have been those who have suggested that this friendship should be considered in terms of a fraternity of sacrificial officiators. I do not share this view; I am in agreement with Frits Staal, who suggests that this verse deals with a much broader issue—the universal sense of companionship that exists between humans. As in the first verse, language is characterized, here too, in eroto-aesthetic terms: it resides in a certain human inwardness (that of the ṛṣis) and from there it needs to be gently and subtly extracted, much like the inward relationships of love and friendship.

This characterization, so I contend, is most pronounced in the third verse. This verse describes the communicative dimension of speech, its nature as a means whereby humans successfully communicate with one another. The verse portrays speech as something both active and dynamic, and thus it comes as no surprise that it is seen as analogous to the paradigmatic form of Vedic activity, i.e., ritual. The connection between ritual activity and linguistic communication is plainly visible, and it would seem that this hymn goes so far as to suggest that these are but two sides of the same coin.[5] The link between language and ritual is intriguing. The unraveling of the origin of language through ritual activity turns language into the spoken facet of ritual performance. And so long as this act is associated with human activity, so long as at the core of this ritual we find an active human agent rather than a transcendent God—language too is conceived as independent of and unconditioned by a transcendent source. Again we stumble upon a typical intercultural misunderstanding: attributing language to the goddess Vāc is in effect divorcing language from a divine external source, in the "Western" sense of these terms.

In the previous chapter I noted that in India divinity was awarded a secondary role in the performance of rituals. At times they were even dependent upon man's ritual activity (in the sense that the gods were conceived as dependent upon the "seers" or, by substitution, "reasoning"). Now we can add the precedence of the interiority of language over the world of the gods and their dependence upon the latter as the deepest inner level of language and linguistic activity. For a notable illustration of this dependence, one can adduce the interpretative philosophical work of the Indian philosopher Śabara, a follower of the Mīmāṃsā (one of the six Hindu darśanas, or "schools of thought"). One of the key issues in Śabara's philosophy is his willingness to participate in the Mīmāṃsic extensive project of demythologization of Vedic religion. The Mīmāṃsā tried to expunge all mythology from religion. Part of this process of demythologization took the form of removing the gods from sacrificial rites. The Mīmāṃsā claimed that the motive lying behind sacrifice arose solely from the sacrificial act itself. Accordingly, Śabara devised the following interesting explanation to account for the relationship between ritual activity and the Vedic gods. He compared this to a grammatical relationship. As an example, he suggested the following sentence: "The king's servant deserves to be respected." It is evident that the subject of this sentence is "the servant." The word *king* is merely a qualification and as such simply aids in the identification of the proper subject: which servant is worthy of respect. For Śabara, every mention of the gods the in the Vedas operates in this grammatically qualifying sense. He thus deduced that the gods do not precede ritualistic religious activity, but rather are derived from it. In this manner Śabara turned the divinities into linguistic entities, mere grammatical qualifiers of actions and nothing more.

This theoretical exposition is conveyed more poetically by those Indian texts that chose to highlight the independence of linguistic activity vis-à-vis external reality (in the sense that external reality is contained within it). One might want to consider, for example, the explanations put forward in support of the timelessness and sanctity of the syllable *aum*. This syllable holds within it "everything"—a totality including the gods too. In one of the early Upaniṣads there is a fascinating description of the gods becoming fearful of Death, which in turn makes them hide away from Death's watchful eyes. They decide to insert themselves into the Veda, cloaking themselves in Vedic meters. Yet Death immediately recognized the hiding gods as one sees a fish in clear water. Realizing that they had been found out, they sought refuge in the holy syllable *aum* and entered it. Thus, they became immortal and the fear of Death departed from them.[6]

To return to the first four verses of the hymn to Vāc, it is clear that the way of speech is the way of the ritual and this twofold path is contained inside the "seven singers." In simple words: language is located inside humanity in exactly the same manner that the ritualistic acts of sacrifice are situated there. The radical Indian idea of the internalization of the external, which later evolved into a description of ritual as something occurring inside the mind of its officiator, has its roots here. This claim, without doubt, sounds strange to Western ears: ritualistic activity as something sustained through internalization, sustained as ritualistic activity but shifted into the mind of whoever performs it. The nature of this internalization needs further elaboration, and this shall be done in later chapters discussing the self in India.

According to my reading of the hymn to Vāc, language is formed and crystallized in three discrete stages. To begin with, language was considered a name-giving activity motivated by the power of love. Language was then connected to meaning by filtration and purification, driven by the power of friendship. In the third stage language is consolidated as a means of communication by assimilating itself to the principle of internalized ritual. The fourth verse of this hymn expands on the previous three: after naming, construction, and dissemination, the next stage speaks of the pragmatic reception of speech by the hearer(s) or, in more general terms, of aural comprehension. The metaphorical framework does not change much: understanding is likened to intimate sexual relations between two lovers. The necessary conditions of understanding do not exist in extralinguistic reality. On the contrary, the "one who looked did not see speech, and another who listens did not hear it." The objects that form the world are evoked by means of fancy dress, that is, besides being capable of deceiving us (undoubtedly on account of its beauty too), it is also an obstacle that needs to be removed if one is to attain that supposed bodily understanding brought about by sexual coupling. The sexual imagery used here tries to balance two opposing poles: on the one hand, to characterize understanding as a uniquely private and personal process, but, on the other hand, not as solipsistic understanding because it transpires between two separate minds.

Do the first four verses of the hymn to Vāc give rise to a unique and special kind of logos? Not a logos that has materialized according to the universal laws of an all-encompassing wisdom, but rather a logos that has been radically eroticized and expressed aesthetically as intimate interpersonal relationships? Or perhaps *logos* is not the appropriate term here? There can be little doubt that the vision of language this hymn espouses is radically different from the corresponding Western outlook. The presupposition of transcendence found forceful expression in the Western worldview; the idea of language as a representation of external reality is the natural—and perhaps even necessary—outcome. That presupposition is absent from the Indian worldview; accordingly, the minor role allotted to the notion of truth as a correspondent representation of reality inevitably follows from this absence. Needless to say, it is clear that, in a certain weak sense, there does exist some kind of correspondence in Indian thought no less than in Western philosophy. By this I mean the seeking and the motivation behind the seeking; in this sense, there is no doubt that Indian thinkers sought a certain degree of correspondence between mental images, ideas, and thoughts and what appeared to be beyond the perceiving self's internal world. Still, it is less common to find in India (with the exception of one philosophical school) the presumption of a correspondence in the strong sense, namely, the realist assumption according to which perceived reality is completely independent of our perception of it. In the fourth chapter we shall consider in detail a radical Buddhist outlook (formulated by Nāgārjuna) that conceived of human language as a set of conventions resorting to no representation of external reality in any form whatsoever. This Buddhist view of language is, in a certain sense, immensely different from the Vedic idea of language since the latter is endowed with absolute inner harmony, while language as envisaged by the Buddhists is dissonant and illusive (the rules governing it are no more than conventions and thus the relation between words and what they represent is conventional). Nevertheless, these two opposing conceptions of language do have something in common: both, each in its own way, undermine the principle of correspondence between language and the world. In other words, both the Vedic approach and the Buddhist approach, each for reasons of its own, reject the supposition that the meaning of words and their truth-value hinges upon the degree of correspondence with an external, extra- and prelinguistic reality.

Not only did the poetic and somewhat permissive worldview of Vedic hymns fail to find a place for the assumption that there is a correspondence between language and the external world; there is evidence to this effect in the more abstract, and technical, philosophical doctrines regarding the nature and origin of language. Thus, for example, the Mīmāṃsā defined human language in terms of an internal principle, independent of and unconditioned by the external world. This philosophical assumption enabled the Mīmāṃsā to explain how Vedic language operates and, moreover, how everyday language functions, which according to them, is not essentially different from the language of the Vedas. These philosophers called the relationship between a word and its sense *autpattika*, which could mean "natural" or perhaps even "innate." That is, the link between a word and its sense is based on an internal mechanism, residing within man. This relationship is not the result of accumulated empirical experiences. We speak a language the way we do because of our mind's innate structure or because of our mental makeup.

This approach to the absolute inner source of language is also prominent in the work of the grammarian and philosopher Bhartṛhari (probably of the second half of the fifth century CE). Bhartṛhari's detailed and systematic treatise deals with the major problems in the philosophy of language, but this need not concern us here. Yet, one should mention in the present context that, like the Mīmāṃsā, Bhartṛhari also saw the connection between words and their meaning as internal. Bhartṛhari went even further than the Mīmāṃsā: for him our perception is *entirely conditioned* by internal linguistic structures. According to him, ideal language is the perfect structure of the world, while the empirical world, the world our senses perceive, is an imperfect reflection of this language. This is also true of natural language—it too is but a partial embodiment of an ideal language residing within us as pure form. Accordingly, our perception is determined by our linguistic capabilities. Language makes things known to us through the rules governing it. It is impossible to immediately perceive external objects; each is mediated by universal linguistic entities. Understanding language is therefore understanding the world. This is, of course, a radical approach, referred to in the West as linguistic idealism. In chapter 5 we shall examine in detail Western and Indian expressions of idealism, but here it is imperative to mention Bhartṛhari's linguistic idealism, if only to draw attention to yet another manifestation of the harmonic, nonrepresentational understanding of language prevalent in Indian thought. This harmonic approach to language is a repudiation of the idea that language supposedly represents things and events beyond itself. Generally speaking, it would seem that most Indian thinkers did not adhere to a direct, strict correspondence theory of truth. To them the meaning of events and the nature of things are, in the main, determined by some kind of inner structure. There is a fair amount of disagreement in Indian thought about what the exact nature of this internal structure is—there are those who try to erect a system in which the self occupies a central position and there are others (mainly Buddhists) who take a more radical approach and whose worldview is subsumed by an idea of interiority drenched in the complete annihilation of the self. In the following chapters we shall encounter such views in greater detail.

———————

So long as transcendence is assumed as preceding immanence, it is difficult to encounter this kind of a harmonic view of language in the West. In order to illustrate this difficulty I would like to dwell on one of the most enduring portrayals of language in Western culture. This will offer an incisive, condensed, and penetrating illustration of the presence of the presupposition of transcendence in determining truth and in characterizing language as relating to an exteriority independent of it. Let us consider man's attempt to build a tower in Babel, which, as is well known, is a reflection on the origin of languages. The dominant theme surrounding the construction of the tower and the creation of many different languages is not love, friendship, or any other kind of intimate relationship, but—quite the contrary—violence, the implementation of force, and its dire consequences.

The first thing we have to note is that such stories abound in other cultures too. Yet, in all likelihood, there is something unique in the biblical version of this story and it is for this reason that it has captured the intellect and the imagination of philosophers, writers, painters, and artists throughout the ages. Merely nine verses—terse, succinct, with no superfluity and devoid of any emotion or undue judgment: a case of verbal virtuosity from which all flourish is absent (except, perhaps, the last verse, to which we shall return). Curiously, all this sublime use of language is geared merely to describe the monumental failure of language as such.

It would not be amiss to recall the words that recount the construction of Babel and its tower.

[1] And the whole earth was of one language, and of one speech. [2] And it came to pass, as they journeyed from the east, that they found a plain in the land of Shinar; and they dwelt there. [3] And

they said one to another, Go to, let us make brick, and burn them thoroughly. And they had brick for stone, and slime had they for mortar. [4] And they said, Go to, let us build us a city and a tower, whose top may reach unto heaven; and let us make us a name, lest we be scattered abroad upon the face of the whole earth. [5] And the Lord came down to see the city and the tower, which the children of men builded. [6] And the Lord said, Behold, the people is one, and they have all one language; and this they begin to do: and now nothing will be restrained from them, which they have imagined to do. [7] Go to, let us go down, and there confound their language, that they may not understand one another's speech. [8] So the Lord scattered them abroad from thence upon the face of all the earth: and they left off to build the city. [9] Therefore is the name of it called Babel; because the Lord did there confound the language of all the earth: and from thence did the Lord scatter them abroad upon the face of all the earth.

(Genesis 11)

The biblical scholar Claus Westermann has said of the first eleven chapters of the book of Genesis (those that end with the story of Babel) that their main concern is the description of an ever growing chasm, replacing primal harmonic order with a cosmic and social disorder. Chaos commences with that primal precreational formlessness (*tohu va-vohu*) that divine creation blots out, but nonetheless is indelibly imprinted in the realm of human affairs—the relational breakdown between man and woman, followed by the murderous rapture afflicting their two sons, and then the murder, violence, and incest that characterize the human race as a whole. This violent disorder culminates in the throes of a horrific deluge wiping out all life from the face of the earth. The much-coveted order is not reinstalled even after the waters assuage; instead we hear that God acquiesces to the presence of perpetual disorder. The attempt to build a tower comes as a sort of epilogue to this state of affairs.

The received view is that this story did not originate in Babylon and, furthermore, it does not relate to the building of any specific tower there. It was composed in Israel by an author (or authors) who were well aware of Babylon's enormous tower-temples. The story's final verse offers an explanation of the name *Babel* (*Babylon* in Hebrew), and it would seem that the author quite intentionally distorts the root from which the name of the city is supposedly derived (from b.b.l to b.l.l),[7] probably with the intention of obliquely deriding the city and its dwellers. Be it as it may, this historical setting of the story need not be one's primary concern when one is attempting to uncover the story's philosophical import. Indeed, this story seems to beseech its reader, begging interpretation and pleading for explanation. I would like to present two sets of interpretative gambits from the vast commentaries that have been offered to this story. One cluster of interpretations mostly stresses the human aspect of building the city and the tower—activity that, at varying degrees, signifies a confrontation with God. According to this view, the gist of the story lies in the land dwellers' defiance of the celestial one; the confounding of language is but the outcome of this defiance or a punishment for it. The other cluster of interpretations sees the gist of the story as residing in the author's attitude to the nature and origin of languages; the confusion and dispersal upon the face of the earth, each according to his language, occupies center stage. Alongside these two interpretational moves, I will offer yet another possible reading that will demonstrate the need to combine these two clusters, since it seems to me that there is a close connection between the act of defying the heavens and the splintered nature of human language.

The first cluster of interpretations regards the construction of the tower of Babel as an act of defiance against God. The creation of many languages is the outcome of God's response to this act of defiance. The story assumes that to begin with there was one original language, an *Ursprache*, perhaps a remnant of Adam's paradisial condition. This language enabled men to speak freely with each other. The whole human race spoke one "original" language: "And the whole earth was of one language, and of one speech." (In all likelihood, the author's contention was that the multiplicity of language evident in his own times was not a favorable condition and that, in the not too distant past, things were different.) The people who spoke one language traveled from the east and found a plain in the land of Shinar (probably Mesopotamia), a place that was amenable to settlement. In that region it would have been difficult to find stones for building. Thus these settlers devised the technique of burning bricks in kilns. Employing this technology, they constructed a city, at the center of which they built a tower, and their unity and solidarity supposedly enabled them to achieve this undertaking. Its professed goal was to make themselves "a name." By means of this "name" these people hoped to revolt against God their creator. This rebelliousness brought about a firm and resolute response from God—He intervened directly in the affairs of men, stopping them from completing their task.

In this interpretational cluster, God's response is described in different ways, each account being conditioned by the background and religious outlook of its respective interpreter. According to one commentarial approach—more contemporary and not religiously committed—God's response demonstrates a father's anxiety at his children's ganging together to be one ("one language, and of one speech"); in other words, God was fearful of the human attempt to instigate the idea of humanity (and perhaps even the very idea of culture), and, moreover, fearful that His rebellious offspring were attempting to eliminate His fatherhood. What God most feared was that, as the building progressed, human autonomy would begin to take a recognizable shape and push man to transcend his finality, thereby undermining God's transcendence.

The second portrayal of God we come across in this interpretational cluster was suggested by, among others, traditional Jewish commentators. These commentators also perceived the construction of the tower as an act of defiance, perhaps even revolt. Thus, for instance, one midrash says:

> "And of one speech": that means that they spoke against two who were unique [lit. "one"], viz. against *Abraham* who *was one* [Ezek. xxxiii, 24] and against The *Lord our God, The Lord is One* [Deut vi. 4]. Said they: "This Abraham is a barren mule, and cannot produce offspring." Against *"The lord our God, the Lord is One"*: "He has no right to choose the celestial spheres for Himself and assign us the terrestrial world! But come, let us build a tower at the top of which we will set an idol holding a sword in its hand, which will thus appear to wage war against Him."

These commentators saw the builders as people who were sinning against the heavens; yet most of them did not see this revolt as a genuine threat against the heavens and, needless to say, they did not think that God's response indicated any fear on His part. On the contrary, His decision to confound language is directly derived from His omnipotence in contradistinction to man's failings. Moreover, these commentators did not see God's response as cowardly punishment. After the powerful ways in which God was characterized in the preceding chapters of the book of Genesis, it is difficult to imagine Him suddenly frightened of a tower. Rather, and contrarily, his reaction was meant to preempt the children of man from harming themselves. Arising from their will to rebel against God, the settlers created for themselves a life-enslaving mission that, in turn, made them captives of a totalitarian monolith. One midrash eloquently describes their compulsive devotion to the task of building the tower:

> There were no stones to build the city and the tower, so what did they do? They would bake bricks and burn them in the manner of a potter so that finally the tower was seven miles high. [The tower] had ramps facing the east and the west, and those who would bring up the bricks would ascend on the eastern ramp and those descending, would do so on the western ramp. If a man fell and die, they would heed no attention, yet if a brick were to fall, they would sit to lament it, saying: when will another one come in place of it!

The traditional commentaries thus saw the attempt to build the tower as yet another testimony of human frailty. The construction of the tower foreshadows the implementation of ideological totalitarianism. It is not God who is being threatened, but humanity itself, and the threat arrives from within. The more power humanity accumulates, the more likely it is to harm itself. Thus, dispersal upon the face of the earth is not a punitive act but a preventive one: God demolishes man's sense of unanimity and instead installs division and fragmentation. The creation of distinct linguistic groups brings a halt to the construction of the city. By eradicating the hegemony of language, God in fact prohibits totalitarianism.

Within this cluster, there is one interpretation that I think is especially interesting. The philosopher and sociologist Michael Oakeshott has suggested a reading of the story that merges the traditional and modern points of view. The attempt to build the tower and the city, according to Oakeshott, is a form of nostalgic longing, it is man's attempt to overcome his exile and secure his return to his primordial lost paradise. This longing was not perceived as a (perforce, limited) rebellion against God, but rather as a veritable revolution. Humans were aspiring to found a commonwealth capable of expressing the human yearning of heaven on earth, embodying, if only to a degree, the hope to regain their long-lost—and now utterly deformed—utopia. Building the city and the tower embodies a motion that is in fact a retreat, the retreat from what is to what is aspired to, and perhaps from what is to what ought to be. And so God has to be destroyed. Only then will it be possible to complete the city enclosing the tower—only then will it be possible to establish Babel as a truly liberated city.

For Oakeshott, the mainstay of this episode is to offer an account of man's collective effort to achieve perfection. This is a shameless and uninhibited act of defiance that brings with it both reward and punishment. The reward is the very existence of the attempt to obtain perfection, whereas the punishment lies in its failure and the ensuing, inexorable dispersion. Indeed, the revolution's failure was inevitable. The confusion of languages is a symbolic expression of the finality and totality of this failure. What outdoes what? The reward or the punishment? So long as we concentrate on the individual, and only on the individual, we can assume that the reward outweighs the punishment; that the price of dispersal is worth paying for the very attempt to obtain perfection. And yet, according to Oakeshott, the story's moral has little to do with the individual, but rather with the collective—with human society. Seen from this point of view, the price is not worth paying since it incurs a torn society. Not only are these tears irreparable, they will also engender a chaotic social condition in which a clash of opposing ideals will reign, bringing about the complete disintegration of any form of communal life.

This description of the attempt to transform the relationships between heaven and earth, between God and man, reveals the essential differences between the Western and the Indian worldviews. Rebellion, revolution, or just childish defiance—all these clearly spring from a discernible sense of frustration; the construction of the tower occurs when the rift between God and the "children of man" is at its most acute: not only has the violent expulsion from Eden killed off any innocence, but a horrendous deluge has destroyed all breath of life from the face of the earth. From now on, all life is perpetually and irreconcilably vestigial, "that which has survived." The human response to the construction of the tower basks in the shade of the inevitable frustration begot of these events. One would find it difficult to imagine such a frustration in India, for reasons outlined in the previous chapter. India abounds in stories about men defying the gods or openly rebelling against them—even at the price of being punished—yet, these stories are completely different from the story of the builders of the tower. Since Indian culture is not committed to the presupposition of transcendence, when a man revolts against God it is but one expression of the dialectical tension that exists in the relationships between humans and God or gods. We have seen that these relationships are entirely bilateral. And so we find that in India the reason for rebelling against a god (or goddess) is the will to change places with them—if only the gods were to descend slightly so that we could slightly ascend. On the other hand, the rebellion of those building the tower, at least as perceived by this interpretational cluster, is not man's desire to exchange places with God, but rather to eliminate God altogether. To use a thespian analogy, we might want to say that the dialectical relationships between man and god in India are motivated by the desire to reshuffle the actors' different roles in the drama that is the world. On the other hand, in the West this frustration does not bring about the desire to exchange roles (which would be quite pointless). Satisfaction will be obtained only by changing the very text of the play, that is, staging a different play altogether. This cathartic provision is bound to fail, since the presupposition of transcendence, so long as it lies at the foundation of a culture, prevents any alteration in the repertoire. Thus only if one were to eradicate the presupposition could one alter the text.

Let us now consider the second commentarial cluster. Here, the story of Babel—the city and the tower—is mainly considered as expressing ideas about the nature and origin of language. Jacques Derrida is one of the most prominent exponents of this approach. According to him, the tower of Babel is, primarily, a story about deficiencies: the lack of correspondence between any two languages, the lack of correspondence between any two places, the lack of correspondence between language to itself and language to meaning. These deficiencies render translation impossible; at the same time, the story demonstrates the need we have to label different discernible linguistic forms and the existence of (noncorresponding!) translations that supposedly will compensate us for the plurality (including linguistic plurality) denied us. Derrida writes:

> The "tower of Babel" does not merely figure the irreducible multiplicity of tongues; it exhibits an incompletion, the impossibility of finishing, of totalizing, of saturating, of completing something on the order of edification, architectural construction, system and architectonics. What the multiplicity of idioms actually limits is not only a "true" translation, a transparent and adequate interexpression, it is also a structural order, a coherence of construct. There is then (let us translate) something like an internal limit to formalization, an incompleteness of the con-structure. It would be easy and up to a certain point justified to see there the translation of a system in deconstruction.

At the hub of this imperfection, the limitation of structural order, lies the ambiguity imbedded in the name *Babel*. Derrida is well aware of what biblical scholars know too and what even Voltaire was familiar with: the etymological sense of *Babel* is probably derived from the compound *bab-ili*, meaning "the gate of the gods," or, broadly speaking, the house of god or the city of god (much like, for instance, the "gates of heaven" that Jacob saw in his famous ladder dream and after which he named the place he dwelt in *Beit El*, the house of God). On the other hand, the biblical author attributes the confusion of language to *Babel*, despite the fact that in doing so he confounds the root from which the name of the city is derived (from b.b.l to b.l.l). Derrida claims that this ambiguity is emblematic: the confusion even resides in the name itself. The name of the city, which according to the text was given by God Himself, confuses between it being the city of God and the city of confusion (how remarkable that even Derrida is among the confused, since the Hebrew word *balal*—derived from the root b.l.l.—does not mean "confusion" but rather "mixing").

Thus, for Derrida, building the city and the tower is not necessarily an attempt to construct an edifice whose top is in the heavens (although he does not necessarily exclude this) but, more important, this endeavour expresses the will of the children of man "to make [themselves] a name," to appropriate for themselves a name, to consolidate the unity of language while keeping it in one place and in one tower ("lest we be scattered abroad upon the face of the whole earth"). The children of man, to use Derrida's terminology, tried to establish a unified genealogy by means of a universal language, and it was for this that they were punished. God, infuriated by the name these people have chosen for themselves, imposes His name upon the city. In doing so, he instigates the demolition of the tower, which is no less than the utter collapse of universal language. God destroys "one language," replacing it with "languages"—translations that are, paradoxically, both compulsory and forbidden. By doing this God keeps to Himself the role of naming. Babel is the city of God and it is God and only God who can name the city ("Therefore He called its name Babel").

Derrida's interpretation prefers not to stress the presence of the actual paradigm of crime and punishment in which men act, God responds, and humans bear his punishment. Instead, Derrida offers a much more abstract paradigm, that of man's failed aspiration to attain a sense of completeness that in turn ushers in want. This want, or absence, is characteristic of human languages, and this is most eloquently expressed by God himself, by His choice of an ambiguous name that has become the most potent symbol of linguistic activity as such. I cannot resist a slight digression that will illuminate Derrida's point from different textual angle. Consider one of the many philosophical reflections that abound in Ecclesiastes: "He has made every thing perfect in its time also, he has set the world in their heart, without man finding out the work that God made from beginning to end" (3:11).[8] Despite the fact that in all likelihood Ecclesiastes stems from the wisdom literature of the East, East and West are, as we know, relative concepts, and, in the context of this book, Ecclesiastes is a Western book par excellence: at its core is not man, but rather a transcendent God separated from man by a vast and unbridgeable abyss. This much is evident from the verse quoted above. God "has made every thing perfect in its time," but this world, having been created by God, is inaccessible (much like God himself) to the human mind. Compared to God, human identity seems not only limited but also lacking autonomy: this identity resides inside a world that God has "set in their heart." If we stop to consider this act of setting the world in men's heart from a (hypothetical) divine point of view, then it seems like a very simple operation: the world is forged in man's mind. Yet, if we care to look at it from the human perspective, we end up facing a vicious circle: I assume that God created the world, a world that is beyond my understanding, since the creation of the world includes within it the act of implanting the world in my mind.

The connection between Derrida's perception of want and the above verse is apparent in the exegesis offered by one of the classical Jewish hermeneutists. In the midrash *Koheleth Rabbah* the verse "also he hath set the world in their heart" is interpreted in several different ways. The first, the simplest, tries to defuse it by turning it into a description of a state of mind. *World* is glossed as a desire for the world; a sort of life instinct naturally imbedded inside human life. God inserted "the desire for the world" in the hearts of man (without them noticing it). It is as if God decreed that the relationship between man and the world would be some sort of adaptive relationship necessary for existence of life.

There is in this midrash a different, and seemingly more profound, interpretation of the same verse ("also he hath set the world in their heart"). *World* is glossed as fear or anxiety. God instills man with the fear, creating a condition in which the life of man will always be set against the backdrop of a basic, fundamental, primordial fear—the fear of death.[9]

The third interpretation, and to my mind the most interesting, draws us nearer to Derrida's understanding of the tower of Babel. Setting the *world* in the hearts of men is not the planting of desire or the installation of fear, but the amalgamation of "world" (*olam*) with "vanish/disappear" (*he'alem*).[10] That which God "set in their hearts" is merely a "vanishing" (it is interesting to note how the paronomasia here is similar to the one surrounding the word *Babel*). Man was created in such a way that his nature has an internal "want" that can neither be fulfilled nor eliminated. What is missing? Obviously, perfection, wholeness—that which Derrida has called "name." The midrashic commentator similarly refers to it when he relates to that "vanishing" as the withdrawal of the Tetragrammaton, God's explicit name. This commentator is suggesting that God is preventing man from attaining the absolute wholeness contained in His explicit name and thus condemns man to a life of want. According to this commentary, the condition of *not* knowing God's explicit name has enormous advantages; knowing it would have made human life impossible.[11]

Let us return to the story of the tower of Babel and the second commentarial cluster. In his book *After Babel* George Steiner suggests an interpretation similar to that of Derrida, even though it is set in different terms. Steiner describes the primordial, ideal, human language as characterizing human existence as such. He sees the tower of Babel as the catastrophic breakdown of man's ability to employ his ideal primordial language. The biblical tradition, says Steiner, draws attention to the presence of an ideal language that resides in the foundation of our linguistic condition before it turns into a discord, because of the collapse of the tower. Adam, before the fall, is said to have given names to all the living beasts. Steiner sees this as the ideal and natural state of language. He is relying here on an article by Walter Benjamin, which, coincidentally, Derrida also mentions in the same context. In this article Benjamin draws attention to what he considers to be the most distinguished feature of the human species: the fact that human language is a language capable of "naming all other beings." Accordingly, "it is . . . the linguistic being of man to name things." A certain degree of collaboration between man and God is achieved through language. "In the name, the mental being of man communicates itself to God." Imbued with Benjamin's ideas, Steiner points out that "this Adamic vernacular not only enabled all men to understand one another, to communicate with perfect ease. It bodied forth, to a greater or lesser degree, the original Logos, the act of immediate calling into being whereby God had literally 'spoken the world.'" Adam's language was therefore blessed by an eternal syntax. Every time Adam spoke, he reenacted the mechanism of creation. There was complete and perfect correspondence (in the strong sense of the word, obviously)—here was a language that perfectly mapped the true nature of things as they really are. Adam's paradisial language was lucid and unblemished glass, through which the "light of total understanding" shone brilliantly. It is for this reason that Babel, according to Steiner, is the story of man's second fall, since Man failed to maintain that direct relation between language and reality. Man was banished from the garden of Eden, and now, on account of the construction of the tower of Babel, he is again banished, except that this time round he is exiled from the ability to fully comprehend and form the ability to generate a language that clearly corresponds to external reality. Man's primordial language was lost, and the only thing left, according to Steiner, was hope (Steiner notes that this is the very hope underlying the name of Zamenhof's universal language, *Esperanto*). This hope, says Steiner, can be summed up thus:

If man could break down the prison walls of scattered and pol-
luted speech (the rubble of the smashed tower), he would again
have access to the inner penetralia of reality. He would know the
truth as he spoke it. Moreover, his alienation from other peoples,
his ostracism into gibberish and ambiguity, would be over.

In other words, let that immediate, transparent, original language, the
language spoken by Adam and all of mankind before the tower of Babel, be reconstructed and revealed to us again.

The interpretation that I would like to put forward is something
of an attempt to conflate the two commentarial clusters I have been
outlining; that is, I concede that the story of the tower of Babel princi-
pally highlights the close connection between the picture of language
it offers and the inconceivable rebellion against transcendent deity. My
interpretation follows the trail set out by Derrida and Steiner, who
considered the story of the tower of Babel as a story about the most
fundamental characteristics of human nature. And yet my proposed
interpretation departs from Steiner when it considers what the biblical story actually claims about the nature of this ideal primordial language. Contrary to Benjamin—and Steiner, who in this respect follows
him—it does not seem to me that divine language is perceived as a language granted to its speakers directly, immediately and transparently.
An ideal language is indeed a divine language, and, as such, it is (by
definition?) profoundly and painfully severed from all its actual, human manifestations. Gershom Scholem managed to portray this rift,
in all its severity, by quoting "one of the greatest Kabbalists" who saw
the worlds as "the names written on the paper of God's being," or, in
Scholem's words, "the worlds are nothing but names written upon a
piece of paper of divine essence." No doubt this bears testimony to
the presence of a deep mystical outlook, one that attempts to relocate
the plurality and manifold nature of external reality onto the Oneness
of the divine plane. Yet it would seem that it is possible to apply the
relocation that Scholem mentions to realms other than the esoteric
discussions of this or that mystical doctrine and see it as reflecting not
only the role of language but also, more pertinently, the question of
the divine status of language and the differing degrees of man's ability
to appropriate this divine language. If language is divine and endowed
by the transcendence of a supreme being, every actual manifestation

of language in a nonmystical perception of reality is but a wound—or maybe just a probing of this wound, that is to say, an attempt to numb the pain of an open abyss spanning the possibility of human expressiveness and the perfect divine foundation upon which it is founded. My suggested reading of the story of the tower of Babel is an acerbic illumination of this linguistic abyss.

To begin with, this reading asks us to consider what is missing from the story. Here I revert to the comparative method. Let us note that this story completely lacks any notion of human language as something arising from the depths of human interiority, from profound feeling of intimacy (i.e., love, friendship, or eroticism). These points of departure are not to be found in the story of the tower of Babel. Instead of such internal, intimate sources, language (as expressing human nature) is presented in terms of violence. Let us dwell on the presentation of this violence. "And the whole earth was of one language, and of one speech." Consider, as Steiner suggests, that this connotes a primordial language that binds humanity. This, Steiner claims, was a completely transparent language, a language that made it possible for a perfect correspondence between words and the world: it exhibited no vagueness, there were no ambiguities, no pragmatic considerations that overrode a word's semantics.

Thus, Steiner; yet I think he is mistaken. Not only in his commentary on the Tower of Babel, but, more pertinently, in his underlying assumption about the existence of a "primal, ideal language." If such was the primeval state of language, how are we then to explain the motives that made these people, speaking an original, transparent, perfectly corresponding language, to aspire to build a city with a tower whose top is in the heavens? The text offers us two explanations. The first is affirmative: "let us make us a name" (Derrida has highlighted this as the key element in his reading of the story). But besides this the text also mentions a negative reason: "lest we be scattered abroad upon the face of the whole earth." That is to say, besides the constructive urge to obtain and actualize perfection (expressed by "making a name"), there is another motivation at the heart of which lies great anxiety: dispersion is seen as a threat, as a harbinger of weakness and an inability to actualize all that they strove to accomplish by being located in one place. Here, inevitably, a thorny question presents itself before us: if the whole earth was of one language and one speech, what is the source of this anxiety of dispersion? Why should a society characterized by a determinedly harmonic language, immediate and transparent, feel anxious about dispersion and diffusion? How does such a society arrive at a point where it is oblivious to that great sense of security—that insurance policy—embedded in the presence of "one language"? Why should they fear dispersion? This gives rise to yet another question: why did these settlers feel they could avoid dispersion by building a tower whose top is in the heavens? It would seem that they used this tower as an anti-anxiety pill, and it is not apparent why. But before we consider this question, one should regretfully note the inefficiency of this anti-anxiety pill: not only did it fail to deliver its purported effect (it did not prevent anxiety), but, quite contrarily, in retrospect, it would seem that this very drug only served to increase their anxiety. After all, the building of the tower results in the everlasting dispersal of the human race.

Perhaps, instead, we should admit that at the heart of this endeavour there is nothing but confusion? It is quite simple to determine the meaning of this confusion by listing the misconceptions that afflicted the builders—their perplexity, their bewilderment, even their primal ignorance—that together combined to make them feel unhappy with their lot. Is not the attempt to build a tower some kind of early variation on the theme of Pandora's box? Bewildered and weary of their nomadic life, always on the look out for fear of slipping into one of the great diluvial swamps, a pointless anxiety about "overscattering" takes hold, propelling the story to its somewhat ironic finale in which they are desperately scattered upon the face of the earth. This is quite unlikely. The tower is not the Mesopotamian equivalent of Pandora's box. It was built quite intentionally and with deliberation. The builders were well aware of their motives and gave this awareness succinct verbal expression (and, in all likelihood, quite eloquently too: "And they said one to another"). If the anxiety that brought about the construction of the tower did indeed stem from confusion, it was a necessary confusion, an inevitable, archetypal confusion, arising from a clear understanding of their true condition. The origin of the settlers' primal language was indeed of divine origins, but, to prevent human dispersion and enable them to obtain a comforting linguistic transparency, it had to be appropriated by man. The construction of the tower had to eradicate, or at least to lessen, the builders' sense of anxiety. What is evident beyond doubt is that the existence of a primary language failed to prevent this anxiety. The reason for this is quite simple: their primary and original language was a divine language, and, as divinity is transcendent, transcendence must lie at the hub of this ideal language. Elsewhere Steiner has drawn our attention to the fact that man was born out of a dialogue the creator God had with an interlocutor (or a complete entourage of interlocutors) since, before he creates man, God says, in the plural, "Let us make man" (Genesis 1:26). According to Steiner, this address to an unidentified entourage reveals the close connection between human speech and its transcendent origins. But Steiner does not dwell on one interesting aspect of God's dialogue before the creation of man. The whole world was created by speech; evidently, the authors of this text saw God's soliloquy as *preceding* human language as such (God made use of language before man was created). With the creation of man (or perhaps a split second before it) the monologue becomes a dialogue, but this does not suffice to turn language into something more human, since even this dialogual aspect of speech, by which man was created, necessarily precedes human language. Hence man cannot be the real master of human language. Language belongs to God and thus when man employs language it is bound to be deficient. Benjamin's idyllic account of the language of man as a bona fide name giver before the fall, is misleading, since it ignores the plain and obvious textual context of the occasion of name giving. I have already argued that this context shows that the first linguistic act in the Bible is not name giving, but *God*'s attempt to find man his helpmeet. Man, facing nothing but God, is a man alone, and this solitariness in the face of God is so drastic that the only way to overcome it is by increasing the rift, by creating a distinctly human surrounding—spouse, family, society. Language is seen as part of that divine master plan to define man in such a way that it will perpetuate the rift, the unbridgeable abyss that lies between man and God. Thus the attempt to find man a helpmeet by means of language is also an attempt to establish man only by means of humanity. That is to say, once more to show man how apart he is from his transcendent creator. Fear of dispersal and scattering is therefore inherent to the condition in which language is employed. The attempt to reach the heavens, to redress the crooked, to redeem humanity from the intolerable pressure of a divine essence was drenched in this fear. At its core, the attempt to build a tower is an attempt to induce a one-way movement, from below to above, from the soft margins to the center, from the phenomenal and material to the world of form. The tower is seen as an effective "anti-anxiety pill" since it brings about a unilateral movement countering the other unilateral movement. No longer will man be in a condition in which divine language, despite it being "one language and one speech," widens the rift between man and God. Instead man will generate a new situation in which, through a language of his *own*, he will make himself a name so as to perpetuate himself through eternity and thus induce a movement in the direction of God.

But hope recedes. The tower's unilateral movement is an illusory movement since concurrent with the attempt to bring about this movement there is necessarily a countermovement too. The movement to the top of the tower, as a movement from the fringe to the center, is at the same time a more forceful outward movement from the tower to the four corners of humanity, a movement that is typified by the brutal execution of the meaning of that primary language: disengaging man from his transcendent core. Thus any attempt to quell the builders' linguistic anxiety simultaneously draws them deeper into it. If only we could remain immobile—but human nature is such that it has no alternative but to seek antidotes to anxiety, and this only unleashes even greater anxiety. From now on building the tower is a necessity. There is no one who isn't building a tower. But this is a strange sort of endeavor. In a certain sense one is not building upward but burrowing downward. Maybe it is for this reason that God needs to "descend" to the tower; not only because he is in the heavens and the tower is upon the earth, but because every upward movement of the tower is accompanied, by necessity, by burrowing to the depths of the earth. This is another of Kafka's astonishing insights:

> What are you building?
> I want to dig a subterranean passage. Some progress must be made. My station up there is much too high.
> We are digging the pit of Babel.

Anyone who actively builds a tower—that is, digging—is, at the same time, causing the rift to set and perpetuating the anxiety enshrined in it. Veering away from the center is primarily veering away from the ideal of lucid understanding, from the naive assumption that language is a polished looking glass through which meaning is to be transparently reflected. The effort to reduce or even abolish the gap between words and the world can end only in one kind of failure, which turns it into a Sisyphean task, that is, a task perpetually repeating itself. Kakfa was well aware of this. For him, this is an archetypal condition—"Kafkaesque"—the impossibility of necessity alongside the necessity of the impossible. This is the only course open for someone seeking to articulate her or his humanity. Indeed, it is a necessary condition of any such pronouncement. But, what is necessary is, alas, impossible:

> Destroying this world would be the task to set oneself only, first, if the world were evil, that is, contradictory to our meaning, and secondly, if we were capable of destroying it. The first seems so to us; of the second we are not capable. We cannot destroy this world, for we have not constructed it as something independent; what we have done is to stray into it; indeed, this world is our going astray, but as such it is itself something indestructible, or, rather, something that can be destroyed only by means of being carried to its logical conclusion, and not by renunciation; and this means, of course, that carrying it to its logical conclusion can only be a series of acts of destruction, but within the framework of this world.

Human beings have been condemned to define themselves in the face of exteriority and thus "human" language is obtainable only by means of a struggle that is doomed to fail. But we are confronted by a lethal paradox: inside this struggle lies, by necessity, our defeat. This paradoxical struggle turns understanding itself into a paradox. For Kafka, every act of understanding is a failure, by virtue of the identity of opposing unilateral movements. Every upward motion, every ascent, ends with an inevitable collapse. But this is only the collapse of the tower, not the collapse of the attempt to build it. If only it were possible to build the tower of Babel without ascending it, cries out Kafka in scathing irony. If only we were not human.

THREE

My-Self

DESCARTES AND EARLY UPANIṢADS
ON THE SELF

By space the universe grasps me and swallows me up
like a fleck; by thought, I grasp it.
—Pascal, *Pensées*, §348

In the sixth and final section of his *Discourse on the Method*, Descartes
(1596–1650) broods on the misapprehension of his philosophical ideas.
It seems to him that the reason most philosophers fail to understand
him is because they are so entrenched in the past, unable to free themselves from the shackles of philosophical convention or relax their rigid
doctrines. He describes the struggle with his philosophical opponents
in quite an exceptional manner:

> In this they seem to resemble a blind man who, in order to fight
> without disadvantage against someone who can see, lures him into
> the depths of a very dark cellar. These philosophers, I may say,
> have an interest in my refraining from publishing the principles

of the philosophy I use. For my principles are so very simple and evident that in publishing them I should, as it were, be opening windows and admitting daylight into that cellar where they have gone down to fight.

Descartes sees himself cast against philosophers who seem to him to have found refuge in tangled expressions and complicated truths and have failed to see the simplicity that emanates from his handling of the fundamental issues of philosophy. In this respect he is no different from other past innovators who also felt that they had to oppose the rigidity and reserve of their contemporaries. Still, one cannot help noting the curious imagery with which this struggle is described. Descartes sees himself in a violent struggle with the philosophers of yore, in a darkness they have imposed upon him. Given that they are groping in the dark, they are unable to bear the light of true wisdom, and thus they have no recourse but to draw him to "a very dark cellar" in order to quash his intellectual advantage. One of the most celebrated images of Western philosophy immediately comes to mind, that of Plato's cave, in which a darkened cave is contrasted with an open space directly lit by the sun. But even if we take into account the reference to Plato, the picture of Descartes' struggle in the cellar is as bizarre as it is unconvincing. We shall return to this later on.

Few would contest that Descartes' philosophy occupies a singular place in the course of Western philosophy. Some have labeled him the father of modern philosophy or the inaugurator of the idea of modern man as an autonomous subject. Indeed, more than any other philosopher of his time, Descartes has come to epitomize the transition from a traditional religious outlook of the medieval world to the scientific and humanistic modern worldview. In philosophical literature, and in nonphilosophical literature too, one can detect two primary focal points stressed by commentators. The first hinges on Descartes' aspiration to find objectivity. In this respect, Descartes is seen by some as occupying the role of a great innovator, as someone who gave philosophical expression to the main tenets of the scientific revolution of the sixteenth and seventeenth centuries, especially to Galileo's astronomical application of Copernican doctrine. Other interpreters choose to differ and seek to portray Descartes as an essentially conservative thinker, pledged to the deductive model of science. Either way, it is clear that Descartes' aspiration is to establish a philosophy endowed with complete objectivity, exempt from any kind of doubt. His new philosophy was supposed to articulate unequivocally the autonomy of the new sciences and, at the same time, to make a meaningful contribution to its theoretical foundation. Indeed, more than once Descartes expressed his complete confidence in the ability of science to offer this new philosophy a secure foundation and his sincere belief that mathematics is the preferable method for understanding the world. In the same manner, Descartes explicitly stated that he was confident the new philosophy could offer a secure foundation for the sciences, or, in his words, "to establish a firm and abiding foundation for the sciences" by presenting self-evident truths clearly and distinctly.

The second focal point hinges on the idea designating Descartes as the founder of subjectivity. His philosophy is identified, primarily, with his discovery of the "thinking subject." That is, mental substance that can never be doubted, since the very act of doubting it (in itself a mental act) only reaffirms its presence. Human thought is posited as the cornerstone of every conceivable worldview, being an autonomous activity that is not reliant on anything beyond it, activated solely by itself.

These two focal points are not mutually exclusive and are not intended as two competing interpretations of Cartesian philosophy. On the contrary, they constitute two different points of emphasis in one philosophical system that interconnects an objective scientific understanding of the world with the institution of subjectivity. They share a common thread: the idea of certainty or, more precisely, the vigorous quest for certainty. Descartes was motivated by an obsessive urge, nearly a mania, for that one thing: to establish indubitable knowledge. The search for truth was replaced by the search for certainty. As I noted in the previous chapter, truth was generally conceived to be that which perfectly corresponds to the things or events to which it refers; as such, truth was seen as entirely dependent on the reality being described. Certainty, on the other hand, is a condition of the knower and relates to his mental capacity. In other words—while truth (for instance, in Plato's philosophy) "resides" in the world of Forms, Cartesian certainty "resides" in the acquisition of knowledge. The whole of Descartes' philosophical enterprise concentrates on the urge to know with certainty—to uphold knowledge on such a secure and firm foundation that it will be irrefutable. This obsessive urge was accompanied by a mordant fear—the dread of making a mistake, of tripping from the heights of certainty to the lowlands of probability, a place prone to error and fault. Descartes clearly articulated this fear, so much so that he gave error a seemingly theological role: that of sin or guilt. In Descartes' time, advancements in science, in society, in religious and cultural matters reached a certain peak. This may offer a partial explanation of Descartes' fear, since these advancements may have induced in him a strong feeling of insecurity arising from the weakening, and even collapse, of theories and cultural establishments that were previously considered the bedrock of existence in general and of human life in particular. With this kind of backdrop, Descartes' obsessive search for complete certainty is easily explained. So is its upshot: the attempt to reveal an inner world, i.e., the human being as an autonomous subject whose mental existence is irrefutable.

This is not the place to peruse the intricacies of Descartes' philosophical enterprise, especially since they are part of the common heritage of modern philosophical thought. It will suffice merely to highlight the major steps to certainty as described in Descartes' lucid and vivid prose. Interestingly, these stages are cumulative acts of casting doubt. For Descartes, doubting is primarily methodical—it is meant to free the philosopher from the influence of opinions or normative judgments that he would mostly absorb from his surroundings. But, as we shall see, this method of doubting is an indispensable part of the process of acquiring certainty. Descartes begins his project by casting doubt on the evidence of his senses, since these testimonies are sometimes clearly deceptive (e.g., in situations when one is confused or when the objects of perception are far from the center of one's cognitive field). The next stage considers such cases where the evidence of the senses is supposedly infallible since it is located at the center of the perceiver's cognitive field. Descartes asks whether it is really possible to cast doubt on the immediate evidence of the senses without simultaneously running the risk of losing one's mind or being considered insane (we shall return to these musings later on). Yet, on second thought, he offers the dream argument as evidence for a perfectly normal situation in which our most immediate perceptions can turn out to be erroneous. In the midst of dreaming we are utterly convinced that what we perceive is indeed external reality—despite the obvious differences that exist between dream states and wakefulness. In the next stage Descartes broadens his methodical doubting to include epistemological domains that are not reliant on the evidence of the senses. Such domains are supposedly indubitable even when not supported by our sensual apparatus (and thus are not liable to be doubted even whilst dreaming). What he is referring to are our thoughts and the valid conclusions we draw (e.g., in mathematics and geometry) based on the rules of thought. For Descartes, these conclusions rely on the kind of things that he calls "the simplest and most general things." Apparently, it would be impossible to err in thoughts endowed with *clarity* (thoughts that are self-evident and immediately transparent) and also endowed with being *distinctive* (i.e., being differentiated from other thoughts). But Descartes is willing to expand his methodical doubt so that even these kinds of truths will also be challenged. This expansion is achieved by conjuring a "malicious demon of the utmost power and cunning," a demon capable of deceiving each of us wherever we turn—including our basic inferences that were obtained in a clear and distinct manner and whose veracity seems to us certain and indubitable. Here his methodical doubting not only reaches it apogee but also reveals its true nature and purpose. At this stage, for Descartes, it is evident that—unlike the sceptics preceding him, for whom doubt arose out of a penetrating understanding of the nature of things—doubt is in fact an artificial product, a fictional supposition.

At its most contrived moment, just when methodical doubting seems to have reached its apex, it also instantly collapses into a singular point of full and firm certainty. This certainty is subjective, because it is located at the core of the mental act of doubting whose apogee, as mentioned earlier, is the contrived supposition of a malicious demon whose sole purpose is to deceive us. If the process that creates the possibility of a malicious demon is a mental one, then this process must certainly exist. Descartes offers an interesting demonstration of this certainty while toying with the idea that even methodical doubting itself, including all its different stages, is the product of confusion and is therefore also contrived. This idea opens up an introspective window with which to gaze at the source of this contrivance, namely, at himself. This introspection turns out to be the Archimedean point of the new certainty that he originates. As is well known, Archimedes sought an external point beyond earth that would enable him, so he thought, to divert the planet off its course. Descartes too sought such a location, but, curiously, he did not seek it in the far and beyond, but in the core of his inwardness. Evidently, the Archimedean point of certainty comprises the discovery of thinking as a mental activity. It is uncovered in the course of pursuing an answer to the question "Am not I, at least, something?" To which he definitely replies in the affirmative: "if I convinced myself of something then I certainly existed."

In his *Discourse on the Method of Rightly Conducting Reason and Reaching the Truth in the Sciences* Descartes characterizes this apodictic knowledge by the following ambiguous claim, *"cogito ergo sum"* (it is ambiguous since there are two possible readings: either as seeing the "I am" as being derived from the "I think" and thus understanding the whole claim a some kind of inference; the other reading sees the "I am" merely as a performance of the "I think"). In a somewhat later work, *Meditations on First Philosophy*, Descartes conveyed the presence of apodictic certainty by the claim "I am, I exist." Here there is no doubt that it was his intention to highlight a singular point of obstinate subjectivity, presenting itself in such a way that no kind of activity could eliminate it (since it is present in any kind of activity). Either way, in the thinking subject Descartes found apodictic certainty—the irrefutable knowledge of its own existence as a thinking self. The thinking subject is thus the outcome of methodical doubt, but, in retrospect, it is also what enabled doubt in the first place. Following his discovery of the "I-think" (ego cogito), Descartes came to regard it as a "thinking substance," *res cogitans* (since according to the tenets of Aristotelian thought, wholly endorsed by Descartes, no action is possible without the existence of a substance that performs it—a *res cogitans*, in this case).

Metaphorically speaking, the apodictic self-knowledge of the "I-think" must take place in a sealed room whose heavy curtains are drawn together. Complete impermeability of this room is necessary. This will keep opinions, norms, customs, habits, and predispositions from entering the room in which the quest for certainty takes place. Disengaging from culture and society, from the world of convention, is highly desirable and indeed encouraged, since the very presence of these intrusions is liable to create a real obstacle in the mind's way to knowing itself and thus it is imperative to eliminate that stumbling block from the philosophical path:

The simple resolution to abandon all the opinions one has hitherto accepted is not an example that everyone ought to follow. The world is largely composed of two types of minds for whom it is quite unsuitable. First, there are those who, believing themselves cleverer than they are, cannot avoid precipitate judgements and never have the patience to direct all their thoughts in an orderly manner; consequently, if they once took the liberty of doubting the principles they accepted and of straying from the common path, they could never stick to the track that must be taken as a short-cut, and they would remain lost all their lives. Secondly, there are those who have enough reason or modesty to recognize that they are less capable of distinguishing the true from the false than certain others by whom they can be taught; such people should be content to follow the opinions of these others rather than seek better opinions themselves.

On the whole, human beings are not endowed with abundant wisdom. He distinguishes between those who do not admit their mental deficiency and those who, "having sufficient reason or modesty," admit to their stupidity. Both parties, however, are incapable of treading the path of certainty that Descartes has paved. Philosophy is too serious and intricate a pursuit to be done publicly. The philosopher takes on the airs of a hermit (albeit a secular hermit) at least in the sense that his solitude is indispensable to his philosophy. We should bear in mind that the word *meditation*, adorning the title of Descartes' essay *Meditations on First Philosophy*, directly alludes to the introspective gaze—the kind of contemplative act that is always conducted on one's own, in the serenity of one's own solitude. Solitariness is indeed a becoming condition for these meditations, and Descartes blesses the opportunity that enabled him to "arrange for myself a clear stretch of free time" when his mind is "free of all worry." It would seem that for him the certainty of knowing one's self-existence is achievable *only* by means of deep contemplation undertaken in complete isolation. It becomes apparent that solitude, for Descartes, was not just a personal preference. The ivory tower in which a philosopher locks himself is not merely a matter of preference or a tactical retreat: it exhibits an element of necessity. For Descartes, solitude is paramount: his complete philosophical enterprise was conducted under the shadow of a dire menace, namely, our inability to discern between truth and falsehood. Moreover, it was undertaken at a time clouded by a sense of insecurity. This menace prescribes drastic measures, as in a case when one discovers that the house in which one lives is safe no more: "Admittedly, we never see people pulling down all the houses of a city for the sole purpose of rebuilding them in a different style to make the streets more attractive; but we do see many individuals having their houses pulled down in order to rebuild them, some even being forced to do so when the houses are in danger of falling down and their foundations are insecure." Descartes often described the urgency in which his "closed-room" philosophy was being conducted by extreme allusions to foundational disintegration and the spreading of rot. His solitude is therefore more than just a mere physical and cultural dislocation; it is a philosophical style dictated by the vicissitudes of reality. Not only is the philosophical soliloquy preferable to the philosophical dialogue, but, moreover, in a dialogue one runs the risk of being diverted from one's true spiritual-philosophical path.[1] This situation is somewhat ironical. While it would seem that the isolation or uniqueness of the I-think is meant to be the *outcome* of an investigation (namely, the stage in which certainty reveals itself in the singularity of the ego cogito), it now transpires that this singularity was present right from the beginning as the indispensable solitude within which doubting should take place. Later on, we shall encounter a similar irony.

The novelty of Descartes' discovery that certainty resides within the I-think has given us the impression that his philosophy undermines the role of transcendence in the West and that this diminishes, in part, the presupposition of transcendence. In other words, Descartes is often seen a precursor of Hegel and Nietzsche, rather than a follower of Plato, Aristotle, or Aquinas. (Indeed, many of Descartes' contemporaries saw in his writings, for better or for worse, a dramatic devaluation in the role of the divine.) This view is shared by some Cartesian scholars, who, when noting this devaluation, explain it as the outcome of Descartes' radical redefinition of man and his basic traits. Man, as conceived by Descartes, is an autonomous subject, whose recognition of himself does not come about by means of some outward mediator, but rather takes place immediately and directly within himself. The I-think now occupies center stage, taking on constructive roles that beforehand were naturally attributed to an external-transcendent entity. It would seem that the only plausible conclusion we could make as readers of Descartes' oeuvre is that he incurs a point of view in which the presupposition of transcendence has been thrust out of its foundational role. As we shall see, this conclusion is somewhat premature. But before we take this on board, we should review the way in which Descartes introduces inwardness into modern Western philosophy.

There is no doubt that the discovery of the I-think as the cornerstone of our knowledge of the world is an ingenious approach to the problem of human existence. Whereas the Platonic self was not considered in subjective terms (since it was a projection of the universal kingdom of Forms) and the Pauline inward man was not considered autonomous (since he was conditioned by God as a being exterior to him)—the novelty of Descartes' approach lies in the creation of a thinking self whose self-awareness is not the product of, or a part of, some external whole. In our times this sounds like such a perfectly natural assumption (natural, that is, for us to consider ourselves as subjects, to think of ourselves by means of inward terms) that we often attribute it, quite naturally and even somewhat offhandedly, to our predecessors, failing to note that the very distinction between subject and object, between inside and outside, is, in a certain sense, quite a modern distinction. Charles Taylor has expressed this issue lucidly:

> In our languages of self-understanding, the opposition "inside-outside" plays an important role. We think of our thoughts, ideas, or feelings as being "within" us, while the objects in the world which these mental states bear on are "without." Or else we think of our capacities or potentialities as "inner," awaiting the development which will manifest them or realize them in the public world. The unconscious is for us within, and we think of the depths of the unsaid, the unsayable, the powerful inchoate feelings and affinities and fears which dispute with us the control of our lives, as inner. We are creatures, with inner depths; with partly unexplored and dark interiors. We all feel the force of Conrad's image in *Heart of Darkness*.
>
> But strong as this partitioning of the world appears to us, as solid as this localization may seem, and anchored in the very nature of the human agent, it is in large part a feature of our world, the world of modern, Western people.

The self's place inside—this "localization"—continues Taylor, is not a natural point of view, one that men have held to since time immemorial, but the product of a certain historical epoch that is associated with Western modernity. Taylor's insight is clearly demonstrated in literature by Anne Ferry who, on the basis of linguistic and literary evidence, convincingly argues that the beginning of our self-determination as individual selves, or as beings endowed with an inward selfhood, is typical of the modern age. Thus, for example, Ferry shows that the first known use of the word *individual*—a term that clearly expresses the picture modern man has of himself—occurred in the middle of the sixteenth century and was consolidated only at the close of that century. Seeing man as an individual brought with it a new and expanded vocabulary in which a key role was assigned to expressions that represent internal events, hidden experiences, and mental life as a whole. The rise of modern subjectivity, then, incurred new uses of old terms. Allowing ourselves some leeway, we could say that the use of the pronoun *I* turned from a grammatical declension to a reference of what man really is.[2]

This innovation in the perception of man's individuality needs to be briefly explained. Clearly, the natural inclination to regard man in inward-mental terms is *not* an innovation, neither of Western modernity, nor, for that matter, of any other known historical epoch. There are countless instances that attest to the proliferation of the use of mental terms throughout the history of Western philosophy; moreover, examples of its use abound in the sacred Scriptures of Western religions. This much is well known. Suffice it to recall the manner in which Plato talks of the soul as being superior to the body, or Saint Paul praising the "inward man" (Romans 7:22–23). Plato distinguished between our sensual perception of external reality, prone to contingency and error, and the innermost soul, where the truth abides. In a similar manner, Saint Paul saw the inward man as the location in which the true struggle between sin and salvation takes place. These are merely two examples out of many that demonstrate the ancient metaphysical idea of seeing the essence of being human as residing in the soul rather than body—giving precedence to spirit over flesh.

However, the modern perception of man as a subject, or as an individual, is more than just a specific instance of characterizing him in mental terms. Here we evidence the soul or the mind as being more than something internal or hidden; mental space is considered as personal or *private* space. Plato's main interest lay in what was common to all souls. He was barely interested in the individual soul's mental modes of self-expression. Had he been familiar with modern attempts to base humanity on its subjective core, in all probability he would have loathed it. As I mentioned earlier, the modern notion of human autonomy is rarely present among ancient Greek philosophers (with the exception of, perhaps, Socrates). It is also absent from early and medieval Christian doctrines of the soul. Louis Dumont quite rightly notes that if it is at all possible to talk of Christian man, in early and medieval Christianity, as an individual, then, unlike the modern individual man, he should be addressed as an individual-in-relation-to God (by the same token, it would be possible to describe Platonic man as an individual-in relation-to-Form). This takes us right back to the presupposition of transcendence. Both the Platonic and the Judeo-Christian points of view observe human inwardness (soul, spirit, thought) as arising from the inevitable gulf between an external being and man. The kind of inwardness that these doctrines allow is such that the autonomy man is granted is limited and delimited. In Descartes' philosophy the process of the self's internalization, and the pivotal position it assumes, cannot be seen as yet another philosophical version of the discovery of the soul as an immaterial and perhaps even eternal entity, wholly distinguishable from matter. Descartes' modernity suggests something altogether novel. He was among the first and foremost exponents that regarded this entity as an active being, exhibiting complete ownership over its worldview and the different angles through which each and every one of us perceives the world. There is no way to disengage whatever is conceived as real from that primary, independent, separated presence of the self—a presence that is considered capable of generating the self-identity of an individual person, limited merely by the boundaries of his thought.

According to Taylor, one of the apparently covert sources of this discovery of the inward self can be traced back to Saint Augustine's (354–430 CE) highly innovative philosophy. Augustine, he says, precedes Descartes in establishing the prominence of internalization (and in this he is extremely at odds with his era). Augustine distinguishes between the outward man and the inward man, a distinction he drew from the New Testament. Yet, in suggesting that religious truths reside in man's inwardness, he adopts a much more radical stance. Taylor cites a famous passage from Augustine in which he calls upon man not to go outward but to venture within himself, since "In the inward man dwells truth." Essentially, Augustine's path to God is through inwardness. This is so, says Taylor, because God is not only the "transcendent object" but also the "basic support of the underlying principle of our knowing activity."[3]

To find an underpinning for this inward activity, Augustine employs, among others, an argument that, prima facie, recalls Descartes. Augustine shows his interlocutor that it is impossible for him to deny his own existence, since were he not to exist, he could not be deluded or confused. Here Augustine utilizes the first-person standpoint, making it the most fundamental means by which truth can be obtained. In appealing to the self, Augustine is instigating reflexivity—the self taking up a reflexive stance. According to Taylor, it would not be an exaggeration to claim that Augustine was the first philosopher to introduce radical reflexivity; he bequeathed it to Western thought.

Is it possible, then, to view Augustine abandoning the Platonic predisposition for the precedence of the outward, anticipating modernity by claiming that God should be sought in man's inwardness? An affirmative reply to this crucial question will be all too premature. Although it is reasonable to portray him as a philosopher who managed to unite a transcendent vision of God with a view that emphasizes the importance of the believer's inward, spiritual reality, it is still a far cry from assigning him the role of the ancient father of modern subjectivity. To be more specific, I think one should not overstress the importance of Augustine's emphasis on inwardness since at the core of his worldview we still find the transcendent Godhead in all its outwardness. In this context Brian Stock has drawn attention to the fact that the starting point of self-knowledge in Augustinian thought is situated in the sad recognition that the soul is set apart and severed from a divine being located beyond it. Self-knowledge is the result of this severance, which, in itself, is the outcome of man's original sin. The inward gaze draws the believer close to the realization of God's presence inside her or him. But it is possible, indeed inevitable, to trace the foundation of the "inward" in the transcendent existence of the outward. Even though God is to be discovered in man's inwardness, since it is the only place where it can be revealed, Augustine keeps the Platonic preference: like Plato's Forms, Augustine's God is ontologically prior to every created being. As such, He resides above humans and beyond boundaries of any human mind. Thus, even though Augustine's didactic-psychological approach constitutes a move from the outward to the inward, his conceptual framework still espouses the unidirectional inward gaze that proceeds from the inside to the outside; the concept of divine outwardness hovers above the depths of inwardness. Accordingly, the role played by reflexivity in uncovering divine truth does not impinge on the ontological precedence transcendence has over immanence. One could say that Augustine's thought is yet another version of the transcendent type, despite the presence of an evident tension between the immanent and the transcendent. Hence, the wording of Augustine's argument in favor of the certainty imbued in mental activity is indeed similar to Descartes', but the use Descartes made of this argument is different from Augustine's—on account, among other things, of the fact that Descartes' I-think signifies the activity of a creative mind functioning independently of divine truth. As Stock puts it, the most telling difference between Augustine and Descartes becomes clear when we consider that inwardness for Descartes is perceived as wholly autonomous, whereas for Augustine it is dependent on the external authority of Scripture. The French philosopher and theologian Jean Luc Marion saw Descartes as holding a key position in transforming the traditional priority given to ontology over epistemology. From a concern with being as such Descartes turns his attention to an inquiry on the role of self as subjectivity. Marion sees Descartes as draining ontological investigation of its prior significance. The only ontological residue in Descartes' thought (Marion refers to it as "grey ontology") is the intended movement from the inside to the outside where the fundamental structure of the target of this intended movement consists of a "reduction of *ens* to pure objectivity." This is a radical interpretation, which will be mostly refuted in what follows. Yet, one can still agree with Marion when he draws out attention to the considerable differences that exist between Augustine and Descartes. What for the former is fully fledged ontology, for the latter is only a "grey" one. But it remains to be seen whether Descartes, by offering the transition from "truth" to "certainty," is really shifting the core of gravity from ontology to epistemology.

In any case, the transition from "truth" to "certainty" left an indelible mark on the course of the history of philosophy. Taylor further expands our understanding of this transition by pointing out how

Descartes altered our grasp of rationality. It is no longer understood as thinking in accordance (not to say harmony) with the right (not to say perfected) order of the world; instead it is seen as a "method" or a procedure of thought. For Plato, as for Augustine, to be rational means to think rightly about the order of things, but for Descartes to be rational means to think according to given standards. Rationality is now seen as no more than an internal attribute of the "I-think." The emphasis laid by Taylor on the procedural nature of thinking is crucial not only for understanding the way the subject thinks but also for apprehending the very nature of this thinking self. Descartes' thinking self is impersonal. Adding a personal dimension to the I-think would turn it to a self thinking a *certain content* and thus lacking a general objective status. It is in this respect that Descartes despises psychologism: the subjectivity that he is arguing for is a "philosophical" subjectivity severed from the world of content of the individual's psychology. It contains only thought, void of any specific content. Only such impersonal subjectivity could lead to an apposite, accurate, errorless worldview.

Can this subjective self vouch for the certainty we hope to find in the recognition of the objects that comprise the external world? Descartes senses that "a slight reason for doubt" might remain—not serious doubt but merely "a metaphysical one"—with regard to the correspondence between our inward mental activity and external reality. In order to get rid of this slight metaphysical doubt, "as soon as the opportunity arises I must examine whether there is God, and, if there is, whether he can be a deceiver. For if I do not know this, it seems that I can never be quite certain about anything else."

As we noted, the I-think is an activity that manifests itself in the immediacy of thought, so long as this thought is focused on its instantaneous ideas—all that is known to me as a thinking subject are my current indubitable thoughts. Yet the moment the immediacy of this thinking passes, so too does our experience of certainty vanish. I cannot be absolutely certain that these thoughts correspond to something external to me. Thoughts, says Descartes, are certain only as self-awareness, regardless of whether they accord with some kind of external reality:

Even though the objects of my sensory experience and imagination may have no existence outside me, nonetheless the modes of thinking which I refer to as cases of sensory perception and imagination, in so far as they are simply modes of thinking, do exist within me—of that I am certain.

This is a captivating idea since Descartes refers here to "sensory perception and imagination"—that part of one's inwardness to which he does not ascribe any kind of external reality, save in its appearance as a thinking self. Nevertheless, Descartes is certain that the "cases of sensory perception and imagination, in so far as they are simply modes of thinking, do exist within me." Herein lies the force of epistemic certainty, but this is also its limitation, since it cannot validate the relationship of thought to that which is external to it. Descartes therefore sees pure subjectivity as standing on its own and only so long as it is conceived as the immediate intuition of thought. But thought is more than such a momentary intuition, and it must, in fact, rely on the presence of some sort of coherent continuum of intuitive thoughts. The I-think itself cannot be the sole executor of such a coherent continuum, since it is in man's nature not to be able to think persistently on one thing only:

> Admittedly my nature is such that so long as I perceive something very clearly and distinctly I cannot but believe it to be true. But my nature is also such that I cannot fix my mental vision continually on the same thing, so as to keep perceiving it clearly; and often the memory of a previously made judgement may come back, when I am no longer attending to the arguments which led me to make it. And so other arguments can now occur to me which might easily undermine my opinion, if I did not possess knowledge of God; and I should thus never have true and certain knowledge about anything, but only shifting and changeable opinions.

For there to be a sense of continuity going beyond our immediate act of thinking there needs to be an external being, and this being must be endowed with its own exceptional continuity. Only such a being can accord continuity to our mental operations:

> What I took just now as a rule, namely that everything we conceive very clearly and very distinctly is true, is assured only for

the reasons that God is or exists, that he is a perfect being, and that everything in us comes from him. . . . But if we did not know that everything real and true within us comes from a perfect and infinite being, then, however clear and distinct our ideas were, we would have no reason to be sure that they had the perfection of being true.

Nothing, not even certainty as clarity and distinctness, can persist beyond the immediate and momentary appearance of thought. That which guarantees the persistence of the activity of the thinking "I" must necessarily be a being that is not dependent on thinking (even though it can surely be an object of thought). It is God, an omniscient and self-contained Being, that enables continuity beyond the bounds of a unitary moment appearing in the present. Evidently, inasmuch as the matter pertains to the "I-think," there is no need for this divine guarantor because the thinking self has an immediate and direct aware- ness of its own existence. But validating clear and distinct thoughts by God is necessary in those situations where they have no immediate presence in thought. In this respect the presence of an omnipotent and undeceiving God supplies us with the framework that enables us to grasp our inward life as a unity. For Descartes, therefore, God is the paradigm of objectivity. It is not pertinent to the issue at hand to dwell upon the different ways in which Descartes attempts to prove the existence of God, nor to consider the rest of his philosophical system once he has, to his satisfaction, proven the existence of this omnipotent and undeceiving God. What we are seeking to understand here is the true character of Descartes' suggested internalization, for which he had gained the reputation of being one of the principal founders of the modern Western concept of subjectivity. The question I am con- cerned with asks what role the presupposition of transcendence has in the evolution of the Cartesian picture of man. Does the decisive transition from the outward to the inward eradicate this presupposi- tion, eliminating it from the conceptual framework of the Cartesian worldview? Or is it perhaps still present somewhere at the bedrock of this framework, whether hidden or apparent?

This question elicits an immediate and unequivocal reply: right after disclosing the I-think as the kernel of certainty, God is admitted into the framework of subjectivity. Evidently, the Cartesian description of

God is not commensurate with that of mainstream Western religious monotheism. For Descartes, the presupposition of transcendence is manifested as something much more abstract and philosophical. His God is not the subject of admiration, fear, or love (much to Pascal's sorrow); he is rather "the God of the philosophers"—a Being whose main task is to serve as the permanent guarantor of clear and distinct ideas. It would seem that God is what enables the inward journey to retrace its steps, allowing it to return from the inside back to the outside world with the renewed vigor of certainty. Let me reiterate: I-think cannot do this by itself, since its world is comprised solely of mental states, and even though these mental states are admittedly indubitable, they are conceived so only while the mind is focused. To use the words of Jonathan Bennett, so long as the mind is indeed focused on its object, the thinker has an "epistemic advantage," even without any prior assumptions about God. Yet, the moment the thinking self no longer focuses on the object of his thought, he loses his epistemic advantage and can reestablish it only if he acknowledges the existence of an undeceiving, omnipotent God.

Descartes' understanding of the I-think wavers between two positions. On the one hand, we detect an audacious inward motion—an unprecedented shift from the external world (whose existence is not endowed with certainty since it is prone to doubt) to human inwardness, where we encounter the whole range of ideas that we have of the world. But even this is but an intermediate stage, since the final destination of this inward movement is one singular mental event that offers indubitable knowledge from which all else springs. On the other hand, it would seem that this inward motion only leads to a subdued and delimited internalization, bridled and replete with self-imposed restrictions. Moreover, the inward movement is not as unrestrained and spontaneous as it would first seem since it is fraught with the problem of how to return, that is, how to move back from the inside to the outside.

This is where the meaning of the presence of the presupposition of transcendence in Descartes' philosophical enterprise is most explicit. But it is possible to detect it beneath the surface too. The omnipotent and undeceiving God is indeed assumed and proven *after* certainty has been obtained by means of the I-think; but, to my mind, the terms and presuppositions that Descartes has recourse to are still very much steeped in that conceptual distinction between the inner and the outer, granting the latter evident ontological precedence. In this sense, Descartes' proof of the existence of God resembles someone looking for a lost object, not necessarily beneath the proverbial lamp, but all over, only to realize at the end of a fraught search (in which anxiety and desperation go hand in hand, the way it always does in such cases) that it was in its proper place, the place where it was meant to be all along.

Let us now return to Descartes' description of his struggle with the philosophers of yore, who, on account of their blindness, try to lull him into a darkened cellar so that he may not have an advantage over them. I have noted that there is something unconvincing in this allegory. Descartes sees himself dwelling in a well-lit room, then he goes on to complain about those who, immersed in perpetual mental darkness, try to cast this darkness over him. This, it would seem, is a conventional application of the standard allegory used to contrast the old with the new. Yet the imagery he uses reveals something else: the blind philosophers of yore understand the true nature of the darkness in which they are immersed and, what is more, they have a surprising ability to find an adequately darkened cellar to where they can tow our enlightened philosopher. That is to say, these philosophers have a "visual" faculty that does not fall short of Descartes', since not only can they readily distinguish between light and dark (they might have gained this ability through analogies or by evoking the sort of childhood memories that took root in their minds before they had lost their sight) but they are also able to find by themselves a "place of darkness" from which to conduct their philosophical struggle (this ability being diametrically opposed to their blindness). Descartes, it would seem, misappropriates this allegory. It might be, however, that this reveals more about Descartes' position than the use he intends to make of it. The conspicuous differences that exist between the blind and the sighted are irrelevant to an understanding of the differences between Descartes and the philosophers of yore. After all, they *do* have something in common, and this common ground is precisely what enables these supposedly blind philosophers to perceive lucidly the darkness of the cellar and the difference between it and the well-lit space outside. Undoubtedly, Descartes would have much preferred a struggle between the past and the present not to be conducted in a darkened cellar, but rather in the "open," outdoors, amid unadulterated concepts and in uninvolved anonymity (the "outdoors" in this case is analogous to being released from beliefs, conventions, and norms of the past). Unfortunately, the darkened cellar is as much part of Descartes' world as it is of the supposedly blind philosophers'. Descartes turns out to be a wavering philosopher: he is palpably trying to denounce the past, yet at the same time he draws heavily on assumptions from the past in order to do so. It is thus difficult to justify the imagery that he employs in order to distinguish between his clarity of vision and the blindness of his predecessors.

The presupposition that Descartes draws from the past, and on which he heavily relies from the beginning of his philosophical enterprise, is the conceptual presupposition of transcendence. In this respect the certainty that he claims to have discovered at the end of his methodical doubting, i.e., the "I-think," is, in fact, presupposed right from the start and hovers above his complete philosophical enterprise.[4] To put it more bluntly, were Descartes not to presuppose the logical and ontological precedence of the outward over the inward, then he could not have embarked on a philosophical enterprise that employs methodical doubt, since what bothered him, more than anything else, were errors in the judgment of reality. His quest for certainty was meant to eliminate such errors so as to enable him to arrive at an outcome completely independent of its starting point. That is to say, Descartes' "discovery" of subjectivity was made possible only by his persistent—almost obsessive—drive to retain a picture of the world as wholly "objective," that is, as totally independent of any particular subjective cognition of it. In a certain sense, clear and distinct ideas are possible because of the underlying presence of the presupposition of the transcendence. In the same vein, the subjective viewpoint Descartes adopts is meant to reach its opposite, that is, allowing us to hold an irrefutable knowledge of a wholly objective, impersonal, point of view without any particular personal involvement. In this context Harry Frankfurt draws attention to what he has termed "the paradox of the anonymous autobiography": Descartes mostly wrote in the first person, in a personal and, at times, even intimate style. Yet, even though his writing is autobiographical, the story he tells us recounts his efforts to break away from the confines of the merely personal—that is, from the psychological, historical, and social framework of a particular person—in order to find his impersonal identity as a rational being. Charles Taylor, reviewing this state of affairs, labeled it the "paradox of modernity"—a situation in which "radical objectivity is only intelligible and accessible through radical subjectivity." Yet I doubt if we are face to face with a paradox. Instead I suggest thinking of Descartes as a great innovator who introduced the autonomous subject to the core of Western philosophy but who, at the same time, still hung onto a traditional presupposition of transcendence. And so his philosophical journey ends exactly where it began: the I-think is the only epistemic possibility on which to establish objectivity, but this very I-think can only be established as a person by presupposing the ontological and logical precedence of objectivity.

Surely a curious way to define a person—on the one hand it is huddled around itself, on the other, it is held captive within the conceptual framework of the presupposition of transcendence (conceived in the abstract and impersonal, as opposed to personal, religious understandings of God). An impersonal objectivity—dare I say, antipersonal objectivity—manifests itself at the very core of subjectivity, presenting us with an I-think whose mental activity is divorced from any specific content. An important feature of this thinking self is the procedure by which it ascertains itself rather than the content of its thinking. Yet, having said that, it is impossible to ignore the presence of the presupposition of transcendence even while the process of ascertaining certainty is taking place. Note, for instance, how Descartes examines the boundaries of sanity and his unease when forced to consider the possibility that he himself might be insane. So long as he is actually casting doubt, he has to reject this terrifying possibility. Indeed, Descartes goes to great extremes to avoid thinking of the possibility that insanity lurks at the edge of consciousness. But why? Why not just accept this as part of the process of doubting everything, despite it being, admittedly, somewhat farfetched? The answer seems self-evident: if the possibility of insanity will not to be removed out of hand at this exploratory stage then Descartes' whole quest for certainty will be in jeopardy. It is essential for him to eliminate the possibility that the person casting doubt is insane because of his (i.e., Descartes') obsessive need to locate a foundation for objectivity—an objectivity he accepts a priori, even while in the process of casting doubt! Stated more explicitly, one could say that the presupposition of transcendence is apparent in the foundation of Descartes' philosophy, and it is precisely what enables him (perhaps even obliges him) to ignore, at all costs, the possibility of insanity. In granting the outward an ontological precedence over the inward, Descartes obliges himself to suppose that there must be a criterion capable of clearly distinguishing between sanity and insanity; armed with this supposition, he allows himself conveniently to shrug off the possibility that he is in fact insane. Thus, for example, he argues that it is impossible to assume that he is insane, since, if this were so, he would lose the very ability to utilize his mental faculties. To be more precise: if one assumes insanity at the outset, one will lose the possibility of establishing a criterion of rationality. That is, this "objective" criterion must exist as a procedural form, even *before* establishing the "I-think." Moreover, this enables it.

Insanity is thus rejected, but casting doubt carries on until it is expressed as exaggerated doubt (in the guise of a malicious demon) functioning as the Archimedean point of certainty. And then—lo and behold—the possibility of insanity vanishes. The malicious demon has emptied inwardness of any specific content and has established the existence of the "I-think." As Derrida rightly notes, at this point the "I-think," depleted of any specific contents, is indubitable, regardless of whether it is perceived as being mad or deemed as such: "There is a value and a meaning of the Cogito, as of existence, which escape the alternative of a determined madness of determined reason." Here the severance between the "I-think" and the specific contents of its thoughts reaches a dramatic climax. The price Descartes is willing to pay for the autonomy of inward mental activity, and for subscribing to an individual, albeit impersonal, definition of his existence, is the risk of a mental situation in which the ability to distinguish between sanity and insanity collapses. We have already mentioned the necessity of dislocating the mind from culture and convention. Now we face yet another dislocation—severing our ability to determine normative standards with which to tell sanity apart from insanity. The obsessive search for ideal certainty leaves no room for probabilistic definitions of norms and deviancy. Still, we are offered an alternative to culture and to a quantitative criterion of sanity. The alternative is a mental state of affairs in which individuality is considered intransitively: the more intensified it gets, the less personal it is. In this state the risk of insanity poses no threat since the reality principle and reality testing (which are, as is well known, the accepted standard employed to distinguish between sanity and insanity) become irrelevant and cannot be applied to a self that is not dependent on its contents. Undoubtedly, there is a touch of irony here: Descartes was anxious lest he be accused of insanity, but having arrived at the end of his long journey into certainty, it turns out that this anxiety was no more than a rhetorical expedient, or perhaps it was a genuine anxiety functioning as a defense mechanism. Be that as it may, the mechanism is now replaced by the certainty of the "I-think," and consequently the need for a defense mechanism has subsided so that anxiety can be psychologically liquidated—there is nothing to defend, since all the contents of my mind (whether real or imaginary) have collapsed into the certainty of the cogito.

This situation, in which the presupposition of transcendence is present in the formation of the idea of a self and, moreover, in the bedrock of its existence, has some very interesting philosophical repercussions, especially with regard to the boundaries of the "internalized" self. To achieve a better understanding of these repercussions, I shall again resort to a comparison with ancient India. The comparison I have in mind draws on a very lucid and clear picture of selfhood and subjectivity. This radical picture is to be found in the Upaniṣads. It is not my intention here to expand on the different elements that comprise the whole Upaniṣadic view of selfhood, but only to concentrate on one Upaniṣadic view in which the boundaries of the self are explained within a conceptual framework that is not bound by the definitions and observations arising in a framework operating under the canopy of the presupposition of transcendence.

As I have already noted in chapter 1, the Upaniṣads are a compilation of texts composed around the middle of the first millennium BCE by a group of renouncers who forsook, in varying degrees, the ritualistic householder's life, opting instead to follow a path of personal development in which the exercise of self-control played a crucial role. At the core of the Upaniṣadic worldview we find a sharp turn from the outward to the inward—from the domain of public ritualism to reflexivity at the individual level. The renouncer tradition of ancient India sprang up at a time of dramatic political and social upheavals, gaining a foothold during the ensuing loss of confidence. Even after the crisis elapsed and the social map of India was completely redrawn, the renouncer tradition remained and exists to this very day.

From a social point of view, the renunciation was seen as a form of a protest. The renouncer, by adopting his chosen way of life, rejected, at least de facto, the collectivity of ritual. The renouncer advocates a radical departure from customary norms: rather than a public ceremony, constrained by strict and unalterable rules and regulations, he creates a completely private and personal ritual, for example, the manner in which he subjugates his body to severe penance as means to purify the soul. Rather than abide by rules, obey injunctions, and enforce prohibitions, he forces himself to follow a strict regime of inner-directed psychophysical meditative exercises. Instead of living according to the dictates of his social class, his caste, and his family, he takes on the life of a wandering ascetic in the forest, renouncing both property and social obligations. There is something defiant in renunciation; it constitutes an open revolt against the collective foundation of contemporaneous Indian culture. There is no doubt whatever that the renouncer tradition contributed toward undermining ancient India's ritualistic worldview, though it never managed to completely uproot it. Perhaps rather than say that it became enfeebled, one could claim that the renouncer tradition is, in some form or other, its outcome: once the mystery of cosmogenic sacrifices was eroded, even among the Brahmins, its officiators, the road was paved to a more personal form of life, not within society, but alongside it.

The world of the Indian renouncer is an inward world. The renowned sociologist Louis Dumont has said that its dominant feature, sociologically speaking, is the fact that it arises from philosophical activity that negates, that rejects, culture itself and with it the idea of man as a social, ritualistic "animal." Renunciation, says Dumont, is what brought about the idea of man as an individual in ancient India. Dumont uses this term in its philosophical sense (to use his expression): man, as an individual, is an autonomous, self-contained being, capable of establishing his own worldview. According to Dumont, the India of the Upaniṣads and of early Buddhism was the first culture to entertain this "modern" outlook. Much like Descartes, who also sought apodictic subjectivity in a closed room, yearning for a wildernesslike solitariness, the Indian renouncers sought the subjective self in the depths of the forest.

The Upaniṣads express an obvious predilection for the ascetic life of the renouncer, much preferring it to the householder's active life. This predilection subsumes a new kind of knowledge, radically different from the traditional notion of knowledge gained by means of ritualistic-social activity. The province of this new knowledge is the process of internalization, and the Upaniṣads often refer to it as *prajñā* (wisdom): a subtle mental activity difficult to describe, yet evidently diametrically opposed to the kind of cultural, public, and institutional wisdom acquired at the feet of a guru or in a classroom. One of the best-known expressions of this dichotomy is the distinction between the "path of the gods" (designating human personal wisdom) and the "path of the ancestors" (designating institutional public wisdom). Jaivali Pravāhaṇa, a great Upaniṣadic sage, refers to it thus:

> Have you not heard the seer's words?—
> Two paths mortals have, I've heard:
> the paths to fathers and to gods.
> By these travel all that live
> between the earth and sky.

The distinction between the path of the gods and the path of the ancestors is a distinction between two planes of knowledge. Whoever obtains knowledge only from his cultural surroundings need not acknowledge this distinction because he is completely entrenched in the path of the ancestors and sees the world only from a cultural vantage point. On the other hand, the renouncer undertakes to follow (or rather to pave) the path of the gods, which is an intricate personal path taking him on a profound inward journey. For the poet who distinguishes between the two paths, following the path of the gods is supposed to bring about a state of homology between the inward and the outward, the microcosmic and the macrocosmic. One of the most celebrated views in the early Upaniṣads, best known in its philosophical formulation, asserts the identity of a person's basic "selfhood"—referred to in Sanskrit as *ātman*—with the power that comprises absolute reality, namely, *brahman*.[5] This brahman is diametrically opposed to the manifold, to variance, and to evolution as these manifest themselves in the phenomenal world experienced in our daily lives. The Upaniṣadic sage saw in his inner "self" the means by which to know brahman and, accordingly, the means by which to control it. On account of the identity between brahman and ātman, knowledge of the inner "self" is also the knowledge of everything that exists. Accordingly, controlling the "self" is manifestly the control of all existence. Initially, this claim may sound very similar to many mystical declarations on the nature of the ineffable, claims that gallantly sail toward the boundaries of sense, the twilight zone of metaphorical expressions where the obscure provinces of contradictory speech abound. Yet, here, this first impression is unwarranted. The process of internalization described by the Upaniṣads and the place of ātman as the utmost inward essence should not be taken face value. A thorough examination is needed, one that will focus on the very distinction between the inward and the outward. This examination will show that the Upaniṣadic pronouncements on the nature of the ātman are none other than a set of arguments that undermine this very distinction.

This idea will be demonstrated through two separate depictions of the ātman, both drawn from one of the earliest Upaniṣads, the Bṛhadāraṇyaka Upaniṣad. The first depiction of the ātman can be found in a mythic account of the creation of the world, the second is drawn from a philosophical dialogue between an Upaniṣadic sage and a king. The mythic description begins in this way:

1: In the beginning this world was just a single body (*ātman*) shaped like a man. He looked around and saw nothing but himself. The first thing he said was, "Here I am!" and from that the name "I" came into being. Therefore, even today when you call someone, he first says, "It's I," and then states whatever other name he may have. That first being received the name "man" (*Puruṣa*), because ahead (*pūrva*) of all this he burnt up (*uṣ*) all evils. When someone knows this, he burns up anyone who may try to get ahead of him.

2: That first being became afraid; therefore, one becomes afraid when one is alone. Then he thought to himself: "Of what should I be afraid, when there is no one but me?" So his fear left him, for what was he going to be afraid of? One is, after all, afraid of another.

3: He found no pleasure at all; so one finds no pleasure when one is alone. He wanted to have a companion. Now he was as large as a man and a woman in close embrace. So he split (*pat*) his body into two, giving rise to husband (*pati*) and wife (*patnī*).

Surely this is why Yājñavalkya used to say: "The two of us are like two halves of a block." The space here, therefore, is completely filled by the woman. He copulated with her, and from their union human beings were born.

4: She then thought to herself: "After begetting me from his own body (ātman), how could he copulate with me? I know—I'll hide myself." So she became a cow. But he became a bull and copulated with her. From their union cattle were born. Then she became a mare, and he a stallion; she became a female donkey, and he, a male donkey. And again he copulated with her, and from their union one-hoofed animals were born. Then she became a female goat, and he, a male goat; she became a ewe, and he, a ram. And again he copulated with her, and from their union goats and sheep were born. In this way he created every male and female pair that exists, down to the very ants.

One of the questions that captivated the imagination of ancient and classical Indian thinkers was the question of origins: is there a beginning? And if so, what is it? And what connections are there between this beginning and all that ensues? In response to this quest for beginnings and origins, many varied and interlaced replies were suggested. These replies would blend into each other or exclude one another, yet they all pointed to some source from which "everything" sprang. It is not easy to understand the precise meaning of these ideas, as they are cloaked by a veil of myth. Nevertheless, it is possible to uncover some of the assumptions that these different cosmologies share. One such assumption is the obvious predisposition toward cyclic explanations as opposed to linear accounts of creation. One would be hard-pressed to find in the large variety of Indian cosmologies a description of creation as something with a singular beginning, occurring only once and arising out of nothing. On the whole, the relation between originator and originated is expressed in cyclic and organic terms that evoke the imagery of birth, germination, evolution, emanation, entailment, and transformation. In contradistinction to the prevalent traditional Western accounts of creation, Indian narratives, on the whole, lack an evident divide between creator and created. The Upaniṣadic emanation story, quoted above, follows the path laid down by Vedic myths of the dismemberment of primordial man, *Puruṣa*, from whose parts the universe was formed in its entirety. And yet the Upaniṣadic myth goes further than the Vedic hymns on Puruṣa, since this myth gives prominence to the subjective selfhood of the primordial man. Accordingly, I propose a philosophical reading of the above verses, especially those that deal with the place of the ātman as a primordial originator of the cosmos from which all else comes into being.

First, though, a preamble on method. Anyone who is even remotely familiar with Indian philosophy will have come across a philosophical reading of the Upaniṣads. One of the better-known schools of Indian philosophy, the Advaita Vedānta, has set itself the task of offering a systematic interpretation of the ideas of the different Upaniṣads, most notably those that deal with ātman/brahman identity. This school (and especially its founding figure, Śaṅkara) provided the Upaniṣads with a metaphysical interpretation whereby the ātman is understood as an overarching spiritual principle, a uniform being resistant to any flux, plurality, or movement, which are mere illusions, especially when juxtaposed with the metaphysical spiritual principle. This interpretation of the Upaniṣads has been very influential, both in the world of Indian spirituality and its Western counterpart, so much so that at times there is a tendency to unwittingly see the Upaniṣads through Śaṅkara's eyes. In such cases, Śaṅkara's own philosophy, whose explicit goal is to repudiate duality (advaita means "nonduality") is unequivocally projected onto the Upaniṣadic texts, and accordingly they are read as representing the metaphysical idea of nonduality. I think this projection is false. I fail to detect in the Upaniṣads the nondual metaphysical speculation that Śaṅkara supposedly sees in them (and, in fact, forces upon them). The reading I suggest avoids projecting a nondual metaphysics onto the Upaniṣadic texts. Instead, it looks at the basic ideas found in these texts without at the same time superimposing on them any kind of conceptual framework that inevitably forces upon these disparate texts a dogmatic intellectual hegemony.

The opening sentence of the above quotation's initial paragraph from the Bṛhadāraṇyaka Upaniṣad begins with a declaration: the "self" is unique, that is, it is a primary, spontaneous manifestation of being. Yet it would be difficult to claim the text intimates that the "self" is blessed with the objective status of an omnipresent and overarching being. (Subscribing to such a view would demonstrate what it is to project one's own metaphysical stance onto the text.) What is actually being said is something completely different: the "self" appears in the text as pure subjectivity. It is brought into being only through an act of self-awareness. This awareness is articulated in the self's ability to apply the first-person singular to itself: "Here I am (*aham*)."[6] The true point of departure of "everything" (are we not dealing with the story of beginnings?) is that crucial primary appearance of self-awareness whose only attribute is the self's reflexivity. In this Upaniṣadic passage, selfhood predates its nominal formation. Undoubtedly, for a Western mind this is a problematic claim. This attribute of selfhood as relating to or as reflecting upon itself may sound strange to anyone who thinks that reflection necessitates a division between observer and observed. It would seem that this myth is not bothered by this difficulty, perhaps because its author relies on the experiential dimension of self-awareness rather than on an intellectual analysis of the origin of such concepts (we shall encounter such an analysis later on in a different Upaniṣadic text). The reliance on the experiential dimension of awareness is carried over to the next sentence of the first paragraph where, so it seems, an etiological explanation is put forward. This is supposed to explain the kind of behavior familiar to each and every one of us: the fact that one responds with the first-person pronoun ("I"), even prior to recognizing oneself by one's own name. This pattern is explained as arising from that first reflexive act ("Here I am") of the primordial man. This etiological explanation will become a philosophical generalization if we turn it the other way round: everyday behavior, in the course of which each of us first recognizes herself or himself by the designation "I," enables us to arrive at a general conclusion about the primacy and predominance of selfhood knowing itself. Undoubtedly, this is a somewhat naive idea, and, as mentioned earlier, the author does not identify any difficulties in his supposition of reflexivity, despite the conceptual problems that arise from assuming a state of identity between the observer and observed. I ask myself if, in finding it necessary to emphasize this difficulty, I am not unconsciously imposing the presupposition of transcendence (which necessitates a clear division between knower and known) on the Indian mythical narrative that knows of no such thing.[7] After all, the conceptual demarcation between the knower and the known is justified on the basis of a preconceived differentiation between inside and outside. It might be that emphasizing this conceptual difficulty is merely another version of Descartes' trick of weaving the presupposition of transcendence into the notion of subjectivity. I shall return in chapter 5 to the problem of self-awareness and its attributes in both the West and in India.

The Upaniṣadic narrative, as mentioned previously, sees the ātman's self-realization as predating the world and preceding any concept of outwardness. How then is it possible for the world to originate from the self's experience of self-awareness? How can the inward break through to the outward? Descartes, let us recall, had to bring God to his aid. He could do that (and from his point of view he was compelled) because his whole philosophical enterprise is cloaked right from its inception in the presupposition of transcendence. Assumptions such as these were missing from India's conceptual archives and were thus unavailable to the Upaniṣadic authors. What then can explain selfhood going beyond itself? The text offers a complex description of the *internal processes* that occur within the ātmanic self and offers it as the reason for the rich expansion of existence that this unique ātman brings about. These processes are triggered off by the sense of fear that suddenly enwraps the solitary self: "The first being became afraid; therefore, one becomes afraid when one is alone." Later on, the feeling of fear dissipates. "Then he thought to himself: 'Of what should I be afraid, when there is no one but me?' So his fear left him, for what was he going to be afraid of?" But the sense of fear was now replaced by a different inner sensation, that of dissatisfaction arising from the solitary self's feeling of boredom: "He found no pleasure at all; so one finds no pleasure when one is alone." This boredom brought about desire, on account of which woman was born out of the ātman. Here too, like in many other Indian texts, desire is perceived as a primary force motivating any action.

Yet, this desiring, motivating force did not arise directly from the ātman as a unique form of selfhood. The boredom that evolved into desire was preceded by a different inward condition—the state of fear that arose on account of the self's solitude—the same solitude that eventually brings about its cessation. The reading I suggest sees the account of fear that overcame the solitary self as a necessary stage in understanding the efficacy of desire that enabled the self, later on, to create, from within himself, woman, and then, through persistent copulation, every living species. In the very first sentence of the quoted passage, the self is described in an apparent narcissistic condition that contains only self-awareness (self-identity void of any specified content). In the second paragraph this narcissism is transformed into fear. The text is offering us an etiological explanation of the fear that overwhelms us when we are faced with extreme solitude. But if we again turn this etiological explanation around, we will obtain a fascinating psychological generalization about the structure of human behavior. This generalization maps a diffuse condition of fear—the sensation of fear not caused by the presence of any external agent. Our modern vocabulary calls this condition "anxiety" (or *angst*), to be distinguished from the condition where fear arises from something external and is, on the whole, distinct from the fearing self. If we subscribe to this terminology, the fear that the ātman is experiencing is anxiety, and this condition, according to the text, has psychological precedence over the condition of fear. Anxiety fades away the moment it transforms itself into fear. This is an important conceptual shift: anxiety arises from the inwardness of the self knowing itself. This anxiety gives rise to the idea of the "other," that which is not "self," and this in turn brings about the transformation of anxiety into "fear" and thereby the possibility to uproot anxiety from within the self. Uprooting anxiety involves projecting the idea of the other. "Of what should I be afraid, when there is no one but me?" It is noteworthy that anxiety was not dispelled empirically, but by means of conceptual revision. The self does not discover the *existence* of the "other"; rather, it creates the *idea* of the "other," drawing the other from its innermost depths as something that was present within, albeit as an inexpressible, diffused condition of anxiety, now crystallized into something definable. Stated in more general terms, this account portrays the self as containing *within itself* the very possibility of the idea of objectivity. The fact that objectivity resides in the subjective self is what enables the sense of displeasure, frustration, or boredom mentioned in the third paragraph. The idea of an external object now begins to take on flesh and bones, that is, it becomes the object of desire. This desire is what enables the self to generate from within itself its complementary feminine side and from then on to try repeatedly to reunite through copulation with its other, severed, part. Copulation, it realizes, while uniting, creates, at the same time, diversity through the offspring begotten from it. This happens over and over again: the self divides only to desire its newly formed other half. Desire reunifies the separated parts, but it does not find satisfaction (desire never reaches satisfaction) and so again tries to attain the union of the self with it-self. The other (feminine) half understands this circularity all too well and tries, , to escape from that merry-go-round of fertility: "She then thought to herself: 'After begetting me from his own body (ātman), how could he copulate with me? I know—I'll hide myself.'" Here the myth gives voice to the female aspiration for radical separation from the (male) self, but this feminine aspiration evidently fails. The female perceives the sexual intimacy of these two bodies as a form of incest that will inhibit her from taking on an independent female identity. Her attempts to go into hiding are supposed to prevent the fertiliza-tion of the world; hiding is no less than the attempt to establish wom-en's identity apart from masculine fecundity. But the Upaniṣadic myth does not let her succeed in hiding herself. The birth of independent female identity is blocked by man's capacity to adapt himself to each of woman's different transformations and thus to subjugate her identity over and over again. Even though this endless violent cycle curbs the development of separate woman's identity, interestingly, the male is in-capable of eradicating the feminine vitality in the creative process: it is femininity that generates the different forms of existence; masculinity only adapts itself to these different forms and thus enables their fertil-ization. This fascinating account of woman's generativity needs to be further investigated, but it is beyond the scope of the present book. To return to the Upaniṣadic narrative, erotic desire is seen as the creative force that initiates the cosmos in its entirety.

In the beginning, then, was the self. This self was pure self-aware-ness, which is expressed by uttering "Here I am."[8] We have ques-tioned before the possibility of the outward being born from the in-ward. How is it possible for the world to originate from the ātman's experience of self-awareness? We have just seen that this expansive motion is not dependent on any prior assumptions (not even implied ones) regarding the ontological precedence of the external over the internal or the objective over the subjective. On the contrary, origina-tion is explained only by means of a psychological observation about the dynamic mental processes extant in the self's inwardness and by revealing the ideas of outwardness as manifested in these dynamic processes. Later on the myth describes the birth of the external world in two ways: primordial man blows fire from his mouth (blowing fire represents the feminine half while Puruṣa's mouth is likened to a vagina) and, secondly, by insemination. This form of birth gives rise to the different components of the external world, including the gods. Ironically, the author makes no attempt to conceal his disdain for those who devote themselves completely to ritual. "Sacrifice to this god. Sacrifice to that god—people do say these things, but in reality each of these gods is his [Puruṣa's] own creation." The author knows well that the source of this birth is not divine but human. Puruṣa gives birth to the gods from his body; the gods are indeed superior to mortals, but mortals create them! It would seem that they display a special kind of mutual dependency. Again we note the ambiguity that prevails in descriptions of the relations between the gods and mortals (with which I dealt in the first chapter of this book).

The Upaniṣadic narrative on Puruṣa attributes the self with the power of creating external reality; furthermore, ātman is in fact the originator of the very distinction between inward and outward. Outwardness is the product of a great anxiety that befell the self, and the abatement of this anxiety constitutes the self's first act of projecting the outward—imagining the other or the outsider as an object of fear. This gives rise to a fascinating idea, namely, that the first stage in the world's formation out of the self begins as a sort of fiction; the self is anxious, and this anxiety causes it to create or project the idea of the other. This imaginary projection sets off the story of creation, which is, ultimately, the story of the world and everything in it.[9] Interestingly, the other or the outsider also appears in one of the early stages of Descartes' philosophical enterprise, but the role of fictionality there is categorically different from its role in the Upaniṣadic mythic narrative. There, the other appears in the guise of a highly competent malicious demon. It is an invention meant to bring about the much aspired certainty by revealing the I-think that necessarily gives rise to it. But the malicious demon is neither the outcome of spontaneous self-awareness nor is he the product of an inner feeling of anxiety. Instead, he is invented for one purpose only: to enable us to reach the Archimedean point of certainty. How ironic it is that certainty is established here by means of fiction. No wonder that this is an exceptional fiction, since it is supposed to eliminate, as it were, any future fiction. The excessive story of the malicious demon is not just another imaginary story but it is, in a certain sense, the ultimate story, a fiction describing the death of fiction (how apt that its death need be described in a fiction).

Doubt comes disguised as an outsider, an other, a malicious demon to which the doubter has no ontological commitment. This other is meant to finally eliminate otherness, to impart objective indubitability on inward subjectivity. Descartes' transcendent conceptual framework has him perform one last act of mercy in his role as an imagining self: the curtain comes down, never to rise again, on this other, this demon who has just played the role of doubt, and, much like in a play by Ibsen, the fall of the curtain is accompanied by the sound of a single gunshot, that of the outsider shooting himself. Fiction has blown itself to bits. The place where animated fiction begins in the Upaniṣadic narrative is where it ends in Descartes' philosophical drama.[10]

I would like to consider a second depiction of the ātman. Like the Upaniṣadic narrative just discussed, this too is taken from the Bṛhadā-raṇyaka Upaniṣad. Unlike the mythic character of the narrative about Puruṣa, this account tends to be more in the abstract. It figures in a conversation between Yājñavalkya, one of the principal characters of the early Upaniṣads, and King Janaka of Videha. In this dialogue the sage shows the king what the ātman is—and does it by way of a set of diminishing alternatives:

One day Yājñavalkya paid a visit to Janaka, the king of Videha, thinking to himself, "I won't tell him." But once, when the two were engaged in a discussion about the daily fire sacrifice, Yāj-ñavalkya had granted Janaka of Videha a wish. The wish he chose was the freedom to ask any question at will, and Yājñavalkya had granted it to him. So it was the king who now put the question to him first.

"Yājñavalkya, what is the source of light for a person here?"

"The sun, Your Majesty, is his source of light," he replied. "It is by the light of the sun that a person sits down, goes about, does his work, and returns.

"Quite right, Yājñavalkya.

But when the sun has set, Yājñavalkya, what then is the source of light for a person here?"

"The moon is then his source of light. It is by the light of the moon that a person sits down, goes about, does his work, and returns."

"Quite right, Yājñavalkya.

But when both the sun and the moon have set, Yājñavalkya, what then is the source of light for a person here?"

"A fire is then his source of light. It is by the light of a fire that a person sits down, goes about, does his work, and returns."

"Quite right, Yājñavalkya.

But when both the sun and the moon have set, Yājñavalkya, and the fire has died out, what then is the source of light for a person here?"

"The voice is then his source of light. It is by the light of the voice that a person sits down, goes about, does his work, and returns. Therefore, Your Majesty, when someone cannot make out even his own hand, he goes straightway towards the spot from where he hears a voice."

"Quite right, Yājñavalkya.

"But when both the sun and the moon have set, the fire has died out, and the voice is stilled, Yājñavalkya, what then is the source of light for a person here?"

"The self [ātman] is then his source of light. It is by the light of the self that a person sits down, goes about, does his work, and returns."

Right from the start, we note the obvious structural differences between this exposition—in which ātman is understood as the source of light in man—and the previous one—in which the birth of the world is attributed to the ātman as Puruṣa. In the mythic account the ātman is conceived of as the narrative's point of departure, whereas in the dialogue between the king and the sage the ātman is gradually revealed following a set of preliminary clarifications. It would seem that the mythic narrative does not care much for the dialectics of discovery and, moreover, shows an obvious lack of interest in epistemic problems. The knowledge of ātman as "Here I am" is, for the myth, immediate, intuitive, and performative, that is to say, it does not necessitate any kind of proof whatsoever and clearly does not feel the need for a systematic appraisal of the process of recognition by which this primordial subjective entity is recognized. The philosophical narrative, on the other hand, exhibits a genuine interest in epistemic problems, especially in the distinction between the real and the phenomenal, as also between waking and dreaming experiences. Accordingly, the ātman's role as "self" is, in the mythic story, based on his ability to induce an active cycle of birth and origination. On the other hand, in the philosophical narrative the ātman is a more passive form of selfhood, characterized by the image of light rather than the image of a power or desire (light does not produce, it merely radiates). Nevertheless, as we shall see, this difference cannot obliterate the similarity that exists between these two approaches to ātman as self.

In order that we may properly understand the ātman's role as self in Yājñavalkya's dialogue with King Janaka's, we need to look at the different stages that comprise this dialogue. Quite purposefully, I broke off the quotation just before the king's inevitable next question, "Which self is that?" Yājñavalkya's reply to this question outlines the nature of the ātman as a knowing self. His reply here is among the most celebrated Upaniṣadic excerpts, and is quoted and treated so often that one tends to forget that the account of ātman in this dialogue is prefaced with elaborate explanations on the source of light that take the sage and the king from the sun to the moon, then to fire, from there to sound, and then, only then, to the ātman. It seems to me that a careful scrutiny of these different stages will allow us to fully appreciate Yājñavalkya's response to King Janaka.

At first glance, these stages seem like mere didactic explanations. An interlocutor is gently led through four intermediate stages only to arrive at the final destination of the search (the ātman) in dialogue form, slightly reminiscent of the style attributed to Socrates. These minutely calculated steps are designed to lead the quest confidently, allowing it to reach its final destination. And yet, so I contend, dwelling on these different stages does not merely constitute a didactic matter.

The king asks about the "the source of light for a person here?" A somewhat obscure question, but the repetitive wording of each of the replies illuminates the question posed. Bear in mind that the source of light changes in each reply, but the object remains constant throughout: the light is directed to a person "sitting down, going about, doing his work and returning." Since no objection is raised against this pattern, we must assume that the king has no intention of searching for a source of light as some abstract entity or general principle. Rather, he is seeking a source of light for a sentient being, someone endowed with personhood and a body, someone known to us through his mundane practices that involve transportation, being present in a given location, or being recognized by virtue of the fact that he is going somewhere and returning. The motive underlying this dialogue between king and sage concerns an actual physical need to identify the source of light for mundane and tangible human practices. Moreover, these questions are asked in a very down-to-earth manner. The two interlocutors are not interested in light either as a physical particle or as a spiritual abstraction. They are genuinely engaged with the different ways in which light can be detected in everyday situations. Notice that the king does not ask a general, abstract question concerning the source of light, but rather looks for "the source of light *for a person here*" (my emphasis). However, the reply the king expects is unrelated to a factual description of the world. Instead he is eager to find out the necessary conditions for human action. Given that a person is incapable of doing things without there being light (for reasons that need to be explored), the king seeks the source of this activity-enabling light (i.e., sitting, going about, working, returning, etc.)

This question elicits different responses, and none is rejected. On the contrary, each reply is considered plausible, but second thoughts deem it not wholly satisfactory. Each intermediate reply is only partially adequate. The different transitory stages—sun, moon, fire, sound—do not function as a didactic tool; their true meaning is revealed by observing the shift in the relation of the different sources of light to the active agent. One readily notes a certain retreat in the transition from one source of light to the other. It is common practice to see this as expressing a withdrawal from the outward into the inward, from the public and distant to the personal and private. I have yet to be convinced of this reading. All the replies given by the sage relate to an active person—sitting, going about, working, resting—and the different sources of light, though distinguishable in terms of brilliance and amplitude, are all, right down to the ātman, similarly external—they are extant in an extrapersonal world and recognized by our senses. The shift from sun to moon, from there to fire and then to sound, do not, at this point, betray a movement from the outward to the inward. Such internalization will only become evident in the last stage, in the shift to the ātman. But, as I mentioned previously, there is in these intermediate stages an obvious sense of retreat—from large to small, from open to closed. What we see in this account is a rendition of altering spatial orientation through different metaphors. To look for the "source of light for a person here" is to look for the different modes by means of which people find their way in space. What is it that enables a person to leave one place and reach another? How can he find his way? What will guarantee that he won't be lost in his everyday activities? No doubt, these questions impart an existential flavor. They do not assume a hidden external structure, motive, or objective. The search for the conditions of spatial orientation is existential in at least one sense: it tacitly acknowledges the futility of looking for a transcendent framework that will serve as an external navigator, providing orientation "for the person here." It seems that this person will have fended for himself. In so doing, Yājñavalkya highlights the different degrees of orientation that are obviously dependent on the space within which orientation is needed. The light source is supposed to enable man to move, that is, to pilot him through space. The sun fulfills the role in open space; the moon satisfies it when space is more limited, and fire (probably from a torch) functions as a source of orientation in more confined space (one should not ignore, of course, the fact that what defines the breadth of space of orientation is the source of light itself).

Underlying these quests for the sources of light is the need for orientation. The shift between each intermediary stage signals a contracting horizon, and following every such contraction a new source of light is introduced to take the place of its predecessor. The transition from one stage to another is not an inner meditative movement of the psyche but rather an orientating motion of the body in space. This is most apparent in the stage preceding the ātman, when Yājñavalkya adds a few explanatory words about the way in which "sound" can act as a source of "light": "When someone cannot make out even his own hand, he goes straightway towards the spot from where he hears a voice." The sun allows for orientation in open space, the moon operates when sun-drenched space no longer exists. Fire functions as the source of orientation in ever more darkened and closed space. Then sound operates in pitch darkness, when one can't even sense one's own body. One sees that these are different modes of self-perception, different ways for " a person" to distinguish her uniqueness as an active human agent (sitting, moving about, etc.). When all other modes of orientation have been consumed, Yājñavalkya introduces the simile of sound bursting forth from a heart of darkness as a means by which a person can recognize herself, making use of a specific range of activities that belong solely to that person and by which self-identity is defined. Sound delivers the person seeking refuge from the loss of identity arising from a lack of orientation.

It would seem then, that what characterizes the different sources of light is a unique concept of person, one in which an individual's major stumbling in his path to self-awareness is the fear of *going astray*. Let us recall Socrates' declaration at his trial (in what has become one of the hallmarks of Western civilization): "Life without . . . examination is not worth living." Life is deemed worthwhile only if a constant effort is made to understand it, whatever the price may be; and it includes, of course, the drive to overcome error at all costs. In the case of Descartes, this becomes an obsession. Yājñavalkya, on the other hand, is wary of only one kind of error—something akin to the feeling one gets in misreading a roadmap. The Upaniṣadic parallel to Socrates' erring man is the man gone astray. Let us recall that Descartes began his methodical doubt by declaring that our senses are liable to delude us and, accordingly, we should not put our trust in them. Note how different Yājñavalkya's point of departure is. Descartes clearly understands that an error arising from sensual misperception can be recognized as error only after it has been actually corrected, being superseded by an alternative "correcting" perception. This is precisely the source of doubt: my perceptions, at this very moment, may be erroneous, but it is impossible that I will realize this instantaneously, which means that I cannot really know right away if my perceptions are indeed erroneous. Yājñavalkya and King Janaka, on the other hand, are bothered by a different problem: that of going astray. What is paramount here is how the one gone astray feels about being lost. Anyone who has, even momentarily, experienced a loss of orientation knows well the immediate impact of this terrifying sensation. But the possibility of going astray does not bother Descartes in the least, since he is perhaps completely confident that his path will indeed bring him to his coveted certainty and all he has to do is remove the different obstacles—be they substantial or cultural—that may stand in his way.[11] We have already noted that an obstinate quest for an indubitable certainty is conceptually rooted on the presupposition of transcendence. Is it really possible to imagine Yājñavalkya turning into a Descartes and consoling himself that when a person is disoriented, when he goes astray, he is in fact experiencing only a particular epistemic error, an error that can somehow be overcome? Evidently, donning Yājñavalkya with a Cartesian mask will not do: Descartes commences his philosophical quest with the firm intention of finding "anything at all in the sciences that was stable and likely to last," but for Yājñavalkya this "stable and likely to last" scientific knowledge—the possibility of scientific knowledge that is completely objective and independent of any specific point of view—is no more than a figment of one's imagination. In order to find parallels for Yājñavalkya's philosophy in Western thought, we will have to shift our attention to the philosophies emerging in the West in the nineteenth century, that is to say, some two hundred years after Descartes.

The Upaniṣadic sage suggests voice as the penultimate stage in man's quest for the source of light. The king's final question seeks the source of light in that situation when even sound fades away: "But when both the sun and the moon have set, the fire has died out, and the voice is stilled, Yājñavalkya, what then is the source of light for a person here?" Yājñavalkya's reply heads toward the final destination of this journey: "The self (ātman) is then his source of light. It is by the light of the self that a person sits down, goes about, does his work, and returns." The search for the source of light arrives at its final destination the moment it becomes apparent that the ātman is the source of a person's orientation in those bewildering situations when things are so "darkened," so obscure, that every other source of light, including sound, is inoperative. At the end of this flashback we reach the subjective starting point, but, in contrast to the I-think of Descartes as a singular point of full certainty, what we find in Yājñavalkya's inner realm is not the I-think but, metaphorically, the "I blink."

The description of ātman following the quoted passage is one suffused with color and laden with metaphors. I will mention only two similes with which Yājñavalkya evokes that special quality of the self as source of light—the first dreaming and the second deep dreamless sleep.[12] By means of the first simile, the ātman is described as residing in that twilight zone called "the place of dreams"; this is, supposedly, its point of departure, the place from which it observes all other worlds. According to Yājñavalkya, the ātman draws its dream contents from its wakeful experiences and impressions; he then dismantles them, only to reform them in his dream. But if its dream contents are reliant on external reality, the very occurrence of a dream is not dependent upon its contents. The ātman "dreams with his own radiance, with his own

light." Yājñavalkya considers dreaming without attributing any precedence to transcendent existence over subjective "inwardness." Thus, in
that dream place, Yājñavalkya continues, "this person becomes his own
light." This application of the dream metaphor suggests a conception
of self-awareness (or perhaps preself-awareness) that deliberately blurs
the very boundary between inward and outward and a fortiori diminishes ability to identify the exact location of this boundary. Indeed,
elsewhere in the Upaniṣads dreams are seen as outbursts of creativ-
ity in which the dreamer's mind is subjugated to dynamic processes
that create massive mental upheavals. So long as the dream continues,
these upheavals themselves transfigure external reality. This notion of
a dream forces us to make a clear-cut philosophical decision: if external reality is altered from within, then it will be of value only if you
presuppose that internal changes are useful for defining the boundaries of external reality. Alterations are thus inevitably conditioned by
one's understanding of external reality's soft boundaries. One of the
most famous extracts from the Upaniṣads clearly speaks of dreaming
in terms of a dreamer's active journey: "Wherever he may travel in
his dream, those regions become his worlds." In the aforementioned
passage Yājñavalkya exceeds in his description of the creative side of
dreaming: "In that place there are no carriages, there are no tandems,
and there are no roads; but he creates for himself carriages, tandems,
and roads. . . . In that place there are no pools, ponds, or rivers; but he
creates for himself pools, ponds, and rivers." Elsewhere other qualities
of dreaming are described quite vividly and imaginatively: a dreamer
is likened to a god since he too takes "many a visible forms," a dreamer may "dally with women"; at times he laughs and at times it sees
frightful things; it appears that people try to kill it or vanquish it; or a
dreamer is undressed or sees itself falling into a deep precipice—to cite
just a few examples.

The most characteristic feature of the use of these metaphors in
Yājñavalkya's philosophy is the thorough espousal of an internal point
of view as forming the groundwork of the self's true existence. This
strong inward movement is different from Descartes' inward movement. Thomas Nagel is right in claiming that Descartes' internalization is put forward so as to enable man's *outward* gaze, his ability to
look at himself from without, to critically examine the ways in which
his beliefs might arise from wrong and invalid reasons. Following Na-

gel's line of thought, I suggest that Descartes' idea of self-awareness is a much more limited form of self-awareness compared to that of the dreaming ātman. The Upaniṣadic self serves as a source of orienting light and enables a form of self-awareness that is highly reminiscent of the "Here I am" evidenced in the ātman-as-primordial-man. As a dreamer, the ātman is self-illuminating and creates, by means of his dreams, the boundaries of reality. In the preceding two examples— that of mythical narrative and that of philosophical dialogue—ātman is portrayed as an obvious corollary of the search for orientation. The imagery of darkness is not coincidental. The narrative myth refers to it obliquely; the philosophical dialogue mentions it explicitly. The self bursts forth from this darkness as a body of light—not as a Cartesian thinking substance, but rather as an illuminating beacon.

On the other hand, Cartesian self-awareness is restricted, since there is, as it were, something forced upon it from the outside: thought that is ineluctable (this is yet another manifestation of the presence of the presupposition of transcendence in any mental act of reflexivity). In this sense the I-think functions as a censor, curbing its own reflexive activity. As such, it is not much different from Augustine's inward man. For the latter, every form of self-awareness finally leads to God, and this ensures that reflexivity will not transgress the limiting boundaries in which Augustine's notion of the presupposition of transcendence has enclosed it. Similarly, Descartes limits the mind's reflexivity by means of a fetter of certainty that inevitably functions in his scheme as a transcendent buffer. In accordance with this, Descartes fixes the I-think as a thinking substance and grants this substance precedence over experience; thus he cannot relate to the immediacy of experience since he has locked this immediacy inside a rigid framework of abstract objectivity. In this respect, Descartes not only follows in Augustine's footsteps but also in those of the whole Platonic tradition and the Western religions.

The difference between Descartes' notion of consciousness and that of Yājñavalkya becomes even more pronounced when we turn to the second of the two similes that Yājñavalkya employs in order to express the primacy of the ātman's role as a subjective self. Here we encounter the simile of deep dreamless sleep, in which even the self's own orienting activity is internalized. The simile distances the dreaming ātman from his dreams and thus presents him in his most primordial form. In other words, the simile of deep sleep is used to express a mental condition in which the sleeping self lacks any form of experience whatsoever, not even experience projected from within itself—and this gives rise to a complete and purged form of subjectivity in which the ideas of boundary, demarcation, and differentiation are lost forever. If while dreaming the boundaries between inward and outward have become less rigid and more supple, less defined and more blurry, then in deep sleep the mind faces only itself, void of content, lacking even the remotest ability to discern between the inner and the outer. Removing these boundaries presents the self as being "beyond what appears to be good, freed from what is bad and without fear." One of the secondary images that the Upaniṣads use to explain the meaning of deep sleep is that of love or sexual ecstasy—the condition in which one is completely immersed in one's sensations. Yājñavalkya likens deep sleep to a man being embraced by the woman he loves, "oblivious to everything within or without." Elsewhere in the Bṛhadāraṇyaka Upaniṣad we read that "when a man is in deep dreamless sleep, on the other hand, and is not aware of anything at all, this is what happens. . . . He rests there oblivious to everything, just as a young man, a great king, or an eminent Brahmin remains oblivious to everything at the height of sexual bliss." Deep sleep releases the self from everything contained within its personal world as well as from every kind of social framework to which it subscribes. This is how Yājñavalkya describes it:

> Here a father is not a father, a mother is not a mother, worlds are not worlds, gods are not gods, and Vedas are not Vedas. Here a thief is not a thief, an abortionist is not an abortionist, an outcaste is not an outcaste, a pariah is not a pariah, a recluse is not a recluse, and an ascetic is not an ascetic.[13]

The use of sleep imagery reveals the problems that taint any attempt to compare the thought processes of different cultures. These comparisons have to be conducted very cautiously and must be sensitive to the difficulties that arise when one tries to assimilate similes and analogies from other cultures; all too often we err by endowing a simile taken from one culture with the linguistic practices familiar to us from our own. A Western understanding of the Indian simile of deep sleep is a case in point. We tend to see sleep as something that happens to us involuntarily—and not always welcome at that. A complete person—a person in the full sense of the word—is someone awake (someone who is an inseparable part of external reality as a whole). Wakefulness, the state of total control, is the ideal state for one to be in, while sleep is a kind of partial, and sometimes even entire, retreat—it is a state of re-gressive "surrender" into a stubborn (and perhaps hopeless) struggle to remain awake. Indian thought sees sleep in a radically different light. Sleep, in the Upaniṣads, does not refer to physiological slumber, a very corporeal idea; it expresses a unique state of consciousness, at which the individual arrives after a long and laborious journey, whose one and only goal is the discovery of one's self-identity. This self-aware-ness takes us immediately back to the simile of the ātman in the mythic story mentioned earlier, that is, to the ātman as a *singular* experience of "Here I am," since self-identity is ascertained here without it needing a specific object (and not even the conceptual differentiation between an external object and internal subject).

Needless to say, Descartes' process of internalization does not reach this condition and, moreover, it neither wills it nor aspires to it. In my mind, the reason for this lies in the fact that reflexivity for Descartes is firmly rooted in spatial imagery. Perhaps it is difficult for us to recog-nize this since it is all too obvious, i.e., to a certain extent our concep-tual presuppositions are not that different from those of Descartes. But a comparative point of view can help us uncover hidden premises. In this sense, the comparativist is not likely to find herself as astonished as Molière's notorious Monsieur Jourdain who suddenly realized that he was "speaking prose" all his life and didn't even know it! I have already mentioned the novelty of the modern Western approach in which the self is located in internal space as opposed to external, public, and dis-closed space. Augustine, by evoking this kind of spatial imagery, is a pioneering thinker, whose philosophical language is, in this respect at least, well ahead of his time. It was ushered into the modern mind by two prominent sixteenth-century figures: Montaigne, among philoso-phers, and Shakespeare, among men of letters. Both of them position mental activity as an internal event. In Descartes' able hands, this im-agery became one the foundations of modern Western thought.

The Upaniṣadic simile of deep sleep can, with hindsight, be con-sidered as something diametrically opposed to the modern use of spatial metaphors in characterizing human subjectivity. So long as

Yājñavalkya, in his account, refrains from evoking the metaphor of deep sleep, it is still possible to encounter extensive characterizations of the self by means of spatial imagery. Such images abound in the dialogue between him and King Janaka—the very question on the source of light, repeated over and over again, attempted to "place," to locate, the ātman in some kind of spatial condition. The king tries to solve the question "who am I?" with questions such as "where am I?" or "where is the place in which I perceive, act, return?" or "which path should I follow?" All these questions make use of imagery drawn from space—place, direction, path, etc. Despite the profound differences that exist between Descartes and Yājñavalkya with regard to the role of transcendence, for the time being, Yājñavalkya, much like Descartes, still relies on spatial imagery when referring to his subjectivity. And yet, since he is not bound by the conceptual presupposition of transcendence, he can go one step further. From the point of view of Western thought (represented here by Descartes), this is an extremely radical, not to say implausible, move: the shift from dream imagery to the imagery of dreamless deep sleep is a dramatic elimination of spatial imagery from the depiction of the self. If the question "where is a dream located?" is meaningful (since, somewhat pressed, one may respond to it by claiming that it is now located "inside" the dreamer, thus offering a spatial answer to a spatial question)—it is doubtful if it is possible to give any sense to the question "where is he who sleeps a dreamless sleep located?" The only conceivable reply will be to point at the one sleeping, perhaps lying on his bed. But, evidently, this misses the point. Moreover, is the dreamless sleeper really here now? And if he is not here, is he anywhere? Both alternatives seem quite dubious. It is not possible to comfortably attribute spatial imagery to deep sleep. Indeed, Yājñavalkya emphatically affirms the use of spatial metaphors to describe dreams, while emphasizing, at the same time, how pointless it is to do so in describing deep, dreamless sleep. The only way to refer to this state is by using *temporal*, not spatial, similes. But this will hardly do. After all, deep sleep is a metaphor disconnecting the ātman, as a self, not only from any kind of spatial presence but also from its "presence" in a determined temporal continuum—since this very continuum can be defined only through reliance on spatial terms (Freud clearly understood this when he talked about the subconscious in spatial-topographic terms seeking to establish its "place in time").

In deep sleep the self consists of a singularity, completely devoid of any specific content and characterized only by self-awareness. Let me repeat what I have already said: this point of view may sound bizarre to the Western ear, since reflexivity in Western eyes would seem to necessitate a conceptual division of knower and known. Hence the claim that the known is identical to the knowing subject sounds senseless. This may explain why Western philosophy regularly inserts an "other" at the core of any reflexive activity. This approach determines at the outset the impossibility of any total self-awareness: as often happens, the limits of sense are determined by one's choice of vocabulary, of basic terms and similes. In the history of Western thought we do indeed find a clear commitment to a scheme of spatial imageries by which reflexivity is referred to. Charles Taylor, when pondering over this commitment, allows himself to arrive at some generalizations, which, to his mind, stem from our essence as human beings. He claims that humans define themselves by means of spatial metaphors and that there is nothing coincidental or incidental in this. On the contrary, he thinks that there are clear signs that the need for spatial orientation lies deep within the human psyche. The generalization underlying Taylor's appraisal of this issue is, of course, mistaken—but we are not concerned here with empirical psychology, only with the comparison of conceptual schemes. I have already demonstrated the conceptual differences that exist between the West and India, and it would seem that Taylor's appraisal is a fair representation of only the Western perspective. The scheme of spatial imagery used to describe self-identity, enabled, on the one hand, the characteristic internalization typical of the Western idea of man prevalent since the end of the sixteenth century; on the other hand, it made introspection into a very problematic idea. This quandary will be considered in chapters 4 and 5.

Returning to the Upaniṣads, let us say that even though spatial imagery prevails in the description of the ātman's preliminary groping stages of its recognition of its subjectivity (the imageries of sun, moon, fire, voice, and even dream), following my suggested reading of the dialogue between Yājñavalkya and King Janaka, I would say that this spatial imagery is only connected with the quest, not with its final goal. In the initial, probing phase, self-awareness indeed finds its expression by means of a strong need for orientation, and this need is described by a series of spatial images. Having been revealed, the ātman is still cloaked by a scheme of spatial images, only as long as it is associated with the dream metaphor; in a dream any introspection is interlaced with some kind of partition, since the ātman knows itself by means of its various dreams; the objects seen in dreams are naturally perceived as independent of the dreaming mind. Yet, the moment the dream metaphor is substituted by the metaphor of dreamless deep sleep, a significant conceptual change occurs. The sleeping ātman ceases to occupy any place whatsoever.

How are we to understand this claim? Underlying it, there seems to be a radical outlook, namely, that self-knowledge, the state in which the "self" is united with itself, is a singular situation in which self-awareness exists in such a way that it is not dependent on the presupposition of outwardness. It is clear that this state of mind defies succinct verbal expression, since every such expression will eventually necessitate a spatial imagery with which to qualify the "presence" of self-awareness. As we shall see in the next chapter, when this is applied to language it has far-reaching consequences, notably when it serves as a basic assumption for Buddhist philosophers who challenged the Upaniṣadic notion of selfhood. Their concern was not that the self went too far from space to time, but rather that it stopped too early, that it didn't travel far enough, reaching that ultimate and final destination where the pure self, knowing only itself, will be empty and void.

But Descartes labors within the framework of the presupposition of transcendence, so he will not allow himself to show interest in the kind of metapsychology that could be constructed on the basis of the indubitable existence of the I-think. Engaging in metapsychological speculations would mean that the I-think can function reflexively and this, for Descartes, is inconceivable, because it is impossible to refrain from assuming a subject-object duality, a distinction between the knower and the known. It seems to me that Descartes feels slightly uncomfortable with the kind of self that his philosophy gives rise to. He has no choice but to describe it in spatial terms, despite the fact that Descartes' I-think is not, by nature, extended in space. He attaches the ego cogito to the transcendent framework of certainty and objectivity, and consequently the self appears based on inscrutable logical principles that are taken for granted. Thus Descartes cannot distinguish between the ways in which the knowing self actually knows and the conditions that make the process of knowing possible. The transcendent structure of his philosophy arrests reflexivity at precisely the moment its inward journey could have begun. And so we are faced with a curious self whose imminent disappearance is preordained by the very conditions that led to its emergence. In this he betrays a striking similarity to Mozart's Don Giovanni.

––––––––––––

Don Giovanni's appearance here is not coincidental. I wish to conclude this chapter by drawing attention to the character of the seducing Don as one who, in a certain sense, bridges the Cartesian self and the Upaniṣadic self and, in another sense, contests both. In the latter sense he anticipates certain philosophical developments to be discussed in chapter 4. My concern here is only with Don Giovanni as the main character of Mozart's opera and Da Ponte's libretto. I shall quite intentionally ignore the many other depictions of Don Juan in the course of Western art, literature, and music. My appeal to Don Giovanni will be strictly philosophical, and in this I follow in the footsteps of the Danish philosopher Søren Kierkegaard (1813–1855), who, more than any other philosopher, contributed to a philosophical understanding of music and especially to Mozart's magnificent opera.

Kierkegaard makes no attempt to hide his profound admiration for Mozart's *Don Giovanni*. He tells us that he does not fear lest some future generation vie to depose Mozart from his place among the immortals, adding, with a typical pinch of self-irony, that he is prepared to accept the accusation that his emphatic insistence on Mozart standing *highest* among the immortals is somewhat childish. According to Kierkegaard, Mozart takes his place there on account of *Don Giovanni*. Mozart's other works please us, make us content, cause admiration, enrich the soul, and satisfy the ear, but heaven forbid that we see any other of Mozart's works, separately or together as a whole, as "equally great" as *Don Giovanni*.

Don Giovanni's greatness, according to Kierkegaard, arises from the combination of the abstractness extant in the idea that the Don represents and the abstractness that exists in the musical medium through which that idea is expressed. In this opera there is a double abstractedness, both of the subject matter and the medium through which it is presented. Kierkegaard's intention here is to emphasize that Mozart had the good fortune to find a subject for opera that is intrinsically and in its very essence a musical subject. Thus, Kierkegaard adds, if any other composer were to try to surpass Mozart, all he could do was merely rewrite *Don Giovanni*. This opera is a perfect paradigm of pure musical form: its idea is absolutely musical in that the music does not enter as an accompaniment, but "in bringing the idea to light, reveals its inner most being." What, then, is this musical idea? Kierkegaard retorts thus: Don Giovanni himself expresses the erotic, that is to say, he manifests "the spirit of sensuality," the immediacy of desire, the life force that animates sensuality itself.

The spirit of sensuality can find direct expression only in music:

> It must of course not be forgotten, therefore, that it is not a question here of desire in a particular individual but of desire as a principle, spiritually specified as that which spirit excludes. This is the idea of the spirit of sensuality. . . . The expression of this idea is Don Giovanni, and the expression of Don Giovanni is, again, solely music.

According to Kierkegaard, Don Giovanni is motivated by one thing and one thing only—desire. It stands by itself, it is not aimed at achieving any goal or as a symbol behind which something else lies. Don Giovanni is not a character but an idea. It would be wrong to perceive him as some particular individual and less so as a dramatic character, since he is a "power of nature, the demonic, which as little tires of seducing, or is done with seducing, as the wind is tired of raging, the sea of surging, or a waterfall of cascading down from its height. In this respect, the number of the seduced might just as well be any number at all, or a far greater one." Not surprisingly, in the catalogue that Leporello (the Don's manservant) carries in his pocket, there are "already" the names of a thousand and three of his conquests in Spain alone; more than anything else, the feature of this number is that it is odd and accidental. The list is by no means closed; on the contrary, Don Giovanni is still on the move.

In a fascinating article entitled "Don Giovanni as an Idea," the present-day philosopher Bernard Williams continues Kierkegaard's line of thought, claiming that as a straightforward operatic character Don Giovanni is beyond doubt quite a feeble character. The opera doesn't offer us any insights to explain who the Don is and what motivates him. It seems as if there is nothing to be found in the depths of his soul. He has no reflective aria—he never sings about himself in the manner that many other Mozart characters do. We do not know how he behaves when he is alone; he is perpetually on the move, and this perpetual motion lacks any self-awareness, it is entirely prereflective. Relying on Kierkegaard, who noted that it would be a mistake to think of the Don as a genuine "seducer," Williams adds that the act of seduction necessitates a certain degree of awareness, and this is precisely what Don Giovanni lacks; he is not a seducer but a desirer. A seducer needs a power that in Don Giovanni is missing, namely, the power of speech. Don Giovanni attracts by another force—the force of sensuality. His desire marks the flow of life and expresses unbounded vitality. Kierkegaard calls him "the liberating joy of life." All the other characters of this opera exist merely as "derivatives," while the Don is the force that animates them, the life force pounding within. The idea of Don Giovanni as a principle of life is what draws Leporello to him and holds him in a bond he cannot undo. The hero himself is always energetic, abundant, and flowing. He needs no preparation, never hesitates, and never makes any long-term plans. He is always prepared; that is, the force is always within him. It cannot be expressed verbally. Only music can show us what this energy is. That is why Don Giovanni is absolutely musical.

I would like to use Kierkegaard's analysis of Don Giovanni in order to explain his uniqueness as a desiring self. Don Giovanni's force is internal. This internal force, this power of eroticism, tries by way of perpetual desire to create for itself an external world. But this creation is void of any specific content and predetermined purpose. Much like the birth of ātman of the Upaniṣadic narrative and Yājñavalkya's orienting ātman, Don Giovanni too is a creating self, empty of any content, whose sole feature is being active. What is the nature of this self? Is it, like Descartes' I-think, a self linked to certain logical and ontological frameworks wrapping it in an invisible network of outwardness? Or is it like the Upaniṣadic self, immersed in the erotic condition of absolute indistinguishability between the outward and the inward, its purpose being to attain the ultimate mental ecstasy that expresses the transition from dream to deep dreamless sleep in which the self is completely liberated to gaze solely at itself?

This is an intricate question; its answer is comprised of a dense network of similarities and dissimilarities between the hero of the opera and Descartes' I-think as well as between the Don and the Upaniṣadic ātman. But Don Giovanni also contains certain unique Mozartian characteristics that cannot to be found either in the ego cogito or in the knowing ātman. In one respect, Don Giovanni is seemingly more akin to the Upaniṣadic self than to its Western counterpart. The musical flow in which he expresses himself is more reminiscent of the mythical ātman than the I-think. However, Don Giovanni as self is also similar to Descartes' self. Descartes, it will be remembered, tries to present the self as a firm foundation from which to draw objectivity and, in order to extract objectivity from experience, he tries to make experience impersonal. Clear and distinct ideas require that each of us will travel outside ourselves and adopt that impersonal point of view which Thomas Nagel aptly termed "the view from nowhere." Don Giovanni too has nothing personal inside him. He is a pure self in the sense that he is impersonal. He too views and acts from nowhere, from an impersonal, disconnected condition.

But then again, philosophically speaking, he is, interestingly, clearly different from Descartes. Mozart "solves" the problem of reflexivity that so bothered Descartes in typically operatic manner. To reiterate, Descartes faces a dilemma arising from the fact that reflexivity is necessarily limited; the dilemma being that, on the one hand, he is compelled to endorse an unequivocal act of internalization, but, on the other hand, he still relies on the conceptual framework of transcendence and thus not only is internalization incomplete but moreover it does not enable complete reflexivity. Stated somewhat differently, on the one hand, inwardness is necessary in order to conceive reality, but, on the other hand, it cannot undermine the foundational concepts that locate reality outside of mental activity. It would seem that Mozart tries to overcome this ambiguity, and so in his music he depicts a self that manages, by means of his unbridled desire, to achieve a violent breach of the inward that propels itself forcefully outward. This act of violence completely obliterates the Cartesian form of (curtailed) reflexivity. From a Cartesian point of view, desire does not have metaphysical status; at most, it is an annoying background noise damaging the harmony of rationality. By comparison, the self's desire as epitomized by Don Giovanni is so total that it leaves no place for any reflexivity. One can almost hear Mozart saying to us: if reflexivity is in any way limited and presupposes boundaries beyond itself, why not completely give it up and substitute it with blind creative activity? Perhaps Mozart has thus "solved" the dilemma of reflexivity that so bothered Descartes. The elimination of reflexivity establishes an authenticity evident in the Don's musical character, in contradistinction to the duplicitous and false nature of the opera's other characters. In this sense, Don Giovanni's authenticity is akin to Job's authenticity and dissimilar to the latter's consoling friends. Both Job and Don Giovanni seek to break loose from the circle of reflexivity and thence to venture outward. They both have to contend with deceitful emissaries of this outwardness. Bildad the Shuhite and Don Ottavio, the arrogant youngster Elihu and the clumsy peasant Masetto—all are burdened by norms, conventions, and cultural customs. This is not the outwardness either Job or Don Giovanni had in mind when they attempted to break loose, clinging to the outward. But the similarity between the two ends here, since what Job is trying to uncover by breaking out is the unequivocal presence (perhaps even the revelation) of God, while Don Giovanni is interested in a completely different kind of encounter with outwardness. He is interested in meeting himself out there as the externalization of his erotic desire. In this respect the Don's eruptive desire is like the primordial ātman's desire when it sought a companion that was but a part of itself. Again, in that dense network of similarities and dissimilarities, it would seem that Don Giovanni is more akin to the Indian ātman than to the Cartesian I-think. Yet there is a notable difference, and this needs be underscored: the Don fails precisely where the ātmanic Puruṣa succeeds. It is true that Kierkegaard states emphatically that Don Giovanni manifests the life force of the other characters. "Don Giovanni's own life is the principle of life in them. His passion sets in motion the passions of others." The Don is accordingly not only the hero of the opera but also "its common denominator," because the life of the others is derived from his. These characters, concludes Kierkegaard with typical incisiveness, are "the outward consequences constantly posited by his life." Notwithstanding the presence of Don Giovanni in the life of other characters, he fails in all his amorous exploits. His ability to control external reality is not really that impressive. It would seem that the objects of his erotic desire do not yield to his desirous urge.

The attempt to break out while eradicating reflexivity fails. What will be the self's fate in a case such as this?

Mozart composed *Don Giovanni* roughly 150 years after Descartes wrote his key philosophical texts. By then the self's pivotal role as an agent enabling knowledge of the world and its construction had been completely ingrained in the Western mindset. In *Don Giovanni* I see Mozart as presenting us with a thought-provoking response to the Cartesian enterprise. More precisely, in composing it he demonstrates the post-Cartesian attempt to let the subject break away from the trap that Descartes had set for it. As I mentioned earlier, this attempt fails, but Mozart's notion of subjectivity, in contrast to that of other characters in opera, cannot bring about *Don Giovanni*'s close in the manner in which most operas end where the hero or heroine (or both) follow the natural way of all flesh. A desiring subject cannot die, yet, having failed, neither can he persist. And so Da Ponte and Mozart choose to hide subjectivity in the throes of the underworld, beneath the surface but near enough for a susceptible ear to pick up the murmurings of its song.

It would seem that the I-think (whose reflexivity is anyway limited) is in the process of becoming a desiring subject without any ability to be reflexive and so taking its place only in the innermost depths of unconsciousness. Indeed, it is not that difficult to perceive the Freudian underpinnings apparent in this sketch of the Don's musical character. But it seems to me that Mozart outlines the fate of the desiring subject in a much deeper sense. Musically speaking, he does this somewhat strangely: he concludes the opera with two endings. In the first finale Don Giovanni is dining. This dinner is purportedly his last supper. It will be recalled that he has invited to this meal a guest from another world—the marble statue of the Commendatore, Donna Anna's father, whom Don Giovanni slew in a dual at the opening of the opera, after the aged Commendatore was called to protect his daughter's chastity before being violated by the Don's relentless sexual drive. The musical rendition of this eventful meeting constitutes one of the highest peaks in the history of Western music. After the statue arrives and commands the Don to repent (which he blatantly refuses to do) the dramatic tension rises at every turn; in this manner the music climbs up and up, weaving one harmony into another until finally it cannot contain itself any more. Accompanied by the harrowingly beautiful voices of infernal spirits, the Don vanishes into hell, making this colossal ending none other than the ultimate annihilation of opera as opera. It appears that it is not only Don Giovanni that Mozart whisks off to the inferno, but the very possibility of any other music in the future. Indeed, a definitive finale.

But then Mozart presents us with another ending. Making their way through the disappearing smokes of inferno (the flames of which have just devoured the Don) six characters appear on stage, six survivors. They wind up the story in a sextet that begins by extolling the Don's just punishment and then proceed to tell, each in his or her turn, what the future has in store for each of them: some to marriage, another to the convent, yet another to the employment office, or to a life devoted to perpetual longing for the inextinguishable desire of Giovanni. And all this—in the blandest piece of music, indistinguishable from hundreds of other such pieces evident in works of contemporaneous court musicians: professional music, somewhat superficial, steeped in exterior gaiety and conventionality. Consider this: an opera that did not know of even one banal moment, musically speaking, finishes off just like that, in tedious, one might say almost gloomy, music. Can this be the most appropriate way to end a piece whose musical expression has until now been unrivaled? Such an unimaginative ending, especially when juxtaposed against the exciting and incomparable finale preceding it. This curious epilogue has been the subject of endless debates, analyses, and examinations. Some have chosen to condemn it and have prayed for its everlasting demise (there have been conductors who did, in fact, scrap it from their performance); some have sought to defend it—each choosing his own preferred angle: historical, political, and even religious—finding cultural attenuating circumstances for the inclusion of this insipid epilogue. Mozart, so they say, knew well that this finale was of little musical value but had to include it for reasons wholly unrelated to music or art. There have been musicians who have tried to rehabilitate this ending in the hope of proving that Mozart's genius resides even there. Both salvage campaigns, in my opinion, feel somewhat strained and unconvincing. Admittedly, the extramusical apologetics of one side is no less awkward than the musical apologetics of the other. Mozart, as an opera composer, found little difficulty in writing sublime music for odious characters, the kind that lie, deceive, and betray, but do it to musical perfection. Why then should we force ourselves to entertain the exact opposite of this, namely, that Mozart suddenly felt compelled to write music tainted by superficial conventionality? I suggest a different explanation of *Don Giovanni's* dual ending. This suggestion takes a simple approach: Mozart knowingly wrote a second ending of little musical worth and drenched it in conventionality. But not for extramusical reasons. On the contrary: artistically speaking, such an ending was inevitable, a necessary component with which to demonstrate the failure and disappearance of the opera's hero, the desiring subject.

The opera's second ending constitutes a direct and bitter appearance of outwardness, of the external world. Six characters that have come into contact with Don Giovanni—three women and three men—are now for the first time divorced from his immediate presence in their lives. Kierkegaard hints at this when he characterizes this lot as being nourished by a Giovannesque desire and thus inherently dependent on the bursting presence of the Don. The second ending of the opera is in fact the first instance of a post-Giovannian era—a world without the subject as a desiring self. Now the time has come for the non-Giovannian characters to commence their victory parade. Yet, drained of the desiring subjectivity from which they drew their vitality, they are merely cardboard characters. As such, their final appearance is not intended to reveal something about themselves, but rather about the *outwardness* of which they are now the sole representatives. After having extolled and celebrated the justice Don Giovanni met with, they sing their final song, which is nothing more than a hollow moralizing tale recounting the past and—what is equally insipid—an account of their lifeless prospects in the future. This is a testimony of outwardness lacking the "I" as subject since the Don has departed. The second ending of the opera is completely lackluster, devoid of any splendour, as it should be. It is conventional, nearly vapid, and in its intentional vapidity lies its only meaning. These cardboard characters representing external reality are the sad remnants of the struggle between the inward and the outward. The inward's attempt to possess the outward has indeed failed, and he pays the price of this failure in hell. The outward has admittedly survived, but its existence is vacant—being drained of any "supporting" substance, be it a transcendent being that could give meaning to its post-Giovanni life or a thinking subject that will occupy the place of transcendent meaning in its creative activity. What is left is empty outwardness—conventional, vulgar, and tasteless. There is only one kind of music that can aptly depict this perverse situation: the plain conventional music with which Mozart ended the opera. Mozart portrayed conventionality by the use of musical conventions. When subconscious desire is confined, when it is brutally dispatched to the infernal regions of the nether world, the medium's external awareness is left to its own devices, aware only of its own conventions since the medium, opera, has now become only a form of expression of outward objectivity. In this respect, perhaps *Don Giovanni* is the first modern work of art.

The self made three appearances in this chapter. The Upaniṣadic alternative offered it complete self-awareness, obliging a radical internalization in which the inward has complete precedence over the outward. In the absence of a basic transcendent framework, the Upaniṣadic thinkers presented the knowing self as the author of absolute immanence. Descartes comes up with a different self, an ego cogito that allows for the requirements and conditions of the presupposition of transcendence. Because of this, subjective introspection is necessarily limited since it is confined by the objectivity that the self is supposed to give rise to—something it is predestined to do. These limitations decree that Descartes' self must be empty of any specific content without at the same time replenishing it in absolute reflexivity: Descartes' terminology does not allow it, just as it will not allow the radical psychologization of external reality. Thus, Descartes' self is left to play a mere procedural role. Don Giovanni epitomizes the third alternative. Here we evidence a self that expresses the condition of extreme internalization, except that this condition is never accompanied by introspection; quite the contrary, the possibility of establishing the self here is conditioned by its ability to break violently out into reality, like a pillaging colonial power in which the inward is forever conquering the outward. The failure of this attempted takeover erases the self's presence from the outward and thus it is left afflicted by the emptiness that Mozart expressed so eloquently in the opera's epilogue.

Throughout this chapter I have, on several occasions, raised possible responses by Yājñavalkya to emerging Cartesian ideas. One wonders how

Yājñavalkya would respond to the character of Mozart's Don Giovanni? How would he react to Job's story, the Don's nonidentical twin? It seems to me that he would find it difficult to identify with either. Moreover, it is very likely that he would fail to comprehend them. Job's demand for outwardly divine revelation on which to base the meaning of life would seem to him like someone who, having completely lost his sense of direction, is groping in the dark. Moreover, for Job to make this claim and to root it in a transcendent divinity that, by definition, is supposed to prevent unjust suffering would seem to indicate a misguided, immature projection of suffering and unhappiness that are, in fact, one's own. This projection onto an outward entity is meant to relegate each individual to his or her own share of meaning, according to its autonomous considerations. It would seem that the only part in Job's story that Yājñavalkya would properly understand is the horrific jest with which the book begins, the capricious bet between God and Satan (which would have reminded him of no less capricious bets that certain Indian gods were confronted with). Perhaps he would have offered Job some timely advice relying on Indian myths on how to thwart such bets, mostly by exploiting the hidden weaknesses that both contestants (God and Satan) have. He would find it difficult to understand Don Giovanni, Job's twin. If Don Giovanni is a subject whose complete essence is desire, and if therefore the boundaries of outwardness do not apply to him, what is there to stop him from fully realizing his desire? Why does his breaking out necessarily entail the complete eradication of the possibility of introspection? Why can't outwardness be overcome by simply understanding it as yet another facet of the immanent? Perhaps the only thing that Yājñavalkya would appreciate in this opera is the final disappearance of the Don, as a being that does not and will never die. But it is highly unlikely that he could truly understand the ensuing nihilism that this disappearance will bring about in Western thought.

FOUR

No-Self

KANT, KAFKA, AND NĀGĀRJUNA ON THE DISAPPEARING SELF

How pathetically scanty my self-knowledge is compared with, say, my knowledge of my room.
—Franz Kakfa, *Octavo Notebooks*

Roughly three hundred years after the I-think had been established as
the Archimedean point of Descartes' urge for certainty, we find Franz
Kafka standing on the ruins of this thinking self lamenting its death or,
more precisely, realizing its unavoidable vacuity:

> The observer of the soul cannot penetrate into the soul, but
> there doubtless is a margin where he comes into contact with it.
> Recognition of this contact is the fact that even the soul does not
> know of itself. Hence it must remain unknown. That would be
> sad only if there were anything apart from the soul, but there is
> nothing else.

We shall return to this declaration, but, even at this preliminary stage, it is clear that, according to Kafka, the soul is impermeable and even if it were possible to penetrate it (merely touching the margins) this would reveal a deadlock in which the possibility of self-knowledge is precluded by the very urge the soul has for self-knowledge. It is bound to fail for two interconnected reasons: the observer's limitations and the soul's vacuity. The reason for this failure or, rather, inner collapse, is not because, in the manner of Freud, we conceive the soul as a multilayered architectonic structure built around a hermetic inner storehouse, accessible only through mediation. There is a much more transparent reason for this. Kafka notes, in another aphorism, that "there is no such thing as observation of the inner world, as there is of the outer world."

More than half a millennium after the composition of the principal Upaniṣads, Nāgārjuna (an Indian Buddhist philosopher who probably lived around the second century CE or maybe even a hundred years earlier) defied Yājñavalkya's idea of the ātman as a self that has within it the capacity to create worlds. Opening his key work is a dedication to the Buddha (a customary practice) in which Nāgārjuna outlines the character of Buddhist liberation, saying that it is no more than seeing things as they really are:

> I bow down to the most sublime of teachers,
> the completely awakened one
> who taught dependent arising:
> No cessation, no birth,
> No annihilation, no permanence,
> No coming, no going,
> No difference, no identity
> Without verbal expansion.

We shall return to this dedication and look at it in greater detail, but, to begin with, we should eradicate a conceptual obstacle that might hamper the understanding of those versed in the canons of Western religions. Nāgārjuna's dedication is *not* yet another case of negative theology; he is not suggesting that the Buddha (or the Buddhist doctrine) is beyond all descriptions. An interpretation of this sort would be a misrepresentation of Nāgārjuna's philosophy and of Buddhist thought in general. Nāgārjuna's dedication concerns a specific doctrine expounded by the Buddha, that of the "dependent arising" of all things. In his dedication Nāgārjuna claims that dependent arising is beyond any classification—it is neither created nor does it cease, it does not appear, nor does it disappear, it is neither a unity nor a plurality—but this supposed elusiveness is not rooted in a metaphysical outlook. On the contrary, not being subject to any meaningful description shows us the right way to approach reality—viewing it as "empty." We shall deal with Nāgārjuna's emptiness later on in the chapter, but it should be clear that his view, peculiar as it may seem, is essentially different from the conclusion that a monotheistic theologian might derive from similar premises.

Within their respective cultures Nāgārjuna and Kafka are considered as enigmatic characters; thus it has always been and thus it is still. What exactly did each of them say? What did they mean? How are they to be understood? The countless interpretations of Kafka's work no doubt testify to certain confusion. Adorno rightly notes that "each sentence says 'interpret me,' and none will permit it." The many interpretations of Nāgārjuna give rise to a similar situation. In between his immediate disciples and contemporary scholarship, everyone has sought to come up with a proper interpretation aimed at establishing the right import of his teaching. Kafka, as I hope to demonstrate, is part and parcel of the philosophical revolution brought about by Immanuel Kant (1724–1804). Nāgārjuna occupies a key position in Buddhist philosophy. At first glance it may seem that Kafka's meditative stance closely resembles Nāgārjuna's philosophical outlook. After all, both seem to reach similar conclusions about what some may hastily call "the demise of the empty self." However, in suggesting this comparison, I have no intention of implying that they are in any way profoundly similar. On the contrary, even though Kafka's claims about the self's emptiness are no less incisive than Nāgārjuna's, the difference between the two is unfathomable!

———————

I doubt there is a simple key to unlocking Kafka's world. Still, it does seem possible to identify the requisite philosophical background with which to assess the quest for such a key. A cursory glance at this

background will show that it is steeped in the thought of one philosopher, Immanuel Kant, and especially his proposal for a Copernican revolution in philosophy. I will say little about Kant himself or
his philosophical enterprise as a whole; instead, we shall concentrate
on only that which I deem necessary in order to understand Kafka's
entangled world.

Kant likened the goal of his philosophy to the revolution Copernicus brought about in astronomy. Copernicus claimed the old astronomical system that envisaged the sun revolving around the earth was
untenable. He suggested changing the order around: let the earth revolve around the sun—that which lay at the center will now be at the
periphery and that which was peripheral will now lay at the center.
Similarly, Kant also saw himself as reversing the traditional philosophical priorities that described human knowledge and its objects. Before
Kant it was customary to assume that the objects of knowledge (things)
occupy center stage while our knowledge of them is a satellite revolving around these objects. That is to say, knowledge was seen as being
conditioned by its objects, not unlike a photographer encircling his
subject matter, trying to get to "know" it with his camera so as to capture the best possible image. Kant does the opposite: he places that act
of knowing objects at the center, considering this an a priori function
of the mind—preceding experience and independent. To use his own
language: instead of seeing knowledge as conforming to objects, he
suggests that "objects must conform to our knowledge." Knowledge is
likened to the necessary "spectacles" through which, and only through
which, reality is perceived and understood. The object (as the object
of the senses) must conform to the constitution of our faculty of intuition, while experience directs itself according to our concepts. Human
cognition determines what an object is and how objects are related to
each other. Kant did not hesitate to state this unequivocally: "We can
know a priori of things only what we ourselves put into them."

Kant's famous question "how is knowledge possible?" resolves itself
by determining the importance of the a priori mental constructs that allow us to perceive and understand. He refers to these mental constructs
as transcendental. One should not confuse the notion of transcendence
as it appears elsewhere in these chapters and the term *transcendental* in
its specific Kantian sense (despite the fact that they are cognate). To
say of something that it is transcendent is to make a claim about its

exteriority; in this sense, the opposite of *transcendent* is *immanent* or internal. On the other hand, *transcendental* is something that does not belong to the world of experience. It precedes it, exists prior to it, and even exceeds it (in the sense of "pure" experience). Kant defines the transcendental thus: "I entitle transcendental all knowledge which is occupied not so much with objects as with the mode of our knowledge of objects in so far as this mode of knowledge is to be possible *a priori*." Transcendental inquiry does not deal with the knowledge of objects themselves, but rather with how objects of experience are known.

Kant distinguished between two modes of knowledge. The first he called intuition, by which the object appears as immediately "given to us." The second he called concept, and here he refers not to the receptivity of objects but rather to the mind's capacity to refer to them by thought. Thus Kant names the receptive power of the mind to receive representations sensibility, and calls the spontaneous thinking power of the mind understanding. With regard to intuitions, Kant makes an important subdistinction between "empirical intuitions" and "pure intuitions." Empirical intuitions are the modes through which our mind relates to its objects, and the immediacy of this relation is evident in that the object is perceived by us as that which determines it (that is, our mind perceives itself as being activated by it). However, Kant was mostly interested in the forms of intuition that precede experience (hence they are called pure rather than empirical in the sense that they are not determined by any particular experience). He recognized two such forms—space and time. For him, space and time lie within the scope of human experience; they are not real essences residing beyond it. Nor are they qualities of such real essences. Space and time are but "two pure forms of sensible intuition" determining the conditions of any experience. Knowledge operates in such a manner that anything presenting itself before it as activated by our senses (in relation to which knowledge is passive) and appears in space and time. These are thus a priori conditions of sensibility—the *way* in which objects are subject to intuition. While space is the pure "form of outer sense," time is the pure "form of inner sense." But Kant is cautious here: even though space and time are pure conditions for the appearance of knowable objects, their actual appearance is conditioned by empirical intuition.[1]

Besides intuition, Kant also recognized an active mental form that he referred to as concept (*Begriff*). If intuition relates to the pure empirical dimension of knowledge, concepts relate to thought or understanding. In his treatment of understanding, Kant searched for the conceptual conditions that enable the mind to think its objects, where the mind has an active role, unlike its passivity in the reception of sensibility. Kant identified twelve a priori concepts (referring to them as categories) and these are "pure concepts of human understanding." Every judgment makes use of these concepts (and for Kant every act of understanding is a judgment). They are the foundation upon which all other empirical concepts are formed. Anything we know empirically is conditioned by these categories, which are considered the transcendental conditions underlying all experience. But these categories, emphasizes Kant, "have no kind of application, save only in regard to things which may be objects of possible experience." Concepts without empirical intuition are empty, and this assertion is true even of the abstract concepts of mathematics.

But humans have another, third, mental faculty besides intuition and understanding, namely, reason. This human faculty has a dialectal nature, i.e., it is an entwining kind of thinking. Kant called the objects of reason "ideas"; they exhibit the human aspiration for the absolute and unconditioned. Ideas surpass pure experience and thus, unlike the categories, are not the pure conceptual conditions of empirical knowledge; on the contrary, reason generates ideas that are used in order to break the boundaries that space, time, and the categories have set for human knowledge. To put it more generally, reason constitutes the attempt to reach the transcendent; this attempt is what Kant calls metaphysics.

Here lies the well-known Kantian distinction between appearance and reality—between phenomenon, as things that appear in experience, opposite the noumenon as thing-in-itself. Phenomena are the totality of empirical experience, namely, all known objects. This is the only mode of knowledge given to us, that which always assumes the existence of empirical (sensual) intuition whose conceptual foundation precedes experience. The whole perceived world surrounding us is a world that is determined by the a priori structure of knowledge. On the other hand, contained in the noumenon—the thing-in-itself—is all that is forever concealed from us: things existing separately and in their own right, without epistemic construction or mediation. The thing-in-itself is thus clearly outside space and time and beyond the categories of understanding. It is imperceptible and definable only in negative terms; for example, as something that exists nowhere (since in order for something to be in a particular place it has to be mediated in space and time—and the noumenon is beyond space and time). This needs some clarification: the distinction between phenomenon and thing-in-itself is not a distinction between different things, but between two aspects of the very same thing; to use Kant's own words, "the object is to be taken *in a twofold sense*, namely as appearance and as thing in itself." What then is the status of the noumenon? Kant's reply is interesting: the thing-in-itself is the (independent) origin of our knowledge. The noumenon is the origin of the phenomenon: it is possible to "think" of the thing-in-itself (the noumenon) as a source of our sensual and conceptual experience, but under no circumstances is it possible to know the thing-in-itself.

Kant offers a radical critique of metaphysics. We shall not enter the thicket of this critique here; suffice it to draw attention to its general framework. The impression one gets is that Kant has embarked on a crusade against any explicit manifestation of the traditional presupposition of transcendence, whether in its philosophical guise or in the diverse ways in which it was presented within the canons of monotheistic religions. For example, well known is his critique of Plato's metaphysics that posits the ultimate objects of our knowledge somewhere evidently far beyond the bounds of the knowing subject. Kant called this, perhaps somewhat dismissively, a deus ex machina approach to knowledge—assuming some kind of vague eternal being that suddenly appears out of nowhere in order to facilitate the act of human knowledge. He regarded this deus ex machina as "the greatest absurdity one could hit upon in the determination of the origin and validity of our knowledge." Kant is objecting to Plato's version of transcendence, which is indeed quite absurd if one accepts as self-evident the assumptions upon which Kant's Copernican revolution is based.

Kant's rejection of the idea that God acts as a guarantor of the possibility of human knowledge runs along similar lines. Kant detects a circular argument here. If the external and mind-independent God guarantees knowledge, clearly the correspondence between our ideas and reality is warranted and is valid even before it actually transpires. The only trouble is that assuming God as a guarantor can be justified only if we find a representation of God in each act of knowledge. But this is precisely our goal, hence we inevitably presuppose that which we are trying to prove. Platonic Forms or God are meant to scrupulously uphold the outwardness of experience and yet. in order to do so, the outwardness of these Forms had to be presupposed without first seeking their guarantor. This constitutes a petitio principii.

We thus end up with Kant willing to accede to our knowledge of "external" reality, but only at the price of double-edged concession. First, we should give up any naive wish to establish an unmediated relation with what lies out there. It is impossible to retain the prephilosophical sense of external objects as something directly accessible to human knowledge. The world for us is only that which can appear in experience. And experience, it will be recalled, is conditioned by the a priori structure of our mind. This is a structural conditioning: Kant was eager to distinguish his view from that of Berkeley (which we shall consider in the next chapter), according to which external objects are nothing but ideas in the mind perceiving them. According to Kant, in contradistinction to Berkeley, the dependence of exteriority upon knowledge is structural, that is to say, it is not an empirical but rather a formal dependence.

Given the unavoidability of this dependence, the Kantian world finds itself chained to experience and impervious to any metaphysical aspiration. In the same vein, Kant has also blocked theology—i.e., the attempt to comprehend the nature and attributes of the transcendent God. God cannot be part of human experience; therefore nothing meaningful can be said about his existence. Since God avails himself neither to the faculty of intuition nor to the faculty of understanding, it remains a contentless, empty concept once and for all banished from the phenomenal world.[2]

Nevertheless, Kant's philosophy still has remnants of the presupposition of transcendence since, as we have seen, he maintains the assumption of the existence of a thing-in-itself. A strange assumption, by all accounts: the only reason it can be sustained is because it is completely empty. In principle, the thing-in-itself does not appear empirically, but somehow, inexplicably, it underlies all our experiences. It would be wrong to equate this with God (or Platonic Form) and, similarly, it would be a mistake to see Kant's attitude to it as taking the rhetorical track of a negative theology. Our inability to know the thing-in-itself or to make any claims about it was not derived from God's boundlessness or from the (unbridgeable) gap that lies between this omnipotent presence and the world. This is not yet another theological proposition about man's insignificance or about his short-sightedness, which prevents him from perceiving the transcendent being and understanding its nature. Kant has a completely different agenda: our epistemic and verbal incapacity is derived from the a priori structure of human knowledge. The thing-in-itself derives its status from the delineation of the boundaries of knowledge. As we have seen, Kant rejects the better-known appearances of Western transcendence—divinity, form, substance, etc.—but nevertheless maintains the inherent structure of the presupposition of transcendence, though the price paid for this is extremely high. In Kant's world it is possible to preserve transcendence only by banishing it from the world of empirical experience and the world of objects. Transcendence, that presence of the other, is shrunken down to a hollow remnant called the thing-in-itself.[3]

I mentioned previously that our knowledge of "external" reality is conditioned by a double-edged concession. I pointed to the emptiness of transcendence as its first aspect. I now turn to the second aspect, which is the emptiness of the "I" as a thinking subject. When Kant deals with the faculty of understanding, he introduces the concept of pure self-consciousness. He refers to it as "pure apperception," and the "transcendental unity of self-consciousness" and also the "transcendental I." This "I" has nothing in common with circumstances familiar to us from everyday life where each of us is aware of himself or herself through the course of different events and our responses to these events. In such circumstances we know our empirical "I" and construct from it an empirical self-identity. This phenomenal "I" is the object of experience, much like any other empirical object. But, unlike it, Kant places the transcendental "I" as the unifying framework of all representations. According to him, the "I" is the necessary condition for every cognitive action. As a transcendental "I," it is attributed with the role of a primary assumption; it needs to precede all experience and thus to appear as consciousness that enables every experience:

It must be possible for the "I think" to accompany all my representations; for otherwise something would be represented in me which could not be thought at all, and that is equivalent to saying that the representation would be impossible, or at least would be nothing to me. . . . This representation is an act of *spontaneity*, that is, it cannot be regarded as belonging to sensibility.

The transcendental "I think" is posited as a substratum for the categories' activity and the possibility of making judgements of understanding through which experience is turned into something we can perceive and understand. Representation is impossible without consciousness preceding it. In Kantian philosophy, there are no "orphaned" representations—representations are necessarily bound up to something that "carries" them, and this ownership necessitates the presence of a formal "I." In itself, it is not the object of intuition and cannot be known through the categories of understanding. It is not identified with a specific person and is in effect indifferent to personal discriminations. It is an a priori self-consciousness and its purpose is only to assign a basis for the unity of different representations under one consciousness; this is why it is called the unity of apperception. It has no empirical content and it exceeds every objective conceptual framework since it is the condition for its very existence. But—and this is an important Kantian qualification—the transcendental "I think" that accompanies all my representations must also appear as a phenomenal-empirical "I." Evidently, it is *not* an empirical representation; "on the contrary," adds Kant, "it is purely intellectual because it belongs to thought in general." But Kant hurriedly adds the qualification: "Without some empirical representation to supply the material for thought, the *actus*, 'I think,' would not, indeed, take place; but the empirical is only the condition of the application, or of the employment, of the pure intellectual faculty."

This "I" is a mere formality, since Kant was not interested in elaborating it or identifying its actuality except to note that we *necessarily* need to see it as accompanying all our representations. It is not his intention to claim that each one of my representations is *actually* accompanied by a thought that I can recognize as my own, but rather to argue for the existence of a necessary "I" that will allow me to see each of the mind's representations as *my* representations and to unite them as a synthesis of the manifold representations in one consciousness.[4]

The relationship between Kant's thinking "I" and the experienced world is very intricate, and herein lies its beauty. Because it is given to us through experience, Kant's experienced world is not conditioned by the thinking "I." Nevertheless, it is quite clear that this thinking self is not identical with any given content of experience, but—as mentioned above—is formally equivalent to every possible representation, while the relation between the representations is determined a priori by means of the categories. Hence, without that relation between the representations through the categories of understanding, the self-knowledge of "I" would be impossible. This "I think" is not, therefore, a phenomenon, but, concurrently, is not a thing-in-itself. Rather, it exists "as something which actually exists, and which in the proposition, 'I think,' is denoted as such." This is an "I" that turns only to itself—with a self-consciousness in which "I am conscious of myself, not as I appear to myself, nor as I am in myself, but only that I am." It comes then as no surprise that Kant characterizes this "I think" as "the simple, and in itself completely empty, representation 'I,'" and, he adds, "We cannot even say that this is a concept, but only that it is a bare consciousness which accompanies all concepts." Having said that, we know this "I" only by means of our thoughts, and it is impossible that we should know it any other way. In other words, I know myself as someone who is in possession of all these representations (and not as someone who knows himself "through" these representations or "by means" of these representations and is consequently distinct from them). It is impossible to know this self-consciousness as an abstraction, precisely because it is empty; this is why it can be known only through the mental operations in which it identifies itself with its thoughts. Kant envisaged thought as somehow perpetually encircling the "I":

> We can assign no other basis for this teaching than the simple, and in itself completely empty, representation "I"; and we cannot even say that this is a concept, but only that it is a bare consciousness which accompanies all concepts. Through this I or he or it (the thing) which thinks, nothing further is represented than a transcendental subject of the thoughts = X. It is known only through the thoughts which are its predicates, and of it, apart from them, we cannot have any concept whatsoever, *but can only revolve in a perpetual circle*, since any judgment upon it has always already made use of its representation. And the reason why this *inconvenience is inseparably bound up with it*, is that consciousness in

itself is not a representation distinguishing a particular object, but a form of representation in general, that is, of representation in so far as it is to be entitled knowledge. (My emphasis)

This "revolving in a perpetual circle" around the "I" (which is no more than an X—a structure of thought-predicates)—caused Kant to feel an "inconvenience." Like many other philosophers in the West, it seems that Kant too was averse to circularity. This is why he felt inconvenienced when facing a situation in which we cannot know the empty transcendental "I," except as an X around which we (with our thoughts) "can only revolve in a perpetual circle." Moreover, besides this gloomy revolving repetition, the "inconvenience" of going around and around in circles has another problem: the circumference, by definition, never nears the center around which it revolves. It is doomed to remain at a permanent inalterable distance from it. This is so because the transcendental "I" that is the central axis around which our thoughts revolve—despite its necessity and perhaps because of it—is unreachable in itself: "we cannot even say that this is a concept." How then shall we refer to the condition in which circular motion is inevitable? Forever prudent, Kant regarded this circling movement as an "inconvenience." Perhaps he should have been more assertive. Perhaps we should say it is "Kafkaesque"? "Necessity" turns out to be a strange conjunction of the vacuous with the concrete, and this combination leads us straight to Kafka's oeuvre.

The days are past when, in a philosophically oriented book, one needs to justify one's reference to Kafka. It is now commonly acclaimed that his writings are deeply rooted in modern philosophical thought, in Kant, Kierkegaard, and Pascal as well as in Greek philosophy. His affiliation with philosophy is borne out not only by its effect on him but also by his influence on the development of twentieth-century philosophy, specifically postmodernism and poststructuralism. Philosophers, historians of ideas, literary scholars, hermeneuts, phenomenologists—and even theologians—constantly refer to Kafka. In Adorno's witty description, Kafka's writings have served as "an information bureau of the human condition, be it eternal or modern." Apparently,

Adorno did not approve of much of what he read on Kafka. Indeed it seems impossible to say anything incisive about Kafka's writings; one interpretation glides into another, competing explanations chase each other, budding hypotheses are cut down as quickly as they surface, theories rise and fall—but Kafka's writings stand aloof, untouched, only reluctantly lending themselves to interpretation and frequently defying it. Kafkaesquely, most of these interpretations are defeated by the texts to which they refer. Kafka's readers are familiar with that bizarre state of affairs in which an interpretation seems utterly plausible and yet entirely inconceivable. Not only do readers find themselves in this unenviable situation; Kafka's literary creations do so too—Karl Rossmann, Gregor Samsa, Joseph K., K the land surveyor—each of whom, in a certain sense, represent more than merely themselves, yet none of them is capable of satisfactorily representing even themselves. The way that each character interprets his own life is, by way of necessity, only the expression of his frustration at not being able to come up with such an interpretation, or any other kind of interpretation for that matter. In *The Trial*, at the height of the debate between Joseph K. and the prison chaplain in the cathedral, while K. is trying to refute the interpretation offered by the chaplain for the Parable of the Law, the chaplain famously retorts: "Don't misunderstand me, I am only showing you the various opinions concerning that point. You must not pay too much attention to them. The scriptures are unalterable and the comments often enough merely express the commentator's despair."

It would seem that the very essence of Kafka's works, if there is such thing, lies in their ability to defeat a commentator. They are concerned with the quest for grace as much as forsaking it, in lamenting total destruction and yet yearning for it, in recognizing the inevitability of the modern condition and so, too, in ironically sneering at those who cannot find their way out of it. One should thus avoid succumbing to the enticing urge to generalize, the urge that all too often compels us to bestow upon Kafka's work a comprehensive explanation, as if the commentator were an omnipotent God that can, at will, marry content to form and weave it all into one faultless fabric.

Can one really abide by this worthy counsel? It is doubtful that a reader will resist interpreting, since, as one commentator has aptly noted, the only way to avoid interpreting Kafka is by not reading him.

There seems no way out of this hermeneutical trap and thus whatever will be said here about Kafka is bound to fall prey to it. Nevertheless, it is possible to lessen, if only partially, the severity of this trap if we think of our understanding of Kafka as merely a method of "reciting" the text—where certain topics are emphasized and certain structures are accentuated. Obviously, this recitation is still an interpretation that ultimately, according to Kafka, is doomed to failure.

Kafka's role as one of the most significant harbingers of modernism in the twentieth century is well attested. His preoccupation with selfhood—the boundaries of the subject and the limits of its epistemic horizon—is deeply embedded in a complex set of historical, cultural, philosophical and literary developments. From a philosophical point of view, it is possible to consider the journey of subjectivity in the West as a kind of race in which Descartes fires the starter's pistol and Kant, in charge of both the finishing line and the stopper, informs subjectivity where the track is and, at the same time, systematically and critically prevents it from traversing the only track on which such a race can take place. Kafka can be seen here as a worried, even skeptical, observer, reporting back to us on what he considers to be the grim consequences of this futile race from the outward to the inward. On the one hand, Descartes has made such a race unavoidable; on the other hand, Kant, with his compulsive need for order and structure, has shown that the race is in fact impossible. We may well ask why this is so. It seems that Kafka's tacit answer would point to the Kantian inevitability of the I-think as being "capable of accompanying all our representations" as that which makes the inevitable, at the same time, the impossible. As we have seen, Kant left the transcendental "I think" void of any content, alluding to a feeling of "inconvenience" that is "inseparably bound up with" our strange acquaintance of our innermost self. The transcendental, abstract "I" cannot be known, except through its concrete appearances. What for Kant was an "inconvenience" is for Kafka a conceptual as well as existential snare. The "I" always appears in one of its copious empirical manifestations. As such, its emptiness is irreversible.

For Kafka, the self's emptiness is an outrageous scandal. The thinking self is a precondition of all our representations, but since this thinking self is empty, representations cannot be sustained by experience. Rather, as they arise from this self, they tend to collapse right in front of our eyes—their creation becomes their demise. It would seem that Kafka sees this collapse as a conceptual disassembly manifesting itself in the malignant condition of a lack of synchronization between the multifarious empirical representations and their conceptual construction by the empty self. Like Nāgārjuna, whom we shall consider further on, Kafka shows that the formation of these conceptual constructs is a process in which language brings about its own doom by being persistently and increasingly preoccupied with the construction of concepts. This state of affairs dominates Kafka's writing. It comes to the fore in the vicissitudes of his literary characters as well as in the structure and style with which these events are recounted. The medium is not only the means whereby these events are described; it is, prior to anything else, a way of "performing" this linguistic failure. No wonder that Kafka's language is anything but linear. His sentences writhe around each other or else turn and twist around imperceptible axes. Either way, be it the characters themselves or their anonymous narrators, everyone ends up failing miserably; a character will set out to say whatever he has to say, only to immediately retract, then to uphold what he had said to begin with, only to have reservations about his very retraction. A lot happens, though no progress is made: it is a dialectics lacking an upward movement, that *Aufhebung* so characteristic of Hegelian dialectics. Some commentators claim that Kafka's language is at its core paradoxical. Other commentators perceive a more intricate view in which the logical is dressed up in psychological garb—and so, instead of paradox and contradiction, they see in Kafka undercurrents of hesitancy and ambivalence. But Maurice Blanchot—to my mind one of the most profound thinkers to have written about Kafka—rightly notes that these attributes will be of little use in trying to unravel Kafka's oeuvre since each of the above-mentioned expressions refers to a reality—albeit an elusive and fluid reality. And yet Kafka, so it seems, cannot commit himself to any picture of reality, however precarious and unstable it may be. If descriptions of reality are confounded by paradoxes, the same holds true of the paradoxical descriptions itself—they are no less paradoxical than their alleged subject matter. Paradox, vagueness, hesitation, and ambivalence are all entangled around each other in Kafka's literature. Consider a typical structure of a course of events narrated by Kafka: several alternatives present themselves and, ostensibly, a decision has to be made (that is, one option has to be chosen, thereby excluding all others). Making a choice seems possible, and indeed a choice is made: one option is reckoned as preferable to all others and, having been decided upon, it inevitably excludes its contradictory counterparts. But then it transpires that the option chosen, surprisingly, includes its contradictory alternative. Thus the very option that has just been eliminated is in effect chosen by virtue of its opposite having been chosen. In this manner the first alternative negates itself and becomes its opposite.

Some might think that this is sheer nonsense; anyone acquainted with and abiding to Aristotle's laws of thought knows that two contradictory statements cannot reside within one logical framework, and thus it may seem that Kafka, barring appearances, nevertheless creates paradoxes. Furthermore, in his eager pursuit of paradoxes, he finds them everywhere, even in everyday linguistic practices where they may hardly be detected. And yet, in my suggested reading, Kafka is not interested in paradoxes as such, but is concerned, rather, with the pragmatic inefficiency of ordinary language. Whereas paradoxes stem from the conjunction of two contradictory propositions, the Kafkaesque situation is such that even contradictions fail to materialize—every proposition, by being performed, somehow "entails" its contradiction. In saying one thing—its exact opposite is concurrently "performed." Again, the very act of choosing one possibility (which indeed excludes all other options) binds one to the opposite option: try imagining an attempt to sew together two pieces of cloth with a needle in whose eye there is a minute blade that unstitches whatever this needle sews together. Yet even this analogy is somewhat off the mark, since, in effect, the unstitching blade is not a part of the needle, but attached to the fingers of the hand clutching it. We end up with a sorry state of affairs where stitching is unstitching and unstitching is stitching, affirmation is negation, progress is retreat, and vice versa. The futility of language is not a semantic matter but rather inheres in its pragmatics—in the way language is put to use, which, like the above stitching, is always fruitless. Stated ontologically, the failure of language is unrelated to reality's linguistic elusiveness, i.e., that it lies beyond the reach of language. In this respect, Kafka's world is a far cry from the world of the biblical narrator recounting the story of the tower of Babel. For the latter, language's failure is the result of a yawning gap between the transcendent and the human, whereas, for Kafka, the failure of language is inherent to it. More specifically, it is caused by a lack of correspondence between the inward and the outward—or, as Kafka puts it, a lack of synchronization between the intentional process of knowing (in which consciousness refers to the outside world) and the innermost self that is supposed to generate it. In a diary entry dated January 16, 1922, Kafka refers to waking up (the perceiving of the outside world) and sleep (the inward self) as two clocks that are not in unison. The lack of synchronization between these two clocks is brought about by the fact that "the inner one runs crazily on" while "the outer one limps along at its usual speed." Inevitably, this lack of synchronization brings about tragic results: "What else can happen but that the two worlds split apart, and they do split apart, or at least clash in a fearful manner."

Claiming that Kafka's world is paradoxical is too simple an egress from the clutches of his modernistic nightmare. While it may be perfectly acceptable to conduct one's life without paying too much attention to problems of logical consistency, it is far more exasperating, as is the case with Kafka, to conceive the human condition as a vacuous singularity, the empty space right at the dead center, more or less like a mathematical zero.

Herein, perhaps, lies the horror that Kafka casts upon his readers and the true sense of that ubiquitous adjective *Kafkaesque*, which has managed to lodge itself so securely in contemporary idiom. This is unlike the more humdrum uses of this term, where it usually evokes a bureaucratic world that operates according to strict, unbending, and obstinate rules. Notwithstanding the ubiquity of these clichés, the Kafkaesque menace is not brought about by the world's arbitrariness but, on the contrary, by its richness and variety. It is a world that is "uncommonly manifold," and this "can be put to the test at any moment if one just takes up a handful of the World and looks at it a little more closely." But the many faces of its manifoldness and variability chase themselves around, forever failing in their attempt to exclude one another, and thus they continue to move about, crossing their respective paths, fusing into each other, only to break up again. One might want to say that it is this circular movement that gives rise to the Kafkaesque nightmare in which every possibility contains within itself the very obstacle that prevents its actualization.

One can mull at length over the manifold nature of the world in Kafka's oeuvre. Here, however, it will suffice to concentrate on one salient, yet complex, feature of Kafka's narrative, namely the abstruse interconnection between the malignant manifoldness of the world and the post-Kantian shadow of the presupposition of transcendence. As we have seen, Kant blurred this presupposition, leaving it as an empty horizon of our knowledge of the world. More specifically, he preserved relics of the presupposition of transcendence at the price of rendering it completely futile; Kafka, as I see him, follows suit. In his writings God is conspicuously absent, but every claim confirming His absence simultaneously proclaims His presence. The very attempt to dispose of the presupposition of transcendence seems to draw attention to its vacant existence. The demise of transcendence has been proclaimed no less voraciously in Kafka's world than in Nietzsche's. There is no need to expand on Nietzsche's tirelessly quoted allegory about the death of God in *The Gay Science*. Still, one should not forget that Nietzsche concerned himself both with the question of the presence of the *concept* of a transcendent God in Western culture and, no less, with the question of the character of the Judeo-Christian "personal" God. In his flowery style he urged his readers not only to overcome God but also to combat his shadow: "But when shall we ever be done with our caution and care? When will all these shadows of God cease to darken our minds? When will we complete our de-deification of nature?"

But while Nietzsche calls for the abolition of the shadow of transcendence from our cultural and conceptual groundwork, declaring the Kantian thing-in-itself to be empty, Kafka could not abide this optimistic wish. Longing for the "de-deification of nature" is no other than longing to be absolutely free of the presupposition of transcendence: if, formerly, man faced a living transcendence, now he has to struggle with a dead transcendence. But its demise does not eliminate its presence; on the contrary, it is present by virtue of its demise. Blanchot has eloquently expressed this: God's death does not enfeeble Him nor does it diminish His complete authority or His infallibility. In death He is more dreadful than in life, since, being dead, empty transcendence cannot be got rid of, cannot be abolished or denied. This vacuous transcendence has a marked appearance in many of Kafka's writings. The injunction to build the Great Wall of China (in a story bearing that name) comes from a dead emperor and the implementation of an exceptionally cruel sentence in his story "In the Penal Colony" derives its authority from a deceased commander. The most obvious example of this is, of course, the position allotted to "the Law" in *The Trial.* The judicial system that accuses Joseph K. and finds him guilty, is so transcendent that "you [are] condemned not only in innocence but also in ignorance"—so profound is the gulf separating it from man. The prison chaplain eloquently expresses this transcendence in that incisive proclamation with which he concludes his conversation with Joseph K. in the cathedral: "The Court wants nothing from you. It receives you when you come and it dismisses you when you go." But in the law books of that transcendent judicial system—"old dog's eared volumes, the cover of one was almost completely split down the middle, the two halves were held together by mere threads"—one finds a pornographic picture of a man and a woman, drawn crudely and unskilfully, the couple sitting rigidly upright, finding it difficult to turn toward each other; beside it there is also a sordid (sadistic?) novel entitled "How Grete was Plagued by her Husband Hans." Indeed, firm evidence for the world's manifoldness! In a world where transcendence wallows in vacuity, it is surely no surprise that it also gives rise to ridicule, mockery and the kind of mistaken identities that have given rise to many a farce.

One of the biblical stories in which Kafka sees such a farce of mistaken identity is the story of the '*aqedah* (Isaacs' binding). Kafka was familiar with Kierkegaard's *Fear and Trembling*, a book that deals, in the main, with the horrendous affair of Abraham being called to bind and sacrifice his son. Kierkegaard attempts to understand what lies behind God's command to sacrifice Isaac and also tries to understand the nature of Abraham as a sacrificer, that is, someone who has been ordered to do something that seems utterly preposterous. On different occasions Kafka made some pertinent observations about the character of Abraham as a sacrificer. Who is this Abraham who was ordered by God to sacrifice his one and only beloved son? This is a quintessentially Kierkegaardian dilemma, but not, let us note, a problem Kant, who showed no inclination whatsoever to delve into such questions of self-identity, would occupy himself with. Kant had a different axe to grind: who could have commanded Abraham to perform such an abominable crime? His response to this question not only drains God of his omnipotence but also rebuts the possibility of his existence. According to Kant, it will be recalled, God does not reside within the bounds of human experience. Thus, Kant can claim that even if God were to speak to this or that person, such a discourse would be quite pointless, since the person being spoken to could not know that it was God calling on him (as Kant puts it, "It is quite impossible for man to apprehend the infinite by his senses, distinguish it from sensible beings, and *recognize* it as such." Yet if, epistemically speaking, God's voice is empty, it must be, according to Kant, a morally repugnant voice. Being a morally autonomous self, man's relationship with God is typically asymmetrical. Or, more precisely, no symmetry can be detected between hearing the voice of God and responding to it. When a man hears a voice he cannot, in principle, be sure that it is indeed God, but he can categorically and emphatically reject what the voice is telling him, if it obliges him to act against his autonomous moral categorical imperative and perform an immoral deed. In cases such as these, it is man's supreme moral duty, despite the supposed sublimity of the revelation he experiences, to deem the voice illusory. In a footnote Kant makes the following remark:

> We can use, as an example, the myth of the sacrifice that Abraham was going to make by butchering and burning his only son at God's command (the poor child, without knowing it, even brought the wood for the fire). Abraham should have replied to this supposedly divine voice: "That I ought not to kill my good son is quite certain but that you, this apparition, are God—of that I am not certain, and never can he, not even if this voice rings down to me from (visible) heaven."

We can be quite sure that Kafka was not familiar with Kant's remarks on Abraham, but he certainly read Kierkegaard's ideas on the 'aqedah, and Kierkegaard himself was in all likelihood well aware of the Kantian moral stand in this matter. In fact, Kierkegaard was even ready to endorse the Kantian view according to which God's decrees may well be immoral. Yet he reaches a conclusion that is diametrically opposed to Kant. Moral repugnancy does not shake religious determination. On the contrary, Kierkegaard manages to extract from it the figure of a true believer, the "knight of faith" whose belief is by necessity absurd. Much has been written about the nature of Kierkegaard's religious believer, and there is no point in expanding on this. Returning to Kafka, however, it will be more suitable to position his view alongside Kant's skepticism rather than Kierkegaard's absurd. In fact, I prefer seeing him as endorsing the Kantian view on the '*aqedah*, even though he was not interested in the least in Kant's moral abstractions. I suggest seeing his remarks on Abraham's trial as the reflection of a post-Kantian, yet very personal, attitude toward Kierkegaard's idea of the absurd. Actually, when he reflects upon the Kierkegardian absurd one can hear him wavering: how can one express the absurd when any verbal expression brings about its opposite? How is the absurd possible in a world that is atrociously concrete, in which the plurality of possibilities is the only trace of necessity left over from the presupposition of transcendence? How is it possible to make a generalization when the moment one does so one is inevitably defying the very possibility of a meaningful generalization?

In short, the absurd is impossible. And so too is the sacrifice of Isaac. The absurd is splintering into a disconcerting plurality of appearances: the infinite possibilities and infinite modes of action bring about their own downfall: there are simply too many instances of it for it to actually happen. Thus, Kafka imagines many different Abrahams, none of whom bind their son and, worse still, Abrahams that do bind their son, but not quite now, a little later perhaps, say tomorrow morning, or perhaps even later. One of these Abrahams, for example, is as eager to sacrifice his son as an obsequious waiter to serve his customers, but right now there are so many domestic problems to attend to that he really cannot undertake the journey to Mount Moriah. Another Abraham—maybe a set of Abrahams—rush to the mountain immediately upon being instructed to do so, but unfortunately, none of these Abrahams has a son. This last alternative is so ludicrous it explains why Sarah laughed when she heard the transcendent annunciation about her bearing a son to Abraham. Even more ludicrous is the possibility of an Abraham that is willing to sacrifice his son and "who has the right feeling for the whole affair, but who cannot believe that he has been chosen, [this] repulsive old man and his dirty son." His hesitation makes the whole '*aqedah* seem quite improbable, since who will vouch that after his departure with his son to Mount Moriah he will not be transformed, en route, to Don Quixote? What could be worse than a sacrifice that is nothing but a mistaken-identify farce? Not only, says Kafka, "will the world laugh itself to death," Abraham might also even join in the laughter and "his greatest fear was that, if he were laughed at, he would look even older and even more repulsive, and his son even dirtier. An Abraham who comes unworthy of being really called!" Kafka imagines a prize-giving ceremony at the end of the school year in which the best pupil is eagerly waiting to receive his prize and then suddenly the worst pupil, mistakenly having thought that the teacher has called his name, rises from his dirty desk at the back of the room "whereupon the whole class roars with laughter." But maybe he was not mistaken—perhaps "his name was really called, it having been the teacher's intention to make the rewarding of the best student at the same time a punishment for the worst one."

This description of Abraham should draw our attention to the fact that it would be wrong simply to reduce Kafka's world to a means for pointing out the presence of an empty transcendence. Though Blanchot has managed to capture this terrifying presence marvellously, he did not mention its Kantian aspect. Let us not forget: the emptiness of transcendence is a direct outcome of the a priori structure of knowledge. Hence the 'aqedah is inconceivable. If only Abraham could actually sacrifice! If only the act of sacrifice would not annul itself. It is like a few unforgettable scenes from a Chaplin movie when something blocks the tramp from achieving one goal or another, but that something is the very act of trying to obtain it. This is perhaps the reason why Kafka chose to portray Abraham the patriarch in a Chaplinesque manner, as an "old-clothes dealer." Just imagine: Abraham, a perpetual wanderer, roaming about in endless circles, disappearing only so as to reappear, traveling with a sack on his back that forever spills it contents, never enabling him to hold his wares. If only Abraham could sacrifice! Then peace could be regained—through death or annihilation or that deep sleep so yearned for by Kafka at many critical points in his novels and stories. But these provinces are beyond our reach: sleep is never deep enough, it is never sleep in the real sense. Even death is not "death in the real sense":

> The cruelty of death lies in the fact that it brings the real sorrow of the end, but not the end.
> The lamentation around the deathbed is actually the lamentation over the fact that here no dying in the true sense has taken place. We must still content ourselves with this sort of dying, we are still playing the game.
> Our salvation is death, but not this one.

Neither is Abraham's wish to sacrifice his son an '*aqedah* in the real sense. Were it to happen "in the real sense," Abraham would finally pass through the gate of eternity. But how could he possibly cross the gate? Entering eternity necessitates a departure from the transient world and, unfortunately, it is impossible to synchronize between these two movements. You can either be on the way in or on the way out, but never both. Kafka describes this through the impossibility of Abraham drifting into eternity:

> The transient world is not adequate to Abraham's carefulness for the future, hence he decides to emigrate with it into eternity. But whether it is the gate on the way out or the gate on the way in that is too narrow, he cannot get the furniture wagon through. He puts the blame on the weakness of his voice uttering the commands. It is the agony of his life.

In this brilliant and succinct comic portrait, Kafka conveys the figure of an ancient vagabond transporting the world in his furniture wagon, a wagon that gets stuck either on the way out or on the way in. One of the two gates is too narrow, and, to confound things even more, we don't know, and never will, which gate it is. The incompatibility between the furniture wagon and the gate is, similarly, the incompatibility between the entrance and exit gate; it might be that they are one and the same gate, only that this vagabond wants to go out and come in simultaneously. An impossible mission, indeed—not to mention the furniture wagon, the "uncommonly manifold" world trailing along. Perhaps it would have been possible for the vagabond to execute this self-negating dual motion if only he did not have a wagon (in the same manner in which death could have been our salvation, if only it was death in the "real sense"); but this lies beyond the Kantian scope of comprehensibility. Within the realm of Kantian epistemology the Kafkaesque man heaves the world in his wagon, or on his back, or on the hard armor plate of a gigantic insect that one morning has taken the place of his back. Within this Kantian framework, it will never be possible to synchronize between the world and the self. On the contrary, the world's dependency on the self decrees that every struggle between the self and the world is doomed to fail.

How can Kafka's empty subject be characterized in a world where transcendence is present only as a vacuity? What possibilities are there for self-awareness where, to quote Blanchot, "from which faith but not the pursuit of faith is banished, hope but not the hope for hope, truth here and hereafter but not the need for an absolute truth."

What is the status of language, its role in knowing the world? In trying to deal with these questions, we should return to the Kantian notion of the knowing subject. This is a solitary subject, obsessively seeking the a priori sources of its knowledge of the world. But Kant knew very well that an "objective" worldview could be maintained only by forsaking the world's exteriority. For him, the concept of objectivity is situated not in the world, but in our mind. At the end of the day, there is something illusory in this idea of objectivity, even though it is a necessary illusion:

> The cause of this is that there are fundamental rules and maxims for the employment of our reason (subjectively regarded as a faculty of human knowledge), and that these have all the appearance of being objective principles. We therefore take the subjective necessity of a connection of our concepts, which is to the advantage of the understanding, for an objective necessity in the determination of things in themselves. This is an *illusion* which can no more be prevented than we can prevent the sea appearing higher at the horizon than at the shore.

Kant recognized transcendence as an idea of his inwardness (rather than attributing it to the external world)—by positing the thing-in-itself as something quite beyond our senses and understanding. Needless to say, the thing-in-itself lacks any content—it is no more than an a priori expression of our inwardness and its limitations. Accordingly, we will never be able to understand what is meant by the claim that a thing-in-itself has a specific content. Similarly, this inevitable misunderstanding pertains to the Kantian "I-think," who is nothing but its own self-existence. Let us recall: The "I-think" is "simple, and in itself completely empty representation 'I'; and we cannot even say that this is a concept, but only that it is a bare consciousness which accompanies all concepts." At the risk of wildly putting the cart before the horse, dare I say that this Kantian reflection has a distinctly "Kafkaesque" flavor to it? As is Kant, so is Kafka. Not only does Kafka undermine the presupposition of transcendence but he also ravages the foundations of the Cartesian subject, pushing the whole Kantian enterprise to the brink and leaving both the world and the self entangled in one another in a virulent state of paralytic indeterminacy. Earlier, we asked ourselves what likelihood there is for self-awareness in world such as this. Now, the answer seems unequivocal: none whatever. Self-knowledge is impossible within an indeterminate framework.

To demonstrate this, we turn to one of Kafka's short stories. Toward the end of the second chapter I drew attention to Kafka's enigmatic treatment of the tower of Babel that turned out, at closer inspection, not be a tower at all but a pit, not built upward but dug into the ground— the burrowing substituting for the construction that was supposed to burst into the heavens. In Kafka's last, unfinished, story, "The Burrow," a subterranean creature offers us an eloquent account, in the first person, of his burrow. This account, written as if by someone submitting an official report, concerns his burrow, which is not only his home but mostly a "castle keep" of security. He (or it?) describes in great detail the innumerable measures he has taken to protect himself against his enemies—whether camouflaging the entrance of his burrow or the construction of an inner castle keep at the burrow's dead center. Silence pervades the burrow; this supposedly enables this creature to attain a certain degree of equanimity. Unlike the "poor homeless wanderers in the roads and woods, creeping for warmth into a heap of leaves or a herd of their comrades delivered to all the perils of heaven and earth!" Our narrator peacefully occupies one of the fifty chambers of his burrow; he can choose whether to nap or to fall into a deep, unconscious sleep. Alas, the creature does not dwell in an Indian forest, but rather in a Kafkaesque world, and thus he knows all too well that the confidence that his burrow offers him can only be attained if one looks at it *from the outside*. For this reason he occasionally ventures out of his burrow to observe it from a hiding place close to the entrance. It is then, supposedly, that his sense of confidence turns into veritable certainty:

> The burrow has probably protected me in more ways than I thought or dared think while I was inside it. This fancy used to have such a hold over me that sometimes I have been seized by the childish desire never to return to the burrow again, but to settle down somewhere close to the entrance, to pass my life watching

the entrance, and gloat perpetually upon the reflection—and in that find my happiness—how steadfast a protection my burrow would be if I were inside it.

Thus this creature that constantly yearns for security wallows in his hiding place, next to the entrance, gazing at his burrow from the outside. This is supposed to grant him complete certainty—a complete sense of confidence and resilience that can counter any foreseeable calamity. It is difficult not to be impressed by the unique manner in which Kafka describes this state of affairs:

> I seek out a good hiding place and keep watch on the entrance of my house—this time from outside—for whole days and nights. Call it foolish if you like; it gives me infinite pleasure and reassures me. At such times it is as if I were not so much looking at my house as at myself sleeping, and had *the joy of being in a profound slumber and simultaneously of keeping vigilant guard over myself.*
>   (My emphasis)

Indeed, there is nothing more noble than this aspiration: to fall into deep sleep—to be completely immersed in one's own narcissism, one's own burrow, one's own inwardness, in a state of near senselessness, with boundaries blurred and barriers hazy—and all the while to be completely outside, to stand guard, to observe diligently the sleeping self. In Kafka's world, all this is of course impossible, it is no more than an illusion. Indeed, disillusionment duly arrives: "No, I do not watch over my own sleep, as I imagined; rather it is I who sleep, while the destroyer watches." Since it is imperative to be *outside* in order to look *inside*—it is bound to fail. Perhaps it is best to abandon the outside right away and return instantly to the inside. But this seemingly Ulyssesian return ends in a miserable failure. He hurriedly returns to his burrow, then fatigue induces sleep and later on the creature is woken up by a barely audible whistling noise. This continual murmur never relents; at times it gets louder while at others it is so soft that one might just believe that it is has disappeared, but then it reappears, getting closer, yet receding if one tries to approach it. The destroyer is perpetually awake. He is not necessarily the product of the outside. He might be inside the burrow—and not merely inside it, but in its innermost core, in a place that even the burrower cannot reach:

> And it is not only by external enemies that I am threatened. There are also enemies in the bowels of the earth. I have never seen them, but legend tells of them and I firmly believe in them. They are creatures of the inner earth; not even legend can describe them. Their very victims can scarcely have seen them; they come, you hear the scratching of their claws just under you in the ground, which is their element, and already you are lost. Here it is of no avail to console yourself with the thought that you are in your own house; for rather are you in theirs.

The intruder, the destroyer, the scratching power that even legends cannot describe is both inside and outside. It is more internal than the burrower even when he is in the depths of his lodging. But at the same time it is outside the burrow; its distinct whistling can be clearly heard beyond the walls. And perhaps not? The most threatening aspect of it all is that it has become impossible to distinguish between inside and outside. The last part of Kafka's story is dedicated to the burrower's destructive struggle against his burrow, driven by repeated attempts to find the source of that whistling.[5] This description is cut short—Kafka died before he had a chance to finish the story. But then again, maybe he did? The story ends thus: "But all remained unchanged." Maybe this indicates that after all the story has no end: that which was is what will be; the noise of the burrowing will follow the creature and might even ruin him for the simple reason that it happens in the present, as a whistling—and that is the cause of his ruin.

Empty transcendence has a compelling presence in the burrower's world. The murmur coming from outside the burrow is no more than an (actual? imaginary?) realization of what lies at the foundation of the burrow right from its inception. Remember that the burrow is an upside down tower of Babel. The urge to dig down is but another facet of the urge to break loose upward. Kafka's description of the painstaking thoroughness with which the creature digs his burrow is uncannily similar to a fragmentary description of how the workmen's city was built prior to the construction of the tower. And yet the two are not the same: the builders of the tower intended to reach the heavens, yet they failed to do so because of the weakness of its foundation (Kafka informs us of this in "The Great Wall of China"). The burrower digging the pit of Babel is supposedly concentrating on the foundations. The movement is not outward but rather inward, to the depths rather than to the horizon. Erecting the tower of Babel is supposed to be achieved at the end of a long and laborious process that is represented by a dual movement that moves simultaneously both upward and downward. The builder's failure is thus necessarily also the burrower's failure. This foundering is inevitable and the presence of the (actual? imaginary?) enemy beyond the walls changes nothing whatsoever. After all, it was there right from the beginning, as we know from the ancient legends handed down to us about these primeval and terrifying creatures. The route to exteriority is blocked, since in a post-Kantian world it is conditioned by a strong inward motion—only by means of a motion such as this can one discover exteriority. But it is a strange kind of exteriority, residing inside—and only inside. This ever present "inward exteriority" is empty, because no synchronization between the internal and the external is possible. A notable feature of this entanglement is the inevitable failure of representation, which is due, of course, to the failure in synchronizing between the internal and the external. Freud's notion of the unconscious might be one salient example of the failure of representation. His unconscious is not only unrepresented, but, moreover, unrepresentable. To return to Kafka's burrow, it is clear that interiority as such allows for no security since there is, in fact, no "interiority as such"—there are always the remnants of exteriority residing within it, draining the self of anything that might have allowed it to be in that deep sleep. Indeed, there is a vast difference between the Western burrower and the Indian Yājñavalkya whose "selfhood" found itself a dreamless sleep without a furniture wagon or an old clothes dealer's sack, in the form of a philosophical and religious heritage, dragged after anyone seeking self-knowledge and preventing him or her from making any real progress. It is not surprising that the legends and songs of the builders of the tower betray a "longing for a prophesized day when the city would be destroyed by five successive blows from a gigantic fist." Similarly, subterranean legends recount stories about creatures that reside inside bowels of the earth that "not even legend can describe," that scratch their claws just under you and ultimately bring about your utter destruction.

It is in this manner that the self gradually begins to recede from the West's cultural horizon. The idea of the "I" or the self as subjectivity was a distinctly modern approach that originated in Descartes' attempt to undermine the presupposition of transcendence (but, as we saw in chapter 3, he did not manage to disassociate completely himself from it). With Kant, subjectivity was pushed further afield and took up a key position in the possibility of human knowledge. In order to place subjectivity so centrally, Kant had to wilt the presupposition of transcendence. Yet undermining transcendence also brought about the complete disappearance of the self-as-subjectivity. The Copernican revolution was of no avail here; what benefits are there in recognizing oneself as a subjective self, if this mental recognition leaves behind it a trail of empty transcendence that demolishes the possibility of full self-knowledge, but not, alas, the yearning for it? Perhaps it might have been possible to subdue this vicious circularity if it were possible to be at one and the same time both outside—literally outside—and inside. This, in my mind, is the essence of Kafka's outlook on man and the world: "At such times it is as if I were not so much looking at my house as at myself sleeping, and had the joy of being in a profound slumber and simultaneously of keeping vigilant guard over myself." This aspiration—to enter into a profound slumber but at the same time to keep vigilant guard over it—is but a fallacy, a delusion, since evidently this creature knows that in fact he is merely sleeping, while his mysterious destroyer remains wide awake, keeping constant vigil over him. But this awareness is not capable of grinding this circularity to halt. This is the condition of being an "observer of the soul" mentioned at the very beginning of this chapter. Self-knowledge is supposed to be possible only if two conditions are simultaneously met with: the soul is observed from the outside and self-awareness exists from within. But this occurs only in as much as it is needed for a person to understand that it is, in principle, impossible: "The observer of the soul cannot penetrate into the soul, but doubtless there is a margin where he comes into contact with it." From that "contactless" contact, that touching of the "margins," one also learns that "the soul does not know itself," and there is little doubt that this lack of knowledge is brought about by the compulsion to gaze at it from without and from the fact that it cannot be done. This vicious circularity turns our inability to know the soul into a *necessary* condition ("Hence it must remain unknown"). To make things still worse, there is little comfort in this necessity: "That would be sad only if there were anything apart from the soul, but there is nothing else."

The unattainable goal—to fall into a deep slumber while at the same time to stay vigilant—is the gist of Nāgārjuna's proposal. In Nāgārjuna's philosophical milieu the quest for man's interiority and his limits is conducted without at the same time attributing the outward precedence over the inward. Nāgārjuna's Buddhist philosophy, and that of his disciples too, much like Upaniṣadic thought, expresses itself through absolute immanence; an immanence that is in no way circumscribed by the assumption of a delimiting exteriority. Yet, unlike Upaniṣadic thought, Nāgārjuna's philosophy does not reach its goal the moment the self recognizes its selfhood, but, contrarily, by realizing the emptiness of the knowing ātman.

It will be recalled that Upaniṣadic thought maintained that the inner depths of human interiority generate the "self" as a subject who is, in turn, the creator of external reality. Buddhism rejected the self's role as expounded in Upaniṣadic thought. This defiance was evident in, among other things, the way in which the Buddha's awakening was conceived: as a "seeing-of-things-as-they-really-are" (yathābhū-ta-darśanam), as a perception of reality as it is. This true perception contains within it a tacit, yet piercing, critique of our basic linguistic practices, concentrating mostly on concepts such as permanence and self—permanence as a foundational term in which we contain the will to unify the world and self as a foundational term under which we contain the will to unify perception and experience. In this respect the Buddha is to be seen as a genuine innovator. His critique is aimed primarily at the Upaniṣadic understanding of the world, even though, like Upaniṣadic thought, Buddhism also sprang from the renouncer tradition. Moreover, like the Upaniṣadic renouncer, the Buddhist monk too constructed his individualism through his relinquishment of culture. Furthermore, both Upaniṣadic thought and Buddhism denounced the prevalent ritualism that was characteristic of the beginnings of ancient Indian civilization (and from a social standpoint, Buddhism's denunciation was more pungent and its conclusions were more radical than those of the Upaniṣads). But let there be no doubt: Buddhism rejected the Upaniṣadic worldview and chiefly the Upaniṣadic renouncers' prevailing understanding of selfhood. As we have seen in Nāgārjuna's dedication quoted above, he claimed that the Buddha's teaching was epitomized by the idea of "dependent arising" (pratītya-samutpāda) (in this Nāgārjuna follows Buddhist tradition). "Dependent arising" can be seen as the inability to base reality on well-defined, permanent foundations, and accordingly the only thing that can be said to be true of reality is that it is in constant flux, impermanent, momentary, perpetually and rapidly changing from one moment to another. This is aptly captured by the oft-quoted formulaic epigram common to most forms of early Buddhism: "When this exists, that comes to be; with the arising of this, that arises. When this does not exist, that does not come to be; with the cessation of this, that ceases." The circular and somewhat peculiar characterization of dependent arising of this formula is quite intentional. According to the Buddha, this is a character of events in the external world. This world defies a simple linear description; and so it is inaccessible to linear description in which events are presented in a teleological manner. According to the Buddhist worldview, nothing contained within the bounds of the phenomenal, empirical world (be it objective or subjective) exists in its own right, in itself. Rather, every occurrence is dynamic, that is to say, it arises from the activity of minute particles that are constantly in flux. Dependent arising is the character of something that occurs in a conditioned world or a world where everything is mutually dependent upon everything else.

There have been, and there are, many different attempts to elucidate this radical Buddhist position that seems to defy some of the most basic intuitions we have about how to conduct our daily lives, i.e., our regular, customary understanding of reality that treats objects as permanent and our inclination to acknowledge the presence of a knowing "self" underlying all our perceptions, a "self" that we endow with a consistent, continuous, and perhaps even everlasting, identity.[6] Among Buddhologists, there is profuse disagreement not only about the philosophical import of the Buddha's pronouncements but also whether he actually made them. There are bitter arguments about what the Buddha actually said, and then, given how one resolves this question, what it ultimately means. Thus, for example, one line of interpretation claims that the Buddha had no interest whatsoever in making any philosophical claims and that on more than one occasion he expressed his disgust and repugnance at the fruitlessness of philosophical speculation as such.[7] An alternative line admits that Buddha's positions are philosophically potent, but insinuates that his philosophical goals were mostly of an antimetaphysical nature disclosing his inclination to uproot general, dogmatic. and unsubstantiated metaphysical pronouncements on personal identity and the nature of external reality. According to this interpretation, the Buddha's rejection of selfhood and of permanence is not a total negation of the meaning of these terms, but only a partial or limited rejection concentrating mainly on a few misuses of these terms, namely, the metaphysical. Scholars who support this interpretation would suggest that claims surrounding the annihilation of permanence and the demise of selfhood in the Buddha's teaching are premature and too hastily drawn. In truth, his philosophical position merely sought to supplant abstract dogmatism with empirical sensations and unsubstantiated generalizations with common sense judgments; thus the Buddha did not doubt the actual meaning of the concept of the self, only repudiated the unbridled metaphysical applications conducted in its name. The same holds true for permanence: the Buddha did not deny the place of objects in external reality as they appear by means of mental cognition, he only denied the unrestrained generalization that made these objects out to be substantive universals.

This chapter suggests a third line of interpretation, repudiating the former two. Not only do I want to endorse the idea that what we have in the Buddha's teaching is a philosophical viewpoint that explicitly tries to expunge metaphysical generalizations and dogmatic worldviews, but this antimetaphysical philosophy is an attempt as well to scrutinize critically the very legitimacy of the different uses people make of the concepts of permanence and selfhood, and that this critical inspection is focused on the everyday, common, regular uses of concepts—those that supposedly docilely follow the dictates of common sense. In short, the Buddha's philosophy not only tries to target metaphysical propositions but is an antiessentialist standpoint that attempts to expose the spurious philosophical status of some of the most basic intuitions that we have about the world and about our selves, and, moreover, the conceptual framework that is constructed around these erroneous intuitions. In the different sayings attributed to the

Buddha, in the sermons ascribed to him and in the dialogues associated with his name—in all these the Buddha casts doubt on the adequacy of concepts such as permanence and self. He supplies many examples that demonstrate that these concepts are void of any reference, i.e., they relate to nothing in particular;[8] rather, they are mental constructions per se. For the Buddha, general terms, claims, and arguments are fictitious (including the present claim, of course). Accordingly, the unity of our perceptions and the unity of the knowing self are none other than the outcome of mental activity, that, like a film projector, casts the unity of objects and the unity of the self that recognizes them upon our mental screen. In effect, repudiating the general meaning of the concept of permanence as a characteristic mark of reality and the concept of self as a characteristic mark of the knowing agent arises directly from a broader intellectual outlook that tries to comprehend reality and human nature without assuming the presence of a substratum, a source, a support, or anything else that cannot be empirically ascertained. In this sense, it is erroneous to think of the world as something permanently endowed with well-defined attributes and to regard the self as having its foundation in a static and enduring mental core. (These errors have, according to the Buddha, very hazardous psychological and religious repercussions, but we shall not consider these here). The Buddha, as I understand his philosophical message, tried to demonstrate the futility of the very distinction between internal and external, subject and object—since this distinction itself is no more than a mental construction. And if you ask: do specific personal experiences have objective correlates? Buddhism will answer in the affirmative: subjectivity necessitates objectivity. Yet, from this it does not follow that the distinction between subjective and objective has any ontological status. Nor is objectivity identical to something real out there, independent of the minds perceiving it. The call for objectivity, and actually the yearning for it, is a mental state that arises from mental impulses that are not necessarily under the control of the will or of thought. These impulses bring about the creation of permanent mental constructs (conceptual categories) and their outward projection—it is thus that a picture of external reality is formed in our imagination. The ensuing picture is obviously a distortion since its actual existence arises from human interiority. According to the Buddha, the attempt to convey such an external world, be it in metaphysical abstractions or, more complacently, in common sense terms, is but an expression of the mental structures that give rise to our perception of "exteriority" or "selfhood" as enduring essences. As later Buddhist philosophers see it, the very polarity between an inner "self" and an external "world" constitutes part of our mental makeup.

This is not the place to debate which of the three interpretational approaches mentioned above is the most fitting representation of the Buddha's teaching. I shall refrain from taking part in this Buddhological and philosophical discussion by dealing not with an attempt to uncover the Buddha's "original" teaching—whatever that may be—but rather by dealing with its eventual philosophical explications in the works of one of the most prominent of all Buddhist philosophers. It would be difficult to object that Nāgārjuna's outlook only has therapeutic merit and that it lacks any philosophical standing, as claimed by the first line of interpretation about the Buddha's teaching. Unlike the Buddha's narrative, Nāgārjuna's rhetoric is distinctly and overtly philosophical— at least in one sense: his claims are put forward by means of carefully articulated *arguments* and, concurrently, his criticism of his opponents' views is conducted according to a strict logical procedure. Moreover, the philosophical nature of Nāgārjuna's works cannot be reduced to the repudiation of metaphysical speculations in the manner advocated by the second interpretational approach to the Buddha's teaching. It would seem that Nāgārjuna's philosophical outlook goes further and tries to critically examine the foundational core of our mental activity when applied both to our understanding of the world and ourselves.[9]

Nāgārjuna is considered the founder and most prominent figure of the Madhyamaka ["Middling"] school. In my mind, he is as profound as he is thorough, making him one of the most fascinating philosophers India has known. Most scholars place him around the middle of the second century CE, though a few have suggested that he may have been active even a hundred years prior to this date. As its name testifies, the Madhyamaka school is an attempt to follow the middle path. But this middle is a very extreme middle.

The extremeness of Nāgārjuna's philosophy becomes immediately apparent the moment one examines the key concept underlying his whole viewpoint. This concept is abundant in Buddhist literature and, with the expansion of Buddhism to major areas of East Asia, it took on a plethora of different meanings and variegated uses. The concept

I have in mind is *śūnya*. In the past this term was sometimes translated as "nothingness," but this is a misleading and erroneous translation. It wasn't Nāgārjuna's intention to find a way of articulating a certain kind of lack or absence, nor was he trying to describe the metaphysical condition of nothingness, or even trying to express in words the mystical experience of turning from being to nonbeing. A more appropriate translation of *śūnya* is "emptiness" or "voidness," keeping in mind the mathematical zero—that absolute middle point lying in between positive and negative integers. The Buddha himself articulated his experience of awakening in terms of a middle way. During the centuries preceding Nāgārjuna there were many different spiritual outlooks in Indian Buddhism, and they all were genuinely interested in understanding the nature of the term *śūnya*, which lay at the heart of the Buddhist path to enlightenment. It was deemed that *śūnya* could be realized through intense meditative practices in which perceived reality was broken down to its core elements. There is little doubt that Nāgārjuna was familiar with his predecessors' views, yet he sought to uncover the Buddha's original designation of the term. The Buddha said that emptiness is the opposite of all opinions and points of view (*dṛṣṭi*). The expression *point of view* is the Indian designation for an intellectual standpoint, a philosophical system or "academic" school. Nāgārjuna vehemently rejected the idea that emptiness was a theory or theoretical point of view saying that: "emptiness is the relinquishing of all views. For whomever emptiness is a view—that one will accomplish nothing."

How then did Nāgārjuna understand emptiness? Behind this question there lies a great conceit, since trying to unravel Nāgārjuna's exact use of this term is nothing short of a complete exposition of his philosophy, but—and here such conceit might verge on the ridiculous—a complete exposition of Nāgārjuna philosophy is just as elusive as seeking a definitive interpretation of Kafka. Nāgārjuna is an enigmatic philosopher whose work has never shunned controversy. His seemingly indecipherable texts have given rise to a mass of different and opposing philosophical interpretations. It would seem that Erich Heller's claim that the only way to avoid interpreting Kafka's *The Trial* is by not reading it applies equally to Nāgārjuna's major works. Indeed, how can one "interpret the doctrine" of a philosopher who has been described by different commentators in, among others, the following terms: a great philosopher, a worthless philosopher, a skeptic, a pragmatist, an antirealist, a nihilistic antiphilosopher embracing no views, a metaphysician advocating absolutism, a mystic attempting to attain salvation by means of self-annihilation, an intrepid critic on any kind of essentialism, Wittgenstein's precursor, the founder of Indian deconstructionism? And to confound things even more, it would seem to me that the majority of these claims (barring two) are indeed applicable to Nāgārjuna, in one way or another. It is too voluminous a task to draw a detailed map, outlining all the many routes, pathways, and sidetracks of his complex. Instead, I shall mostly concentrate on Nāgārjuna's notion of emptiness as an expression of an essentially radical position on the nature of subjectivity, the limits of knowledge and the nature of reality.

Nāgārjuna was well acquainted with the Buddhist philosophical doctrines of his time. On the whole, these doctrines tried to induce a subtle form of ontology into Buddhism. One of these, for example, not coincidentally called the Sarvāstivāda ("the doctrine that all exists"), regarded reality as made up of basic "atoms," certain minute particles called *dharmas*, some of which were endowed with self-existence, namely, existing by their own nature and of their own accord. The term *self-existence* or *self-being* is a quite literal translation of the Sanskrit term *svabhāva*," but, as Siderits rightly points out, "it is increasingly recognized that it should instead be rendered as 'intrinsic nature' or 'intrinsic essence.'" Nāgārjuna himself, when he examines the meaning of this term, is responding to two widespread definitions that appear in Sarvāstivāda texts: "that which is not constructed" (i.e., has no components and is neither created nor devised as part of the fabric of human conventions)[10] and "that which is not conditioned by anything else." According to the Sarvāstivāda, sensible objects are but a complex manifestation of simple primary particles. That is to say, our mind, in a normal state of affairs, perceives a compound of minute elements that are inaccessible in themselves to our regular modes of cognition. These form the elementary building blocks from which reality is constructed; elementary dharmas are irreducible and moreover cannot be analyzed through any other element. As mentioned before, they are endowed with *intrinsic nature*, that is to say, each and every particle exists of its own accord, totally independent of all other particles.

Nāgārjuna repudiates this concept of *svabhāva*. With logical flair and argumentative fervor he attacks the very possibility that at the foundation of phenomena there is any kind of essence whatsoever, even the most minuscule or momentary. Obviously, this constitutes a complete rejection of an ontology that seeks to affirm the existence of self-reliant substance or substances, entirely independent of the mind that perceives them.[11] Among Nāgārjuna's commentators, there are those who saw him as concentrating only, or mainly, on an attempt to uproot ontology from Buddhism. This is wrong, in my opinion, and distorts his views, mostly since Nāgārjuna was not interested in ontology as such—he had a much more ambitious and daring agenda. Though it is obvious that he strongly objected to any kind of ontological stance and saw emptiness as a kind of negation of substance. Still, a more careful assessment of the major thrust of his philosophy will reveal that this antiontologism is merely one stage in a much more fundamental inquiry. At the core of this process stands an analysis of linguistic concepts. He saw this repudiation of all ontological assumptions merely as part of a much more thorough, critical, and radical philosophical enterprise whose goal was to undermine completely the representational status of human language.

Hence, the main thrust of Nāgārjuna's philosophy is the radical nature of his conceptual analysis. He extracts one concept after another from the building blocks of the Indian philosophical schools known to him and assesses these concepts, trying to see if they actually relate to something real. His conclusion, in each and every instance, is negative. Hence Nāgārjuna, as mentioned before, is not concerned in setting up a negative ontology, but rather in using this negation as an instrumental part of a complex process meant to criticize devastatingly our linguistic misconceptions and thus to point to the emptiness of the language employed when referring to extralinguistic reality. For the Buddha, direct contact with external reality occurs when a sense organ makes contact with its object (i.e., that which appears before us while making contact). One early Buddhist text tells us of the following incident: during a brief meeting with his disciples the Buddha made a philosophical pronouncement, but it was so terse that his disciples were left in utter perplexity. Since the Buddha retreated to the forest, they decided to seek a comprehensive explanation from one of the most senior disciples, a monk by the name of Mahākaccāna who was frequently extolled by the Buddha and considered by him an exceptional expositor of his most complex teachings. Mahākaccāna did in fact systematically elucidate the Buddha's cryptic words: a man *perceives* that which he senses, only then does he *understand* that which he has perceived; next, he *conceives* in words that which he has understood. But even Mahākaccāna, the great expositor, did not explicitly touch upon the role of language. Only later on was language made the subject of direct investigation, this by the Sarvāstivāda, for whom linguistic reference was contextual, though they did not reject its phenomenal status. By comparison, Nāgārjuna declared that any kind of linguistic utterance was empty—not only metaphysically speaking but also phenomenally. His objection to the Sarvāstivāda's viewpoint was, in the main, an objection to the assumption of a substratum that enables the existence of linguistic references. That is to say, Nāgārjuna did not repudiate trust in things, but, rather, trust in words.

In this respect, a Western gaze at the Madhyamaka easily identifies what a Western philosopher will consider as something uniquely modern, that is, a great concern with the role of language and with the referential status of sentences that relate to extralinguistic reality.[12] One example of the kind of linguistic usage that Nāgārjuna criticizes is the term *ātman*—the Upaniṣadic notion of "selfhood" we met with in the previous chapter. In exploring the underlying assumptions of the ātman as a substance that generates the self's knowing activity, Nāgārjuna asks us to consider what might the exact meaning of this *self* be. He considers two possible replies: either the self is identical to its psychophysical constituents, or else it is not identical to them (possibly because there is something in it that is more than the sum of its parts). Either way, the concept fails to live up to the expectations we have of it, namely, to relate to a well-defined entity or to pinpoint a unique and exclusive form of mental existence (to put it, somewhat ironically, in Cartesian terms, one could say that for Nāgārjuna the concept of self is neither clear nor distinct). When Nāgārjuna mentions the psychophysical components that form the concept of ātman, he is responding to a ubiquitous psychological classification prevalent in Buddhism from its inception. According to this psychological classification, a sentient being is seen as composed of five aggregates or heaps of psychological and physical conditions: form (or body), feeling, recognition, volitional formations, and basic consciousness. This classification has little philosophical import and it merely indicates an attempt to supply an explanatory framework meant to cover the totality of Buddhist phenomenology, to be put at the disposal of a Buddhist practitioner whilst meditating. If the "self" was identical to these aggregates, which comprise the totality of psychophysical events, then it would have to be described only in terms that are applicable to each of the aggregates. In the aggregate of "form" one cannot find self-awareness and thus the concept of "selfhood" cannot refer to it. Hence, it must relate to one of the four "mental" aggregates, or to part of them, or to all of them. But this is bound to end up in failure, since each of these aggregates refers to states of mind that are forever changing. At any one given moment: one feels, one recognizes, one experiences volitional formations, and immediate self-awareness is present. All these vanish when the given moment elapses. Another moment arises, and with it a different combination of these aggregates. It is impossible to stabilize or to fix permanently the sum total of all these mental events beyond any discrete given moment. But these moments offer endless possibilities and thus if the ātman, as a selfhood, is identical with these momentary aggregates, then it would be an ātman constantly changing its nature by virtue of the frequent alterations that occur to the aggregates. Instead of a unique Upaniṣadic "self" that recognizes itself in a primary act of self-awareness, and rather than ātman as the ultimate source of light that gives rise to external reality while still residing in that metaphorical dream (or else establishing its selfhood in a temporal singularity while occupying the metaphorical world of deep sleep)—we now have a flickering "self," appearing and disappearing right after its appearance, only to reappear at some different "place" (since it now appears in a different formation of aggregates), again, only to flicker rapidly and disappear, so as to reappear and so on and so forth. It is difficult to organize this psychological picture into an enduring linguistic concept with distinct boundaries and a well-defined meaning.[13]

We are thus left with the second alternative: the ātmanic self is not identical with the aggregates. The reason for this dissimilarity is that, in all likelihood, "selfhood" is more than the sum of its psychophysical constituents. But this alternative makes us none the wiser. Here we encounter an evasive, even somewhat mysterious, self that is by necessity divorced from experience and from how we know ourselves. Needless to say, Nāgārjuna rejects this metaphysical possibility offhand: it is unfounded and unintelligible.

The philosophical attempt to clarify the referential role of the concept of self reaches a dead end. Applying this concept to the totality of our psychophysical experiences makes it infinitesimal and hence dysfunctional. Alternately, if we think of the self as relating to more than the sum of our psychophysical experiences, it will expand to such an extent that it again fails to function properly. Thus, the concept of self has no definite reference since, upon analyzing it, it either shrinks or expands in excess. We are thus incapable of relating this concept to anything, and it is thus reduced to an empty concept.[14] According to Nāgārjuna, this voidance of the concept of self entails the voidance of the idea of mine and so too of every other concept that is characterized as a predicate of that "I" or empty "self."

Nāgārjuna's argument demonstrating the self's emptiness is but one in a long series of arguments that critically examine philosophical concepts in such a way that they emerge as void of any extralinguistic reference. Causality, time, motion, substance, essence—these concepts and others like them are all subject to an insidious critical examination at the end of which they all turn out to be empty. Claiming that a concept is empty is not intended to prevent us from seeing it as an external, existential thing. Instead, this claim dispels the assumption that words can correspond to an extralinguistic reality. In Nāgārjuna's writing there are ample examples of him demonstrating the voidness of concepts. In the present context it will suffice to offer one more example. Nāgārjuna critically examines ocular vision and sees it as an event in which "someone" sees "something." Can there be a conceptual discrimination between "seer" and "that which is being seen"? Can we separate the observer from the object that he or she is observing? Superficially speaking, the answer is affirmative: this is, after all, how language functions. Nāgārjuna does not take issue with linguistics, although he seriously doubts whether linguistic practices justify the distinction between subject and object and our reliance on there being an independent "exteriority" out there. How is it in fact possible to distinguish between the process of vision as a sensory activity and the existence of the seer? Or consider the following dilemma: is it possible to separate the seer from his vision? Obviously not, since such a separation, if it were possible, would prevent us from referring to the subject as "seer" (if he has no sight, how can he be called seer?). On the other hand, how is it possible not to separate between the seer and whatever he sees? Is this not what resides underneath every attempt to speak of a seer? Thus, we find ourselves in a very bizarre situation: the observing agent, at one and the same time, *has* to be dependent upon his act of observing, but *cannot* be dependent upon it. Needless to say, Nāgārjuna is not trying to understand the actual visual process, but rather to supply us with a critical analysis of the linguistic possibilities needed to describe satisfactorily and distinguish this process and its interrelations. This criticism does not bring about the collapse of our visual faculties, nor is it a blatant denial of the possibility of an ultimate ontology. Rather, it manifests our ability to talk about it, that is, language's ability to relate to any kind of activity as something that exists independently of it.

The kind of argumentation that seems to be, prima facie, similar to Nāgārjuna's argumentative ploy has been frequently referred to in the West as reductio ad absurdum: the procedure in which one tries to prove to one's opponent that the premises of her argument are inconceivable because the conclusion drawn from them is false or patently absurd. In this manner an opponent is pushed to the extremity of her position and shown that from this vantage point her doctrine is groundless. With hindsight, it would seem that Nāgārjuna both endorsed this kind of argumentation and made extensive use of it: he offered his opponents all logical alternatives encompassing each possible alternative and then proceeded to demolish them one by one. The inevitable outcome of this kind of reasoning is the inability to endorse successfully any one exclusive conclusion. The opponent is left in a sort of equilibrium that, of course, is devastating for philosophy, since there is no way to decide between opposing views and, accordingly, any hopes there might have been of obtaining any knowledge are irrevocably crushed. Affirmation and negation are balanced out at a zero point of intellectual indetermination. But it is crucial, in my mind, to emphasize an important difference between the more general procedure of reductio ad absurdum and the specific use Nāgārjuna makes of it in his assaults on language. Whoever uses a reductio ad absurdum argument is trying to force his opponent through a forest of obstacles at the end of which lies an abyss of meaninglessness. The whole point of the argument is to show the opponent that, having adopted these premises and this line of reasoning, he will inevitably find himself rolling down this abyss. On the other hand, Nāgārjuna wants to use this argument for a completely different purpose: he is primarily trying to demonstrate the complete emptiness of our conceptual scheme and accordingly to point to the emptiness of the reality these concepts refer to. Yet here he is confronted by a serious linguistic difficulty; how can he argue, by means of language, that our linguistic conceptual scheme is empty? Is this not another instance of oversophistication that ultimately brings about self-defeat, since in trying to denounce language he has in fact found himself endorsing it by using it? I am reminded here of that caterpillar-philosopher who, sitting on his mushroom and smoking his hookah, demanded of Alice that she define in clear and distinct terms, once and for all, who she was. Alice finds it somewhat difficult to comply with this request since she is forever changing. She attempts to explain to the aggressive caterpillar just how empty her "self" is here in Wonderland. "I can't explain myself, I'm afraid, sir," she says, "because I'm not myself, you see." Then, all of a sudden, this astute Anglo-Saxon philosopher cuts her short and, showing his great philosophical acumen, says: "You! Who are you?" What would Nāgārjuna have replied to this inquisitive caterpillar? What would he have replied to someone asking: who is this Nāgārjuna that proclaims, by means of language and its concepts, that concepts are empty? If the self is an empty concept, then all the more is a personal name like *Nāgārjuna* empty, itself nothing but an empty concept, void of meaning. It follows that whoever makes any claims about the nature of emptiness—he himself is empty. Thus, if the claim regarding the emptiness of all concepts is meaningful, then the caterpillar may be right after all, and is, in fact, not an Anglo-Saxon philosopher, but rather a French one, and it is just possible to hear him repeating Descartes: "let him deceive me as much as he can, he will never bring it about that I am nothing so long as I think that I am something" or, slightly altered, "let him deplete me as much as he can, he will never bring it about that my concepts will be nothing so long as I use them for my depletion."

Nāgārjuna is well aware of this linguistic predicament and thus constructs his reductio ad absurdum not as an argument that is supposed to push an opponent in the direction of abysmal meaninglessness, but rather as a pragmatic program that draws him back to that point of departure from whence he began to develop his concepts, showing him that the moment he took his very first conceptual step he had already set upon the path of meaninglessness. This is an interesting case of philosophical "flashback"—a return to the beginning, to that imaginary point of departure where the philosopher took his first fateful and rash decision—to embark on an intellectual journey: to move, to progress, even if only slightly, in order to bring to light those concealed truths hidden beyond the deep, to draw out the universal from the particular, to vindicate the grip abstractions have on the diversity of tangible appearances. When Nāgārjuna, by means of the reductio ad absurdum, draws attention to the inevitable failure of the philosopher's journey, his intention is, in fact, to show that the journey was doomed right from the start. What may seem like a failure that occurred en route is, in reality, the deluded idea that the journey itself was possible. Here one can't help recalling Kafka's remark that "there is a goal, but no way; what we call a way is hesitation."

In other words, demonstrating the emptiness of the concept of the self, and of the other concepts too, is *not* itself a claim, even though it would initially seem to be using language in a declarative sense. As a matter of fact, language is employed here not as a set of predicating sentences but as a performance: the use of language is not assertive but performative; it is as if language were a sort of signpost preventing the philosopher from setting out on his perilous journey by warning him that each conceptual analysis he or she is going to make will only divulge the emptiness of the very concept whose meaning he or she is trying to uncover. This is how I understand Nāgārjuna's intention in bringing forward the seemingly puzzling reaction to his aggressive opponents' accusation that he is contradicting himself: "If I would make any proposition whatever, then by that I would have a logical error; but I do not make a proposition; therefore I am not in error." In this seemingly audacious assertion, Nāgārjuna establishes the fact that he himself does not subscribe to any philosophical doctrine whatsoever, not even the doctrine of emptiness. It is as if he can see through any philosophy, revealing its defects with X-ray eyes, but in doing so forms no allegiance with a philosophical doctrine, including his own antiphilosophical arguments. He himself does not argue, he merely mirrors. As I have already said, in this sense emptiness is no more than an admonition placed as a signpost at the starting line of the philosophical path warning us: Beware! Do not commence this journey, since what seems like a path is not a path; this philosophical path (as much as any other philosophical path) does not exist—it is empty, and so those traversing it are destined to fall into an abyss. A courageous philosopher might rise up and say: since the signpost alerting us to emptiness is itself empty, why need I pay heed to its warning? However, such reaction will not betray great wisdom; it will only reveal a sorrowful myopia, an inability to distinguish properly between claims that try to assert something as opposed to preventive performatives, like those of Nāgārjuna. Nāgārjuna himself clearly emphasizes the preventive-performative function of his claims, likening them to the action of an imaginary person preventing someone from doing something. An imaginary woman, for example, is coveted by man who mistakenly thinks that she is a flesh-and-blood woman. Then a doctor arrives and draws the man's attention to his error, to the fact the he should not have set out on his lustful path in the first place since the object of his desire is but a product of his imagination. Dispensing a course of preventive therapy, the doctor successfully cures the deluded man; he prevents the desperate lover from erring, revealing the illusory nature of the woman he covets. At this point Nāgārjuna surprises us: the doctor preventing the illusion is himself illusory—he too is imagined. Would this illusory doctor fail to cure this man just because he himself is a fictitious character? Since he employs only preventive measures, Nāgārjuna is willing to assess it pragmatically, judging it only according to its therapeutic efficiency without taking into consideration in any way the doctor's ontological status. Nāgārjuna thus decrees that so long as he has only a preventive role, notwithstanding his linguistic activity, he lacks a firm conceptual grounding, so there is nothing to make this therapeutic intervention inefficacious. Likewise, this is how Nāgārjuna sees himself; the use he makes of language is analogical to a kind of admonition: "Danger! Beware!" At this point I cannot resist the temptation to make a slightly facetious comparison between Nāgārjuna's illusory doctor and Descartes' malicious demon. Both these fictional "characters" make their entry at a climactic moment, when skeptical analysis reaches its peak; they both slice through their respective objects of investigation with the sharpest of all scalpels and both willingly bear the consequences arising from this delicate procedure. The malicious demon and the preventing doctor both "perform." The demon's deception, it will be recalled, gives rise to the thinking self; that cogitating subject that knows with certainty it exists since it can be deceived. Nāgārjuna's illusory doctor precludes the formation of a self and thus brings about its downfall, and this he does, to put it figuratively, while pointing to the vicious circularity of fiction. For Descartes, it is the last fiction, whereas, for Nāgārjuna, fiction curls itself around like a coiling serpent choking any possibility of certainty, not to mention truth; this is so since fiction is conspicuously present in any account given of external reality (the coveted woman) as well as in the very declaration of external reality being fictive (the doctor). The malicious demon transports us from the fictive framework within which he functions to the Archimedean point of certainty. The preventive doctor, on the other hand, demonstrates more than anything else, the pointlessness of hoping to cut through the fetters of the fictional trap. The demon destroys "fictionality," the doctor perpetuates it.[15]

The self's emptiness is a particular instance of the emptiness of our conceptual scheme as such. As I have already stated, this emptiness comes to the fore the moment one attempts to distinguish between concepts, to decide between different alternatives, to form an opinion, and to construct an immutable worldview that has an element of stability to it—at least to the extent that the speakers of language trust the ability of words and sentences to point clearly to distinct objects. We can thus detect in Nāgārjuna's critique of language a radical exposition of an early Buddhist idea according to which reality is no more than a web of linguistic uses that reside nowhere (neither outside the mind perceiving them nor in its interiority), but rather is the product of convention and custom. It seems that Nāgārjuna tacitly rejects the hypothesis that it is possible to describe and represent the world without the description itself being an active part in the object it describes. That is to say, it is misleading to assume that it is possible to portray the world without the act of describing it being present in the description itself and influencing it. This mutual dependence is indicated by emptiness, and underlying it there is a tenacious refusal to see things, or for that matter the subject who knows them, as endowed with intrinsic nature (*svabhāva*). Nāgārjuna is very specific about this point: to say of things in the world that they are empty is to attribute them with a "name" and in this sense the word *emptiness* is as arbitrary as any other word. Nothing lies behind this designation. One could therefore see reality as lacking self-being. But even this lack is but a designation that exhibits the mutual dependence of all our sense data—void of any inner logic, lacking a central axis, a point of departure, or a finishing line. Language is a prison from which there is no escape because it is an open prison whose walls (i.e., the boundaries of meaning) are perpetually on the move, forever determined by our linguistic performance. One cannot go beyond these boundaries, since they are solely dependent on us. When we break out it is merely an imaginary escape, nothing but a shifting of the boundary. Nāgārjuna does not tire of repeating that *emptiness* itself is but a designation, an empty name, a way of putting one's finger on the mutual dependency that obstructs language's ability to refer to anything external and independent of it:

> Whatever comes into being dependent on another,
> Is not identical to that thing.
> Nor is it different from that.
> Therefore it is neither nonexistent in time nor permanent.

This outlook of emptiness is clearly sensed in Nāgārjuna's dedication to the Buddha quoted at the beginning of this chapter. On the whole, dedications of this kind are intended to evoke in the reader and writer a certain frame of mind—attentiveness, thoughtfulness, and, at times, even devotion. This is deemed imperative in order to gain a proper understanding of the text. But here, besides this, a concise preface manages to offer a poetic summary of the whole work. Four contrary dyads appear in this preface. Each of the dyads sheds its own particular light on a certain aspect of Nāgārjuna's thought. Dependent arising, that is, emptiness, is

> No cessation, no birth,
> No annihilation, no permanence,
> No coming, no going,
> No difference, no identity
> Without verbal expansion.

As I mentioned earlier, this characterization of dependent arising might, at first glance, look similar to what is usually referred to as negative theology—the claim that the Divine Being (be it God, the Absolute, or whatever) cannot be contained within language on account of the yawning fissure that exists between our linguistic ability and the infinite qualities of that Being. Accordingly, we have no other recourse but to refer to it through negating terms, that is, to use language in order to signal out its *non*corresponding attributes. In other words, all that can be meaningfully said about the divine subject is what it is *not*. No wonder that some scholars of Buddhism have been led astray by this apparent similarity and presented Nāgārjuna's list of negations as yet another appearance of negative theology. However, despite appearances, Nāgārjuna's view has nothing to do with Western negative theology. As is often the case, similarities turn out to be quite deceptive. Negative theology represents God as the opposite of certain contrary dyads, and being the opposite of every conceivable dyad, He, as it were, dwells beyond thought, beyond comprehension, and beyond the boundaries of language. This form of negative theology is typically Western: it asserts that anything opposing a contrary dyad must reside "beyond" these dyads (as an essentially metaphysical form of existence). And if it doesn't exist beyond these dyads, then it perforce must exist beneath them in a sort of mental junkyard of nonsensical metaphysical musings that have no meaning whatsoever and signify nothing more than the intellectual vapidity of whoever churns them out. Those theologians and metaphysicians who adhere to negative theology as the only possible way of speaking about the absolute, and those equally agnostic philosophers who utterly abhor such metaphysics, share between them the same logical ground: they both unfailingly and unquestioningly obey Aristotle's Law of Excluded Middle, according to which every proposition is either true or false, and these two alternatives exhaust all possibilities. Acceding to this law forces one to reject any other kind of possibility: the raven is either black or not black and, on account of this law, any other alternative, such as "black and not black" is excluded a priori from the realm of possibility. Thus the opposite of contrary dyads must reside either "beyond" any realm of logical application of the Law of Excluded Middle (in that twilight zone of "negative theology") or "beneath" any realm of application of the law (in that scintillating world of nonsense); in this sense, the opposite of contrary dyads is beyond comprehension, either because of its absoluteness or because of its meaninglessness. Nāgārjuna's interpreters who tacitly assumed that he maintains some version of the Law of Excluded Middle have thus sought either to turn Nāgārjuna into a closet metaphysician who upholds emptiness as a "metaphysical absolute" or else saw him as a nihilist trying to negate every possibility of understanding by pointing to the universality of emptiness.[16] Both these interpretations impose upon Nāgārjuna a Western conceptual framework quite alien to his way of thinking. The Indian logic prevailing in his time did not formulate a formal equivalent to Aristotle's Law of Excluded Middle. At least, as far as Nāgārjuna is concerned, the rejection of all four logical possibilities seems to violate it. Thus Nāgārjuna need not have assumed that the opposite of contrary dyads must "reside beyond" or "beneath" the realm of application of the Law of Excluded Middle. Recall that emptiness, as the negation of contrary dyads, is a point (empty!)—an arithmetical zero in which there is neither origination nor annihilation, neither permanent nor transient, neither one, nor many—empty precisely because there is no need to assume that every proposition is either true or false and nothing else. In that sense Nāgārjuna is antirealist, mainly because of his refusal to acknowledge that there is only one true account of reality. Siderits, who considers Nāgārjuna to be an antirealist, has presented his case convincingly: "It is by showing that any given proposition can be neither ultimately true nor ultimately false (nor, for that matter, ultimately both true and false, nor ultimately lacking in truth-value) that the Buddhist anti-realist aims to demonstrate the ultimate incoherence of the notion of ultimate truth." Contrarily, accounts of reality are necessarily mediated by language, which invariably fails to disclose an external, mind-independent reality. Language for Nāgārjuna, as much as for Kafka, is speaking itself into death or, better still, into emptiness.

This last point is well attested by the verse in the above dedication in which Nāgārjuna characterizes dependent arising as the absence of "verbal expansion." "Verbal expansion" is the translation I am offering for the Sanskrit *prapañca*. Nāgārjuna frequently uses this term in his writings. It is, I think, the key term in his (anti)philosophy. Different translators have glossed this term as "objectification" or "conceptual construction" (Garfield), "conceptual play," "provisional" or "a phenomenal play of words or thought process" (Inada), "verbal proliferation" (Matilal), "conceptual diffusion" (Burton) and "linguistic proliferation" (Lusthaus). *Prapañca* literally means "expansion" or "elaboration." Its appearances in Nāgārjuna's work tend to be associated with a certain kind of unrestrained, generative activity that is, in the main, either verbal or conceptual. By calling it "verbal expansion"

I am hoping to convey the complete freedom that characterizes the emergence of mental concepts and verbal constructs—insofar as this emergence denotes the bursting forth, coming apart, and perpetual eruption of mental concepts and verbal expressions. Verbal expansion is but the mutual ensnarement of language and thought coiled round each other.

This outlook is quite often referred to as "the emptiness of emptiness." Identifying language with an infinite activity of verbal expansion defeats an essentialist explanation of language. The emptiness of reality is therefore demonstrated by the emptiness of verbal expansion. In fact, what is expected of us is merely to talk, since the moment words begin to take form, sentences to take shape, descriptions and arguments to be moulded into something tangible—inevitably, false representations will start forming of their own accord and it will immediately become apparent that everything is empty. In one of Nāgārjuna's texts (concerned with his attempt to quell the objections of Buddhist and non-Buddhist opponents), a certain objector tries to portray his whole philosophy as if it were established upon a blatant self-contradiction. The opponent's heady argument runs thus: if you are right, Nāgārjuna, and everything is void of intrinsic nature, then even the words "void of intrinsic nature" are void of intrinsic nature; thus they cannot function as linguistic entities since, so at least according to the opponent, a word must have an object to which it refers. Nāgārjuna's reply to this objection leaves no doubt whatsoever: indeed, "we have already established in detail the voidness of all things. Even the name has already been stated to be void. . . . We do not say, indeed, that the name is existent." The opponent's objection is neither refuted nor negated, it is simply dissolved. Like any other verbal utterance, it too refers to nothing! While even this assertion seems to refer to something, it is, in fact, empty: "We do not say, indeed, that the name is existent." In this little squabble there is more than meets the eye: there is no doubt Nāgārjuna was well aware that he was adopting here an extremely radical position. Wishing to cast a new light on the Buddha's remedy to the problem of human suffering, Nāgārjuna opined that the more lucidly we diagnose the human condition (as empty linguistic events), then the easier it will be to understand the Buddha's remedy.

Verbal expansion is not yet another attribute of the mind and even less an attribute of the thinking self. On the contrary, it generates the underpinning of mental structure that enables man to perceive objects as external and refer to them linguistically. B. K. Matilal has noted that for Nāgārjuna *prapañca* is man's "obsessive tendency" to form concepts. I doubt if Nāgārjuna himself would have acceded to this Kantian-like characterization of prapañca as an a priori structure of the mind; in his treatment of prapañca Nāgārjuna doesn't award it a transcendental status but uses it exclusively as a descriptive (i.e., empirical) term. In this he remains true to the Buddha, who, it will be recalled, sought to remedy human suffering by seeing things as they are—the erasure of error, the eradication of ignorance.[17] What is intended here is not an intellectual error, a sort of mistaken reasoning that fails to arrive at valid deductions. The error is more fundamental. It resides in the assumption that there are such things as valid deductions. An error of this kind is more reminiscent of a hallucination than an error arising from fallacious reasoning contracted along the arduous route from premise to conclusion. Among other things, Nāgārjuna likens this error to a desert mirage that gives rise to an imaginary city. The forces that Nāgārjuna identifies in language and that create such delusions, operate, according to him, like the bewitching powers of a magic incantation. Language is a spell, since every use we make of it determines, whether directly or indirectly, its meaning. Prapañca—verbal expansion—endows language with enormous powers because, like an immense trapper's net, it covers every aspect of human activity, perception, and response, enmeshing language in the totality of one's life. Seen from within this net, speech acts are nothing but to and fro movements inside an impermeable maze (lacking any kind of correspondence to anything that might lay outside it). These movements determine or generate meaning arbitrarily or, at best, conventionally. This callous approach to language and the understanding that its utterances are void of any reference is, in one sense, the opposite of the Vedic depiction of Vāc as absolute internal harmony. And yet, in another sense, there is a certain kind of similarity between them: both reject the idea that the meaning of words is determined by the degree to which it corresponds to an extralinguistic reality. To put it more bluntly, both reject linguistic realism. But, of course, each of them does so differently, in a manner diametrically opposed to the other. While the Vedic thinkers, and those associated with them, substituted correspondence to reality with language's complete self-awareness, Nāgārjuna and those following him made language empty, forever dependent on its tirelessly changing context and functioning only within the conjectural framework of *convention*.

Nāgārjuna rejects the idea that linguistic utterances are representational, but he does not reject their ability to operate in everyday situations. On the contrary, the elimination of linguistic essentialism (and, concomitantly, basing language on utterances void of any reference) does not impair its efficacy in everyday situations. In fact, this is the only way in which language can function properly. One might want to call this approach fictionalism, since the world is conceived as being populated by objects and events lacking a clear ontological standing; a linguistic approach to these fictional objects does not bind one—not even faintly—to any kind of ontology. In order for language to retain its efficacy, it is necessary to suspend all judgments about the existential status of the objects to which language refers. After all, this suspension is the very essence of fiction as such. What is evident here is Nāgārjuna's reliance on convention when considering the efficacy of linguistic utterances; for him, language is determined by social conventions—empty linguistic utterances present themselves before us, and we consider them as real only by virtue of certain conventions. In this manner "things like a cart, a pot, a cloth, etc., though void of an intrinsic nature, [and] because of being dependently originated, are occupied with their respective functions, e.g., carrying wood, grass and earth, containing honey, water and milk, and protecting from cold, wind and heat." The possibility that chariots, jars etc., will be efficacious is determined by their emptiness; that is to say, by their mutual dependence, or, to look at it from another angle, by our inability to free ourselves from the circular, malicious grip of language when using it. Consequently, if language were not empty, everyday activity would not be possible:

> If dependent arising is denied,
> Emptiness itself is rejected.
> This would contradict
> All of the worldly conventions

If emptiness itself is rejected,
No action will be appropriate.
There would be action which did not begin,
And there would be agent without action.

In other words, an essentialist stance that awards objects a nonempty status (of a sort) will preclude everyday activities that form the basis of how we know the world and how we respond to it from within our overall experience of the world.[18]

Is fictionality possible without presupposing, at some subliminal level or other, a nonfictional reality? Can reality be conceived merely as an aggregate of conventions? One of the more common arguments against fictionalism or conventionalism assumes that a thing's fictionality invariably depends on a definition of fiction in relation to a nonfictional reality and that the making of a convention requires that there be obtainable facts that do not rely on any convention. Clearly this is a realist argument, and whoever subscribes to it should concomitantly subscribe to the idea that there is a reality independent of our concepts. In other words, there is a reality that is not conceptually constructed. However, this is precisely what Nāgārjuna rejects, and this is what Siderits means when he claims that he is an antirealist. Garfield states this quite eloquently when he says that, for Nāgārjuna, "our conventions and our conceptual framework can never be justified by demonstrating their correspondence to an independent reality. Rather, what counts as real depends precisely upon our conventions." Admittedly, language operates, among other ways, by juxtaposing opposing concepts, but, for the antirealist, the realist relies too heavily on these opposing concepts and is consequently trapped by them, falling prey to what I would call the ontologistic fallacy: he derives an ontological conclusion from the existence of opposing concepts. It is true that conventionalism is impossible without presupposing a nonconventional reality—but this last premise is itself also conceptually constructed. From a conceptual point of view, the aspired-for opposition remains intact. According to the antirealist, it would be a grave error to derive from this a realist conclusion concerning the existence of an external reality independent of our concepts. This is what is so daring about Nāgārjuna's philosophy: even absolute reality is not independent of our concepts, and it too is subject to the all-pervading effect of prapañca.

In one of his key pronouncements Nāgārjuna summarizes his position thus:

> Whatever is dependently co-arisen
> That is explained to be emptiness
> That, being a dependent designation,
> Is itself the middle way.

Dependent arising is, for Nāgārjuna, emptiness. As Siderits puts it, there is an equivalence between arising in dependence and being devoid of intrinsic nature, i.e., empty. Furthermore: dependent arising is itself dependent upon its verbal expression, since, as Nāgārjuna claims here, emptiness is merely a designation. As I have already noted, every designation is but a convention; there is no designation that is not itself dependent or conditioned by other designations. This sums up everything in a nutshell: dependent arising is what is meant by emptiness. There is no difference between the way things are and how we speak of them: the world of events and the world of concepts have an equal standing. And so emptiness is no more than a *designation*—that is, it too is an empty word, void of any proper reference. When dependent arising, emptiness, and the world of linguistic concepts are taken together, they turn out to be one and the same thing, the pinnacle of pinnacles—the Buddha's middle path.

Strangely enough, the world that Nāgārjuna portrays here has the same characteristic mark that we encountered in Kafka's world—it is an "uncommonly manifold" world that, to reiterate Kafka, "can be put to the test at any moment if one just takes up a handful of the World and looks at it a little more closely." The same holds true of Nāgārjuna's world: it contains within it illimitable possibilities. Nothing has being as such; things appear within a fictional or conventional framework—including, of course, Buddhist doctrine and even the Buddha himself. Even designations such as *the Buddha* or *nirvāṇa* are empty terms. They do not denote entities or things in themselves. They can only assume the role of fictional or conventional terms that are dependent upon the linguistic use made of them. This point needs to be emphasized: terms such as *Dharma* (the Buddhist teaching) or *Buddha*, despite their immense importance, are yet another case of prapañca. Verbal expansion sets out the ever expanding limits of language and thereby concocts a "world" in which representation is doomed to fail, to be replaced by empty, fictional, or conventional devices. Only conventions can set the world in motion, guaranteeing that intentional acts will be conventionally successful (i.e., efficacious). Gaining an understanding of this empty world by realizing the emptiness of (empty) language consists of the desired nirvāṇa—in which all distinctions collapse into an empty zero point, suspended between any pair of opposites. Realizing that language is no more than prapañca will bring about the pacification of that malignant verbal expansion. Seeing every linguistic activity in mere conventional terms posits one in a blissful state of "no preference." In such a mental state—which for Nāgārjuna is nothing short of the Buddha's nirvāṇa at the moment of his awakening—language is inefficacious, consequently all terms and concepts subside into a contextual dependent arising. In the short verse with which Nāgārjuna concludes the chapter on nirvāṇa in his magnum opus (it has been suggested that this is the final verse of the work as a whole), he characterizes nirvāṇa as a state in which all attachments and verbal expansion have been ceased and are pacified; he then caps the whole text with a claim that in the West, before Kant, would have been totally inconceivable: "No Dharma was taught by the Buddha, at any time, in any place, to anyone."

One must entertain the possibility that it is easier for modern (nineteenth century and on) Western readers to understand these words, readers barred from pre-Kantian naïveté and compelled to see things in a Kantian or neo-Kantian perspective. Post-Kantian thought in the nineteenth and twentieth century is punctuated by some modernist insights whose common ground is the disappearance of the transcendent framework and concurrently the disappearance of man as an autonomous thinking subject in this framework. What we face now is a vacuous ontological framework whose center is entirely depleted—both of God and of the knowing human subject. Derrida, who noted that the postmodern self is fragmentary and that its core cannot be fixed to any center, dramatically highlighted the vacuity of this ontological core. This blurring of the center was implicitly presaged by Kant's Copernican revolution and was explicitly spelled out by Kafka, despite the fact that Derrida welcomes, to a certain extent, that which Kafka's soul could not bear.

I suggest we look at Kafka's empty self (a direct descendent of the

Kantian self) and see it as perpetuating its emptiness in a manner similar to Nāgārjuna's empty self. But how apart these two are! Kafka's emptiness is that horrific failure at being "inside" and "outside" at one and the same time. Cartesian interiority, which Kant began to nullify, is, in Kafka's modernist outlook, reconstructed as an impassable obstacle, blocking the road from opinion to knowledge, or, to put it more dramatically, from doubt to certainty. After all, the prerequisite for knowledge of the external world is to presuppose its exteriority, but this presupposition is empty in Kafka's modernistic view. On the other hand, this presupposition is totally absent from Nāgārjuna's philosophy; his disagreement with the Upaniṣads, profound as it may be, does not revolve around an alleged commitment to a transcendent being. Nāgārjuna is not worried by transcendence but, to the contrary, by what he sees as the erroneous conception of an independent, all-pervading immanence. For him, the Upaniṣadic presupposition granting immanence an autonomous position (exemplified by the metaphors of dream and deep sleep) is no more than a delusion that ignores language's necessary role in any cognition. By stressing the importance language has in shaping the world as we know it and experience it, one might want to think of Nāgārjuna as initiating some sort of linguistic turn.[19]

Needless to say, Nāgārjuna is not fearful of the terror afflicting Kafka's works. In pointing to the emptiness of everything and by diagnosing language as a perpetual verbal expansion, Nāgārjuna is only suggesting an alternative way or other possibilities of experiencing "humanness." The empty self is the liberated self. This is precisely the kind of emptiness with which Kakfa, as the acting representative of a completely different culture, cannot acquiesce: as we have seen, fragmentation of the subject is the dismal outcome of the necessary encounter with a dead, yet present, transcendence. This fragmentation is exactly what makes the world so indifferently manifold. On the other hand, the manifoldness of Nāgārjunas world is no more than the many and countless faces of human language: forever expanding, sloughing, becoming disgracefully unruly, swelling up, pushing its limits even further, coiling around itself, devouring everything it creates, ruthlessly wanton, yet appeasing the rigidity of meaning in a self-revealing linguistic performance. The process of prapañca is not only the distinguishing mark of reality but also the great hope of those who understand it. No other sentence better exemplifies this great hope than the piercing and penetrating claim that "No Dharma was taught by the Buddha, at any time, in any place, to anyone." One may imagine that Kafka would have yearned to accept the message embodied by this verse. But for Kafka hope was banished forever. Even death is no solution: "Our salvation is death, but not this one." It is precisely the "other death" that Kafka cannot attain and the reason underlying this failure is the disparity between his world and Nāgārjuna's. Kafka's world is diversely manifold, but it contains within it the seed of transcendence in all its unbearable emptiness. This is the point where Kant's empty self reaches its apogee in the form of a paralyzing paradox. An inward gaze is necessarily an erroneous gaze. Necessity, which for Kant was the empty existential framework of the transcendent, turns with Kafka into a delusion. The empty framework is filled with content, but this content is always self-defeating in the sense that any attempt to verbalize it ends up in contradiction. Let us look at this Kafkaesque situation in greater detail: the drive to disclose the external entails a certain modification of interiority that must end with an explosive contradiction, since this interiority cannot be defined as interiority unless it is, to begin with, somehow seen in relation to an exteriority. Thus every attempt to release oneself from transcendence is bound necessarily to end up with the mind's (or self's) inevitable defeat, since release from transcendence is a release from the very interiority that stands in relation to it. For Kafka, the wish to eliminate the *necessary* ends *necessarily* in a shameful defeat—the eradication of personal identity and, moreover, of humanity. The voice of an emaciated philosophical incarnation of Kafka rises from the tumult, positions itself opposite Kant's death mask, and, gazing at it squarely, says, Did it really never occur to you? How could you not understand that the price of rescuing transcendence by emptying it of any content and establishing it on consciousness will be of no avail? If only we could turn things around, cease being modern and revert to our pre-Kantian condition. If only we could simply accept exteriority ontologically and the presupposition of transcendence again. But the Copernican revolution left us with an empty *framework* of transcendence and thereby aggravated the self's fragmentation.

In contrast to Kafka's hopelessness, Nāgārjuna's emptiness is the object of the hope that it instigates. One can formulate this somewhat

crassly by saying that hope is expressed by the recognition of hopelessness, by the recognition that the world is completely indifferent, lacking both a core and a rim and displaying no qualitative distinctions between them. But Kafkaesque hope is never quite hopeless (no death is
the "real" death). Empty transcendence is powerful enough to retain a
residual hope, rambling around aimlessly. In bygone days, when transcendence was basking gloriously in its abundance, it gave rise to hope
and cultivated its growth. Now that transcendence is present only in
its emptiness, it leaves hope in a state of meaningless or, shall we say,
purposeless, existence. Dead hope survives—as a disobedient predisposition, as an unfulfilled wish, as an unattainable goal. At the end of
Kafka's unfinished (could it be otherwise?) novel *The Trial,* Joseph K. is
towed away to his place of execution by two "tenth-rate old actors" in
frock coats and top hats. At the place of execution they lay him down
ceremoniously on the ground and in a horrifically comic scene begin
passing back and forth a double-edged butcher's knife above him. "K.
now perceived clearly that he was supposed to seize the knife himself,
as it travelled from hand to hand above him, and plunge it into his own
breast. But he did not do so, he merely turned his head, which was still
free to move, and gazed around him." And what K. saw, while turning
his head thus, was a human figure in the window of the top story of a
house, a human figure "faint and insubstantial at that distance and at
that height" who "leaned abruptly far forward and stretched both arms
still farther. Who was it? A good man? Someone who sympathized?
Someone who wanted to help? Was it one person only? Or was it mankind?" This is the kind of hope envisaged by Kafka, utterly cruel in its
emptiness, yet all too burdensome in its presence. The human figure
perched in the window, in the face of death, reasserts *contingency* in all
its violence. Contingency—the presence of vacant transcendence—is
what prevents Abraham from sacrificing his son, since, it will be recalled, he sees the world in all its manifoldness, but, despite this, doubt
persists—perhaps it is all a farce? The figure in the window is what
prevents Joseph K. from reaching "that" death—"real" death—where
he would seize the butcher's knife from his ridiculous executioners and
plunge it deep into his own breast. Because of the contingent multifarious appearances of this hopeless hope, Joseph K. has to make do with
"this" death, in which "the hands of one of the partners were already
at K.'s throat, while the other thrust the knife deep into his heart and

turned it there twice." It is not surprising that, in his last words, the dying K. acknowledges his shameful defeat by uttering a summation of Kafka's emptiness: "Like a dog."

We have already encountered the figure in the window: it was the unbearable presence of an "other" scratching and digging in the burrower's lair. These terrifying outsiders, so the legends say, "scratch the thickness of the earth in such a way that you feel as if you are in their house, far rather than yours." Had transcendence been living then one could anticipate—with suspense or horror or hope—that it would make an appearance in the world of man. But since transcendence is vacuous—whether in the world of those dwelling aboveground or the world of burrowers or even in the levitating world of the builders of the tower of Babel—it can only be present in absentia. A living, veritable transcendence could terminate linguistic writhing—it could slash circularity, push it ahead, and thus guarantee its purposefulness, since its directionality is determined by an aspiration that is, of course, tied to the presence of hope. What can one hope for from a living transcendence but that it would take on the complete and utter annihilation of our wishes, whether by making them come true or by absolutely and irrevocably eradicating them. But if it is empty transcendence that is poised before us, then the only hope allowed us is empty hope, compelling us to construct the tower of Babel but simultaneouly proscribing the builders from climbing it—just as it induces the burrower's yearning for deep sleep and simultaneously his desire to keep vigil over himself from the outside. Indeed, what could be more abominable and horrendous than seeing, at the fatal moment of execution, hope lurching from a high window, embodied in the figure of a feeble and pale man whose contorted body assumes the form of a question mark?

As I see it, Nāgārjuna and Kafka are similar in that they both share the worldview that sees everything as empty. Yet, since each of them arrives at this depiction from a different angle and sees it within the particular gaze of his own culture, needless to say each of them spins a conspicuously different yarn from their respectively different empty worlds. Let us examine these two disparate, and even contrary, yarns by means of two examples—the one contemplative, the other literary. To each of the two we will try to envisage separate responses, both by Kafka and by Nāgārjuna.

In one of his essays on Kafka, Maurice Blanchot describes how words commit suicide:

The idea of the impersonal, mythical tale as faithful to the essence of language obviously raises certain problems. We noticed that language is only real in the perspective of non-language: it tends towards a perilous horizon beyond which it tries to disappear. What is this non-language? That is not the question. But we should however bear in mind that, for all forms of expression, it is a reminder of their inadequacy. What makes language possible is that it strives for the impossible. Thus at every level it involves unavoidable conflicts and anxieties. No sooner is something said than something else must be said to correct the tendency of all that is said to become final, to insinuate itself into the imperturbable realm of objects. There is no end, neither at the level of simple sentences nor at that of complete works. Conflicts, which can never be resolved, are not a solution; but neither is silence a solution. Language cannot be achieved by silence; silence is a form of expression whose dishonesty forces us into speech. Besides, the suicide of words can be only attempted within words—suicidal obsession that can never be realized, that leaves them with the blank page or with the insignificance of vain words. Such solutions are illusive. The ruthlessness of language derives from its ceaseless evocation of a death it cannot achieve.

Blanchot spun this description of language around Kafka, and it feels as if the latter were its ghostwriter. Language can say nothing, but has to say all; it cannot shirk from this empty duty (even silence will be of no use, as this is nothing but a different "form of expression" propelling us back, perforce, to speech). Linguistic death is impossible for that simple Kafkaesque reason that it will never be a terminal death. Even the "suicide of words can be only attempted within words." And so, "The ruthlessness of language derives from its ceaseless evocation of a death it cannot achieve language."

Nāgārjuna could have never written these words, but he would be willing, in my opinion, to accede to the author's premises, even though he would have vehemently rejected his conclusions. There is no doubt that he too thinks that language is real only by virtue of its inability to manifest its reality. Every essentialist conception of language will push the speaker down a precipitous slope of self-contradictions. Any attempt to seek permanent meaning sends us down the slope of meaninglessness. In Blanchot's claim that "language is only real in the perspective of non-language," Nāgārjuna would find an admirable representation of his approach to language—as verbal expansion, always bursting forth from within itself, resisting itself so that every time "something else must be said to correct the tendency of all that is said to become final." In retrospect, Blanchot has managed to beautifully articulate Nāgārjuna's insight on words: prapañca is that condition of restlessness that prevents language from insinuating itself "into the imperturbable realm of objects." But, contrary to Blanchot's understanding of language, according to Nāgārjuna it is capable of bringing about its own demise. What is there to stop it? Every use of language is but another expression of that deathly transition from the essential to the fictional and the conventional. Hence, prapañca can be stilled. Its operation as prapañca is precisely its stillness.

———————

How would Kafka and Nāgārjuna have responded to yet another example of empty reality? This time it appears in Herman Melville's fiction, in the eponymous scrivener Bartleby.[20] *Bartleby* is told in the first person by a rather elderly New York lawyer whose office employs scriveners (a lawyer's job entails a lot of paperwork, and photocopy machines in the middle of the nineteenth century were an idea yet to be conceived). The narrator employs two scriveners; one is called Turkey, and is reasonably sane before twelve o'clock, meridian, after which his reason begins to play havoc (manifesting in manic attacks); the other scrivener (answering to the name of Nippers), owing to certain digestive problems, was prone to a nervous testiness and grinning irritability throughout the morning, though in the afternoon he would become comparatively mild. The lawyer recounting the story sought the services of a third scrivener, and, in answer to his advertisement, one fine morning, upon the threshold of his office, stood "a motionless young" man, "pallidly neat, pitiably respectable, incurably forlorn!" This was Bartleby, who applied himself to the job with particular industry, writing "silently, palely, mechanically." Barely had three days passed and the lawyer discovered, much to his surprise and consternation, that, having been asked to examine a small paper with him, Bartleby replies in a singularly mild and firm voice: "I would prefer not to."

This is the first reply to a request and it immediately becomes the standard reply to a set of other requests—varying in degrees of urgency and importance—that the lawyer puts to Bartleby in the days to come. The latter replies invariably in the same manner: "I would prefer not to." This is not a refusal, but neither is it an assent. This is how Bartleby responds when addressed. For instance, when the lawyer asks him to compare his copy with an original or when, later, after Bartleby's passiveness had caused him some irritation, he requests that they read a copied document in concert. There is more to follow: when the lawyer asks him to "just step round to the Post Office" he prefers not to or, on a different occasion, when he is merely asked to transport himself to an adjoining room. Then, one Sunday morning, upon trying to enter his chambers, the lawyer discovers, when trying to apply his key to the door, that there was something inserted from the inside. It transpires that Bartleby had taken up residence in his chambers. When asked by the lawyer to let him enter into his very own chambers, Bartleby again "prefers not to." Ultimately, the lawyer decides to dismiss the scrivener, notifying him that "the time has come; you must quit this place," but Bartleby again informs him that "I would prefer not."

The lawyer is left no choice but to leave his current chambers and move elsewhere. Some days later, just as he thought all was doing well, a perturbed looking stranger pays him a visit—a representative of his old office's new tenants—informing him that Bartleby has remained, preferring not to move, not to quit the premises or even to reply to any questions. Bartleby is finally sent by the police to the Tombs as a vagrant, where he prefers not to dine, despite the fact that the narrator informs us that he was paying a grub-man to bring Bartleby the best dinners possible. One day Bartleby is found in the yard, huddled at the base of the wall. The lawyer's paid grub-man believes he is sleeping and says so to the lawyer peering at him: "His dinner is ready. Won't he dine today, either? Or does he live without dining?"

"Lives without dining," said I, and closed the eyes.
"Eh!—He's asleep, ain't he?"
"With kings and counsellors," murmured I.

Melville offers us Bartleby as the utmost middling middle figure.[21] Gilles Deleuze has written on the philosophical nature of this expression. He said that the sentence "I'd prefer not to" is neither an affirmation nor a negation:

> The attorney would be relieved if Bartleby did not want to, but Bartleby does not refuse, he simply rejects a nonpreferred (the proofreading, the errands . . .). And he does not accept either, he does not affirm a preference that would consist in continuing to copy, he simply posits its impossibility. In short, the formula that successively refuses every other act has already engulfed the act of copying, which it no longer even needs to refuse. The formula is devastating because it eliminates the preferable just as mercilessly as any nonpreferred. It not only abolishes the term it refers to, and that it rejects, but also abolishes the other term it seemed to preserve, and that becomes impossible. In fact, it renders them indistinct: it hollows out an even expanding zone of indiscernibility or indetermination between some nonpreferred activities and a preferable activity. All particularity, all reference is abolished. . . .
>
> The formula *I prefer not to* excludes any alternative and devours what it claims to conserve no less than it distances itself from everything else. It implies that Bartleby stop copying, that is, that he stop reproducing words; it hollows out a zone of indetermination that renders words indistinguishable, that creates a vacuum within language. But it also stymies the speech acts that a boss uses to command, that a kind of friend uses to ask questions or a man of faith to make promises. If Bartleby had refused, he could still be seen as a rebel or insurrectionary, and as such would still have a social role. But the formula stymies all speech acts, and at the same time, it makes Bartleby a pure outsider to whom no social position can be attributed. This is what the attorney glimpses with dread: all his hopes of bringing Bartleby back to reason are dashed because they rest on a *logic of presuppositions* according to which an employer expects to be obeyed, or a kind of friend listened to, whereas Bartleby has invented a new logic, *a logic of preference*, which is enough to undermine the presuppositions of language as a whole. . . . The formula "disconnects" words and things, words and actions, but also speech acts and words—it

severs language from all reference, in accordance with Bartleby's absolute vocation, *to be a man without references*, someone who appears suddenly and then disappears, without reference to himself or anything else.

We are again face to face with that synchronous entanglement that we recognize in Kafka's literature. Like a genuine Kafkaesque hero, Bartleby does nothing except demonstrate "impossibility." Though, unlike Joseph K., who is completely unaware of the impossible necessity, and in contradistinction to Albert Camus' Outsider, who is completely aware of the absurdity of impossible necessity, Bartleby's consciousness lies in the middle, halfway between awareness and unawareness.

Bartleby's reactions offer readers a profound and piercing modernist proposition on the status of man in a culture void of any transcendent being, a condition in which he is exposed to the demand for self-determination, that, on the one hand, necessitates the existence of an objective set of values but, on the other hand, fails to come up with the requisite standard for this objectivity. In these circumstances, man is exposed to the question of identity without being protected from the forceful radiance of his own inwardness, with this radiance arising mostly from the emptiness of his self or, to put it more bluntly, radiance formed by the process of annihilation. "I would prefer not to" is the expression of that emptiness that, as Deleuze says, mercilessly cancels out the preferable that is now on a par with the nonpreferred. Deleuze has magnificently captured this with the phrase "creat[ing] a vacuum within language," which also simultaneously "stymies the speech acts." Constructing language is also deconstructing language. Bartleby's language, which anticipates the modern protagonists of Kafka, Mann, Agnon, Musil, and others, lacks any reference point, operating as it does in an absolute void. This voidance is what drives Bartleby to equanimity, much as it does Yitzchak Kummer, the protagonist of S. Y. Agnon's novel *Only Yesterday*. Kummer also attained a certain degree of equanimity, only to be bitten in the end—despite the equanimity or maybe because of it—by a mad rabies-infested dog that makes him take on the dog's insanity, i.e., he becomes himself a dog. Kummer, like Joseph K. before him, ends his days like a dog. And yet the same is true of Bartleby, who, even prior to these two, was found dead, lying "strangely huddled at the base of the wall." What can one say of him except quote the verse from the book of Job in which Job claims that he should lie still and quietly sleep "with kings and counsellors." The allusion to Job is no mere coincidence, since sleeping with kings and counsellors—death—is for Job the only possible consolation: the stillness longed for by every creature and the rest coveted by the weary: "For now should I have lain still and been quiet, I should have slept: then had I been at rest, With kings and counsellors of the earth, which built desolate places for themselves" (Job 3:13–14).

In Melville's world, Bartleby fulfills the role of the tragic hero or, better said, the empty modern substitute of the tragic. In Nāgārjuna's world, Bartleby could have assumed the role of no less than the Buddha himself. His complete indifference, his use of the logic of preference rather than the logic of deduction are the conditions of perfect equanimity, an infinitesimal zero point in which the silencing of prapañca is achieved by the irreversible dissolution of language, its abstract meanings and concrete pronouncements. Bartleby-as-the-Buddha serves as an illustration of that empty middling point (a singularly exact middle) that makes it impossible to favor one alternative over the contradictory other; the preferable cannot be favored over the unpreferable, and so one can only "prefer not to prefer," and even this preference is not preferable over its alternative. Both Bartleby and the Buddha operate within the framework of an authorless text. Nietzsche's death of God is Melville's death of the author (long before he was killed by many others in the twentieth century). Not only the death of the textual author but also the death of the *idea of an author*—the death of what is considered to be a fully fledged subject, namely, the yardstick by which preferences are made possible. For Nāgārjuna, Buddhist texts are also authorless texts, since Buddhism likewise refuses to make choices (every preference is a matter of convention).

We are confronted by two authorless "noncharacters"—Bartleby and the Buddha. Yet here ends the similarity difference between them. Bartleby bewails the *disappearance* of his author; his is the wailing of someone who is in despair over his existence. On the other hand, the Buddha (at least as Nāgārjuna sees him), when faced with the absence of an author, will respond with an enigmatic smile. In Buddhism the fragmented self carries with it the promise of liberation, since the author of the Buddha's worldview is not dead, for a simple reason: he was never alive, i.e., he was never anything but a fable to begin with.

There is a grave difference between a text whose author has been re-
linquished and a text that never had, or never meant to have, an author. The fact that transcendence is totally absent from the core of
India's conceptual foundation allows the process of mental disintegration to occur without incurring any trauma. This disintegration is not
brought about by deprivation or severance. No otherness casts its long
shadow on the process of the self's dissolution in this post-Kantian
world in which man has lost the comforting knowledge of there being epistemic boundaries that *precede* mental activity and perhaps even
condition it. With this consolation absent, Joseph K. dies muttering
the words "like a dog" and Yitzchak Kummer departs from the world
in anguish, barking hoarsely. But the Indian worldview is such that the
boundaries of knowledge are flexible, shrinking and expanding, and
thus while Bartleby of the West lies strangely huddled on the floor, this
huddled mass comprises the great promise of the Buddhist Bartleby, of
a culture that to begin with did not seek an outwardness save as a mild
or extreme sort of projection whose source is inwardness.

Let us cast our parting gaze on Bartleby. The lawyer narrating the
story mentioned at the beginning of his tale that "Bartleby was one of
those beings of whom nothing is ascertainable, except from the original sources, and in his case those are very small," hinting that there is
more to come: "What my own astonished eyes saw of Bartleby, that is
all I know of him, except, indeed, one vague report which will appear
in the sequel." And indeed in the last section of the story, after having
mentioned Bartleby's death by alluding to those verses quoted from
Job, the narrator returns to that "vague report":

> Bartleby had been a subordinate clerk in the Dead Letter Office
> at Washington, from which he had been suddenly removed by
> a change in the administration. When I think over this rumor,
> I cannot adequately express the emotions which seize me. Dead
> letters! does it not sound like dead men? Conceive a man by
> nature and misfortune prone to a pallid hopelessness, can any
> business seem more fitted to heighten it than that of continually
> handling these dead letters and assorting them for the flames?
> For by the cart-load they are annually burned. Sometimes from
> out the folded paper the pale clerk takes a ring:—the finger it
> was meant for, perhaps, moulders in the grave; a bank-note sent

in swiftest charity:—he whom it would relieve, nor eats nor hungers any more; pardon for those who died despairing; hope for those who died unhoping; good tidings for those who died stifled by unrelieved calamities. On errands of life, these letters speed to death.

Ah Bartleby! Ah humanity!

This last admission adds another profound dimension to the comparison between Bartleby and the Buddha. The "vague report" is a testimony of his humanity. To be Bartleby is to be human. Bartleby's humanity lies in that redemption that has disappeared without a trace, hopelessly faded away in the hands of a pallid clerk sorting dead letters. And so this is exactly why this mortal must prefer not to prefer. On the other hand, the humanity of the Bartleby-Buddha arises from the profound perception that the limits of my language are the limits of my world, except that my language has no limits, thus the limits of my world are boundless. According to the Bartleby-Buddha, the very act of burning letters is the most profound act of liberation conceivable, and that is what constitutes being an authentic person in the literal (empty) sense. Thus it might just be possible to insert the Buddha's name instead of that of Bartleby in that concluding exhortation, "Ah Bartleby! Ah humanity!" But perhaps this insertion is a scandalous ignominy since even though there is admittedly an uncanny similarity, they are also separated by a great and sundering gulf.

FIVE

"It's All in the Mind"

BERKELEY, VASUBANDHU, AND THE
WORLD OUT THERE

. . . for the eye sees not itself,
But by reflection, by some other things.
—William Shakespeare, *Julius Caesar,* 1.ii

When one means something, it is oneself meaning; so
one is oneself in motion. One is rushing ahead and so
cannot also observe oneself rushing ahead. Indeed not.
—Ludwig Wittgenstein, *Philosophical Investigations*, §456

While Winston Smith, the hero of George Orwell's *Nineteen Eighty-four,* was being brutally tortured in the place where there is no darkness—the permanently lit cellars of the Ministry of Love—O'Brien, the arch-inquisitor and infamous torturer, found the leisure to enlighten Smith on a few general issues:

You preferred to be a lunatic, a minority of one. Only the disciplined mind can see reality, Winston. You believe that reality is something objective, external, existing in its own right. You also believe that the nature of reality is self-evident. When you delude yourself into thinking that you see something, you assume that everyone else sees the same thing as you. But I tell you, Winston, that reality is not external. Reality exists in the human mind, and nowhere else.

Nineteen Eighty-four was published after World War II, and ever since its publication it has been understood, on the whole, in political or social terms. Among its readers, there have been those who saw it as an assault on totalitarian communism, particularly of the Stalinist variety. Indeed, Big Brother's portrait bears an alarming similarity to Stalin; in Goldstein one cannot fail to pick up references to Trotsky; the party is of course the party; Winston Smith, an employee of the Ministry of Truth, rewrites history for a living, undoubtedly inspired by the perpetually modified versions of the Soviet encyclopedia from which names and events would appear and disappear at whim, without these alterations bearing any obvious relation to fact. There are other such allusions in the book, some more explicit, others less so. A different group of readers preferred to extend the novel's interpretative domain and did so by including any form of modern totalitarianism: communism, fascism, the hierarchy of the Catholic church and other institutions or regimes that are comparable, in varying degrees, to the Orwellian nightmare.

Yet now that this supposedly apocalyptic date is past, a more level-headed consideration of Orwell's novel is possible, unburdened by the futuristic baggage that two generations of readers have felt compelled to cast upon it. It is now possible to see the novel's picture of totalitarianism not only as allegorically portraying certain forms of government but also as an expression of the nature of human evil as such. As we shall see, Orwell exposes this idea of evil as something intricately bound up with—perhaps even derived from—a complete abjuration of reality's exteriority. Ivan Karamazov's anarchistic claim about God's death opens wide the portals of all possibilities, including the most horrific, and finds in O'Brien its apotheosis: "But I tell you, Winston, that reality is not external. Reality exists in the human mind, and nowhere else." This is the high point in the dissolution of exteriority, the beginnings of which were encountered in Descartes' philosophy, then amplified with Kant, only to reach a heightened extreme in Kafka's vision of the world. It comes then as no surprise that Orwell has O'Brien make this last pronouncement from within a torture chamber, a labyrinthine inferno whose very existence exemplifies human nature, depicting the latter as a fragmented self that not only generates external reality, and not only struggles against its vacuous necessity, but, moreover, turns out to be its sole creator. What O'Brien does to Winston Smith is a vile manipulation, at the end of which the world's exteriority is substituted by the mind's boundless interiority. This substitution will drive Winston Smith to irrevocable ruin, to his demise as a human being.

Those acquainted with the history of Western philosophy will recall the claim that reality resides solely in the mind from the works of George Berkeley (1685–1753). Berkeley was an Irish bishop who lived for the most part in England. In 1710, when he was barely twenty-five years old, he published his *Treatise Concerning the Principles of Human Knowledge*, which made him the most notorious philosopher of early eighteenth-century England. More than anything else, Berkeley was identified with his epigrammatic claim *esse* is *percipi*. In his view the only things that truly exist are the ideas that inhabit our mind (for this reason his philosophy has often been called idealism while, in fact, he only referred to it as immaterialism, that is, an explicit denial of the existence of matter or, more precisely, a rejection of the prevailing view that things are external and independent of the mind perceiving them). While *esse* is *percipi* quickly came to epitomize the whole of his philosophy, it did not take long before this claim deteriorated into the more common and more vulgar expression "it's all in the mind." Repudiating the exteriority of the perceived world was seen by Berkeley's contemporaries, and by later generations too, as an exercise in self-indulgent vapidity and a case of intellectual deceit—verbal gymnastics by a philosopher with a tendency to make vain proclamations that even he himself does not believe in. Thus, for instance, even a year prior to his death one could still find someone writing a letter to the editor of the *Gentlemen's Magazine* in which he expresses his wish that "it were to be wish'd that his lordship had always employes his fine genius (as indeed he has done of late) in teaching mankind useful truths, and not taken so much delight in displaying its subtlety by astonishing the world with paradoxes, and making impossibilities plausible." Berkeley was certainly not in need of letters such as these, or other affronts, to realize the idiosyncratic nature of his philosophy. In one of his writings he referred to himself as someone who is perceived by the public "as one who maintained the most extravagant opinion that ever entered into the mind of man, to wit, that there is no such thing as *material substance* in the world." Nonetheless, one can't help sensing that he did not, in fact, consider his philosophy that extravagant and, moreover, that he took it to be in complete accord with common sense, being a genuine representation of the common man's convictions, before these were clouded by too many overly abstract philosophical meditations. Berkeley felt that the only reason for his public ridicule was because he was misunderstood.

Even though it is clear that Berkeley was seen as an eccentric philosopher by his contemporaries, there is little doubt that his philosophical views were steeped in his intellectual zeitgeist and reflect the terminological and conceptual framework of philosophers preceding him such as René Descartes and John Locke (1632–1704). Like Descartes, Berkeley also sought to understand the self's true nature and to uncover its boundaries. In this respect, his philosophy should be seen as a natural development of a line of investigation that Descartes instigated, namely, a casting of one's gaze inward in order to reveal by means of this reflexive act the modi operandi of the soul and the manner in which it relates to the external world. Like John Locke (and Descartes too), Berkeley's point of departure can also be seen as the kind of philosophy that requires a firm foundation as a basis for every belief system and every judgment about reality.[1] According to Locke, human knowledge is founded on "ideas" that reside within us and that originate from experience. The immediate and most direct knowledge we have is not of external reality as such, but of ideas that, according to Locke, function as necessary intermediaries between us and the things "out there." The mind itself perceives nothing but these ideas. Locke was well aware that possessing a certain idea does not necessarily mean that one is capable of seeing things as they really are, since one cannot completely rule out illusions: the perception of ideas that are representative of nothing. We can, nevertheless, distinguish between illusions and genuine ideas. The latter, but not the former, represent external objects, which, for Locke, exist independently of the mind. But even if not all ideas are truthful *representations* of external reality, each and every one of us has absolute confidence in the existence of ideas in the mind. Locke has no doubt about this: nothing is less prone to doubt than the certainty one has in the existence of the ideas perceived by one's mind. Berkeley is in complete accord with Locke; their respective philosophies share the same point of departure.

Still, very early on, their paths diverge; before long we find Berkeley set on his own particular philosophical track. If in Locke's worldview there are, on the one hand, ideas and, on the other hand, external objects (represented by ideas), according to Berkeley's view there are only ideas. External objects have been expunged from the philosophical worldview he inherited from Locke. Perhaps it is wrong to say that he expunges external reality; rather, one should say that he amalgamates it: objects are simply ideas. There are no external objects save those that the mind perceives as ideas. In other words, in Berkeley's rendition of the world, things are no more than ideas in the mind. In claiming this seemingly bizarre view, Berkeley nonetheless resorts to commonsense rhetoric. He retains the conceptual distinction between subject and object, between the internal, perceiving mind, and the external, perceived objects. His innovation is in pointing to the origin of this distinction, claiming that it takes place within the mind perceiving the world. "I am not for changing things into ideas, but rather ideas into things; since those immediate objects of perception . . . I take to be the real things themselves." It would seem that Berkeley is trying not only to internalize the external world but also to externalize the mind's internal perceptions. Later on we shall return to this bilateral action.

How does Berkeley manage to justify this philosophical outlook? Even though his writings abound in arguments and proofs, here we shall concentrate only on the most pertinent. Berkeley's main justification of idealism can be found in the arguments he puts forward in repudiating his opponent, the realist. He identifies two kinds of realists: first, those of a philosophical persuasion (Locke being a prime example). The others are what Berkeley refers to as the "illiterate bulk of mankind" or the "brutes"—that is to say, common people who uphold views and beliefs that are not afflicted by problems that bother philosophers and who, in the main, embrace a practical view of the world. Both the philosophers and the brutes entertain the same kind of realism; that is to say, they both accept (whether explicitly or implicitly) there being an external reality independent of our perceptions, and they respond accordingly, that is, they regard reality as not being conditioned in any way by the ideas populating our mind. Berkeley describes nonphilosophical realism thus: "It is indeed an opinion strangely prevailing amongst men, that houses, mountains, rivers, and in a word all sensible objects, have an existence, natural or real, distinct from their being perceived by the understanding." Philosophical realism tends to be more sophisticated. Those who uphold this opinion (first among them being Locke) think that external reality cannot be perceived directly and immediately. Our ideas are the necessary intermediaries between the perceiving subject and sensible objects. And yet the existence of external and independent objects—even though they are not perceived directly—is never doubted, since they are supposed to be represented by ideas, and if there were no objects it is not clear how there could be ideas in the first place. The mainstay of Berkeley's nonrealist argument consists of a series of vigorous assaults against realists of both types (philosophers and commoners). In this respect, it would be more appropriate to call Berkeley an immaterialist (that is, one who denies the existence of matter) than an idealist (that is, one who argues for the exclusivity of ideas). He tries to undermine philosophical realism by addressing the realist with the following question: can your external objects (ideas being merely representations of these) be perceived by the mind? If the answer is in the affirmative, namely, that objects represented by ideas are indeed perceived since they are ideas, then the realist has contradicted himself, "and we have gained our point." If, on the other hand, these objects are imperceptible (which is what the realist contends) then there is no way to know them. Berkeley is employing here an epistemological line of reasoning, and with it he is trying to show that there is no way to ascertain the existence of material objects and thus the claim that necessitates their existence must be rejected on epistemological grounds. In other words, even if matter does exist, one cannot know this by ordinary perceptual means: whether empirically or even through reason. Berkeley resolutely concludes that "if there were external bodies, it is impossible we should ever come to know it; and if there were not, we might have the very same reasons to think there were that we have now."

Next, Berkeley broadens this epistemological line of reasoning and subjugates it to the possibility of knowing matter or material objects and in effect tries to crush the actual framework of the philosophical realists' worldview. This he does by rejecting the notion that ideas *represent* a reality external to them. The target of this onslaught is not only Locke but also the whole philosophical tradition that asserts a correspondence (between ideas and objects, between language and things), which we considered briefly in chapter 2. Berkeley cannot understand how there can be a correspondence between ideas and objects that will enable the former to be representations or images of the latter. If the realist insists that "the ideas we perceive by our senses are not real things, but images or copies of them" it naturally follows that these ideas will be truthful if and only if they faithfully represent the objects. But how can we know this? Who will vouch for us that what is seen as a correspondence between an idea and a thing does indeed correspond? It is Berkeley's contention that, in principle, there can be no such correspondence: if we do not perceive external objects directly, how can we compare them and the ideas that supposedly represent them? In order for us to consider the immediate perception of ideas as the indirect or (mediated) perception of external objects, there has to be something in the ideas themselves that enables them to go beyond themselves—they have to contain within them the relation of *representation* of something external. But Berkeley rejects the notion of representation since it is only possible when there is a shared similarity. That is to say, it is incomprehensible to say that A represents B when there is no way to ascertain this representation:

> It is your opinion, the ideas we perceive by our senses are not real things, but images or copies of them. Our knowledge, therefore, is no farther real than as our ideas are the true representations of those originals. But, as these supposed originals are in themselves unknown, it is impossible to know how far our ideas resemble them; or whether they resemble them at all. We cannot, therefore, be sure we have any real knowledge. Farther, as our ideas are perpetually varied, without any change in the supposed real things, it necessarily follows they cannot all be true copies of them: or, if some are and others are not, it is impossible to distinguish the former from the latter. And this plunges us yet deeper in uncertainty.

The only sense in which it is possible to talk about representation is when there is a similarity between the representation and that which it represents. Accordingly, if ideas represent something, they can only represent something similar to them, that is, other ideas. This is how Berkeley formulates his principle of similarity: "an idea can be like nothing but an idea." He uses this principle to counter all theories of representation and against all forms of materialism or substantial materialism. It is in this manner that Berkeley thinks he can rid philosophy of the curse of skepticism that befell it the day philosophers brought in the distinction between perceived phenomena and true imperceptible things and then sought to overcome it by introducing a criterion capable of distinguishing the perceptual from the real. But since every such attempt is doomed to fail, skepticism will always have the upper hand. Berkeley's solution is the epitome of simplicity: our sensual perceptions are the real things. This simple assumption overcomes skepticism since the gap between appearance and reality (which made the skeptic so anxious) has been eradicated by a phenomenalist approach that *identifies* phenomena with reality.

Undermining the possibility of a correspondence between ideas and things is not only an epistemological argument rallied against the possibility of perceiving material substances but also a linguistic argument whose purpose is to show that the concept matter is meaningless or that it contains within it a blatant contradiction (Berkeley, in fact, adopts both alternatives). How can one understand the existence of something unknown and stripped of any tangible qualities? Matter is supposed to be an unthinking external substance, void of any sensation, yet possessing the qualities of matter—extension, figure, and motion. This is a contradiction since, according to Berkeley, extension, figure, and motion are ideas formed in the mind—were it not so, they could not be apprehended to begin with. Thus "it is absolutely impossible, and a plain contradiction, to suppose any unthinking being should exist without being perceived by a mind." Moreover, when philosophers are asked to describe matter they further complicate things by entangling themselves with words. They end up with such a hazy description that it is in fact utterly meaningless. Thus, for instance, they claim that matter is a substratum that supports extension, but they fail to explain what exactly is meant by "matter's supporting extension." Berkeley concludes that trying to vindicate the existence of material substance—as do philosophers—has no grounding. Apples, stones, trees, and books are ideas blended or combined together, and ideas "cannot exist otherwise than in a mind perceiving them." Accordingly, apples, stones, trees, and books cannot exist if they are not being perceived.

Berkeley is well aware that he still needs to confront the belief in the existence of external material objects when common people, who are neither trained in philosophy nor interested in it, advance this claim. Common people do not bother themselves with explicit pronouncements in support of the existence of the external world; they simply adhere to their firm belief in a reality independent of one's perception of it. The arguments Berkeley used to counter the philosophers will be of no avail in tackling the commonly held convictions on the existence of external objects; it is pointless drawing a common human being's attention to the fact that the concept of matter is imperceptible, self-contradictory, or downright meaningless, since for her matter is not an abstraction, but something fundamentally tangible. Accordingly, Berkeley's argument against the common perception of external reality is addressed mostly to common sense; he tries to convince common people that in fact each of them is no less of an "idealist" than he is himself. That is to say, Berkeley is not disputing a doctrine or learned point of view (since matter, among common people is neither a doctrine nor a learned point of view), but instead insists that *esse* is *percipi* is consistent with what most of them think anyway. To do this, he employs a number of strategies, among them asking his interlocutors to "look into [their] own thoughts." This kind of introspection—a sort of thought experiment—will, in his mind, supply immaterialism with immediate and persuasive corroboration. Berkeley asks us to consider what is implied when I assert the existence of the table in front of which I sit. Is it not merely to state that I perceive it with one or several of my senses? And, were I not to be in the room in which I claim the table to be, am I not claiming, in other words, that if I were in the room I could perceive it? Whether I *actually* perceive the table or I *potentially* perceive the table, its existence for me is a fact only on account of it being an idea in my mind. Existence is inseparable from perception. For Berkeley, this claim epitomizes common sense since, basically, it relies on intuition and the immediacy of introspection. When he tackles the counterclaim, according to which what most people think is that there is an essential difference between the existence of things and their actual perception ("Ask the first man you meet, and he shall tell you, *to be perceived* is one thing, and *to exist* is another"), Berkeley utterly denies that people do in fact uphold such a position, substantiating this view with the results of a little poll he conducts:

Ask the gardener, why he thinks yonder cherry-tree exists in the garden, and he shall tell you, because he sees and feels it; in a word, because he perceives it by his senses. Ask him, why he thinks an orange-tree not to be there, and he shall tell you, because he does not perceive it. What he perceives by sense, that he terms a real being, and saith it *is*, or *exists*; but that which is not perceivable, the same, he saith, hath no being.

Like many of Berkeley's arguments, this too is not as simple as it seems. "Common talk" has challenged him by maintaining that there is a difference between being and being perceived; but Berkeley chooses to evade this contention. He does not go about asking people about the difference, but proceeds immediately to consider the *arguments* they might come up with *were they to be asked* why they uphold the existence of something. In this manner, he transforms the commoners, ex post facto, into philosophers, ignoring the fact that the main difference between them and philosophers is precisely that common people are not overly concerned in seeking proofs for the existence of matter as something apart from perception.

Berkeley averts this specific problem by coming up with yet another articulation of his denial of the existence of mind-independent material substances. Not only does this articulation offer us an interesting account of Berkeley's actual arguments, it also provides us with an interesting vista of his intellectual backdrop:

But, say you, surely there is nothing easier than for me to imagine trees, for instance, in a park, or books existing in a closet, and nobody by to perceive them. I answer, you may so, there is no difficulty in it; but what is all this, I beseech you, more than framing in *your* mind certain ideas which you call books and trees, and at the same time omitting to frame the idea of any one that may perceive them? But do not you yourself perceive or think of them all the while? This therefore is nothing to the purpose: it only shews you have the power of imagining or forming ideas in your mind; but it does not shew that you can conceive it possible the objects of your thought may exist without the mind. To make out this, it is necessary that *you* conceive them existing unconceived or unthought of, which is a manifest repugnancy. When we do our utmost to conceive the existence of external bodies, we are all the while only contemplating our own ideas.

This argument is aimed at both philosophers and commoners. Here too Berkeley asks his interlocutors to cast an inward gaze, hoping that they will reach the inevitable conclusion that it is impossible to conceive of an object of thought as residing *outside* the mind without that object being at the same time *inside* the mind. Clearly this argument shows that Berkeley assumes that what the realist is attempting to do—and miserably failing—is to suggest that an image of a tree in the garden or a book in a room exists (as an image!) without being perceived. And yet the realist, in his philosophical guise and in his guise as a commoner, is not interested in trying to prove the existence of imperceptible *images*. The realist is interested in proving the existence of *objects*, of things, whose existence is independent of their perception, and what he will find unconvincing in Berkeley's argument will be the supposition that it is impossible to assume the existence of an object without first imagining it in the mind as an idea. In other words, Berkeley's argument will only convince someone who, to begin with, accedes to the claim that whatever can be imagined exists concurrently inside the mind. Thus, it is not possible to think of an external object unless we have an idea of it inside the thinking mind. But there might be another alternative: if, per chance, external objects do not exist inside the thinking mind and instead function as a sort of conceptual border. Or consider yet another alternative: an external object could be described by means of a behavioral terminology of actions and dispositions without relying on the necessary presence of its idea in the mind (in this case it might not be an object in the Lockean sense, but it will still be "external"). Yet Berkeley refuses to award an object any other kind of status, limiting it only to that which is present inside the mind.

One thing is clear from all of this, that whatever exists in the mind (namely, ideas) cannot be *equivalent* to the mind itself. Ideas do not generate anything nor are they somehow active, they simply are. Ideas, then, must be passive. They cannot be identical to the mind, since the mind perceives, grasps, and creates something and is thus active. Despite the fact that things perceived (i.e., ideas) "are altogether passive and inert" and that the mind cannot thus be considered to be an idea, Berkeley is nevertheless adamant that the mind exists as something perceiving, thinking, inferring—and he is as certain of this as the fact that he perceives ideas. There is little doubt that in this he deflects from his iron rule (*esse* is *percipi*) since he is willing to assume the mind's existence without actually perceiving it (as mentioned earlier, the mind cannot be an idea!). Interestingly, Berkeley suggests here an additional method by which to recognize real things:

> That ideas should exist in what doth not perceive, or be pro-
> duced by what doth not act, is repugnant. But it is no repug-
> nancy to say, that a perceiving thing should be the subject of
> ideas, or an active thing the cause of them. . . . I say lastly, that
> I have a notion of spirit, though I have not, strictly speaking, an
> idea of it. *I do not perceive it as an idea* or by means of an idea but
> *know it by reflextion.*

Berkeley knows his own mind intuitively and knows it without media-
tion. Even though there are no ideas capable of perceiving the mind or the "self," we experience them by reflection. That is to say, Berkeley not only accepts the existence of ideas but also the existence of something else, a mind, which is not an idea, but contains it and perhaps even creates it.

This reliance on reflection—the directness and immediacy of the inward gaze—enables Berkeley to escape (some would say by the skin of his teeth) a problem that should have irked anyone unwilling to commit himself to the possibility of knowing a reality external to his perception of it: namely, the problem of other minds. Are there other minds or spirits besides the mind of the perceiver? In responding to this pressing question, Berkeley is toying with the limits of reflection or, rather, stretching them to include the possibility of other minds. After all, so he claims, there is nothing in reflection that prohibits us from *assuming* the existence of other finite minds (except my own), which are likewise endowed with the ability to perceive ideas. Needless to say, this is a somewhat strained way of establishing the existence of anything, let alone other minds, and admittedly Berkeley feels that he is unable to offer a conclusive argument for the existence of other such minds. "It is granted we have neither an immediate evidence nor a demonstrative knowledge of the existence of other finite spirits." But, he adds, their existence "is a probability." That is to say, Berkeley is aware

of his mental existence by means of an unmediated act of reflection, whereas he infers the existence of other minds from the immediate reflection he has on the existence of his own mind.[2]

This reflexive, introspective gaze can establish the existence of other finite minds as a mere probability. But, according to Berkeley, it does make the existence of another, *infinite* mind, certain. Introspection shows Berkeley that *his* mind cannot be held responsible for the creation of the ideas lodged in his mind. Quite simply, he does not feel that he creates what he perceives. Ideas exist, and they exist regardless of the will of he in whom they reside: "since I know myself not to be their author, it being out of my power to determine at pleasure what particular ideas I shall be affected with upon opening my eyes or ears: they must therefore exist in some other mind, whose will it is they should be exhibited to me." Berkeley considers this conclusion sufficient proof for the existence of God as an infinite mind: since ideas are passive and cannot create anything themselves, that which creates these ideas inside the mind is an active being that does not itself reside in the mind as an idea—neither in my mind nor in any other mind—hence, it must be an infinite mind. Berkeley proves it thus:

> Sensible things cannot exist otherwise than in a mind or spirit. Whence I conclude, not that they have no real existence, but that, seeing they depend not on my thought, and have all existence distinct from being perceived by me, *there must be some other mind wherein they exist.* As sure, therefore, as the sensible world really exists, so sure is there an infinite omnipresent Spirit who contains and supports it.

Berkeley also has another argument in support of God's existence. This time he does not emphasize the fact that God is the underlying reason of perceived ideas, but regards Him as someone who perceives ideas in the absence of any other perceiver. In this respect, God guarantees the *continuity* of ideas and, according to Berkeley's well-known example, it is God who perceives the tree in the garden when no one else is there to perceive it. God is that which guarantees the tree's continuing existence when it is neither perceived nor residing as something perceived in the mind in the sense of "if I were to be in the garden, I would see it."

When I deny sensible things an existence out of the mind, I do not mean my mind in particular, but all minds. Now, it is plain they have an existence exterior to my mind; since I find them by experience to be independent of it. There is therefore some other Mind wherein they exist, during the intervals between the times of my perceiving them: as likewise they did before my birth, and would do after my supposed annihilation. And, as the same is true with regard to all other finite created spirits, it necessarily follows there is an *omnipresent eternal Mind,* which knows and comprehends all things, and exhibits them to our view in such a manner, and according to such rules, as He Himself hath ordained, and are by us termed the *Laws of Nature.*

Some have read here two separate arguments supporting God's existence—the one moves from the passivity of the mind's ideas to the activity of the infinite spirit that creates them, the other commences by noting that a finite spirit *does not* perceive ideas continuously (since a finite spirit *cannot* continuously perceive an idea) and concludes with its continuous perception by an infinite spirit that perceives ideas when they are not perceived by a finite spirit. The first argument is, prima facie, strikingly similar to customary philosophical proofs for the existence of God, since it is merely another version of positing God as a primary, necessary cause or mover. On the other hand, in Berkeley's second argument, God is consigned to a curious role, to put it mildly: He is supposed to guarantee that ideas projected on the mind's screen (and their existence, it will be recalled, is absolutely conditioned by being perceived by this screen—*esse* is *percipi!*) will not disappear the moment the spectators make for the exist. Like an emergency unit waiting in the metaphorical wings—thus too is Berkeley's God—marshaled and prepared for action, standing to watch over ideas, guaranteeing their continual existence by endlessly perceiving them, especially in those moments when they are not perceived by any other spirit.

One wonders whether Berkeley would have pronounced himself "as one who maintained the most extravagant opinion that ever entered into the mind of man" if he had come across Vasubandhu, an Indian

Buddhist philosopher who lived more than a thousand years before him (in all probability, Vasubandhu flourished in the fifth century CE). Berkeley thought his immaterialism was quite unique, but it had in fact entered Vasubandhu's mind many centuries earlier. Moreover, Vasubandhu devoted several of his key works to advance the claim that to be is identical to being perceived. He debated these issues with the exponents of Indian realism, those who claimed that things exist apart from being perceived by the mind. Berkeley, given his specific vantage point, was justified in sensing that his ideas were a radical departure from much of the prevailing outlook of Western philosophy up until his time. On the other hand, Vasubandhu could not, even had he wanted to, claim that his ideas were at odds with his immediate philosophical milieu. On the contrary, idealism formed an integral part of an influential branch of Indian (and later Tibetan) Mahāyāna Buddhism. This psychophilosophy is referred to by a few different names: in early Mahāyāna literature it is called *Yogācāra*, meaning "Yogic deeds or ways," or the "application of Yoga"; this appellation hints at its psychological character, alluding to the central role meditative practices play in it. The other name extant is *Vijñānavāda*, meaning "the doctrine of consciousness"; lastly, it is also called *Cittamātra*, literally, "Mind Only." This is its most explicit designation. While teaching the "doctrine of mind only," it goes without saying that one of its primary tenets is that worldly objects do not exist outside the realm of the mind. To put it differently, any external object we perceive is, in fact, not external, but rather the projection of a mental image and thus a product of the mind.

Idealism of this kind can be found in the earliest strata of Yogācāra textual developments, those that precede Vasubandhu by at least two centuries. Yet Vasubandhu was, in all likelihood, the first Yogācārin not content with merely supplying an outline of idealism. Of course, he readily subscribed to the terminology and presuppositions of his Yogācārin predecessors (and as a Buddhist he also remained faithful to basic Buddhist terminology). But his writings constitute an attempt to rationally *justify* the Yogācāra idea of "mind only," that is, to offer arguments in support of it and to debate its validity by refuting realism.[3]

Vasubandhu's biography is shrouded in mystery. Like the other major figures of pre-Muslim India, his life story makes impossible demands on a biographer, although there's no lack of fanciful stories about him. These range from the quasi-mythical to the anecdotal: a plethora of mostly incongruent personal details, unattested by either reliable dates or documentation, make this information of little value to a biographer or historian. Generally speaking, classical India's attitude toward history, discussed in chapter 1, is also attested by its attitude to biographical writing. Besides this, part of the mystery surrounding Vasubandhu's biography arises from the fact that he has been attributed with the authorship of an enormous, near encyclopedic, work that meticulously and systematically outlines all the Buddhist schools and doctrines of his time. It is claimed that this text is the product of the realist school of Indian Buddhism. Prima facie, it is difficult to concede to the idea that one philosopher could present so thoroughly both a realist position and its diametrical idealist opposite. Thus some have suggested that there were in fact two different Vasubandhus, the one a realist, the other an idealist. Others have favored the idea of one Vasubandhu who changed his affiliations, shifting to his opponents' views during the different stages of his philosophical development—to begin with he was a realist and later on, under the influence of his brother Asaṅga, he renounced realism so as to become a radical idealist.

Before we take a closer look at Vasubandhu as a philosopher, we should briefly survey his psychological outlook. Vasubandhu drew Yogācāra's main tenets from Yogācāra thinkers who preceded him, and to their doctrines he added his own insights. One of the more interesting elements of this doctrine is its psychodynamic character: Vasubandhu's description of the mind is set in terms of penetrating introspective gazes that expose the different dynamic forces operating on one's mental interiority. This description is, in the main, a propaedeutic for anyone willing to undergo the process of psychoanalysis: consciousness is penetrated and a path to the inner recesses of the mind is diligently followed.[4]

Relying on a well-known Buddhist distinction with which he was evidently familiar, Vasubandhu suggests examining the dynamics of mind from three different aspects or points of view: the imagined (*kalpita*), the conditioned (*paratantra*), and the perfected (*pariniṣpanna*).[5] These three aspects indicate three inward gazes and thus denote different states of mind by means of which Vasubandhu offers us a sort of psychophilosophical journey to the inner depths of human interiority. The imagined aspect refers to the *way* a certain object appears before consciousness and the *way* the mind perceives the object facing it. Thus this aspect is characteristic of the way things are experienced: their appearance hovers around the subjective-objective dichotomy. If the imagined expresses the appearance of an object before the subject, the conditioned is the *very experience* of the imagined appearing. The difference between the conditioned and the imagined is the difference between *what appears* and *the way it appears*. It is clear that empirical sensations are, by necessity, a masquerade—there is no such thing as "immediate sensations" since the conditioned (that which appears) can be accessed by empirical consciousness only through the imagined aspect. That is to say, the only way there can be empirical sensation is under the guise of the imagined, i.e., as a dichotomy. This is highly intriguing: it shows that there is within the mind a kind of necessary severance. Things can never be perceived as they really are since the very act of perceiving them turns them into something else that is "imagined," i.e., different from the conditional, momentary way in which they really exist. This unbridgeable gap between the imagined and the conditioned has a distinctly antirealist flavor: as far as the ordinary way of perceiving the world is concerned, perceived reality is always mediated by the perceiving mind. Hence the repudiation of a representational realism according to which mental images are seen, directly or indirectly, as representing external reality. Representation as such is doomed to fail since there is an unavoidable gap between appearances and the reality they are supposed to represent. The imagined aspect distorts the conditioned aspect; this is inevitable since the conditioned itself is nothing other than an amorphous flow of consciousness forever dependent (hence its designation as conditioned—each moment in this flow is conditioned by all others).

The third aspect is the perfected. Throughout his writings, Vasubandhu offers several definitions of the perfected. But despite this variety—or maybe even because of it—this aspect remains somewhat obscure. This is to be expected. By its very definition, the perfected can only be known as a *negation*—it is no less than the negation of experience. In one place Vasubandhu characterizes it as "the absence of the imagined in the conditioned." That is to say, if you remove from the conditioned the way in which it appears, you will be face to face with the perfected. But this is of course perceptually impossible: when we do remove the imagined from the conditioned we consequently prevent its actual appearance in our consciousness. In this respect, the perfected is an intramental gaze that negates the very mental activity of consciousness. What is especially intriguing here, in this aspect, is the idea that the negation of consciousness dwells within consciousness itself! I shall return to discuss this dynamic stratum when examining the meaning of Vasubandhu's proposed inward journey.

Vasubandhu's psychological doctrine blends in well with his philosophical outlook, which scholars often refer to as idealism. He commences by declaring that the whole world is but an image (vijñāpti)— all there is (or all that we know of) are mental images that occur inside the perceiving mind and only inside it. This is what constitutes his identification of the term *vijñāpti* with the term *mind* (*citta*). In discussing vijñāpti most scholars have gone so far as to call his philosophical outlook "ontological idealism." They claim it is Vasubandhu's contention that there is nothing besides the mind perceiving ideas or images, and thus material bodies (and matter itself) do not exist. According to this interpretation, at the core of Vasubandhu's philosophical doctrine one finds the question "What is there?" to which he would reply decisively: only mind or, more precisely, a plurality of minds, each of them perceiving mental images or objects.

Interpretation of this sort seems to me completely off the mark. To think of Vasubandhu as someone subscribing to ontological idealism is tantamount to making him a scarecrow. If, indeed, he were an ontological idealist who explicitly and decisively argues that there is nothing but consciousness, then it would have been easy, indeed all too easy, to declare him an incompetent philosopher whose reasoning is afflicted by fallacies and who can, at best, raise a few unsophisticated arguments. This, at least, was not the case in classical India. Apparently, Indian philosophers, especially Vasubandhu's realist rivals, took his view—to which they vehemently objected—much more seriously than do some of his modern interpreters. In fact, Vasubandhu did not make any ontological claims about the mind's existence or the inexistence of material substance. This is apparent from the outset, from the way he chose to illustrate the above-mentioned claim, according to which the whole world is but an "image"(vijñāpti). In basing this claim, Vasubandhu refers to situations in which nonexistent objects "appear" in our mind as existent objects: for example when one is mistaken in perceiving something as external when in fact it is the product of the act of perceiving. Vasubandhu exemplifies this claim through a certain ophthalmic disorder (which in Sanskrit is called *timira*) that makes one see strands of hair, minute flies, or sesame seeds in the middle of one's field of vision. At times, this disease can even make one see two moons where there is one. Vasubandhu demonstrates through this example that mental images do not necessarily represent objects outside the mind. He seems to be insinuating that what is applicable to someone afflicted by *timira* applies to regular perception.

What exactly is the philosophical message conveyed by this example? If Vasubandhu were trying through it to argue for the *nonexistence* of external reality, then his argument may indeed seem quite feeble.[6] Such an ontological argument would have reached its diametrically opposed conclusion, namely, it would have brought about yet another reaffirmation of a mind-independent, external reality. Let us look again at the ontological guise of this argument: we are all aware of abnormal conditions in which certain objects—moon, hair, flies—are perceived by certain people as existing independently of their visual faculties despite the fact that they appear to exist only on account of an ophthalmic disorder. Can such argument really refute the existence of external things? Are we genuinely convinced that objects perceived as external are in fact mind dependent? The answer to these questions is negative; on the contrary, it actually presupposes the existence of external objects upon which visual illusions operate. It would have been impossible to demonstrate this through abnormal cases without presupposing that the objects perceived by those whose vision is impaired do indeed exist (albeit not in the shape and form by which they are abnormally perceived). The example of an ophthalmic disorder thus patently fails if it is supposed to illustrate the non*existence* of external objects.

Not surprisingly, scholars who read Vasubandhu's philosophy primarily as an attempt to deny matter and the existence of external objects have been determined to regard his philosophical position as being, in varying degrees, dogmatic or else a labyrinthine thicket of insoluble contradictions. But they are far from convincing. It is my contention that the example of an ophthalmic disorder is not brought up so as to bolster or illustrate a feeble ontological argument that tries to repudiate the existence of external reality but is instead part of a much more radical claim. Moreover, Vasubandhu's choice of example is by no means coincidental.[7]

The ontological interpretation of Vasubandhu's philosophy suggests that the ophthalmic disorder is an exemplification of an illusion—a distortion in one's perception of reality brought about by psychological or physiological malfunction. But an ophthalmic disorder cannot be construed as an example of an illusion. By far the most common example in Indian philosophy for an *illusion* is that of the snake and the rope: a man in near darkness (or whose senses are clouded for some other reason) sees a snake lying on the ground. Understandably, the man is terrified. Yet, the snake is no snake, just a piece of rope. His perception of a snake is merely a perceptual error caused by poor visibility or by mental dispositions. Understanding that the snake is illusory and substituting this faulty perception with that of a rope will soothe and comfort him (even though the perceived rope might itself turn out one day to be an illusion). When someone sees an illusion, the erroneous perception (the snake) is based on a certain supposition about a "correct" external reality (the rope). One cannot understand the illusory perception of the snake without relating it to the existence of the rope. An evident similarity between snake and rope underlies the very error of the perception of "snake." Thus the possibility of correcting the illusory perception lies in the erroneous perception itself, and the illusion will dissipate the moment the object in question is properly illuminated or if the erring onlooker rubs his eyes—literally or metaphorically.

Yet Vasubandhu ignores this stock example. Furthermore, he does not treat the case of an ophthalmic disorder as an exemplification of an illusion. Rubbing the eyes a bit is no balm if the eyes are sick; in fact, this example has nothing to do with erroneous vision. The use of vision here is merely metaphorical. An ophthalmic disorder does not stand for an illusion, but rather a *delusion*. So long as the afflicted person is ill, his worldview cannot be rectified; whether the moon or the flies be better lit, the pupils expanded, the error will persist. The flies or the double moon will be eliminated only by curing the disease itself, that is to say, not by amending some local sensory malfunction, but rather by changing the very framework (the disease being a metaphor of this) in which a double moon or the flies are perceived. Seeing a double moon or having one's field of vision obstructed by strands of hair is not conditioned by a "correct kind of reality." One cannot simply brush aside the hairs appearing in the onlooker's eyes. Moreover, substituting them with threads of rope will be pointless because they are not "based" on anything. This delusion convincingly explains the complete inability to discern between correct and incorrect, external and internal, true and false.

To recapitulate, Vasubandhu is not claiming that we have an illusory grasp of external reality. Were he to do so, his argument would be totally unacceptable since, as mentioned before, an illusion is a clear affirmation that some kind of external reality exists. Vasubandhu proposes something completely different, which has a clear epistemic tinge to it: we can never be sure how we perceive external reality; nothing can satisfactorily vouch that these perceptions actually represent something external and independent of us. Our very grasping of an object (moon, hair, flies or houses, mountains, and rivers) is not enough to determine the exteriority of the perceived object. This then is Vasubandhu's argument: since we can quite easily be deluded into attaching reality to what is perceived by our minds, we must suspend any judgment concerning our ability to deduct "reality" from our perceptual experience. The only thing we can know for sure is that our perceptions contain mental images (vijñāpti), and we have no way of being sure that these perceptions actually represent real objects that exist independently of the mind perceiving them. This is an argument about the boundaries of human knowledge; it is not about the quality or nature of reality as such.

In the course of one of Vasubandhu's philosophical maneuvers in which he tries to embolden his position by replying to objections raised against his epistemic realism, he offers yet another interesting example. In a dream, he says, we determine the presence of perceived objects in space and time. Here too it is impossible to "modify" the experience from within; while dreaming, we see objects and they seem external to us. The only way to get rid of this exteriority is by eradicating the very framework of the dream, i.e., by waking up. In this respect, dreams are similar to delusions since they are misconceptions that traverse our minds while sleeping (let us recall that, in a certain sense, Descartes associated the abnormal delusions of madmen—those who imagine that they are kings or that their bodies are made out of glass—with normal oneiric conditions to which we are exposed every night; Vasubandhu, before him, similarly fused madness with dreams.) Delusions and dreams both give rise to a similar problem: a determining criterion is lost—in neither case can one devise a reliable reality test. Wendy Doniger has described this typically Indian state of affairs

as "an ontological cul-de-sac." Indeed, not only is Vasubandhu's idealism anything but ontological, it is quite the opposite: it undermines the
very possibility of ontology.

The significance of these descriptions is not restricted to the dream
material itself. Dreams cast serious doubts on our capacity to determine the boundaries of external reality and thus they induce a dramatic upheaval in the customary relationships between the inner and the
outer. Dreams testify that exteriority does not logically precede man's
inwardness. Recognition of dreams as an arena in which autonomous
cognitive activity takes place severs the ties between dreams and external reality and draws the philosopher's attention to the possibility that
the very distinction between inner and outer is imbued with a cognitive error or a conceptual fallacy. For Descartes, this is a nightmare,
a terror. In essence, his dream argument is not much different from
Vasubandhu's: it would seem that we have no compelling reason to
doubt that we are now awake and perceive things external to us, since
every one of us perceives herself or himself quite lucidly and is now, at
this very moment, experiencing a particular event (Descartes imagined
himself sitting, cloaked in a dressing gown, opposite the fireplace). But
at times, even whilst dreaming, we occasionally see ourselves in these
same circumstances (Vasubandhu sees himself in space and time and
Descartes casts himself opposite the fireplace)—while we are all, in
truth, nicely tucked in bed. Vasubandhu is well aware of the fact that,
from a practical point of view, we have no difficulties in distinguishing between being awake and dreaming. However, this has no bearing on our ability to draw a clear demarcation line between dreaming
and being awake. We can easily distinguish between these two states
by summoning the "quality" of our respective perceptions. There are
evident differences between these two states; for instance, in a dream
our perceptions tend to be blurry and nebulous, unlike wakeful states
that tend to be experienced with greater clarity and precision.[8] Vasubandhu thus admits that there are differences between dreaming and
being awake of which we may well be aware (so the question "was it a
dream or was I awake?" is, philosophically speaking, uninteresting as
long as it relates to past experiences), but we can never be sure of our
ability to distinguish between them, given that this very distinction,
when made, occurs while dreaming. Even if there are clear differences
between dreaming and wakefulness—both Vasubandhu and Descartes

acknowledge the possibility that my awareness of these differences may take place within my dream. Vasubandhu and Descartes reach the same conclusion: we are incapable of determining whether the mental images that we perceive represent a reality outside them. Notwithstanding the fact that we experience dreams as blurry or confused, their impact on us can be such that we can no longer devise a reality test, nor can we assume a correspondence between our mental images and the reality that lies outside them. Laboring under the daunting shadow of the presupposition of transcendence, Descartes found this philosophically unacceptable, even catastrophic, and decreed that the skepticism ensuing from this state of affairs should be averted come what may. Vasubandhu, on the other hand, sensed no threat. He was a Buddhist philosopher; for him the assumption of exteriority was merely an erroneous belief from which one needs to disengage. In this respect, Vasubandhu plays two "Western roles" in Indian philosophy: to begin with, he assumes Descartes' role by tacitly raising doubts about our ability to be certain of the existence of external reality, but then he proceeds to take on Berkeley's role in canceling out the very threat underlying the complete collapse of our ability to distinguish between inner and outer.

As was the case with Berkeley, Vasubandhu's claim that exteriority is no more than an array of mental images is not only driven by his need to construct an argumentative support for his claims but also, alongside this, by his demolition of the realist position, i.e., his rejection of philosophical realism that in some way or other assumes the existence of an external reality, independent of our perceptions of it and unconditioned by it. The goal of these assaults is to show that the realist's arguments are philosophically untenable and, from the point of view of common sense, absurd.

Generally speaking, this set of arguments is surprisingly similar to Berkeley's. For instance, Vasubandhu cannot imagine how a realist will satisfactorily defend his view that our perceptions are supposed to "correspond" to external objects whose existence is assumed, even if they are not empirically perceived as such. Moreover, he objects to a seemingly Kantian attempt to argue that the fact we recognize in ourselves images of objects we perceive as external sufficiently justifies our assumption that external reality actually exists. According to this last claim, the exteriority of perceived objects is presented as necessarily residing within the epistemic scope of our knowledge. Vasubandhu, however, rejects the realist's assumption both in its ontological and epistemological versions. He claims that it is impossible to understand what it would mean to sensually perceive an "external" object. For such a perception to occur, there has to be a "correspondence" between our image of the object and the object itself. Now, for such a correspondence to materialize, a temporal identity between the image and its subject matter has to persist, but such temporal identity is impossible. The perception of an "object" occurs as a combination of two discrete moments: the first is that infinitesimal moment in which sensory excitation occurs. Like Berkeley, Vasubandhu too sees perception beginning with a momentarily infinitesimal mental event. At this initial moment, the external object has *not yet* been perceived. What there is is only a mental event. In other words, for the duration of the mental event there exists no extramental object that can operate as the object of this perception. Next, the mental event that first occurred as momentary is "stabilized" by undergoing a process of conceptualization (based, among other things, on the memory of past experiences). At this point the external object is *no longer* perceived; rather, it is now being conceptualized. In this second moment of perception, our perceptual recognition stems from the contents of the mind's internal structure. The external object cannot be found in both moments of perception. The first moment is, as it were, preexternal, while the second is, as it were, postexternal. All that occurs is perception, which, metaphorically speaking, always occurs with "eyes wide shut." Imagine the external object as an unfortunate theater actor who is forever missing his cue, making his entrance either a bit too early or a bit too late. If his role depends on his ability to bring to life a well-defined character that replicates something at a certain moment, his missed entrances mean he has completely ceased functioning as an actor. As we have seen, Vasubandhu tries to prove that the assumption of an external object is utterly incoherent since it contradicts everything we know about how perception operates. It is clear that external objects are forever failing to show up "on time."

One of the unresolved difficulties in Berkeley's philosophy was the problem of other minds or other spirits. Berkeley claimed that one knows one's mind by means of a direct and immediate reflexive operation. On the other hand, I can know of the existence of other minds only indirectly, by inferring it from the reflexive quality of my own mind.

Yet this is but an intermediate stage in the argument, since a reflexive investigation of my mind enables me—and perhaps impels me—to acknowledge the existence of God as an infinite spirit that plants in my mind the ideas that I have not authored. Moreover He guarantees the continuity of these ideas while they are not being actively perceived by any finite spirit. Likewise, Vasubandhu faced the problem of how to account for other minds. Yet, as an Indian philosopher immersed in his culture and, moreover, given the underlying assumptions of Buddhist thought, Berkeley's notion of God was not a viable option for him. How then did Vasubandhu explain shared perceptions between different minds?

How did he respond to our basic intuitions about the existence of discrete others? Did he find a way to blend subjective consciousness into the realm of intersubjective communication? If he cannot assume the existence of a supramind whose consciousness contains the totality of all other subjective minds and functions as a vessel for them,[9] then perhaps his only alternative is to admit that he cannot convincingly solve the problem of other minds and the problem of shared perceptions between my mind and other minds. There are scholars that feel that way, i.e., they think that Vasubandhu does indeed concede. Having said that, before we make our final judgment, we should carefully examine what Vasubandhu himself said. In a short polemical treatise that outlines his objections to the realist explanation of the mind and the world, Vasubandhu mentions two sets of objections raised against him:

1. Do other minds exist? And if they do, how do they communicate with each other? Can one mind influence another mind? Is mutual cooperation between different minds conceivable within the framework of a mind-only (*cittamātra*) view? Is it conceivable that in such an idealistic world a person will be morally responsible for his actions? Is it possible to punish criminals and reward the righteous?
2. How do different minds share the contents of the same perceptions? Since perceptions are in essence individual experiences known solely to each of us—how can it be that different minds "see" the very same mental image (tables, chairs, mountains, rivers)? If everything that exists is merely an image,

would it not be more profitable to assume that mental images are essentially private and, as in dreams, can neither be shared nor exchanged?

The first set of questions deals with the linguistic, social, and moral repercussions of epistemic idealism. Its contention is that, in such circumstances where everything is "in the mind," linguistic distinctions are in fact inoperative and it would thereby be impossible to share a common predisposition toward the attainment of social goals and, most seriously, to morally distinguish between right and wrong. On the whole, these questions deal with the apparent discrepancy between idealism and what is seen as common sense.[10]

The second set of questions tends to be of a more general character and challenges the idea of epistemic idealism. In view of these questions, it is unclear how one can accept the claim identifying existence with perception, mainly because we intuitively feel that perceptions are shared: standing in front of a given tree, different people will see the exact same tree and thus the idea of a tree is common to all who perceive it. Vasubandhu's philosophy is apparently incapable of explaining this simple fact. Berkeley, as a last resort, ushered in God as a supramind, as a consciousness that is supposed to allow (among other things) perceptions. Since Vasubandhu cannot employ God as a guarantor for intersubjective perception (he vehemently denies the existence of God), it would seem that he has no choice but to leave this matter unexplained.

Prima facie, this is precisely what Vasubandhu does. His replies to these two sets of questions are at first glance far from satisfying. In answering the first set of questions, he turns to parapsychology (or so it seems): there are, he says, quasi-telepathic states in which one mind can influence another and even transmit, through spiritual means of communication, images of external objects. The reply to the second set of questions considers cases of borderline psychopathology: sharing mental images is possible, Vasubandhu apparently says, in the same manner that a group of people share the same hallucination under extreme mental duress or, alternatively, when a group entertain the same delusions about things and events. And yet it is crucial that we look at these replies in greater detail. Hidden beneath an apparent evasion there is a unique philosophical outlook.

Vasubandhu's reply to the first set of questions is conveyed as a dialogue with a (presumably real) opponent; this opponent is asking him difficult questions, and each reply prompts him to pose an even more difficult query.[11] All the opponent's objections stem from common sense—basic assumptions that a normal sane person would regard as self-evident, without feeling compelled to subjugate these assumptions to an (unnecessary) critical examination. Such an investigation is redundant precisely because of the special circumstances that award these assumptions the status of common sense.

One objection probes Vasubandhu's idealism even further and does so by looking at it from the direction of one mind having an influence upon the other. Does this not constitute a proof that something external to one's mind exists? Does it not compel us, in the sheer name of common sense to assume some sort of exteriority in the form of another person? Berkeley's response assumed the probable existence of other minds; Vasubandhu briefly considers a similar possibility: it is a distinct impression in another mental stream that causes my cognition. This can happen without us necessarily assuming the existence of an external object.

An opponent's other, more pertinent, question hinges on moral norms, social conventions, and societal customs. All these would fail to make sense in a world where everything is but a reflection of what is perceived by my mind. Were it not for the actuality of external reality, neither language nor speech could exist, nor, for that matter, actions. It would be ridiculous to ask someone to take personal responsibility for a morally reprehensible act, because he or she could rightly ask: personal responsibility for what? If external things are but appearances in the mind of whoever perceives them, what is the meaning, for example, of killing someone or something? Would a shepherd be responsible for killing the sheep in his keeping if these sheep were only perceptual images? Would he be responsible for any other act he "performed"? And what is killing, or murder, or any other immoral act? Is there such a thing as murder if there is no such thing as a corpse? And what is death, anyway? It seems that this immaterialistic outlook induces the real, everyday world, with all its manifoldness, to fade out. To paraphrase Alice's down-to-earth question, what is the use of a world without events and conversations?

Vasubandhu offers only a partial reply to these questions. He elides the question of how we can take personal, moral responsibility for our actions; instead, he stubbornly denies the very exteriority of these actions. He seems to be implying that moral questions such as these are irrelevant to his mentalistic world. If determining that a murder has been committed depends on finding a corpse, then, yes, a murder has not been committed: one should abstain from saying that the shepherd killed his sheep and death has no domain. Death is merely a mental event. Vasubandhu explains that a perception of death is but a change or modification of mental states. He sees murder as another case of an impression in one mental stream bringing about an effect in a distinct mental stream—in this case the cessation of the current life course of that mental stream. Again we find ourselves considering the coherence between mental images instead of looking for their correspondence to external things. This coherence can be transmitted between minds. Thus actions and judgments that apparently presuppose a shared external substratum arise because of minds that mutually influence each other—one mind functioning as a screen and the other as a projector capable of projecting its images not only on its own internal screen but also on the screens of other minds too. Like Berkeley, Vasubandhu insists that images arising in our minds as a result of mental activity (in the sense that the mind is the only possible screen on which they can appear) need not necessarily mean that we own them. These projections between different minds are mutual, and there is no reason to assume, as Berkeley did, that there must be a sort of divine supraprojector.

Vasubandhu's appeal to telepathy leaves the philosophical reader somewhat perplexed. This perplexity might even increase as one reads further in the text: Vasubandhu, so it seems, takes his telepathic suggestion seriously enough to support it by relying on folkloristic Buddhist sources. He refers to stories (which would have probably been familiar to his contemporaneous readers) about kings, ascetics, ghosts, demons, and other such creatures that all gravitate around telepathic communication: for example, one story recounts how certain demons caused someone to lose his memory; another, how a paṇḍit used his mental prowess to transmit his dream to a certain king; yet another story—dealt with in even greater detail—recounts a meeting between certain revered seers in the Daṇḍaka Forest and a disrespectful king (he showed up at their hermitage without removing his shoes and his sword). After he had left, the seers took it upon themselves to punish him and—making use of their unique mental powers—cast upon him such horrific nightmares that even after he'd awakened he was still in their throes. It would seem that narratives taken from myths, legends, and epics—stories that evidently form part of the common and received background of Vasubandhu's era of Indian Buddhism—are offered as conclusive evidence attempting to corroborate telepathy.

What are we to make of these puzzling examples? Did Vasubandhu genuinely believe that folktales actually corroborate philosophical arguments? Should we think of him as being naive enough to place his trust in his culture's pervading folk beliefs surrounding parapsychological connections between spirits or minds? Perhaps what he is suggesting here is much more daring and interesting and, moreover, at heart philosophical. To assess these possibilities in the manner that befits them, we should first examine Vasubandhu's reply to the second set of questions mentioned above. These, it will be remembered, concern the problem of shared perceptions. Unlike the first set of questions, which were preoccupied with the possibility of one mind *actively* influencing another mind, here Vasubandhu is asked to account for something completely different: the case of two totally *passive* minds that perceive a given image simultaneously. If the first set of questions considered the possibility of one mind functioning as a projector of images for a mental screen apart from itself, here we are faced with a situation in which identical images are projected on two different mental screens without the one influencing the other. To put it in Berkeleyan terms, this is a question about the passive reception of ideas. Can Vasubandhu explain how identical sensory experiences occur in different minds, given his contention that this experience does not represent external reality, whether directly or indirectly? (One should remember that here too Berkeley assumed what Vasubandhu could not even imagine, namely, that God's infinite mind was capable of implanting ideas in finite human minds and so bring about identical sensible perceptions.

Vasubandhu insists that shared perceptions are possible. He illustrates this by means of extraordinary shared experiences of sensory perceptions that, despite the fact that they are shared, do not represent anything in external reality. Different commentators have called these extraordinary experiences cases of "shared hallucinations." Thomas Wood, for example, calls Vasubandhu's epistemological position "the doctrine of collective hallucination." B.K. Matilal went even further and characterized Vasubandhu's reply as suggesting the possibility of shared experience that arises due to what Matilal calls "common psychosis." Matilal saw no reason to take this reply lightly, since "in our technological-scientific times," so he claimed, "it is not impossible to create conditions for some common delusion which can deceive a number of persons." Wood is unconvinced by all this; after carefully inspecting well-attested cases in psychological literature, he feels that he cannot accept Vasubandhu's account of shared hallucinations since it is scientifically implausible. It would seem that these two scholars have fallen straight into one of the traps that Vasubandhu, with great skill, has laid for his readers. As before, Vasubandhu advocates the idea of collective hallucinations by alluding to myth; both Matilal and Wood failed to take Vasubandhu's recurring use of mythic terminology seriously enough.

The story Vasubandhu recounts is drawn from Mahāyāna lore. Different Indian Buddhist texts attest to the existence of hell-worlds. There the doomed are subject to immense sufferings (for instance: one victim will be chopped up into minute bits, another will be forced to swim in a pool of filth and excrement). Still, being in a hell-world is not conceived as a form of punishment. The Buddhist idea of hell is radically different from its many Western counterparts. It is all too common to picture hell as a place where justice is dispensed, where one is sent by a supreme judge, the lord of the earth, or his court of justice passing sentence. The court of justice makes hell a divine prison, yet another manifestation of divine retribution. Buddhism, as is well known, entirely rejected the idea of such a supreme dispenser of justice. This rejection trickled down to folkloristic Buddhism too; hell-worlds were conceived in such a way that any meddling in the affairs of this world by a transcendent element is effectively blocked out. Hell-worlds are *natural outcomes*, inevitable effects whose necessity is derived from a general and universal law that regulates well-defined relationships between causes and effects in all sentient beings. This is known as the law of karma, which states that everything is begot of sufficient causes and is, accordingly, determinate; moreover, every sentient being is to be held completely responsible for the fruits of his actions. Hell is one expression of the law of karma. It is subject to the inescapable efficaciousness characteristic of every action. Whoever finds himself in hell is there because he has to be there and cannot be anywhere else. No power in the universe can relocate him before the fullness of time or absolve him or undo his previous acts. "To be in hell" is therefore indistinguishable from "to be one whose torment is the natural and inevitable outcome of one's previous actions." It is inconceivable that whoever is there does not "deserve" his torment, nor that he will not actually experience it.

Yet Buddhist lore mentions that besides those doomed to suffer in hell there are also hell-keepers. Hell cannot exist without them, since these wardens function as *torturers* (and there is no torture without a torturer). These wardens are also supposed to make sure that those doomed to dwell in hell will each receive the exact measure of the torture they deserve. Here Vasubandhu intervenes, inquiring into the status of these hell-keepers. If *all* those dwelling *in* hell have to be there, then it follows that the wardens, if they too are in hell, "deserve" to be there, and thus they are there by *necessity*; that is, their very presence in hell necessitates that we see them as deserving infernal torture and being subjected to it. But this is impossible since if the wardens deserve to be tortured and are in fact tortured, then they cannot be wardens, that is to say, they cannot be those who inflict torture—one cannot be both the one tortured and the one inflicting it. On the other hand, if the wardens are those who "do not deserve to be in hell," and thus are not subject to infernal torment, then they cannot be there, since hell is populated only by those who, by necessity, have to be there (in the sense of "deserving" torture). Verily a strange situation: the hell-keepers must be in hell (no hell is without torture) but at the same time cannot be in hell. The very concept of hell-keeper is self-contradictory: whoever dwells in hell is not a warden; and whoever is considered a warden—cannot dwell in hell. But it is a necessity that all hell-beings see these wardens, otherwise Buddhist hell-worlds would be logically inconceivable. Seen from the hell-beings' point of view—they all perceive their wardens. According to Vasubandhu, this proves beyond any doubt that passively shared sensory perceptions (or ideas) are possible, despite the fact that they lack any external representation. There are no hell-keepers, but hell-beings collectively experience them (as torturers!). We have then a situation in which sensory perception is experienced in an *identical* manner by a large number of different beings, despite the fact that the objects of their perception do not exist beyond the confines of their minds.[12]

Matilal, among other notable scholars, fell into the psychological trap by mistakenly reading this example as an attempt to prove empirically that there are such things as collective hallucinations or mass psychoses. Vasubandhu, so he says, is arguing for a state of shared internal reality: in light of his examples, the fact that certain minds "see" the same image does not mean that it necessarily represents an objective state of affairs; it might be that this image is no more than a process of "objectivization"—something that consciousness does when it supposedly projects its inner contents beyond itself, creating thereby a framework and endowing it with "exteriority." Alas, this is a distortion of Vasubandhu's claim. Vasubandhu was not attempting to base his idealism on actual borderline cases of psychopathology or parapsychology. If this were his intention, it is highly improbable that he would resort to dubious examples that fail to bolster the "argument from borderline cases"; on the contrary, they are more likely to weaken his argument, and, needless to say, if he were trying to argue from borderline cases, it would be much better to cite everyday familiar instances of such phenomena. It seems highly unlikely that Vasubandhu thought these stories were a genuine source of factual evidence.[13] Moreover, it is hard to accept that he failed to clearly distinguish between fact and fiction. One should recall that Vasubandhu, as a Buddhist philosopher, was thoroughly committed to critical-analytical thinking and that, for someone like him, even the Buddha's own words could not be taken at face value since they would be only a partial or relative expression of the truth (this was so because these teachings had been directed at people who could not immediately discern the depth of his teaching). And if this is how Vasubandhu understood the nature of Buddhist teaching, one can rest assured that he would not have subscribed to simplistic, uncorroborated and unproven folktales to justify his philosophical position. Having said that, we cannot help noticing that he repeatedly draws upon such stories, and, moreover, at crucial junctures in his philosophical expositions. It is my contention that there is nothing arbitrary in this appeal to myth and that it is, in fact, quite intentional. If this is the case, then the fact that he appeals to myths in his argumentation is no less important then the actual contents of mythical stories themselves.

Let us reexamine the story of the hell-keepers and see what we can glean from it. Many of Vasubandhu's readers have failed to notice that what appeals to Vasubandhu in this story is *not* his attempt to substantiate intersubjective hallucinations. He uses this story differently; the main thrust of the tale is definitely not to draw our attention to the fact that the different minds (of the hell-beings) experience the same perception (of hell-keepers), but rather that this perception is common to them all *even though it is logically impossible*—given the story's basic presuppositions (i.e., the existence of hell). According to the story's own presuppositions, it is impossible to assume that hell-keepers actually exist, despite the fact that is absolutely necessary to do so according to these very presuppositions! Vasubandhu is using the story of hell to illustrate how the mind can generate logically impossible situations. These situations undermine the clear distinction we make between a fictional narrative and an objective nonfictional reality. Vasubandhu has a much more daring proposal: the dichotomy of reality and fiction is supposedly exchanged with a much more subtle classification according to which perceptions and experiences are to be characterized by the degree of coherence that exists between different perceptions. Hence fact cannot be distinguished from fiction (and vice versa) merely by relying on the criterion of representation. Fact does not represent reality any more than fiction does. Fact is in no way more public than fiction is. Intersubjective perceptions do not arise from the existence of a reality out there, but are made possible by a certain inward arrangement of mental images. So, in both cases, that is, both with fact and fiction, one is equally justified in assuming shared perceptual experiences without committing oneself ontologically to the existence of an exteriority that is not dependent upon our perceptions.

This is the gist of Vasubandhu's argument from mythical hell. The anguished hell-beings must see hell-keepers that cannot be seen—a tale about an impossible necessity. What appears to consciousness is not a representation of external reality but an arrangement of images that eventually makes up a "story," and it is pointless to look for what underlies this story. Except for the rules governing the narrative with which reality is portrayed, our cognitive process is subject to no other rules. In this respect, the story about the hell-beings is a paradigm of antirealist epistemology where "true" and "false" are wholly dependent on an internal coherence that is to be found among our perceptions. The necessary appearance of the impossible is therefore a blunt manifestation of our inability to approach "reality" as something separated from the generating frame of consciousness. Vasubandhu is arguing for an extreme antirealist stance, which regards truth as dependent on the mind and thereby denies that truth is correspondence between our cognitions and reality. He is not speculating about whether we can empirically experience collective hallucinations. Matilal was wrong when he compared Vasubandhu's argument from hell to Descartes' malicious demon. To my mind, there is no greater dissimilarity than between these two arguments. It will be recalled that the malicious demon was brought in only after insanity was ruled out. There is something methodological about Descartes' demon: it is a fictional character whose aim is to eliminate fictionality once and for all, including, of course, itself. On the other hand, Vasubandhu's hell (much like Nāgārjuna's emptiness) is meant to perpetuate this fiction. One can escape from the malicious demon's grip if, alongside the *cogito's* epistemic precedence we also assume God's ontological precedence. But, if only because of his insistence that knowledge is always mediated, there is no escape from Vasubandhu's hell to the external world of things. There is nothing outside the human mind to which we turn and that is ontologically independent of the perceiving mind. Vasubandhu's hell—let me emphasize it yet again—perpetuates fictionality. It will forever have hell-keepers that perforce cannot be there. Hell will thus be deprived of a realistic truth-value, exactly like the fictional medium in which it is transmitted. Vasubandhu is interested in collective hallucinations and interpersonal telepathic phenomena only as a way of pushing the boundaries of reasoning to the point where they fall apart so that they can be replaced by the flexible and elastic boundaries of the human imagination. This also explains the way in which Vasubandhu uses the story of the sages of the Daṇḍaka Forest: the influence one mind exerts upon another is possible within a worldview in which our perceptions only represent themselves and, accordingly, any claims we make about them is determined solely by the story's inner logic, while there is no way to ascertain if and how the story corresponds to its allegedly underlying reality. Vasubandhu appeals to these borderline psychopathological or telepathic states so as to demonstrate our incapacity to justifiably distinguish between the limits of imagination and the limits of reality.

Vasubandhu and Berkeley's epistemologies are astonishingly similar, and it is difficult not to be impressed by this resemblance. This is most apparent in their respective argumentation when they attempt to repudiate realist philosophies. These view ideas as representations of external reality, neither dependent nor conditioned by these ideas. The barrage of objections that Berkeley raised against the realist is not much different from that of Vasubandhu's. Besides this argumentative similarity, there is also what one might care to call "similar idiosyncrasies." It will be recalled that Berkeley himself was well aware that his views were considered idiosyncratic. "Subjective" idealism of the Berkeleyan type (in which the self is positioned opposite its ideas) was a rarity in Western philosophy beginning with its Greek origins and up until Berkeley's time.[14] Yogācāra subjectivism was also a novelty, not only for Buddhist philosophy but also, indeed, for the whole of Indian philosophy. The idiosyncrasy and rarity of their respective philosophies meant that both Berkeley and Vasubandhu had to conduct their philosophical battles on two fronts. On one front are poised the realist philosophers and on the other, in all likelihood, the very same philosophers, except that this time they appear guised as commoners, as arbiters of common sense. As with Berkeley, Vasubandhu's position too was attacked not only by non-Buddhist realist philosophers but also by Buddhists who tried to reproach him for the patent absurdity of his rejection of exteriority and denial of representationalism. For example, the Buddhist philosopher Candrakīrti, one of Nāgārjuna's most important expositors, claimed that Yogācārins inflict irreparable damage on common sense. Nāgārjuna, it will be recalled, argued that his philosophy is congruent with our everyday and commonplace assumptions about reality (since it is a philosophy that explains human behavior in terms of conventions). But, according to Candrakīrti, Vasubandhu's outlook (and that upheld by his followers) is incongruent with a conventional picture of reality. With concealed derision Candrakīrti rallies against the idealists saying that

> As for us, we are in a very difficult position to attack the convention of the world. So *you* attack the convention of the world. If the world does not oppose you, we too will go along with you. And if there is opposition from the world, just for that reason we shall stay neutral. Let the world and you dispute; then if you win (since we do desire that) we will follow you. But if you are defeated by the world, then we will follow the world, which had the greater power.

Candrakīrti was willing to accept the Yogācāra argument that rejected the possibility of perceiving the existence of external, mind-independent, objects. However, it is his contention that the Madhyamaka can equally furnish us with arguments, no less conclusive, that repudiate the perception of mental entities. When both realism and idealism are rejected, we are left inevitably with conventionalism. There is little doubt that Candrakīrti was confident of his victory over Yogācāra idealism and saw it defeated by a force superior to it: the "world" and its conventions. Still, his ironical attack did little to unnerve Vasubandhu and his idealist followers. For them, the "world" is not a reliable arbitrator since its very exteriority has been seriously challenged. An appeal to the world is but an appeal to those intermediary mental processes through which our picture of world is constructed.

The promulgators of common sense launched a similar critique of Berkeley's views. The quintessential English intellectual Samuel Johnson authored one of the more famous and most virulent attacks on Berkeley's idealism. Consider the following anecdote, taken, of course, from that Sancho Pancho of all biographers, James Boswell. In his biography of Johnson, Boswell informs us that following a visit to a church in Harwich in which Johnson made him kneel to pray, they stood talking for some time together about "Bishop Berkeley's ingenious sophistry." Boswell recalls saying to Johnson that though Berkeley's doctrine is not true, it is impossible to refute it. Johnson promptly answers, "striking his foot with mighty force against a large stone, till he rebounded from it, 'I refute it *thus.*'" Many consider this sharp quip to be an utter devastation of Berkeleyan idealism. Like Vasubandhu, it would seem that Berkeley was not too impressed by this manner of criticism. No external act, even violently assaulting a large stone, can successfully refute the opinion that exteriority is no more than a structured product of interiority. Argumentation of this sort is wholly fallacious. Striking a stone with force (and, in this respect, any other conceivable act, even raising one's hand) will fail to quash a philosopher who, to begin with, does not admit that a kick or a hand gesture have an exteriority of their own.

At first glance it would seem that Berkeley and Vasubandhu are identical twins—a rare species of a Buddhist philosopher breathing through the nostrils of an Irish bishop. However, besides the obvious similarities between them, Berkeley and Vasubandhu's idealism take different, at times even contrary, courses. Interesting things can be gleaned from their divergent paths. Berkeley is not as indifferent as Vasubandhu about the presupposition of transcendence, and in his own unique and somewhat strange manner he reveals a deep concern with the fate of this presupposition. Berkeley's philosophy gives precedence to internal-mental states and also turns exteriority into the product of this internal state—still, Berkeley stops short of embracing the extreme views that Vasubandhu unhesitatingly endorses. There is a specific point, which we shall identify further on, where Berkeley's philosophy comes to a halt while Vasubandhu, his twin, runs headily along on a course that for Berkeley is much too perilous. It seems to me that Berkeley is trying to *preserve* the presupposition of transcendence at the price of a radical alteration of the conceptual framework in which transcendence is present. This makes him the diametrical opposite of Kant, who responded to Berkeley's position by calling it "illusory idealism" and, as noted in the previous chapter, suggested preserving this conceptual framework at the price of emptying transcendence. If we were to employ the same terminology when speaking of Berkeley, one could say that he tries to avoid the emptying of transcendence. Instead, he suggests a dramatic conceptual shift—a shift that enables him, when all things are said and done, to safeguard and preserve the presupposition of transcendence. The difference between Berkeley and Kant is like the difference between two theater directors, each of whom is trying to keep a certain show running; the one (Berkeley) throws away all the scenery in order to maintain the plot, while the other (Kant) removes the plot and keeps the scenery intact as an empty framework.

In order fully to understand the limits of Berkeley's idealism, it is necessary to trace, in some detail, an idea that Berkeley was forever preoccupied with. I am referring here to his unflappable assault on what he called abstract ideas. This assault takes shape in a set of arguments that run throughout most of his writings.

Some of Berkeley's commentators, even those who saw him in favorable terms, sensed that these arguments were somewhat excessive; for them, it was all just a skirmish between him and Locke, in whose epistemology abstract ideas played a central role. This way of interpretation mistakenly belittles the importance that the repudiation of abstract ideas has in Berkeley's overall philosophical outlook. Berkeley himself was well aware of its importance; he repeatedly stresses throughout his writings that the repudiation of abstract ideas is the foundation upon which his philosophical edifice rests. As early as in section 4 of *The Principles of Human Knowledge* he takes issue with the "opinion strangely prevailing among men that houses, mountains, rivers, and in a word all sensible objects, have an existence, natural or real" and that this existence is "distinct from their being perceived by the understanding." Berkeley asks whether it is not "plainly repugnant" that this opinion should prevail, immediately offering an explanation: the reason for the strange opinion that things exist independently of being perceived is to be found, "at bottom to depend on the doctrine of *abstract ideas.*" In yet another passage in *The Principles of Human Knowledge*, Berkeley notes that the "plainest things in the world, those we are most intimately acquainted with and perfectly know, when they are considered in an abstract way, appear strangely difficult and incomprehensible."

According to Locke (at least as Berkeley understood him) abstract ideas are the only means by which man can think in general terms and thus, for him, they are the necessary foundation upon which it is possible to lay general truths. Locke contends that abstract ideas explain how words become meaningful: generally speaking, the connection between words and ideas gives words their meaning; thus the meaning of any general idea (for example, *triangle*) will be dependent upon how this idea relates to the abstract idea of a triangle. That is to say, I can employ the word *triangle* and apply it to all triangles only because in my mind I have a general and abstract idea of triangle.[15] If such an idea does not present itself to the mind, how can one explain man's faculty for making generalizations?

Berkeley did not deny the existence of general ideas—his idiosyncrasy did not go that far—but he did fervently oppose the possibility of *abstract* general ideas. The act of generalization, to which he accedes, enables us to see qualities or attributes as shared by many particular things. This kind of generalization allows the mind to imagine parts of ideas separated from the "objects" from which they derive, and even to imagine different compounds, thus creating imaginary objects as a combination of existing things. Berkeley concedes that he can generalize by subtracting parts from given objects; he can then reassemble these parts, combining them in his imagination so as to create unreal objects that are the fruits of fancy (for example, "the upper parts of a man joined to the body of horse"). Similarly, it is possible to conceive the smell of a rose without thinking of the rose itself.

On the other hand, an *abstract* general idea involves a kind of "surgical" operation: it requires "to abstract from one another, or conceive separately, those qualities which it is impossible should exist so separated" to the point where the idea is abstracted from any concrete content and from any specific character it may have. According to Berkeley, this "abstractive" surgical operation is not only unwarranted, it is, moreover, unfeasible (cloaked beneath a thin veneer of irony, he says that it is simpler to "divide a thing from itself" than to abstract an object from all its qualities). The mind here exceeds its own limitations: it perceives, for instance, a certain color (say red), but then abstracts this perception from the redness within it and creates an abstract idea of color that cannot be the idea of any specific color. "The mind, by leaving out of the particular colours perceived by sense that which distinguishes them one from another, and retaining that only which is common to all, makes an idea of colour in abstract which is neither red, nor blue, nor white, nor any other determinate colour." For Berkeley, the superimposition of abstraction drives philosophy into the absurd position where abstract ideas are seen as things that are, in principle, inconceivable (were they conceivable they would certainly not be abstract). If such is the case, not only do we find the inconceivable apparently trying to explain the conceivable but also it is the inconceivable that makes the conceivable possible. What could be easier, Berkeley asks his reader, than to look into one's own thoughts and see whether they have or "can attain to have" such abstract ideas—for instance, "the general idea of a triangle, which is, neither oblique, nor rectangle, equilateral, equicrural, nor scalenon, but all and none of these at once?" Indeed, a very odd situation: we expect there to be a triangle but, at the same time, repudiate its existence in every conceivable manner.

This argument concludes with the proposition that abstract ideas are a logical impossibility. Let us recall that Berkeley does not object to general ideas as such. But, according to him, it is logically impossible to deduce that one can *abstract* a triangle from *all* its qualities, while contain them simultaneously within. The crucial difference between a legitimate generalization and an illegitimate abstraction is that a generalization "extends only to the conceiving separately [of] such objects, as it is possible may really exist or be actually perceived asunder." That is to say, the limits of generalization are the limits of our sensory perceptions, and legitimate generalization will never exceed this limit. On the other hand, the notion of abstraction against which Berkeley rallies does not recognize the existence of a perceptual borderline and permits the mind to make constructs that are beyond the range of perceivable objects. Such an abstraction incurs no benefit to anyone and is nothing more than "innocent diversion and amusement." Here Berkeley resorts to more than a touch of irony and says that the "generality of men which are simple and illiterate never pretend to *abstract* notions. It is said they are difficult and not to be attained without pains and study. We may therefore reasonably conclude that, if such there be, they are confined only to the learned."

Not only is it impossible to assume that abstract ideas exist, but it is quite pointless. According to Berkeley, the reason Locke felt compelled to admit to such ideas arose out of a linguistic necessity: were we not to assume the existence of abstract ideas, we could not account for generalizations in language. How it is possible to generate words that do not relate to one definite object but rather to the common denominator of different things? According to Locke, language itself can only be explained by assuming the existence of abstract ideas. What distinguishes between beast and man is the uniqueness of the latter's linguistic faculties. Locke believed that this is explained by man's ability to make abstractions, which beasts obviously lack. Only someone capable of making abstractions can create language. Berkeley does not second this opinion. To begin with, he notes with derision that if the ability to generate abstract ideas is the property distinguishing man and beast then he "fears that a great many of those that pass for men must be reckoned into their number" (i.e., the beasts). More to the point, according to Berkeley, if language presupposes the ability to make generalization, this does not mean that we also have to assume that man is endowed with a unique faculty responsible for the formation of abstractions and the creation of abstract ideas; all that is required is to understand that "a word becomes general by being made the sign, not of an abstract idea, but of several particular ideas, anyone of which it differently suggests to the mind." In this Berkeley is attempting to reduce abstraction to generalizations and to argue that this is sufficient to explain the uniqueness of human language. The difference between generalizations and abstractions becomes highly significant, since it now seems that Berkeley rejects abstraction not only as a mental idea but also as a part of our linguistic faculties. The difference between the "language" of the beasts and human language is not, as Locke believed, a matter of quality—it is by no means the difference between a system of concrete signs and a system of abstract signs. The difference is solely quantitative: the "language" of the beasts has merely particular signs while human language has signs that under one verbal or terminological canopy can generalize several particular perceptions.

The repudiation of abstract ideas had many interesting repercussions on the course of Western philosophy. At times it was endorsed by the advocates of common sense in their assault against pronouncements they saw as being overly obscure and enigmatic. At other times it was advanced as a final rebuttal of metaphysical thinking. In short, Berkeley's repudiation of abstract ideas had many repercussions, some of which can still be sensed to this day. Interestingly, this brings to mind Nāgārjuna's assaults on pretentious philosophers seeking to reach general and absolute conclusions on abstract matters such as the supposedly independent nature of the self. In this context one might want to consider, for example, D. H. Lawrence's acrid pronouncement, which is undoubtedly one of the aforementioned repercussions (though, in spirit, it is more akin to the kind of extremity evident in Nāgārjuna):

> You've got to find a new impulse for new things in mankind, and it's really fatal to find it through abstraction. No, no; philosophy and religion, they've both gone too far on the algebraical tack: Let X stand for sheep and Y for goats: then X minus Y equals Heaven, and X plus Y equals Earth, and Y minus X equals Hell. Thank you! But what coloured shirt does X have on?

Be that as it may, a controversy rages among Berkeley's readers and commentators as to the extent of his success in rejecting abstract ideas and also as to its place in his overall idealistic philosophy. Let us not dwell upon these issues. A short lead into how the denial of abstract ideas works in his idealism will suffice. Berkeley's denial of abstract ideas is less essential for establishing his idealism—rather, its main contribution lies in its ability indirectly to retain the presupposition of transcendence. In more explicit terms, one should examine his assault on abstract ideas from an additional angle, by asking what it is intended to preclude. Put differently, we might ask what damage can the notion of abstract ideas do to Berkeley's worldview.

Berkeley's assault on abstract ideas highlights the limits of language. With the denial of abstract ideas we end up with a much scantier version of language (when compared to its realistic account). A mind-dependent world constitutes a fatal blow to the idea of language as a (direct or indirect) representation of external reality. Abstract language is a companion to external reality; just as it is impossible to grasp an external object—that is, as something that is both divorced from a particular perception and at the same time included within it—so too it is impossible to employ words whose meaning is both disassociated from any of its applications and simultaneously present in all of their applications. Berkeley was well aware of the implicit dangers of what he called "words to no manner or purpose, without any design, or signification whatsoever [. . .] mere jargon." He tried to avoid this danger of meaningless words by precluding the mind running amok in creating abstract ideas and by blocking wild, nonsensical linguistic uses of abstract terms. It seemed to him that if he could successfully eliminate abstractions, not only would his immaterialism be fortified, but, moreover, it would act as a bulwark, protecting the presupposition of transcendence from vehement attacks launched against it by "skeptics" and "atheists." This interpretation does not seem congruent with the manner in which Berkeley's philosophy is usually understood, since, it will be recalled, he was seen as a strange man and a dubious philosopher precisely because people were under the impression that he preferred interiority to exteriority. Yet a careful analysis of how he formulated his ideas will show that Berkeley did not, in fact, relinquish the alienable core of the presupposition of transcendence. This was expressed by his wish to establish a direct line between ideas and things; ultimately, the purpose of his suggested internalization was to maintain the somewhat childish picture of a harmony between a perceiving interiority and the contents of its perceptions. There is more than a touch of naïveté here: if only it were possible to sustain the innocence characterizing the relationship between our perceptions and known things! Berkeley himself admits that he would have liked to reach a point where people would say "thing" and mean "idea." Exorcising the use of abstraction from language is not meant to bring about its deconstruction, but, rather, it is supposed to lead to a refinement and purification:

If by *ideas* you mean immediate objects of the understanding, or sensible things which cannot exist unperceived, or out of a mind, then these things are ideas. But whether you do or do not call them *ideas*, it matters little. The difference is only about a name. And whether that name be retained or rejected, the sense, the truth, and reality of things continues the same. In common talk, the objects of our senses are not termed *ideas*, but *things*. Call them so still; provided you do not attribute to them any absolute external existence, and I shall never quarrel with you for a word.

Berkeley's God takes up an interesting role in his philosophy. Not only is He an active supramind, and not only is He the ultimate guarantor for the continuity of ideas even when they are not perceived by any finite mind or spirit, but he also enables Berkeley to describe exteriority in unequivocal concrete terms. For him, God is something external to our minds, even though He Himself is not an abstract being but, on the contrary, a spirit that perpetually manifests itself by means of the ideas we perceive.

The repudiation of abstract ideas is thus important, among other things, for what it does *not* reject. Language is not deconstructed; instead, it is subjected to a process of cleansing that is meant to avoid the obfuscation of epistemic boundaries by the boundaries of imagination. There is little doubt that Berkeley's idealism evolved as an attempt to confront what he saw as an encroaching evil, which he named *skepticism* and *atheism*. In Berkeley's time these two concepts were umbrella terms under whose canopy one would find a host of doubters, unbelievers, and heretics who all denied the ruling religion and, in fact, any religion whatsoever. Berkeley saw them as bitter enemies, and he took it upon himself to wage a philosophical war against them. But his enthusiasm in taking up this cause did not make him imprudent. Accordingly, he sought to make the idea of a material, external, independent substance something utterly incomprehensible, to turn that which supposedly appears as something external into something dependent upon its perception and, in the process, to refine and redefine our terminology. This was not a mere revision but rather an attempt to reinstate a harmony deposed. And so he rejects abstract ideas; but he does not bring his labors to a complete fruition, since he maintained that it would suffice to reject what is "general and abstract." Needless to say, if this is where we come to a halt, we will never be faced with the perilous prospect of utterly destroying any kind of representation whatsoever and the general structure of the world as dichotomous "subjects" and "objects." "We have first raised a dust and then complain that we cannot see." And so, as in India, there is nothing left to do but to disperse the cloud, to cease trampling imaginary feet that raise dust storms of unfounded and irresponsible abstractions. But—and here India recedes from Berkeley's horizon—we know in advance what we shall see once the dust we so earnestly raised has finally cleared. His secret wish is to safeguard that which was and in this he can be seen as subscribing to a very traditionalist point of view. If Vasubandhu's radicality comes to the fore in the extreme consequences he draws from his epistemic idealism, Berkeley, on the other hand, sees himself as the custodian of traditionalism. Indeed, his aspirations are deeply rooted in the orthodoxy of his times. First, his religious aspirations are to allow for a world in which transcendence is present without this world being subjugated to doubt and disbelief. Second, his philosophical aspirations are to enable a pellucid understanding of reality without engendering an epistemic muddle arising from the fissure between assuming the existence of material, external objects and our ability to know them. Moreover, there is a linguistic aspiration too—the hope that in diminishing the scope of language (by ruling out abstractions) it will be possible to retain the transcendent framework of the world. True, "being" is identical to "being perceived," but this identity persists only so long as "being perceived" is strictly confined to the concrete. Otherwise the world, whose solidity Berkeley was so determined to save, will crumble into unconfined images or, rather, figments of imagination in which the very distinction between inward and outward is irrevocably dissolved. By remaining an "idealist" without abstraction he hopes to maintain a notion of transcendence as a general (but not abstract!) mental content that is strictly mental, but nonetheless retains its "spiritual" exteriority, being independent of my mind.

––––––––––––

The repudiation of abstract ideas is, in my opinion, a kind of compromise. Abstractions are shunned, and we are left with concrete situations: ideas and minds that perceive them. This is how Berkeley supposedly tries to prevent the self's annihilation and, consequently, the annihilation of the world. He does this by restricting our faculty of imagination. By pointing out the inconsistencies involved in accepting abstract ideas, he seeks to prevent a situation in which the human faculty of abstraction will take the genie out of the bottle. The irresponsible use of abstraction will push language to its limits or, even worse, will show that these limits can be endlessly stretched out—a sort of malignant verbal expansion (prapañca) comes to mind. It will eventually turn the transcendent framework into a hell-like impossible necessity. Berkeley then hoped to retain what Kant was forced to relinquish; moreover, doing everything he can to avoid experiencing his Alice-like transformation into a Western version of Vasubandhu. This is a version in which hell-keepers are *necessarily* present, while, at the same time—by force of the same necessity—it is impossible that they be there. This impossible situation deems that the existence of hell, as the existence of everything else, is a mere fiction. For Berkeley, this is a precarious state of affairs.

We have come to that point mentioned before, where Berkeley has to stop, where he abandons Vasubandhu, letting him proceed alone. When Berkeley sees that road sign, "Danger! You are Approaching Hell!" he halts. The philosophical insights Vasubandhu can glean from the story of hell is, for Berkeley, an inferno to be avoided at all costs. From this point of view, Berkeley is, in the deepest sense of the word, inseparable from the presupposition of transcendence, even without taking into account his religious devotion. His attempt to reconstruct the borderline running between exteriority and interiority is categorically different from Vasubandhu's similar, and evidently more radical, proposition. From Berkeley's point of view, Orwell's *Nineteen Eighty-four* is inconceivable. Indeed, for this prophetic vision to become real in the West it needs to have Kant "critically" nudge on the boundaries of reality.

Nineteen Eighty-four is surely one of the most compelling literary expositions of Vasubandhu's hell, at least as it is perceived in the post-Kantian West. As I mentioned in the opening pages of this chapter, I do not consider myself among those who see this book as a political manifesto, neither am I among those who base their social worldview or ideology on it.[16] It is my contention that in this book Berkeley's idealism is pushed beyond Berkeley's self-imposed boundaries, boundaries he himself refused to cross. It is a demonstration of how idealism, in its Western version, inevitably degenerates, culminating in the final and utter destruction of humanity.

The novel's protagonist, Winston Smith, is a man living under an extreme totalitarian regime that deprives individuals of all civil liberties and basic human rights. Society is ruled by Big Brother, pictures of whom abound, though he himself is never seen in person. People are constantly being watched by the dreaded "thought police" who track every man and woman with every disposable means, including helicopters (which can pry through windows), though mostly by "telescreens"—a combination of television and video camera that fifty-five years ago seemed to come from an apocalyptic future (notwithstanding Chaplin's depiction of the very same device in 1936 in *Modern Times*).

The world of *Nineteen Eighty-four* is ruled by Berkeley's interiority; every form of exteriority is but a fetish, the a posteriori outcome of mental manipulation. Nothing but consciousness exists; the mind creates reality according to the Party's random directives, which are decided upon in a completely arbitrary manner. It is unclear whether the party itself exists, and, needless to say, Big Brother too. In the main, the populace knows him as a perceived image in their minds. He is an assumed existence that is repeatedly corroborated, but only as an idea. At the other end of the spectrum lies his exact opposite, his arch-enemy Goldstein, the father of all traitors. But Goldstein too is only an idea. His existence is reaffirmed by exacting collective rituals in which he becomes the target of violent hatred. The real object of these rituals, in which this hatred is merely strengthened and intensified, is the states of mind of its participants. Whether Goldstein (or for that matter Big Brother) actually exists outwardly, is irrelevant, since in Orwell's world there is no method to determine anything beyond the subjectivity perceiving them. One should avoid making the mistake of drawing an analogy between Big Brother and the transcendent Godhead of Western culture. Orwell is portraying a post-transcendent society, so any similarity between Big Brother and God is merely a caricature. The same holds true of Goldstein; he is at best no more than a caricature of the Antichrist. As a matter of fact, the ontological vacuity of Big Brother and his antagonist Goldstein makes these two ideas mutually dependent on one another. Is Goldstein Big Brother's creation? Perhaps. But who created Big Brother? Comrade O'Brien, the high priest of idealism? Or perhaps some Goldstein or other? In this Orwellian world the creator blends into his creation and the traditional onto-logical precedence a creator has over his creation is forsaken. This is a world where the future is completely interlaced with the present.

And not only the future, but the past as well. The recreation of the past is yet another manipulation in which external objects are treated as mere ideas. In this interior world time is relative and subject to in-cessant alteration. It is frozen in some moment in the present on which perpetually changing data is superimposed. The Ministry of Truth deals with the alteration of the past. History is constantly being rewritten; the account of the past is influenced by the vicissitudes of the present. If war is being waged against a certain country, the past will be altered in such a way that every historical document will prove that thus it has always been: since time immemorial war has been waged against that country. Winston Smith, an employee of the Ministry of Truth, works in the department whose duty it is actively to recreate the past. Thus, for example, he retouches photographs, expunging those who latterly have been accused of treason. Destroying the evidence, showing the presence of traitors within a certain picture of reality is no less than the alteration of reality itself—if we do not perceive the idea of this or that traitor standing on a certain balcony, it follows that this traitor did not actually stand on this or that balcony. The perpetual recreation of the past in accordance with the dictates of the present makes no allowance for a correspondence with reality; it cannot be assessed by any external standards. These recreations employ only one criterion: a caricature of coherence—this, and only this, determines the validity of our per-ceptions. The manipulative recreation of exteriority has to present a unified picture void of any contradictions. In other words, every act of reconstruction of a past event is a reconstruction of *all* past events.

Forsaking exteriority, the whole of exteriority is absolute and dras-tic. Whoever refuses to comply with it can expect only one thing: to be destroyed, since he upsets the definition of humanity as something controlled only through the manipulation of the mind. Winston Smith is a flawed person because he insists that exteriority exists independent-ly and unconditionally. He still believes that the ideas we harbor inside us must be subjugated to a correspondence test since they represent a reality that, at least in some sense, is not mind dependent. Winston Smith tries to retain a realistic worldview. The novel recounts in great detail, and with much psychological and literary finesse, how Smith attempts to corroborate the world's exteriority. He commits all his memories to a secret diary. For instance, actual historical events that are now completely denied by means of, among other things, the recreation of the past undertaken by the Ministry of Truth where Smith works. He tries joining a revolutionary cell of Goldstein sympathizers (only later, when it is too late, will he discover that this cell does not exist, that it too is no more than a manipulation orchestrated by the big spirit—the party). The most profound—and the most extreme—expression of Smith's struggle against interiority is Julia, a coworker in his office with whom he has a relationship. Winston and Julia discover their exteriority by means of their bodies, and they discover their bodies through their sexual relationships. Sexual intercourse—intrusive intimacy and mutual togetherness—is for them a continual and repeated affirmation of each other's exteriority. Once, after making love passionately, Julia says to Winston: "They can make you say anything— *anything*—but they can't make you believe it. *They can't get inside you*" (my emphasis). But there is nothing they cannot do. Winston Smith is fighting a lost battle; he stands no chances whatsoever in a post-Berkeleyan and post-Kantian society that has had no choice but to relinquish exteriority and substitute the presupposition of transcendence with inward ideas. In this respect Smith is "The Last Man in Europe" (this is the provisional title that Orwell gave the novel before finally opting for the title we now know).[17] During one of their clandestine meetings, the dreaded Thought Police arrest Julia and Winston. Following his arrest, Smith undergoes a series of terrifying and lengthy sessions of torture that have but one purpose: to persuade him to relinquish his exteriority or, to put it more bluntly, that shred of exteriority he tried to resuscitate and then to protect by all available means. The purpose of torturing Smith is not to extract a confession of his crimes—that would have been quite a simple undertaking, and, indeed, after a relatively short period of torture he willingly signs any confession handed to him. He is tortured in order for the internal man to be recreated as a man lacking even a shred of independent, unconditioned sense of exteriority.

One entry in Winston Smith's secret diary, written before his arrest, unravels the true meaning of O'Brien's relentless torture sessions and helps us understand why he does not cease torturing him even after Smith signs every spurious deposition and incriminates himself in fictitious accusations. It is difficult not to be moved by a simple and painful passage in which the last man attempts to preserve not only his existence as a living human being but also the very framework within which, according to Orwell, humanity and human life as a whole have any meaning:

> Truisms are true, hold on to that! The solid world exists, its laws do not change. Stones are hard, water is wet, objects unsupported fall towards the earth's centre . . . he wrote: *Freedom is the freedom to say that two plus two make four. If that is granted, all else follows.*

A whole culture is encapsulated in these few sentences. Those who think that Winston Smith yearns for his personal freedom are mistaken. Quite the opposite is true. Smith wants to be a Cartesian self—an "I-think." which because it can think is absolutely certain of its existence. In this way he is establishing an *objective* foundation for the world. Like Descartes, Winston Smith too is primarily interested in an Archimedean point of reference, which he finds (in keeping with the Western culture and contrary to Indian civilization) in apodictic mathematical propositions. Given the certainty of "two plus two make four," "all else follows." In chapter 1 I mentioned that both arithmetic and geometry were Plato's paradigmatic model for the doctrine of Forms—a general, abstract, and wholly objective picture of what truly exists. Now, hidden from the prying eyes of the police, the last man jots down in his secret diary the final sentence, the definitive epigraph, the summation of a rich and complex culture that can be preserved only through him. Through memory, Winston Smith attempts to conserve that which has been severed and is independent of memory—even of direct experience. If two and two make four—all else will follow. A world in which this equation exists, and in which it cannot be exchanged by another equation suited to the whims of some "interiority," is a world in which Vasubandhu's hell cannot exist. If this proposition is true—"all else follows," and the most important thing that follows is the rejection of hell as a reality substitute whose fictionality defines its very being.

But in the torture cell, "in the place where there is no darkness," it is necessary to torture Winston Smith until he understands how relative this equation is so that he will be able to grasp that in fact his contention that two and two make four and only four is a sure sign of his insanity. He will then also understand that should O'Brien, his torturer, wish that two and two make five, not four, then they will make five. Perhaps this is beyond his grasp, and he does not really need to grasp this, since all that is needed is that he "internalize" the possibility of the latter equation. Needless to say, this is not a mathematical dispute. O'Brien's conclusion is not a mathematical proposition but a proposition *about* mathematics. The very moment Winston Smith internalizes the equation stating that two and two make five, *every* mathematical equation has become multivalent: it has no possible solution and every solution possible.[18] Given the context, it is ridiculous to see Winston Smith's horrific torture by O'Brien as an exemplification of a sadistic desire for torture—torture for the sake of torture (as Rorty seems to suggest). O'Brien is not a sadist and, moreover, he cannot be one, since he is no more than a "hell-keeper"—an empty being that is perhaps just a figment of Winston Smith's imagination. He tortures Smith in order to make him trust his internal world, to make him change his horizons and to establish a complete identity between reality and consciousness. This will eradicate the malignant lack of correspondence that we found in Kafka's writing. Moreover, empty transcendence will disappear since in Orwell's world it too internalizes itself into oblivion. The doorway to the Ministry of Love is the doorway to Vasubandhu's hell, the place that so frightened Berkeley and the place he was so keen to avoid.

The moment Winston Smith internalizes that two and two make five, the complete annihilation of a realist, of someone presupposing "exteriority," is achieved. But it is not enough merely to destroy exteriority; it must be utterly uprooted. The internalization will be final only with a radical and absolute alteration of identity. Here Orwell's apocalyptic nightmare of a nonrealist society reaches its monstrous climax. Winston Smith is dispatched to Room 101 and, crossing its threshold, he enters hell. In Room 101 the "external" man undergoes his ultimate and final torture. This is meant to transform his identity in the extreme so that he will never again become an "external" man. Room 101 is the place where one finds "the worst thing in the world," but, evidently, in the absence of any standards and any concept that enables us to make objective discriminations, even the worst thing in the word is subjective, i.e., something that resides deep inside one's own mind:

"The worst thing in the world," said O'Brien, "varies from individual to individual. It may be burial alive, or death by fire, or by drowning, or by impalement, or fifty other deaths. There are cases where it is some quite trivial thing, not even fatal."

For Winston Smith the worst thing in the world happens to be rats. And so he is brought to a cell at the center of which was an oblong wire cage in which enormous rats were scurrying. The door of the cage will be slid up and then "these starving brutes will shoot out of it like bullets." O'Brien does not spare Winston a description of what will shortly befall him:

> Have you ever seen a rat leap through the air? They will leap onto your face and bore straight into it. Sometimes they attack the eyes first. Sometimes they burrow through the cheeks and devour the tongue.

In Room 101 Smith stands opposite himself, naked, without even his body separating him from what is to him the worst atrocity. The only thing present is interiority, and the place is teeming with it. Winston Smith is about to confront it in its utmost imaginable directness. There is only one way for him to save himself from the worst of all nightmares, and it involves a change of identity: Winston Smith needs irrevocably and unequivocally to transpose his identity, he must let go of his body, to carry on living only as a perceiving immaterial mind. But how can one let go of one's body? Despite the fact that he has already internalized that two and two make five, he is identified with his body in a most horrendous manner. This is evident with the impending fear of the soon-to-be-opened cage filled with scurrying rats. How does one let go of one's body? Where does one place it? He hears the cage doors beginning to open, the threat of the foul rats confronts him, and then, out of the blackness, he clutches on an idea:

> There was one and only one way to save himself. He must interpose another human being, the *body* of another human being, between himself and the rats. . . . But then he had suddenly understood that in the whole world there was just *one* person to whom he could transfer his punishment—*one* body that he could

thrust between himself and the rats. And he was shouting franti-
cally, over and over:

DO it to Julia! DO it to Julia! Not me! Julia!

He finally yields to interiority: "what happens to you here is for ever,"
O'Brien says to Smith. Winston Smith, after having exchanged his
body—the last vestige of transcendence—with Julia's body, is no longer
a man. His heroic attempt to find exteriority through sexual, physical intercourse between two lovers ends with both of them being turned into
incorporeal apparitions (since Julia too, in her Room 101, exchanged
her body for that of Winston's). The new Smith is then discharged from
O'Brien's, that place where there is no darkness (this is the customary
procedure for those who have acquired new identities—they are set
loose prior to execution). One day, wandering the park, he encounters
Julia by chance. Looking at her, Smith remembers how once, in one of
those endless wars, he had helped drag out a corpse from the ruins of
a house hit by a stray bomb. Since they have each sacrificed the other's
body, there can now be no bond between them. These wraiths can now
see one another only as characters sharing a common narrative. The one
possible bond between them is their mutual betrayal, the betrayal that
transformed Winston and Julia into pure interiority. It is no surprise then
that Orwell sums up the novel by describing the final flickering flames
of the last man in Europe fading out. Smith is sitting in a café, drinking
lousy gin and gazing at a colossal picture of Big Brother hanging in front
of him. In a world ruled by nothing other than mind—and whose framework is no less fictional than a Buddhist hell-world—the only thing one
can do is love, and the only possible object of love is Big Brother:

> He gazed up at the enormous face. Forty years it had taken him to
> learn what kind of smile was hidden beneath the dark moustache.
> O cruel, needless misunderstanding! O stubborn, self-willed exile
> from the loving breast! Two gin-scented tears trickled down the
> sides of his nose. But it was all right, everything was all right, the
> struggle was finished. He had won the victory over himself. He
> loved Big Brother.

Bartleby lies huddled at the base of the prison wall forcing Melville
to cry out "Ah Bartleby! Ah humanity!" He whose life was a continu-

ous emptiness of nonpreference still maintains at death a certain degree of humanity. After Joseph K. ends his life butchered "like a dog!" Kafka remarks that "it was as if the shame of it must outlive him." Joseph K.'s slashed body contains none of Bartleby's humanity. But even though his shameful death did not allow death to be "our salvation," yet something at least was left intact—shame itself. In Orwell's "subjective" world, Bartleby's emptiness and Joseph K.'s shame are devoured by inexorable evil (since its only boundaries are the boundaries of human imagination). Now nothing is left. Not even shame. Loving Big Brother is nothing but clearing up a misunderstanding: "O cruel, needless misunderstanding!"

Berkeley does not set out on Vasubandhu's journey to the heart of interiority. Prima facie, it may seem that he is compliant, that he is willing to venture on a journey to interiority, since at crucial places in his writing he calls for intuitive self-reflection and directs his readers to embark on such a voyage : "It is but looking into your own thoughts," he says, contending that introspection of this sort will show that one cannot find an idea unperceived by the mind. He is so confident of the outcome of this introspection that he is willing to wager that, if the results do not confirm his philosophical method, "I shall readily give up the cause." But this first impression is misleading. In fact, Berkeley is not seriously intent on allowing himself to indulge in uninhibited introspection. He arrests his progress at a self-imposed, probably predetermined, boundary. Clearly, the point he comes to a halt is not the last frontier of introspection. When Berkeley draws his readers' attention to their inwardness, he has no intention of immersing them in it. He will be content if they merely cast a fleeting glance, as if they were a scientist furtively looking at a test tube, refusing to let his gaze invade the depths of his mind. Overimmersion in interiority might have calamitous effects; it might create a new psychological or philosophical commitment that will prevent those gazing inward to return from their interiority to that naive world that Berkeley has created for them—the world of ideas, finite minds, and an infinite mind that is supposed to be seen as identical with the world of things they perceived before Berkeley's philosophical intervention in their lives.

In this Berkeley's position is radically different from that of Vasubandhu's. Needless to say, Vasubandhu too has recourse to that inward gaze, but unlike Berkeley he manages to show, in the minutest possible detail, the mechanics of this introspection and thus he stretches it to its Orwellian extremes. Of course, Vasubandhu would not have stamped hell with the Orwellian idea of evil. Unlike Berkeley's harmonious idealism, Vasubandhu's journey into interiority does not subsume the conceptual framework of transcendence. Like Orwell, Vasubandhu resorts to an extreme analogy. He compares external reality to a situation that occurs in a certain hell-in-the-mind in which there is no hope of discriminating between fact and fiction. Like Orwell, he regards the exteriority of things as no more than a delusion, a "cruel, needless misunderstanding." But, whereas the Orwellian misunderstanding is deeply anchored within the West's presupposition of transcendence (signaling the hellish "idealistic" outcome of its collapse), the nature of this misunderstanding in Buddhist thought is entirely different. To begin with, Indian thought did not rely on such a presupposition. There is no transcendence to misunderstand. In this respect, Vasubandhu is akin to Nāgārjuna. His objection to realism is not much different from Nāgārjuna's assault on the representational faculties of language. Similarly, there is not much difference between Vasubandhu's proposed analogy of the human condition as a (necessary and impossible) sojourn in an imaginary hell-world and Nāgārjuna's designation of language as prapañca, as never ending verbal expansion. And yet, whereas Nāgārjuna did not care to investigate the objects of consciousness nor inquire into the mind's limits (and in this he is somewhat similar to Berkeley, even though it is evident that different motives lay behind their respective impartialities), Vasubandhu does offer us a detailed, multilayered picture of internal reality, a beacon aimed at correcting that "misunderstanding." In simpler words, as a Buddhist philosopher he is attempting to come up with a satisfactory reply to what is for him the ultimate philosophical question: What does the inward gaze reveal? What is there inside?

Many adepts in Western philosophy will find it difficult to accept this as a valid philosophical question. Thus, before we dwell on Vasubandhu's reply to this question, one should briefly consider what exactly is the "misunderstanding" that he is trying to eliminate by means of his inward journey. In Indian philosophy the meaning of this misunderstanding is glossed by several different terms. *Ignorance* is a general and common translation for the collection of these terms. Most schools of Indian philosophy agree that the crux of philosophy lies in its ability to identify and remove ignorance. In India it was not uncommon to think of philosophy as a transformative activity, that is, as an intellectual activity whose purpose was to modify the thinker's self-identity so that it brought about deep transformation of his or her personhood. Besides instructing its practitioners on how to eliminate falsity and instead find the truth, philosophy was also meant to bring about a veritable change, both in terms of a practitioner's self-perception and his ability to acquire new perspectives on how to know the truth. The different schools of Indian philosophy (both Buddhist and other) thus emphasized the importance of overcoming and eradicating ignorance. Evidently, each philosophical school invested the notion of ignorance with its own preferred meaning based on the specific underlying assumptions and philosophical goals the school set for itself. For Vasubandhu, as a Buddhist, the eradication of ignorance is not merely the correction of certain misapprehensions or the removal of occasional sensory confusion. Both Nāgārjuna and Vasubandhu saw the eradication of ignorance as the uprooting of false thoughts. This point needs some elaboration. Western philosophy, for the most part, saw ignorance as stemming from an intellectual deficiency that very often was identified as "dogmatism." The usual portrait of an ignorant person has been of someone incapable of thoroughly investigating or critically examining the issue in question because she accedes to some preconceived beliefs or attitudes or else because he wants only to conform to the masses or yet again because she blindly adheres to an uncritical notion of common sense. More often than not, Western philosophers saw this sheepish longing for the dogmatic, the common, and the received as a contemptible form of ignorance. A philosopher has eyes in his head while an ignorant person treads darkness; the philosopher seeks universal principles. She devotes herself to a rational, critical inquiry of these principles. It is inconceivable that philosophers will settle for anything less than apodictic knowledge; on the other hand, ignorant people ("the masses," "the fools," "those whose imagination got the better of their understanding," "the commoners," and other such unflattering appellations by which the philosophers called them) are satisfied with the conventional, the probable, or, even worse, with unexamined dogmas. Recall Descartes' elitism when he maintained that the majority of people are either those who believe themselves cleverer than they are or those "who have enough reason or modesty to recognize that they are less capable of distinguishing the true from the false than certain others by whom they can be taught." According to this view, philosophy, as the eradication of ignorance, is the corrective to mental or intellectual dogmatism. This antidote willfully disregards beliefs and conventions that, for the most part, are prone to an absence of adequate critical examination and quick to adopt groundless conclusions.

What could be more natural than to think of the ignorance that the Buddha refers to in terms similar or identical to those embraced by Western philosophy? What could be more natural than to measure Indian philosophy with the yardsticks of Western philosophy? But doing this is a regrettable error that many have been liable to commit. Ignorance in Buddhism subsumes that basic assumption upon which Yājñavalkya's philosophy is founded. Ignorance is not seen in terms of a lack or an absence of a certain understanding or even in the rejection of critical knowledge in favor of dogmatic views. Accordingly, removal of ignorance is not merely an intellectual process; it is not restricted to a move from dogmatism to critical reasoning. Indeed, right understanding in Yogācāra Buddhism includes no less than the eradication of the very distinction between dogmatism and critical reasoning. The knower is shown that this distinction between commonsense knowledge and metaphysical knowledge is unfounded since both err by clinging to the view that our knowledge should represent things as they are out there. As I have argued, ignorance is first and foremost a mental state—a deeply rooted condition of confusion, delirium, or even hallucination. It is less akin to a cognitive error of miscalculation or a fallacy and closer to a state of delusion. As such, no simple rational correction of the error will avail here—the philosopher must literally have therapeutic means at his disposal. He is not expected merely to examine his views and concepts using the critical tools of reasoning. Moreover, he is expected to solve an existential philosophical quandary that is, basically, a problem of orientation and navigation. Philosophy is there to provide a much needed guidance not only to those who are intellectually perplexed, but, more urgently, to those who are bewildered, having lost their way on account of a practical error of orientation. Disorientation is a state of delirium, of complete dimness and perhaps even of actual hallucination. This occurs when the mind fails to find its way through the dense thicket of reality that, as mentioned before, lacks any a priori clear distinctions between inside and outside. It is as if the mind has sent a search party to find clear distinctions between external objects and their internal representation, and the search has failed miserably. It may well be the case that the Western dogmatist will also be portrayed as someone who has gone astray, lost the right way. But one could assume that in such a case the wandering of the perplexed will be caused either by his inability to read and understand the map or else because the map at hand is, alas, the wrong map. On the other hand, the Buddhist depiction of an ignorant person shows someone led astray because of an inability to realize that the maps he possesses are nothing but an inseparable part of the internal world, thus the maps will never be able to supply a valid itinerary entirely apart from one's own being. The ignorant person envisaged by Buddhism is thus not Ecclesiastes' fool, Maimonides' masses, or Descartes' less capable person: rather, this is a deranged person who has no path and is not in possession of reliable maps that can assist him along his journey (since no map is reliable anyway). Unlike its Western counterpart, Indian philosophy was not forced to wait for the collapse of its conceptual framework in order to take insanity seriously, regarding it as a highly relevant factor in any epistemic inquiry.

Vasubandhu's journey to the final frontiers of interiority takes the traveler to the inner recesses of her mental being. It is driven by the assumption that such a journey might end ignorance by resolving the misunderstanding on which it has been based. That is to say, in a Buddhist sense, it will subdue ignorance and prevent the loss of one's bearings, which is, as we have seen, more a loss of one's mind. One can't help noting how similar in spirit this suggestion is to the modern Western attempts to arrive at interiority without any external aid, without relying on those transcendent ideas already crushed by Kant. But Vasubandhu sets out on his final voyage to the depth of interiority without any reason to worry about the perils that lie ahead. Were he to envisage the depiction of such a voyage by modernist Western writers, he would have been greatly baffled. No doubt he would have felt compassion for K's tireless, yet endless, efforts to reach the Castle, considering him deluded to think that he was moving forward when he was in fact moving around in circles. He would in all likelihood have been upset to learn about Kurz's catastrophic endeavor to reach "the heart of darkness," seeing his journey as defiled with selfish, uncontrollable desire. The one modernist account that Vasubandhu could sympathize with is Winston Smith's voyage in the permanently lit cellars of the Ministry of Love, in which a "cruel, needless misunderstanding" has been removed, where "everything was all right" and "the struggle was finished." Indeed, Vasubandhu would cherish the fact that Smith "had won the victory over himself." Admittedly, his voyage too, like that of Winston Smith, is meant to achieve a total, irrevocable transformation, which, metaphorically speaking, sees the disappearance of the "last man." But in between the dreadful, despairing way in which Orwell described this transformation and the therapeutic, blissful tone Vasubandhu takes in his treatment of it there lies a yawning cultural gulf. For a Buddhist, a psychodynamic journey to interiority is not like a bird flapping its wings on the caged walls of external reality, which logically and ontologically precedes it; this psychodynamic journey advances calmly, since external reality is forever nothing but a construct. Eradicating ignorance is finding one's bearings, that is, freeing the deluded from his delusions.

Now we can return to the question that Vasubandhu, as a Buddhist philosopher, posed as the ultimate philosophical problem: what is it that one finds when one looks inside? In his reply to this question Vasubandhu makes use of terms and concepts taken from the Yogācāra's psychodynamic outlook (briefly described at the beginning of this chapter). When the wise gaze into the depths of their interiority, they find three aspects or three modes of consciousness. The imagined (*kalpita*) is that through which the external world is perceived. Its characteristic sign is duality, the distinction between subject and object. This is the *way* in which the mind, which itself is termed "the conditioned" (*paratantra*), perceived the world. Being "imagined" amounts to the actual appearance of something in our cognitive field. In contrast, being "conditioned" means being a stream of consciousness void of any constructs; this stream never "appears" in itself and is always in need of the veil of the "imagined" to manifest itself. The third aspect, the perfected (*pariniṣpanna*), is the internal negation of conscious activity. It will be recalled that Vasubandhu emphasizes that there is no essential difference between these three aspects, these three inward gazes—they are nothing but three points of view on the very same mental being.

Why then the need to differentiate between three aspects of self-awareness that are in effect one and the same internal condition? Why distinguish between what is essentially indistinguishable? Vasubandhu's reply emphasizes practical and therapeutical considerations: the division into three aspects or three points of view is meant to present the meditator with a dynamic process of mental self-penetration. This tripartite division is suggested as a journey from the outward to the inward—a person's progressive penetration from the day-to-day empirical, seemingly external, reality, to the inner recesses of interiority. The three aspects are the three stages of analytic and deconstructive penetration. At the first stage of his inward journey the subject grasps the conditioned aspect (and not, as one would expect, the imagined aspect). Turning one's gaze inward, one finds neither a veil nor a cloak, but rather "raw" materials: impulses, predispositions, "seeds" of experience. Further penetration reveals the imagined aspect. It is not, of course, the perceived object as such, which was present before the mind even before the commencement of the penetrating journey. What reveals itself during the second stage of introspection is not the perceived object but rather the *inner experience* of perceiving. It is an experience of an unbridgeable gulf, a yawning chasm, between *what* appears and *how* it appears. The discovery of this gulf is possible only *after* one has acquired a clear understanding that external perceptions are derived from the mental raw materials or seeds. In other words, the gradual insight into the nature of the conditioned and then into the nature of the imagined, enables one to make more progress along the inward path and acquire a deeper understanding of the fact that the conditioned and the imagined are mutually dependent upon one another, like a dog chasing its own tail. These graded insights might be described thus: at first penetration, one acquires the understanding that interiority lacks an enduring and permanent core, an "I," a "selfhood"; that is, there is no such thing as a permanent and enduring self that unites the stream of consciousness. Instead there are only "images" void of a referential mental substratum. Next, in the second stage of penetration, a new understanding is acquired—that the existence of these images represents nothing, that consciousness lacks reference and accordingly that we are incapable of determining anything about the existence of external objects.

We can now examine the last stage of penetration, characterized as the perfected aspect. Here Vasubandhu is quite abstruse, and this has led some of his commentators to come up with explanations that man-age to completely distort his doctrine. They claim that he did in fact subscribe to a fully fledged ontology and that the three levels of self-awareness are, in effect, real entities. In contrast to this ontologically laden interpretation, I think that one should take Vasubandhu's words seriously when he is arguing that the perfected aspect of the mind's penetration constitutes an act of *negation*. It is not only the negation of the imagined as a way of appearance, but the actual collapse of the con-ditioned; this is so since the conditioned cannot empirically exist except by means of the duality of the imagined. One should also remember that this division is relative: it exists only from the point of view of someone commencing the inward journey. The further in one goes, the more the divisions disintegrate. The perfected aspect of consciousness is therefore the total elimination not only of externality but also of the whole perceptual and conceptual framework that enables the very dis-tinction between in and out, internal and external. Let us return to the example of an ophthalmic disorder. The person afflicted sees little flies at the center of his field of vision. As I have argued before, this example does not demonstrate the existence of perceptual illusions (ropes mis-taken for a snakes) but the presence of mental delusions. Curing this disorder amounts to no less than the "annihilation" of the seeing eyes. The disease is an (imaginary) symptom, a stream passing in front of our senses, and is expressed by the dichotomy of a person seeing and the flies he perceives. But, at the final stage of the penetration into interi-ority, the perfected aspect of consciousness negates all empirical sensa-tions and thus negates the very meaning of what experience is for us. For Vasubandhu, the Buddhist, there is nothing morbid about a state of affairs in which absolute darkness is a purified expression of complete self-awareness. Perhaps this is what Kafka, unwittingly, meant when he remarked that "the lamentation around the deathbed is actually the lamentation over the fact that here no dying in the true sense has taken place," since for him the condition of complete self-awareness is, in principle, inconceivable, for reasons dealt with in the previous chap-ter. On the other hand, Vasubandhu can attain that "dying in the true sense": self awareness in which the perfected aspect eliminates experi-ence as well as the raw materials of the mind that give rise to expe-rience. It is of course possible to describe this situation through the imagery of absolute darkness, and it is possible to describe it as a place where there is no darkness—a kind of Room 101 in which the light is so blinding that those who gaze out are destroyed by the consuming light. Unfathomable darkness and blazing light are but similes. It might be that the former is more characteristic of Nāgārjuna than Vasubandhu, the latter more of Vasubandhu than Nāgārjuna. For Vasubandhu, unlike Nāgārjuna, the negation of conditioned awareness is not a mere conceptual void; self-awareness is still viable, albeit as an embryonic self (or embryonic ātman) that knows itself.

In chapter 3, while considering the Upaniṣadic ātman as a self-knowing subject, I noted the apparent difficulty involved in positing a total state of self-awareness. Reflection seems to necessitate a division between observer and observed, some split between a knower and the known. Shakespeare placed this idea in the mouth one of his characters: "for the eye sees not itself, but by reflection, by some other things." Indeed, one of the salient features of Western thought has been this very insight: the known cannot be identical to the subject that knows it; there is no choice but to presuppose the existence of an other in every reflexive act. We cannot think about the unity of the knower and known, because in the very act of thinking we separate thought from the thinker. Schopenhauer, who was acquainted with a variety of Indian texts, elaborates:

> But this double character of our inner being does not rest on a self-existent unity, otherwise it would be possible for us to be conscious of ourselves *in ourselves and independently of the objects of knowing and willing*. Now we simply cannot do this, but as soon as we enter into ourselves in order to attempt it, and wish for once to know our selves fully by directing our knowledge inwards, we lose ourselves in a bottomless void; we find ourselves like a hollow glass globe, from the emptiness of which a voice speaks. But the cause of this voice is not to be found in the globe, and since we want to comprehend ourselves, we grasp with a shudder nothing but a wavering and unstable phantom.

Schopenhauer is convinced that self-awareness is not "a self-existent unity." Thus pure self-knowledge is impossible—"Now we simply cannot do this." Despite his profound interest in Indian thought and his evident acquaintance with Kant's Copernican revolution, which brought about the dissolution of the transcendent framework and the disappearance of the self, Schopenhauer still adheres to the conceptual framework of the presupposition of transcendence.

Schopenhauer's assumption concerning the inevitable split between a knower and the contents of her knowledge and his unequivocal conclusion that every reflexive act is necessarily dualistic are imbued with conceptual presuppositions characteristic of Western thought. As a Western philosopher, he could not willfully disregard the difficulty he found in the condition of self-awareness, nor could he accept that we could "be conscious of ourselves *in ourselves and independently of the objects of knowing and willing.*" But he did not stop there; perhaps he could not resist the Indian temptation to ask himself what, in spite of everything—in spite of the fact that both in theory and in practice there can be no such thing—what really happens there, at that unattainable moment of self-awareness? How are we to respond to that will to "enter into ourselves . . . by directing our knowledge inwards"? In considering this question we found Schopenhauer's words resonating with Nāgārjuna's: "we lose ourselves in a bottomless void; we find ourselves like a hollow glass globe, from the emptiness of which a voice speaks." But following this quintessentially Buddhist description of emptiness, Schopenhauer immediately retracts and, seizing the Western reins, adds that "the cause of this voice *is not* to be found in the globe" (my emphasis). This is precisely the moment that emptiness becomes an "unstable phantom." In this Schopenhauerian philosophical toing and froing, a Western philosopher plays with his Buddhist counterpart; the former is allowed to deal the opening serve, but he also has the final stroke in which self-knowledge is described thus: "we grasp with a shudder [!] nothing but a wavering and unstable phantom." This is how the hollow glass globe is blown to pieces by a voice from the beyond; thus too empty transcendence has delivered its final punishment and has abandoned man inside an interiority that is anything but Buddhist—more likely Orwellian. The wavering and unstable phantom gently and obliquely anticipates Room 101.

Every attempt to describe self-knowledge becomes highly contentious in light of these Schopenhauerian ideas. I emphasized in chapter 1 that when a culture places the presupposition of transcendence in a key position, every psychological investigation that highlights internal processes and tries to show their autonomy is justified will, perforce, be restricted by the very precedence of the outer over the inner and of the objective over the subjective. This restriction is sharply expressed by the assumption that any attempt to venture from the outward to the inward must be accompanied (not always in perfect symmetry, but at least correspondingly) by an opposite movement, from interiority outward. In all events, it was deemed to be bilateral movement. Accordingly, a philosopher's self-identity is not at odds with his culture. It is one of this book's primary assumptions that Western philosophy until Kant (notwithstanding some notable exceptions) had a clear conceptual preference for the external, the general, the objective, and the impersonal over the internal, the private, the subjective, and the personal. There was little expectation that philosophers would take the effort to enquire into internal mental motivations, unless this inquiry was subservient to a more general goal. Similarly, psychologism was seen as an adversary of objectivism even in moral issues. It comes then as no surprise that in the West the exploration of the mental, as such, occurs concurrently with the undermining of the concept of transcendence.

So long as the presupposition of transcendence resides within the framework of Western culture, metapsychology is to be rejected offhand. By metapsychology I refer to a possible inquiry into the *modes* in which states of mind are psychologically analyzed and theoretically presented. Needless to say, to conduct a metapsychological investigation within a culture that is founded on the presupposition of transcendence is a tricky affair. Moreover, it is highly unlikely that metapsychology will be considered a legitimate part of a philosophical inquiry in a tradition that stubbornly continues to prefer, and give precedence to, the "objective" over the "subjective." This is categorically different from the situation in India; there the idea of a detailed and rigorous metapsychological investigation raises no difficulties. Vasubandhu's philosophy is a case in point; he presents us with a psychological theory about mental states and mental actions and, at the same time, a metapsychological inquiry into the nature of mental analysis, namely, a theoretical suggestion about the possibility of an "analysis of analysis." In this respect, Vasubandhu is congruent with his own culture; as mentioned before, Indian thought, having no underlying assumption about the outward's precedence over the interior, found no difficulty in accommodating metapsychology. Consequently, Indian philosophy regularly emphasizes philosophy's therapeutic role—philosophical activity is regarded as transformative. To enable transformative philosophy one has to assume that discursive thinking does not block—even encourages—the possibility of a spiritual penetration into a deep state of total self-awareness. Philosophical thinking should enable, perhaps even necessitate, *altering* one's self-identity and *changing* one's perspectives. Indian philosophy was constantly preoccupied with these alterations and saw it as a legitimate goal of any philosophical activity worth its mettle. In this respect, philosophers in India offered not only wisdom, not only the truth, but also a way of life.[19]

Schopenhauer represents a determinedly Western point of view, and so for him metapsychology is something difficult to contend with. And, then, discovering that self-awareness is a hollow glass globe in bottomless space, he abruptly severs his Buddhist ties, thus revealing his true allegiance, his commitment to the philosophical culture from whence he came. He is convinced that the cause of this voice "is not to be found in the globe." How can Schopenhauer know this for sure? How is it possible in that bottomless void to differentiate clearly between inner and outer? How can emptiness—an absolute middle point!—suddenly be determined spatially and located between it and the voice that comes from the outside? It is quite obvious that for Schopenhauer this penetration into interiority required the use of spatial terminology. In chapter 3 I mentioned this ubiquity and drew attention to the fact that modern Western thought primarily relates to reflexivity through a set of spatial images.[20] As a matter of fact, this book is no exception, since I too speak of self-awareness expressing itself, for instance, as *movement* or *penetration* and use such prepositions as *into* or *inside*. On the other hand, even though the Indian understanding of self-awareness exemplified by Yājñavalkya uses spatial imagery when it explains dreams as a stage toward total self-awareness, it nevertheless moves on to a completely different set of metaphors when it depicts the deep sleep as a deeper stage in the process of self-awareness. Here, it will be recalled, states of mind are depicted by means of temporal metaphors (with space being understood merely as an a posteriori image of time). This predisposition toward temporal imagery is shared both by Yājñavalkya, who thinks of man in terms of selfhood, and the Buddhists who extricate the self out of personhood. Schopenhauer, on the other hand, handles the self exactly the same way it was treated by his Western predecessors.

What then does self-awareness mean in Vasubandhu's psychophilosophical world? A reply to this question inevitably requires us to disassociate ourselves from the assumptions prevailing in Western philosophy, at least up to the time of Schopenhauer. Vasubandhu accepts the need for complete self-awareness free of the duality of an observer confronting the objects of his observation. In this he is in tow with the widespread opinion extant in most Buddhist philosophical texts. These texts claim that in every act of perception two things happen simultaneously: a sensory perception in which the subject-object duality occurs is *simultaneously* accompanied by self-awareness (*svasamvedana*): I perceive a certain object and I simultaneously perceive myself perceiving that object. This can easily give rise to confusion, so one has to be very explicit here. The idea is not that perception occurs in two discrete phases—an occurrence of prereflexive cognition in which the subject perceives the object of perception and then, later on, another phase of reflexive cognition in which the subject perceives himself as someone perceiving the object. Such a two tier account of the process of self-awareness (as a process *derived* from the sensory modes of perceiving the world) is, according to Buddhist philosophy, totally erroneous and carries with it dire philosophical and psychological consequences. Quite the opposite is true; if reflexivity is derived from a prereflexive condition and if the "I" or the "self" is cognized only later on, there can be no doubt that that "I" is but an insubstantial construct. Vasubandhu, as a Buddhist philosopher, thinks that self-awareness is not attached to a state of perception that precedes it, but, rather, it is something that presents itself simultaneously with it. According to him, this simultaneity is obtained in the *perfected* aspect of self-awareness—the aspect in which all appearances are finally negated, however they may appear. In this state of complete self-awareness the here and now seems to swell, to devour everything before and after it.

Needless to say, these last words emit an aura of mysticism. One might prefer to keep it so: empty words, void of any reference, representing nothing, merely pointing at a state of consciousness that is quintessentially mental, or, reverting back to Western idiom, quintessentially internal. But it seems to me that Vasubandhu is not endorsing empty mysticism; that is to say, he does not take it to be the only possible account of the mind's perfected aspect. Instead he makes use of a stock analogy that Buddhist philosophers used excessively when they wanted to convey self-awareness as something that is simultane-ously present whenever an object is known. The analogy in question is that of a lamp illuminating objects in a room. This analogy was used in order to demonstrate that, when a lamp is alight, not only does it illuminate the surrounding objects in the room but, at the same time, it also illuminates itself. In this analogy the room, of course, stands for the world, the things in it are the perceived objects, and the lamp is the perceiving mind. Vasubandhu and other Yogācāra philosophers used this image to put forward two claims. The first, that "to be, is to be illuminated"; that is, nothing can be known to exist save when it is lit (that is, perceived) by the lamp (that is, the perceiving mind). The second claim is this: for exactly the same reasons underlying the first claim, the lamp also exists, in the sense that it too is being illuminated, though, unlike the illuminated objects, it illuminates itself only *by* cast-ing light on the perceived objects. Here one needs to be very precise: from the first premise we can derive that a lamp always illuminates oth-er things. Anything illuminated by a lamp that isn't endowed with an intrinsic light source needs a lamp to light it, but the lamp itself, which is a source of light in itself, does not need a different light source. And thus, inasmuch as this pertains to the bilateral relationships illuminat-ing/being illuminated or perceiver/perceived, it applies only to objects illuminated by a lamp; this bilateral relationship does not apply to the relationship between the lamp and itself. Evidently, the lamp cannot il-luminate itself. On the other hand, it is possible to use the image of the lamp illuminating itself in order to accentuate the performative charac-ter of the condition of self-awareness that is concomitant with the act of perception. Certain Buddhist philosophers (e.g., Dignāga) were willing to regard this as a valid form of knowledge, namely, an awareness that is *reflexively* aware of itself. But regardless of whether we endow this self-perception with the status of knowledge or not—we cannot ignore the performative aspect of self-awareness that happens concomitantly with the lamp illuminating an object in a room.

Henceforth, the mind is aware of itself, since it focuses on the objects of its perception. Like any other philosophical analogy, this too has to be treated with great caution; one should be wary of overextending its original intention. This analogy has one purpose: to emphasize the simultaneity of perception and self-awareness. It would be wrong to assume that Vasubandhu thought of the relationship between the mind and the world in spatial terms (just because he uses such terms as *room*, *furniture*, and *lamp*, etc.). On the contrary, much like Yājñavalkya's explanation of consciousness in a state of deep sleep, Vasubandhu makes use of topographical metaphors as a way of conveying temporality. If even an innovative and original thinker like Schopenhauer failed to comprehend this nuance, all the more then would it have been incomprehensible to those preceding him. It would seem that in the West, among the moderns, Freud was the first person who managed to come up with a clear and incisive expression of spatial topography as a metaphor of time.

If space is used as a metaphor for time, then it follows that Vasubandhu is not investigating the spatial relations between the lamp and the room or between the lamp and itself. It is more likely that he is trying to show that the lamp's self-illumination is not temporally differentiable from what is supposedly (and according to Vasubandhu—merely supposedly) located inside the room. Introspection thus does not require that subject and object be spatially differentiated, or, for that matter, "inside and outside." These distinctions exist only in the "imagined" aspect of the mind. Understanding that perception and self-awareness are temporally identical is the radical dissolution of both the perceived and the perceiver. In this Vasubandhu is akin to Nāgārjuna, but unlike Nāgārjuna he confers on this dissolution the psychological qualities of liberating self-knowledge. One is entitled to assume that Vasubandhu would agree with Schopenhauer[21] that the moment we "wish for once to know our selves fully by directing our knowledge inwards, we lose ourselves in a bottomless void." Also, imagining a hollow glass globe, "from the emptiness of which a voice speaks" is particularly apposite to Vasubandhu's Buddhist viewpoint. At the same time, it should be evident why Vasubandhu would vehemently reject the rest of Schopenhauer's imagery, which informs us that "the cause of this voice is not to be found in the globe." Instead of these Western formulations that make room for complete self-reflexivity, Vasubandhu would be happy to implement his "three aspects doctrine" on the glass globe: if the hollow glass globe does indeed reside in a bottomless void, then the voice it gives rise to can at times sound like an external voice (in the imagined aspect); as far as the "'conditioned' aspect is concerned, it is entirely internal. And yet from the point of view of the "perfected" aspect there is nothing standing between the inner and the outer—both dissolve into an ever present moment of self-awareness. This is the gist of Vasubandhu's argument in favor of the possibility of selfless self-awareness void of the duality to which so many Western philosophers, including the daring Schopenhauer, subscribed. Knowing reality is knowing oneself.

T. S. Eliot understood perfectly well what lies at the core of Yājñavalkya's and Vasubandhu's notion of self-awareness. As is well known, Eliot was drawn to Indian thought (both in spirit and in training), and this came to the fore in his poetry. In *Four Quartets*, which were written in the thirties and the forties of the previous century, Eliot describes his perception of the Indian identification between knowing reality and knowing oneself.

> There would be no dance, and there is only the dance.
> I can only say, there we have been: but I cannot say where.
> And I cannot say, how long, for that is to place it in time.
> The inner freedom from the practical desire,
> The release from action and suffering, release from the inner
> And the outer compulsion, yet surrounded
> By a grace of sense.

Residing in Eliot's poem is the claim that that there can be only meaningful reference point: the extreme, uncompromising inward turn—an introspection that tries to establish itself only upon itself, without relying in any way whatsoever on external criteria that are not already present within reflexivity. "There would be no dance, and there is only the dance." This is consciousness dancing, creating the melody to which it dances. This circularity, the mind's self-dependence on its own activity and the self-dependence of this activity on the reflexive gaze, the resolute renunciation of linearity in favor of circularity—in this Indian philosophy has come up with a unique locus of reality, which can be discovered by taking a bold, unperturbed, and uninhibited journey into the utmost depth of human interiority.

Knowing reality is knowing oneself. And perhaps more audaciously, self-knowledge is self-knowledge. What seems like a tautology in fact unleashes an interesting philosophical insight. We have seen that a metapsychological look at the relations between the mind and the world, which in India was not inhibited by the presupposition of transcendence, enables Vasubandhu to come up with a striking equivalence between what is perceived and how it is perceived, between what is measured and the standards used in this measurement. It is thus obvious that if we inspect this equivalence through the eyes of a Western philosopher trying to establish, at all costs, an apposite *representational* theory of reality at whose crux lies a correspondence between the act of representation and that which is represented—if we do so, there will be no choice but to admit that Vasubandhu's claim for equivalence is utterly meaningless. But the equivalence that Vasubandhu suggests is not attached to an underlying assumption about philosophy as an activity aimed at elucidating and illuminating the representational qualities that exist between our perceptions and language and between reality. Instead of concentrating on the what that is involved in *representation*, it seems Vasubandhu is more interested in uncovering the acts of *presentation*, namely, the inner process of *creation*, which is not that different from artistic creation. The equivalence between that which is perceived and the means by which it is perceived indicates the impossibility of an unmediated act of representation and treats complete self-awareness as a recognition of the necessary presence of a creator in any act of perception, recognition, conceptualization, and verbalization. In other, simpler, words, Vasubandhu shows us a picture of self-awareness in which the inevitable presence of the creating or perceiving *medium* is present in every act of reception or understanding. And so I am convinced that the above tautology is a meaningful claim; it draws attention to the equivalence between that what seems to us externally real and the inner creative processes by which reality appears in our mind. Contemporary idiom will call this "the aesthetization of reality."

At this point, Ingmar Bergman's *Persona* comes to mind. In this film Bergman's preoccupation with the question of self-identity and the possibility of self-knowledge reaches towering heights. It occurs within a visually stunning exploration that seeks to convey—through picture and motion—the delicacy of human interiority lying concealed within the many folds of a masking persona. But this preoccupation with questions of identity is attached, in a seemingly Buddhistlike fashion, to another issue: cinema revealing itself as a medium, its "self-exposure" one could say. The spectator's attention is drawn to this right at the outset. The film begins with an image of a spool of film rushing through a projector. Then, halfway through the film, at the crossover between its two parts, the rushing spool is seen again, only to stop abruptly, tear, and catch fire. Yet again this idea recurs at the film's ending: as Sister Alma walks toward the bus station, the camera pulls out and suddenly, as if out of nowhere, Bergman reveals, momentarily, a cameraman on a crane shooting the scene in which Alma walks to the bus station.

This is a fitting illustration for my explanation of Vasubandhu, for whom self-awareness is an aesthetization of reality. Needless to say, in these images Bergman is not simply trying to show the craft of film-making. Far from it; he is not seeking a way to reveal the secrets of cinema by allowing us a furtive gaze into the director's laboratory so as to satisfy our desire for a behind-the-scenes tour of the film set. Bergman wants cinema to expose itself, to allow the medium to reveal its self-awareness, and, like Vasubandhu, he clearly understands that the medium can do this only from within—that is to say, not from some side stage or backroom, but from its throbbing center. Bergman is not interested in simply revealing his cameraman so that we know that he was there. In revealing the film spool at the beginning and at the heart of the film, and by means of that profound "trick" at the end of the film, Bergman is trying to help us realize that the moment the cameraman's presence is revealed it dawns on us that there must be an-other cameraman too, shooting the first cameraman. And his presence is, of course, simultaneous. Could it be otherwise?

Bergman, the master filmmaker, is an antirealist in the same way that Vasubandhu is an antirealist, even though in this respect he is diametri-cally opposed to Berkeley; the latter would have undoubtedly cut short the circularity of cameramen shooting cameramen by introducing an infinite spiritual Cameraman. Having said that, Bergman's *philosophy* (and there is such a thing) is Western through and through and light years away from Nāgārjuna or from Vasubandhu. For an even better cinematic depiction of Vasubandhu's point of view we need to turn to yet another filmmaker and another film: Federico Fellini's *E la nave va* (*And the Ship Sails On*). The film is set in July 1914. We join a group of devotees of a famous opera diva who set sail on a steam liner for her funereal voyage. Her friends and relations—an opulent assortment of decadents from an old and expiring world—embark on a voyage to the shores of the diva's birthplace in order to scatter her ashes there. At the outset of this voyage, Austria and Serbia are already at war following the assassination of the crown prince archduke Franz Ferdinand. We are merely a few weeks away from the outbreak of a war that will quickly deteriorate into a world war. A journalist, answering to the name of Orlando, acts as our host on this voyage. He constantly speaks to a hidden camera that follows him along with the other passengers. The voyage is a journey to death in more than one sense (not only in its depiction of a group of undertakers attempting to scatter ashes on the face of the sea), but I shall not comment upon this here. I shall only state that the whole film is nothing more than a methodical, thorough, and pitiless deconstruction of external reality. Consider the story's narrator, a babbling journalist reporting to an invisible camera, present only through its incessant purring, speaks much and says little. Supposedly he is reporting, instead he prattles, even confusing the name of the ship's captain, calling him "Leonardo de Robertis" instead of "Roberto de Leonardis." (Is not Nāgārjuna's smile lurking behind his back?). With language in shambles, the ship itself, in its entirety, is about to collapse too: having been hit by a (1914) cannon ball shot by an Austrian warship, the ship starts sinking. And then, much like Bergman, just as the ship is beginning to sink, the camera pulls back, revealing the soundstage in which the film is being shot, showing the crew at work: the director, the cameraman, their assistants—all shooting a sea storm that is in fact nothing other than bluish cardboard shaken about rather clumsily. The inevitable presence of the cinematic medium makes its appearance at the very moment in which the deconstruction of reality reaches its apogee. It is as if Fellini, or Vasubandhu, is telling us that this is the point where perceiving reality amounts to being in a state of total self-awareness. Reality is necessarily mediated by the mind. Self-awareness of the (artistic) medium epitomizes a Buddhist-like view of the way-things-really-are (yathābhūtam). But there is more to come: Fellini's camera leaves the soundstage and scenery and concentrates on the survivors' lifeboat bobbing up and down on the azure cardboard waves like a latter-day Noah's ark. In one of the lifeboats sits the journalist, our host, and we see him recounting a story to one of the ship's previous passengers—a huge brawny rhinoceros. As is his custom, he mumbles on, speaking to some camera or other. And then, to conclude the film, Fellini, in a stroke of masterly self-awareness not much different from Vasubandhu's self-awareness, places the picture inside the diaphragm of a lens, places the lens in front of his eyes, focuses it on what his eyes see in the boat, and then, in a defiant gesture, shuts the diaphragm.

NOTES

1. Far and Beyond

1. Around the middle of the second millennium BCE, the Indian subcontinent was subject to massive changes arising from recurring invasions by marauding nomadic tribes that penetrated India from the northwest. These tribes called themselves Āryas ("noble ones"). They spoke an ancient language that would later be designated as Indo-European, from which, among other languages, Sanskrit is derived (Sanskrit is the principal sacred language of Indian civilization). During the first millennium BCE the Āryans gradually took over northwest India, eventually furthering their conquests toward the east, thus establishing themselves in the rich and fertile plains of northern India. One of the important religiocultural features of invading Āryans was their collection of sacred hymns around which most of their ritualistic life centered. These hymns were grouped together and are referred to collectively as the Ṛg Veda. *Veda* means "knowledge," and this collection became the cornerstone of India's religious and spiritual development. These hymns were most likely composed somewhere between 1500 BCE and 900 BCE.

The Āryan, non-Indian, origin of Vedic culture has of late become a controversial issue, hotly debated by historians, Indologists, and philologists, and often referred to as the Indo-Aryan controversy. One of the key questions fueling this controversy is whether there is sufficient evidence to base the view, which was until recently universally accepted, that an Āryan invasion of the Indian subcontinent actually occurred.

2. The word *idea* is phonetically similar to the Greek original *eidos*, but it seems that "Form" is a better translation since the word *idea* is laden with

psychological usage, mostly referring to mental events, while Platonic Forms, being completely external to the mind, are neither derived from nor created by it. One should mention that Plato is convinced that Forms, despite their exteriority, can be known by philosophers. This is explained by Plato through his celebrated doctrine of recollection, elaborated in *Menon*, according to which all knowledge resides in the soul.

3. I am indebted to Zvi Tauber for this reference to Heine as well as for his other insights.

4. These religions are often referred to as monotheism, despite rich variety that historically distinguishes them one from the other, notably in the degree of their commitment to the unadulterated idea of one God.

5. Certain contemporary philosophers suggested a way to combine between autonomous ethics (in the manner of Kant) and what appears, at least initially, as religious heteronomy. These solutions are, to my mind, no more than a set of mental antics that inevitably fail, since they cannot hide the fact that Kant advocated his view, according to which man is the creator of moral imperatives, in such a manner that it necessitates the rejection of a transcendent authority regulating moral imperatives.

6. Maimonides subscribes to the minority view that claims that idolatry is not a surrender to temptation but, primarily, an intellectual misconception of God. Worshipping false gods, says Maimonides, is simply a case of miscomprehension: for instance, as when one attributes a body or a soul to God. Idolatry, therefore, is a mental defect, brute reliance on imagination rather than intellect. Not only is this typical of the masses and mass religions, but also quite contrary to his form of philosophical "purifying" Judaism that cleanses the concept of God from any form of personalization whatsoever.

7. Negative theology—the supposition that it is impossible to make any positive statement about God's attributes, that one can merely negate incompatible attributes—actually arises from the presupposition of an unbridgeable abyss between God and His creation.

8. For example: for Plotinus, the One is a being in itself, all alone. No otherness is present and thus there is no room for an abyss to form. This is so only on account of the absolute and exclusive existence of the One in its own right. Accordingly, the only thing a mystical attempt to bridge such an abyss can express lies in the attempt to draw attention to the yawning abyss as something that is not part of the divine essence itself.

9. *Bhakti* is a form of nonphilosophical and anti-intellectual devotionalism that began to take form in India somewhere around the second half of the first millennium, exerting much influence on Indian religiosity.

10. A common error is the manner in which Western scholars of Indian philosophy (and their Indian counterparts too) consider Śaṅkara's philosophy

(seventh or eighth century CE). Śaṅkara sees reality, including its manifest plurality, as a whole and as contained in an inclusive, abstract, universal principle which he equated with the *brahman* of certain early Upaniṣads. From here, these erring scholars draw the conclusion that Śaṅkara's philosophy is but an a posteriori variation of Neoplatonism. Notwithstanding the cultural gap, so they say, it would seem that Plotinus's One and Śaṅkara *Brahman* are terms that convey the same idea. Nothing could be more mistaken. Plotinus maintains his notion of the One by means of an ontological commitment to its necessary and independent existence. On the other hand, Śaṅkara's metaphysical position is explained without presupposing any ontological assumptions and, according to Śaṅkara, the existence of *Brahman* cannot be divorced from his indisputable presence in man's inwardness. This is a metaphysics of immanence necessitating the evident denial of ontological presuppositions, and will thus reject, *ab initio*, presuppositions with regard to the logical and ontological precedence of the outward over the inward.

11. The role assumed by the Vedas in the religious practices of ancient India is anything but abstract. These hymns had a very practical function. They formed part of the sacrificial ritual performed for this or that God. The religion of ancient India was distinctly ritualistic; it centered on the performance of a sacrifice to a specific god, and this performance necessitated compliance with a rich and complex set of elaborate regulations. Rituals were performed for different purposes—some overt and explicit (such as health, wealth and victory), others tended to be more subliminal (such as immortality). Generally speaking, ritual was perceived as forming a bridge between the tangible world and the world beyond. The ritual would be performed at two locales—the private, homely, almost immanent sphere of existence and the formal ceremonial public sphere. The practices of the latter were very intricate and highly elaborate. At least four priests officiated at the ceremony (the first, in charge of the ritual itself, the second chanted the appropriate spells, the third recited the Vedic hymns and, finally, the fourth, while not actively engaged in the performance itself, his contemplative silence was an inherent part of the ritual). Major rituals could have as many as sixteen officiating priests. The role allocated to the brahmin was of prime importance. It was assumed that if the sacrificial ritual was intended to achieve a goal, and if it was within the jurisdiction of the god to whom the sacrifice was being made, then this goal would be obtained and the wishes of the person performing the sacrifice would be granted regardless of the individual will of the god to whom the sacrifice was being made (and it is doubtful whether such a will ever existed). The one condition that would guarantee its successful outcome was if the intricate and complicated ceremony, with the act of sacrifice at its core, was properly performed, down to the minutest detail. These rules,

comprising a vast collection of instructions on how to perform the different rituals, are to be found in a set of prose texts appended to the poetic Ṛg Vedas. They are called the Brāhamaṇas. The inevitable conclusion arising from these brimming instruction manuals is that the efficacy of a sacrifice did not stem from the fact that a certain god received his offering, but from the fact that the sacrifice was carried out according to the explicit instructions outlined by the Brāhamaṇa.

12. Prof. K.N. Mishra from Benares Hindu University drew my attention to this passage while visiting Tel Aviv as a guest of Tel Aviv University. Shortly after his visit, this unique scholar passed away, yet the profundity of his reasoning remains.

13. One may want to mention here that the force of *tapas* was understood as a kind of heat or blazing flame. *Tapas* is described in Vedic literature as an omnipotent force and, interestingly, it is ascribed to the man performing a sacrifice and endows him with the power to control the gods.

14. The Upaniṣads are a collection of texts that were composed around the middle of the first millennium BCE. The term *upaniṣad* means "connection" or "equivalence," the nature of which implies an intimate or secret knowledge possessed by select group. In a certain sense the Upaniṣads consider themselves as the textual continuation of the previous layers of the Vedic corpus and thus are also referred to as *Vedānta*—meaning "the end of the Vedas." In another sense the Upaniṣads clearly break away from the ritualistic worldview of the Vedas and constitute a counterresponse to its dominant themes. This counter-response is evidenced by the shift from the attempt to control the world by the means of active ritual to an attempt to cancel the threat imposed by the world through a process of self-control, in other words, through internalization—from the outward to the inward, from a characterization of man acting upon the world to a man acting upon himself, thus releasing himself from the world. According to the renouncers who composed the Upaniṣads, the new ideal of *mokṣa* (liberation) replaces the old ideal of the ritual man. Man's active inner mental activity can completely obliterate the framework of his pubic, social, class life. Rather than descriptions of human nature as motivated by a set of strict dynamic inter-relationships with external reality, the new ideal of human nature is of withdrawal, convergence into one's selfhood in an attempt to completely sever the inter-relationships existing between man and world.

15. Patrick Olivelle has noted that these primordial uses of the word "Whole" (*sarva*) were not quantitative expressions. They refer to the condition of being full or complete (as opposed to being partial or deficient).

16. From the beginning of the first millennium BCE, the religion of Vedic ritualism makes way for a much more complex form of religion that combines

the ritualistic assumptions of Indian culture and other assumptions about the nature of man, the boundaries of reality, and the possibility of controlling it. What lies at the core of this complex outlook is an umbrella concept that has an affinity with the Vedic period, but it is more encompassing and broadens the characterization of man as a "ritualistic animal." This new concept is Dharma—most likely the most general and comprehensive set of ideas in Indian civilization. Its scope and application are so extensive that certain Indologists gave up the attempt to find an adequate definition. The meanings of this term seems to them to be too many, and thus they considered it as equivalent to the term *culture*, a kind of blanket term under which many different meanings seek refuge. Some of these different meanings can be isolated without too many difficulties. Dharma is primarily a term denoting order, harmony, and regularity and is derived from a similar notion called in the Veda *ṛta*. This then is a principle that clearly has a cosmological aspect: the assumption of the existence of Dharma is a prescientific supposition about the nature of the world, about the understanding or permanence in it and its relation to a unified system of laws of nature that enables the perception of every event in the world as inseparable from the general picture of the world. Dharma is then a principle that explains the organization of nature. But this explanation is not only cosmological. By the same token, Dharma also explains the laws and structure of social order. Dharma puts forward an explanation that unites the vast plurality of occurrences in one harmonious pattern—regardless of whether these are physical occurrences or social norms. In other words, Dharma is both a descriptive and a normative term, since it includes laws and injunctions applicable to every aspect of an Indian's way of life, both in the specific ritualistic dimension (in which it carries on within the Vedic worldview) and also the plane of everyday life that it tries to channel or perhaps even bring about.

17. Maimonides, the high priest of transcendence, would, of course, be in absolute disagreement. According to him, Moses, the lord of all prophets, stands apart from the other prophets by having been able to see God "face to face," in an "enlightening reflection," unlike the other prophets to whom God revealed Himself merely in a dream.

18. One should bear in mind that in Hesiod's *Theogeny* the cosmos exists from time immemorial and it marshals itself from within (unaided by a creator). There is no mention of a God creating ex nihilo. According to Hesiod's *Theogeny*, in the beginning there was a primordial chaos containing the earth, the firmament, and Eros; in monotheism, by comparison, a supreme God creates the firmament and the earth that were prior to this in a state of complete chaos (*tohu vavohu*). It was the Greek philosophers that entertained the idea of transcendence, and one would be hard-pressed to find this idea in Greek "folk" religions.

2. One Language, Many Things

1. In his book *Empty Persons* Mark Siderits mentions that the Abhidharma (which he calls "Buddhist Reductionism") upholds the notion of truth as correspondence. I am inclined to agree with him so long as the nature of truth is under discussion; however, it does not seem plausible that the Abhidharma endorsed correspondence as a criterion of truth, if only because it shunned substance-based ontology, substituting it with a process-based ontology.

2. Translator's note: The exact phrase in Hebrew is *ezer ke-negdo,* which means, literally, "help against him" or "help opposite him." The King James Version renders this complex term with the more felicitous but less precise *helpmeet.*

3. This is the position of the Mīmāṃsā and the Advaita Vedānta, but it was rejected by the Nyāya. Indeed, later Nyāya thought grounded the Vedas' authority in their omniscient authorship or in the idea that they stem from the words of a reliable person. However, Nyāya philosophers did not show much interest in the Vedas: they would turn to the Vedas infrequently, did not subject them to serious philosophizing, and only on rare occasions uses the Vedas to bulwark their philosophical position.

4. This may be the result of a kind of ritualism that holds that the mere enunciation of the Vedic mantra has causal power independent of any divine will (so an impeccable performance of the ritual brings about the desired result by compelling the god's performance).

5. Fritz Staal notes a certain kind of circularity here: the seven singers "praise together" (i.e., in one voice) and thus they create language. But, in order to praise, they would have had to have language. In my mind there is nothing problematic about this circularity since the hymn relates to different, parallel facets of mental activity.

6. I am indebted to Rafi Peled for drawing my attention to this passage and to its meaning.

7. Translator's note: Babylon in Hebrew is *bavel,* derived from the root *b.b.l.* "He confounded" in Hebrew is *balal,* derived from the root *b.l.l.,* thus it is plain that Babel cannot be a true gloss for "confounding," and the last verse ("Therefore is the name of it called Babel; because the Lord did there confound the language of all the earth") cannot be taken too literally.

8. My translation from the Hebrew source.

9. "Rabbi Benjamin said, on behalf of Rabbi Levy: 'also he hath set the world in their heart,' that is, the love of the world he hath set in their heart; Rabbi Jonathan said, the fear of the angel of death he set in their hearts."

10. This amalgamation is based on a paronomasia on the Hebrew root

shared by both olam—derived from the root *e.l.m.*—and *he'elam*, also derived from the root *e.l.m.*

11. "Rabbi Achva the son of Rabbi Zaira has said: the world—the explicit name was drawn away from it. This is like a king who prepared a feast and invited guests to attend this feast. After they had eaten and drunk they said to him: give us swords and spears and we shall play with them. He gave them branches of myrtle and they hit one another and wounded each other with these sticks. The king then said: 'I have only given you branches of myrtle and see what you have with them? Imagine then that I should have given thee, all the more, swords and spears.' Thus the Blessed One said: 'Having concealed from them the explicit name, they kill [one another] by using [my] appellations, all the more then, had I given to them the explicit name.'"

3. My-Self

1. As is well known, Descartes devoted much of his time to writing replies to objections that were raised against his philosophy. It thus seems that his preference for the philosophical soliloquy did not hamper the undeniable urgency of dialogue in the development of his philosophical system.

2. This change found its literary expression in Shakespeare, roughly fifty years before Descartes came up with its equivalent philosophical expression. Hamlet, for instance, symbolizes such a new concept of man. Here is a man who can gaze at his inwardness, undertake an internal dialogue that is essentially reflexive (in reply to the question what am I in truth?), and then even portray himself in a way that is completely unrelated to his true real inner self.

3. As mentioned earlier, one should bear in the mind that despite the exteriority of Platonic Forms, in *Meno* Plato argues they are knowable through recollection.

4. Is not Descartes' philosophical enterprise motivated, right from the start, by the ideal of clarity and distinctness as necessary criteria for certainty—an intuition that Descartes drew from the mathematics of his time?

5. This term already appears in the Vedas, where it mostly designates the mystic force present in quasi-magical verbal formulae—the mantras—chanted during the performance of rituals. Later the term took on a much broader meaning and in the Upaniṣads it displays the broadest meaning of all, designating the absolute essence of all that exists.

6. *Aham* is the first-person pronoun, literally meaning "I." Since Sanskrit allows for nominal sentences, this makes perfect sense as an independent clause, though the only way to render its meaning sensibly into English is through the complex verbal phrase "Here I am."

7. Needless to say, Indian thinkers did not deny the subject-object dichotomy, but on the whole they saw it only in a posteriori terms, acknowledging its presence in our daily perceptions and everyday discourse yet rarely relying on it as a representation of things as they really are. This claim needs to be elaborated in greater detail, far beyond what the present space allows.

8. The metaphysical interpretation of this passage, which we have inherited from Śaṅkara and his school, sees the existence of the self (in the guise of primordial man) as a minute error that disrupts primary monism, itself giving rise to the false distinction between inner subject and external object. This reading functioned as the cornerstone of a fascinating philosophical system, but whether it is completely faithful to the bare Upaniṣadic text is in doubt. As I have argued above, extracting a system of monistic metaphysics from this text (and its like) constitutes an "overreading" of the text.

9. Attributing a fictional status to external objects does not mean denying their existence, but, rather, like the status of characters and events in works of fiction, to designate the ontology of their existence as something irresoluble and in fact irrelevant. In claiming that reality is a fiction of a sort, one is suspending judgment on the reality of independently existing external objects. However, this account of *Puruṣa* has sometimes been read as an early version of the idea that the phenomenal world, with its multiplicity of objects and its subject-object dichotomy, is wholly the product of *māyā*.

10. Needless to say, this is somewhat of an exaggeration; Cartesian certainty does not eliminate fiction as such; it simply relegates it to the role of a parasite perched on the back of apodictic knowledge, turning into something vapid, a mere satellite, a worldview basking in the bright light of clear and distinct ideas.

11. Some interpretations of Descartes detect the presence of existential anxiety in his philosophy; even if we concede to this, it is obvious that Descartes' anxiety takes place amidst the presupposition of transcendence and thus it is ultimately "methodic anxiety," in no way similar to the anxiety that befalls the solitary ātman.

12. The use of this imagery is common throughout the Upaniṣads. Here I consider its appearance only in the relevant passage.

13. Śaṅkara suggested a metaphysical reading of this passage, according to which the purpose of the negations is to demonstrate absolute annihilation, both of external objects and the subject knowing them.

4. No-Self

1. That is to say, knowledge of an object is necessarily determined by an empirical intuition, since "things in space and time are given only insofar

as they are perceptions (that is, representations accompanied by sensation), therefore only through empirical representation," and "space and time are only forms of sensible intuition, and so only conditions of the existence of things as appearances."

2. In Kantian moral philosophy, God is seen as "regulative idea," but we shall not concern ourselves with this here.

3. We shall not dwell here on the part played by the thing-in-itself in Kantian ethics and his view on aesthetic judgments.

4. "For otherwise I should have as many-coloured and diverse a self as I have representations of which I am conscious to myself."

5. Francis Ford Coppola has put this Kafkaesque motif to great cinematic effect in his film *The Conversation*.

6. It is worth noting the interesting similarity between the Buddha's rejection of a permanent and stable self and that of a similar position regarding the self upheld by the Scottish philosopher David Hume (1711–1776). For Hume, the self is not permanent, it "is nothing but a bundle or collection of different perceptions, which succeed each other with an inconceivable rapidity, and are in a perpetual flux and movement."

7. According to those who upheld this view, a meticulous analysis of the texts in which the Buddha explains his position on this matter demonstrates that he had no interest in examining general and abstract philosophical questions about the nature of reality and the character of man; his negative appraisal of concepts of permanence and the self arose, according to this interpretation, from the practical issues regarding liberation (nirvāṇa) and his concern with plotting out an alternative way of life meant to supersede the regular way of life, which the Buddha saw as a life void of satisfaction since it was driven by craving and lust, which, necessarily, reduces life to a frustrating form of deprivation.

8. This is my reading of several sections in *Nikāyas*, sections that refer to what the Buddha himself allegedly said. However, according to Abhidharma literature words do in fact relate to something, namely, ultimately real dharmas. The Abhidharmikas see language as a mental construct that is nonetheless grounded in reality. As we shall soon see, Nāgārjuna disagrees.

9. Needless to say, this does not mean that we have found a final explanation of what the Buddha's true intentions were, since those who advocate the first line of interpretation can argue—as indeed they do—that Nāgārjuna exaggerated and took his interpretation of the Buddha's teaching to such extremes that not only did he fail to faithfully represent this teaching, but he even managed to distort it.

10. Nāgārjuna refers here to the Sanskrit word *akṛtma* whose literal meaning is "not-artificial."

11. Richard King has suggested that it might be useful to see Nāgārjuna

as someone who is shifting the traditional debate between those affirming the Upaniṣadic ātman and those in early Buddhist thought who rejected the idea—relegating it to a much broader and more technical debate about the affirmation or rejection of *svabhāva*.

12. Some conservative Buddhologists are anxious about the prospect of Indian philosophy having a "linguistic" character. This anxiety seems to me to be unwarranted; it is as if they fear that Nāgārjuna might, heaven forbid, seem a bit too modern—and may even become accessible to the kind of Western philosophy that has already experienced its own linguistic turn. This fear is but a particular instance of a much broader anxiety that affects the community of conservative scholars: the thought that their professional endeavors might have even a sliver of relevance to a wider intellectual milieu. I find this anxiety repugnant. Can it not be that we in the West are, philosophically speaking, better equipped to understand Nāgārjuna today than we were more than a century ago?

13. Here too one is tempted to turn again to David Hume's writings, where we encounter an argument conspicuously similar to this Buddhist claim. Thus, for example, Hume concluded that the senses "give us no notion of continued existence, because they cannot operate beyond the extent, in which they really operate. They as little produce the opinion of a distinct existence, because they neither can offer it to the mind as represented, nor as original."

14. Further on we shall see that this emptiness is not equivalent to meaninglessness, but it is rather the precondition by means of which meaning is determined conventionally rather than being determined by a certain essence or by actual states of affairs.

15. Matilal referred to this as *panfictionalism*. There are those who claim that this empties fiction itself of meaning, since the term *fiction* necessitates a contrast for it to be meaningful. I shall return to this later in the chapter.

16. It is imperative to make a distinction here between this nihilistic interpretation of Nāgārjuna—put forward in the main by contemporary scholars—and between the accusations of nihilism directed at him by certain Indian philosophers of the first millennium CE. When these accused him of being a nihilist, they meant it in a very specific sense: philosophically speaking, they reproached him for refusing to accept the underlying assumptions that made up the framework of Indian philosophy and its ensuing vigorous disputations (namely, settling epistemic questions by examining the operation of *pramāṇas*, "means of knowledge"). In this context, Nāgārjuna was accused of being nihilist because of his refusal to subscribe to the idea of "means of knowledge" as an epistemological cornerstone, thus emptying it of any possible merit. In the religious sense he was accused of being a nihilist (mostly by fellow Buddhists) because they thought that his doctrine was maliciously undermining the Buddha's proper teaching.

17. One can imagine an interesting and opposing scheme if one juxtaposes the Judeo-Christian idea of human nature dwelling beneath the heavy shadow of original sin with the Indian idea that posits human nature, as evidenced in psychophysical phenomena, as nothing more than a kind of "error," or, in its Nāgārjunian version, a false idea.

18. The Sanskrit word *laukika* means "worldly," or "of the world," in the sense of the totality of things customarily known, common and conventional.

19. One can never be overzealous when following the dictum of not mixing two completely unrelated matters with each other. Applying the expression *linguistic turn*, a quintessential product of the twentieth century, to a second-century Indian philosophical outlook is a clear violation of this dictum. But can one resist the temptation? The most common feature of the linguistic turn in the West is the change in point of view: philosophical questions are now seen through the prism of language and its apparatus. This characterization fits Nāgārjuna's point of view perfectly.

20. *Bartleby* was published in 1856, though it was first published three years earlier in a literary journal.

21. Even before Bartleby commences with his emptying dead-center response of "I would prefer not to," he is presented by the narrator as an in-between character, hovering amidst the two other scriveners: Turkey's afternoon insanity and Nippers morning madness. In this context one cannot but recall the Cheshire cat's incisive observation in *Alice in Wonderland* that both the Hatter and the March Hare—each living at the other's extremity—are equally mad.

5. *"It's All in the Mind"*

1. It is customary to refer to philosophical doctrines that necessitate such points of departure as foundational philosophies.

2. Further on in the chapter I will show that Berkeley's conception of reflection is rather limited, especially when compared to Buddhist idealistic philosophy.

3. Ram-Prasad rightly notes that one should be weary of calling Vasubandhu an idealist—if an idealist is perceived as someone who reduces objects to subjective states of mind—Vasubandhu not only repudiates our ability to perceive independently objects, he even repudiates the very existence of a perceiving self. The only sense in which he can be regarded as an idealist is "in the sense that he maintains that the account of ordinary experience itself should reject any reference to external objects and should instead be put in terms of mental constructs." Garfield has written an illuminating article

analyzing the different proponents of nonidealist interpretations of Yogācāra, showing, convincingly, that these do not do justice to Vasubandhu's texts.

4. I see no reason to shun an explicitly psychological use of the term. The reason for this will be evident further on in the chapter.

5. Vasubandhu calls these natures, yet does not imply that the mind contains three essences or subessences, but rather that these natures are inward, introspective gazes.

6. Vasubandhu's claim here can be seen as challenging his realist opponent: show us the evidence that mental images (the immediate objects of perceptual cognition) are produced by external objects. Both sides agree that the hairs in the moon seen by someone with an opthalmic disorder are nothing but a mental image; the challenge is to show that some perceptual cognitions are different. The seeming weakness of his argument may be a result of a dialectical situation. He is following the standard Indian practice of starting with a simple argument, followed by a statement of objections, and then offering a reply to these.

7. According to some scholars, Vasubandhu's adherence to the theory of karmic seeds means that he is a metaphysical idealist, on the grounds that he rejects the existence of external objects without at the same time denying the existence of some subtle form of enduring self. If this were so than obviously Vasubandhu's philosophy would be in a weak position. Thomas Wood, among others, has drawn our attention to this. As he rightly notes, in order to uphold an idealism of this sort it must, pace Vasubandhu, accede to a certain degree of objectivism that is vaguely reminiscent of the Vedānta's ātmanic presupposition. It is my contention that Vasubandhu is not committed to metaphysical idealism. I do not deny that he makes extensive use of the kind of terminology that abounds in early Yogācāra—among which are *storehouse consciousness* and the karmic seeds contained within it. And yet the use of these terms does not mean that he has in any way reified them.

8. It is interesting to note that Berkeley also makes use of a similar argument: "The ideas formed by the imagination are faint and indistinct; they have besides an entire dependence on the will. But the ideas perceived by sense, that is, real things, are more vivid and clear. . . . There is therefore no danger of confounding these with the foregoing: and there is as little of confounding them with the visions of a dream, which are dim, irregular, and confused. And though they should happen to be never so lively and natural, yet by their not being connected, and of a piece with the preceding and subsequent transactions of our lives, they might easily be distinguished from realities."

9. Deep inside the mind, there is a special kind of consciousness that Yogācārins call storehouse consciousness (*ālayavijñāna*). It is termed thus since

it stores or contains within it the "raw materials" of mental activity—the impulses and predispositions that Yogācārins often refer to as seeds or, occasionally, scents. These are the primary and rudimentary units of mental experience. This storehouse is organic—a vessel more similar to a womb than to a room filled with cupboards and shelves—and constitutes a conserving soil from which the seeds of psychic activity sprout. Storehouse consciousness, frequently compared to the forceful and incessant flow of a strong torrent (constantly changing but still retaining an identity of its own), is mental activity void of any reflective awareness. Many contemporary descriptions of storehouse consciousness tend to refer to it as subconscious or subliminal, evidently suggesting, if only by allusion, that this is the Indian version of the Freudian unconscious. In the course of one's mental development, storehouse consciousness splits into seven different consciousnesses or, more precisely, seven developmental levels of mental states. The intricate details that make up this psychological doctrine are immaterial to our discussion here. But is should be noted that the whole taxonomic process has merely an explanatory purpose. Vasubandhu has no intention of claiming that storehouse consciousness, or any other kind of consciousness derived from it, actually exists; he is merely offering a theoretical, explanatory account of the structure of consciousness, outlining it as a map, "placing" psychic activity topographically, as a hierarchy of mental processes. Most scholars of Vasubandhu are agreed that the theory of *ālayavijñāna* is merely explanatory. According to Waldron, for Vasubandhu the seeds that are supposed to be contained in the storehouse consciousness are in fact "simply ciphers, empty significations" that are "neither ontological nor logical, but primarily psychological." As Griffiths aptly puts it, "the store-consciousness is a philosophical construct designed to account conceptually for the kinds of continuity issue . . . an ad hoc category designed to deal with philosophical problems." Since it is no more than an explanatory construct, it is evident that storehouse consciousness cannot take the place Berkeley's God has in his philosophy.

10. Vasubandhu's philosophical opponent is not only trying to undermine here the possibility of an idealist having a "normal" life but also his espousal of a spiritual goal (liberation). According to him, Vasubandhu's philosophy not only fails at the epistemic level, it also fails as a therapeutic method that is supposed to solve the problem of human suffering. As I mentioned in the introduction, the therapeutic aspect of Indian philosophy will not be considered in this book.

11. Much like other philosophers in India, Vasubandhu too was forced by philosophical propriety to convey his opponents' queries not only fairly but also convincingly. Indian philosophy's strict argumentative practices resulted

in many philosophical texts being written as dialogues, and thus, understandably, these texts are presented as debating matches between the philosopher and his opponents.

12. It is compelling to think of the interesting similarity between the status of Buddhist hell-keepers and the many torturers extant in Kafka's works.

13. The idea that hell-keepers are not sentient beings was a claim conjured by Abhidharmika realists well before Vasubandhu's day. They argued that these beings could not have generated the kind of deeds that would explain their presence in hell and, accordingly, they cannot reside there as the result of their karma. To them these beings are only seemingly animate assemblages of material particles, the collective result of the bad karma of those dwelling in hell. In the Vimśatika, Vasubandhu puts forward a similar claim, suggesting it as *another* way of explaining the existence of hell-keepers. In effect, he is leaving it up to us to choose whether to endorse the traditional Buddhist explanation, which draws on early Buddhist resources and emphasizes the presence of karma, or whether instead to adhere to his philosophical suggestion. It should be noted, however, that even the traditional explanation does not accede to existence external of hell-keepers, only showing that, as with our other perceptual cognitions, we have misinterpreted the experiences that we collect under the term *hell-keepers*. We have taken the experiences to have an external cause when in fact the real cause is our own past desires.

14. Even though Berkeley thought that Plato and Aristotle embraced a sort of proto-idealism, Burnyeat convincingly argues that in this he was completely mistaken. According to Burnyeat, Berkeleyan idealism is precisely one of the philosophical positions missing in ancient philosophy.

15. It is Berkeley's contention that for Locke general terms are, as a matter of fact, proper names, each of which refers to one thing, so that the word *green*, for example, is the proper name of the abstract idea of green.

According to Bennett, there is no reason to assume that Locke treated all general terms as proper names. Moreover, there is no reason to assume that it was Locke's contention that there is one, and only one, abstract idea corresponding to every general term. Bennett thinks that Berkeley opposed the doctrine of abstract ideas not on psychological grounds (as he should have) but rather on logical grounds. He was mistaken in thinking that an abstract idea cannot exist on logical grounds. This explains why he was so confident that the intelligent reader could not but agree that we cannot perceive abstract ideas.

16. Richard Rorty sees here an expression of a liberal ideology, but I think that his reading of the book is somewhat one-sided.

17. For Rorty, this provisional title proves Orwell's parochialism. This is evident from the noun *Europe:* Orwell writes about people he knew and about

the European society in which he lived and completely ignored the rest of the world beyond Europe. It would seem that, for Rorty, the words *last man* are of little importance. Having said that, given the comparative context of this book, it is possible to treat *Europe* not as a geographical designation but rather as a cultural one.

18. In Orwellian idealism the absolute internalization of reality is also the collapse of the whole foundation of formal logic ("War is Peace; Freedom is Slavery; Ignorance is Strength") and of mathematics ($2 + 2 = 5$). A much more incisive and cruel manifestation of this is evident in ordinary language, in the practices of "Newspeak," which is the obvious outcome of this idealism and as such completely unburdened by the need to represent external reality. The role of language in *Nineteen Eighty-four* is a fascinating subject all to itself that is in need of a detailed philosophical inquiry, which the present discussion cannot accommodate.

19. Yet in this book, as I mentioned in the introduction, I do not intend to discuss the nature of liberation (mokṣa, nirvāṇa).

20. See chapter 3, page 161.

21. This is, of course, an anachronism; Schopenhauer was a "student" of various Buddhist texts and was also influenced by them.

BIBLIOGRAPHICAL NOTES

Introduction

p. 5   V. S. Naipul, *An Area of Darkness* (London: Picador, 2002).

1. Far and Beyond

p. 13   The Hebrew *piyyut* is quoted by S. Yahalom, *Priestly Palestinian Poetry: A Narrative Liturgy for the Day of Atonement* ([Hebrew] Jerusalem: Magnes, 1996), 13–14.

p. 14   The quote from Maimonides is from his *Mishneh Torah*, "The Book of Knowledge" 10.1.

p. 16, n1   For the "Indo-Aryan Controversy" see E. F. Bryant and L. L. Patton, eds., *The Indo-Aryan Controversy: Evidence and Inference in Indian History* (London: Routledge, 2005); see also E. Bryant, *The Quest for the Origins of Vedic Culture: The Indo-Aryan Migration Debate* (New York: Oxford University Press, 2001).

p. 16   *Rig Veda* 10.129, in *The Rig Veda: An Anthology*, trans. Wendy Doniger O'Flaherty (London and Harmondsworth: Penguin, 1981), 25–26; translation slightly modified.

pp. 19   The quotations are from Plato, *Phaedo* 66, 78e, trans. Hugh Tredennick in *The Collected Dialogues of Plato*, ed. Edith Hamilton and Huntington Cairns (Princeton: Princeton University Press, 1963).p. 26. "[All things] must be supposed": Plato, *Cratylus* 386d, trans. Benjamin Jowett in *The Collected Dialogues of*

Plato, ed. by Edith Hamilton and Huntington Cairns (Princeton: Princeton University Press, 1963).

p. 20   "that which always is": Plato, *Republic* 7, 527b, trans. Paul Shorey in *The Collected Dialogues of Plato*, ed. by Edith Hamilton and Huntington Cairns (Princeton: Princeton University Press, 1963). For an elaboration of Plato's position on the relationship between the particular and universal see, for example, *Menon*, 74–75.

p. 21   "Since the nature of the 'One' is generative": Plotinus, *Enneads* 6.9.3, trans. A. H. Armstrong, Loeb Classical Library (Cambridge: Harvard University Press, 1988), 7:13.

p. 22   "if the eye is to see itself": *Alcibiades* 1, 133 in *Dialogues of Plato*, vol. 2, trans. B. Jowett (New York: Random House, 1937).

pp. 23–24   H. Heine, "Elemental Spirits" [1837] in *The Poetry and Prose of Heinrich Heine*, trans. F. Ewen (New York: Citadel Press, 1948), 564–569. Citation is from p. 565.

p. 25   the set of beliefs and opinions: J. Amit, *Reading Biblical Stories* ([Hebrew]. Tel Aviv, Ministry of Defense, 2000), 105.

p. 26   "The Hebrew man was well aware": A. Neher, *L'essence du Prophétisme*, trans. into Hebrew by Michael Bar-Zvi (Jerusalem: Magnes, 1999), 67; see also R. M. Schwartz, *The Curse of Cain: The Violent Legacy of Monotheism* (Chicago: University of Chicago Press, 1997).

p. 29   I. Gruenwald, "Changing Conceptions of God in Jewish Thought" in *Researches in Jewish Thought*, ed. S. Heller-Vilensky and M. Idel ([Hebrew] Jerusalem: Magnes, 1989), 42

p. 32   Roberto Calasso discusses the tension between murder and sacrifice in his book *The Marriage of Cadmus and Harmony* (London: Jonathan Cape, 1993).

p. 33   The reference to George Steiner is to his book *The Death of Tragedy* (London: Faber and Faber, 1961).

p. 38   M. Douglas, *Leviticus as Literature* (Oxford: Oxford University Press, 1999).

p. 39   For Śaṅkara's view on God and His moral status, see his commentary on *Brahmā Sūtra* 2.1.33ff.

p. 41   For Ricoeur's view, see A. LaCocque and P. Ricoeur, *Thinking Biblically: Exegetical and Hermeneutical Studies* (Chicago: University of Chicago Press, 1998).

p. 42   Jan Assmann's discussion of monotheism is set against inquiry into the Moses' role in Western culture: See J. Assmann, *Moses the Egyptian: The Memory of Egypt in Western Monotheism* (Cambridge: Harvard University Press, 1997), especially chapter 1.

p. 49   Jean-Luc Marion is quoted in P. Blond, ed., *Post-Secular Philosophy: Between Philosophy and Theology* (London: Routledge, 1998), 34.

p. 50   "God is the immanent": B. Spinoza, *Ethics*, in *The Collected Works of Spinoza*, ed. and trans. Edwin Curley (Princeton: Princeton University Press, 1985), 1:428.
          "All things which are, are in God": B. Spinoza, *Ethics*, trans. R. H. M. Elwes (New York: Dover, 1977), 62.

p. 50   See G. Scholem, *Major Trends in Jewish Mysticism* (New York: Schocken, 1961), 7–8; The article mentioned: G. Scholem, "Ten Unhistorical Sayings on the Kabbalah" in *Od Davar* ([Hebrew] Tel Aviv: Am Oved, 1989).

p. 59   A. Kunst, "Man—The Creator": *Journal of Indian Philosophy*, 4(1): 51–68.

p. 60   Among the many translations of the Upaniṣads, one should highlight Olivelle's excellent rendition into English: *Upaniṣads*, trans. Patrick Olivelle (Oxford: Oxford University Press, 1996). All quotations here are from this edition.

p. 60   "In the beginning": *Bṛhadāraṇyaka Upaniṣad* 1.4.1ff (Olivelle 13–14).

p. 62   The story of Śiva's sojourn in Benares is recounted in D. L. Eck, *Banares: City of Light* (New York: Knopf, 1982), 148–155.

p. 65   "It simply goes without saying": F. Kafka, *Parables and Paradoxes* (New York: Schocken, 1961), 119.

p. 67   Among those who claim that the variety of divinities in India are but different ways of presenting a monotheistic divinity, see F. Hadry, *The Religious Culture of India: Power, Love, and Wisdom* (Cambridge: Cambridge University Press, 1994).

p. 68   "Who, alone, himself without colour": *Śvetāśvatara Upaniandṣad* 4.1–4 (Olivelle 259).

p. 70   For the description of god as an uprooted banyan tree, see *Katha Upaniṣad* 6.1. The scholar who took this description for an insinuation of god's transcendence is S. Dasgupta, *Indian Idealism* (Cambridge: Cambridge University Press, 1962), 33f.

p. 71   See W. Doniger O'Flaherty, *Dreams, Illusion and Other Realities* (Chicago: University of Chicago Press, 1984), 53.

p. 72   On the similarity to the Stoics see, e.g., M. Nussbaum, *The Therapy of Desire: Theory and Practice in Hellenistic Ethics* (Princeton: Princeton University Press, 1994).

p. 74   On how classical India perceived history see, for example, S. Pollock, "Mīmāṃsa and the Problem of History in Traditional India," *Journal of the American Oriental Society*, 109(4): 603–610.

2. One Language, Many Things

p. 78, n1   See M. Siderits, *Personal Identity and Buddhist Philosophy: Empty Persons* (Aldershot: Ashgate, 2003), esp. chapter 8.

p. 79   "Knowledge of things is not to be derived": Plato, *Cratylus* 439b, trans. Benjamin Jowett in *The Collected Dialogues of Plato*, ed. Edith Hamilton and Huntington Cairns (Princeton: Princeton University Press, 1963).

p. 79   Aristotle mentions Antistheses' view on language in *Metaphysics* 1024^b 32.

p. 80   "It is impossible for anything": Aristotle, *Metaphysics* 1006^a 2–3.

p. 80   "It is not possible to assert": ibid, 1008^a 35–36.

p. 80   "A name is an instrument": Plato, *Cratylus* 388a.

p. 82   "When people gave a name": St. Augustine, *Confessions* 1.viii (13), trans. Henry Chadwick (Oxford: Oxford University Press, 1992), 10–11.

p. 83   Hegel's reflections on the meaning of the story of the deluge can be found in G. W. F. Hegel, *Early Theological Writings*, trans. T. M. Knox (Philadelphia: University of Pennsylvania Press), 184–185.

p. 86   Fritz Staal compared the two competing models of certainty, the West's mathematical ideal as opposed to the Indian natural language approach, in several places. See for instance F. Staal, "Euclid and Panini," *Philosophy East and West* 15:99–116 1965.

p. 88   The prohibition of writing and the connection between writing and impurity is mentioned in *Aittareya Āranyaka* 5.5.3. For a fascinating discussion of the oral status if Indian literature see T. B. Coburn, "'Scripture' in India: Towards a Typology of the Word in Hindu Life" in M. Levering, ed., *Rethinking Scripture* (Albany: State University of New York Press, 1989), 102–128.

p. 89   "It is the same with written words": Plato, *Phaedrus* 275d, trans. R. Hackforth in *The Collected Dialogues of Plato*, ed. Edith Hamilton and Huntington Cairns (Princeton: Princeton University Press, 1963).

p. 89   "It is written in the soul": *Phaedrus* 276a.

p. 89   On Derrida's discussion of Plato's *Phaedrus*, see "Plato's Pharmacy" in *Dissemination*, trans. Barbara Johnson (London: Athlone, 1981). See also J. Derrida, *Positions*, trans. A. Bass (Chicago: University of Chicago Press, 1981), 12ff.

p. 91   The image of Vedic man as a monk transcribing an incomprehensible text is in F. Staal, "The Concept of Scripture in the Indian Tradition" in M. Juergensmeyer, ed., *Sikh Studies* (Berkeley: University of California Press, 1979), 121–123.

p. 91   Coburn, "Scripture in India," 111

p. 92   "Certainly, to make a bold declaration": St. Augustine, *Confessions* 12.xxxi (42), trans. Henry Chadwick (Oxford: Oxford University Press, 1992), 271.

p. 94-95   Vāc presents herself as a queen in Ṛg Veda 10.125. The quotation here is from 10.71 in *The Rig Veda: An Anthology*, trans. Wendy Doniger O'Flaherty (London: Penguin, 1981), 61. An illuminating analysis of this hymn can be found in Laurie Patton's article "Hymn to Vāc: Myth or Philosophy?' in F. E. Reynolds and D. Tracy, eds., *Myth and Philosophy* (Albany: State University of New York Press, 1990), 183–214.

p. 97   On the debate between Vedic scholars on the meaning of the hymn, see Patton, "Hymn to Vāc."

p. 97, n5   See F. Staal, "Rgveda 10.71 on the Origin of Language" in H. Coward and K. Sivaraman, eds., *Revelation in Indian Thought* (California: Dharma, 1977), 3–14.

p. 98   For Śabara's explanation, see his commentary on *Mīmāṃsā Sūtra* 8.1.34.

p. 98   The Upaniṣadic story recounting how the gods sought refuge in the holy syllable OM is from *Chāndogya Upaniṣad*, 1.4.2.

p. 100   For a detailed discussion of the religious philosophy of the Mīmāṃsā school see S. Biderman, *Scripture and Knowledge: An Essay on Religious Epistemology* (Leiden: Brill, 1995), chapter 5.

p. 101   On the *autpattika* relation between a word and its meaning, see Śabara's commentary on *Mīmāṃsā Sūtra* 1.1.5. It may be argued that the Mīmāṃsā thought the relation between a word and its sense as natural in the sense of being mind-independent. But this possible interpretation ignores the fact that the interest of the author of the *Mīmāṃsā Sūtra* was in grammar and syntax rather than in epistemology.

p. 101   On the notion of *autpattika* see F. X. D'Sa, *Śabdaprāmāṇyam in Śabara and Kumārila: Towards a Study of the Mīmāṃsā Experience of Language*, vol. 7 (Vienna: Publications of the De Nobili Research Library, 1980).

p. 101   For an exceptionally lucid and detailed discussion of Bhartṛhari's philosophy, see the second chapter of B-A. Scharfstein, *Ineffability: The Failure of Words in Philosophy and Religion* (Albany: State University of New York Press, 1993).

p. 103   On the first eleven chapters of Genesis and an explanation on the attempt to build the tower of Babel see D.E. Gowan, *From Eden to Babel: A Commentary on the Book of Genesis 1–11* (Michigan: Eerdmans, 1988); C. Westermann, *Creation* (London: SPCK, 1971); C. Westermann, *Genesis* (Edinburgh: Clark, 1988).

p. 105   "And of one speech": *Midrash Rabbah, Genesis* 38:6, trans. H. Freedman and M. Simon (London: Soncino, 1939), 1:304–305.

p. 106   "There were no stones": *Pirke de Rabbi Eliezer*, chapter 24 (my translation).

p. 107   For Oakeshott's analysis of the story of the tower of Babel see M. Oakeshott, "The Tower of Babel" in *Rationalism in Politics and Other Essays* (London: Methuen, 1962), 59–79; M. Oakeshott, "The Tower of Babel" in *On History and Other Essays* (Oxford: Blackwell, 1983), 165–194.

p. 109   "The tower of Babel does not merely": J. Derrida, "Des Tours de Babel" in *Acts of Religion*, ed. Gil Anidjar (New York: Routledge, 2002), 104.

p. 111   See *Midrash Koheleth Rabbah* 3:11.

p. 111, n11   "Rabbi Achva the son of Rabbi Zaira . . . the explicit name": *Midrash Koheleth Rabbah* 3:11.

p. 112   See G. Steiner, *After Babel: Aspects of Language and Translation* (Oxford: Oxford University Press, 1975).

p. 112   Benjamin's article was probably written in 1916, but was not published during his lifetime. See W. Benjamin, "On Language as Such and on Language of Man" in *Selected Writings*, vol. 1: *1913–1926* (Cambridge: Harvard University Press, 1996). The quotations are from pp. 64–65.

p. 113   "This Adamic vernacular": see Steiner, *After Babel*, 58.

p. 113   "If man could break down.": see Steiner, *After Babel*, 60.

p. 113   The reference to Scholem is to his Hebrew article "Ten Unhistorical Sayings on the Kabbalah" in *Od Davar* (Tel Aviv: Am Oved, 1989), 37.

p. 116   See G. Steiner, *Grammers of Creation* (London: Faber and Faber, 2001), 28.

p. 117   "What are you building": F. Kafka, *Parables and Paradoxes* (New York: Schocken, 1961), 34 [German], 35 [English].

p. 118   "Destroying the world": F. Kafka, *The Blue Octavo Notebooks*, trans. E. Keiser and E. Wilkins (Cambridge: Exact Change, 1991), 43.

p. 118   "If it had been possible to build the Tower of Babel without ascending it, the work would have been permitted": Kafka, *Parables and Paradoxes*, 35.

3. My-Self

p. 119 — "In this they seem to resemble": R. Descartes, *Discourse on the Method*, part 6, trans. Robert Stoothoff in J. Cottingham et al., eds., *The Philosophical Writings of Descartes* (Cambridge: Cambridge University Press, 1985), 1:147.

p. 121 — "to establish a firm and abiding foundation": R. Descartes, *Meditations on First Philosophy I*, trans. J. Cottingham in J. Cottingham et al., eds., *The Philosophical Writings of Descartes* (Cambridge: Cambridge University Press, 1985), 2:13.

p. 123 — "The simplest and most general things": Descartes, *Meditations I*, 14.

p. 124 — "Am not I, at least, something?": Descartes, *Meditations II*, 16; "if I convinced myself," ibid., 17.

p. 125 — "The simple resolution to abandon": Descartes, *Discourse on the Method II*, 1:118.

p. 125 — "arrange for myself a clear stretch": Descartes, *Meditations II*, 12.

p. 126 — "Admittedly, we never see people": *Discourse on the Method II*, 1:117.

p. 127 — "In our languages of self-understanding": C. Taylor, *Sources of the Self* (Cambridge: Harvard University Press, 1989), 111.

p. 128 — The reference to Anne Ferry is to her book A. Ferry, *The "Inward" Language* (Chicago: University of Chicago Press, 1983).

p. 129 — The reference to Dumont is to his article "The Christian Beginnings: From the Outworldly Individual to the Individual-in-the-World," in L. Dumont, *Essays on Individualism* (Chicago: University of Chicago Press, 1986), 23–59.

p. 129 — The reference to Taylor is to his book, *Sources of the Self*, 127–142.

p. 130 — The reference to Brian Stock is to his book *Augustine the Reader: Meditation, Self-Knowledge, and the Ethics of Interpretation* (Cambridge: Harvard University Press, 1996), 250, 271–273. See also B. Stock, *After Augustine: The Meditative Reader and the Text* (Philadelphia: University of Pennsylvania Press, 2001), 20.

p. 131 — See J.-L. Marion, "Descartes and Onto-Theology," in P. Blond, ed., *Post-Secular Philosophy: Between Philosophy and Theology* (London: Routledge, 1998), 78, 72.

p. 132 — "As soon as the opportunity arises": Descartes, *Meditations III*, 25.

p. 132 — "even though the objects": ibid, 24.

p. 133 — "Admittedly my nature is such that": Descartes, *Meditations V*, 48.

p. 133 — "What I took just now as a rule": Descartes, *Discourse*, 130.

p. 135   See J. Bennett, *Learning from Six Philosophers: Descartes, Spinoza, Leibniz, Locke, Berkeley, Hume* (Oxford: Clarendon, 2001).

p. 137   See H. G. Frankfurt, *Demons, Dreamers and Madmen: The Defense of Reason in Descartes' "Meditations"* (Indianapolis: Bobbs-Merrill, 1970).

p. 137   For Taylor's "paradox of modernity," see Taylor, *Sources of the Self*, 175.

p. 139   For Derrida's discussion of Descartes' attitude to madness, see his article "Cogito and the History of Madness" in *Writing and Difference*, trans. A. Blass (London: Routledge, 1997), 31–63.

p. 139   "There is a value and a meaning of the Cogito": ibid, 55.

p. 141   See L. Dumont, "World Renunciation in Indian Religions," *Contributions to Sociology*, 4:33–62.

p. 142   "Have you heard the seer's words": *Bṛhadāraṇyaka Upaniṣad* 6.2.2 in *Upaniṣads*, trans. Patrick Olivelle (Oxford: Oxford University Press, 1996), 82. See also *Chāndogya Upaniṣad* V.3ff (Olivelle 140ff).

p. 143   "In the beginning this world": *Bṛhadāraṇyaka Upaniṣad* I.4 (Olivelle 13–14).

p. 144   For cosmologies in India, see, for example, W. Halbfass, *On Being and What There Is* (Albany: State University of New York Press, 1992), chapters 1–3.

p. 150   "Sacrifice to this god": *Bṛhadāraṇyaka Upaniṣad* 1.4.6 (Olivelle 14).

p. 151   "One day Yājñavalkhya paid a visit": *Bṛhadāraṇyaka Upaniṣad* 4.3.1–6 (Olivelle 58).

p. 156   Life without . . . examination is not worth living": Plato, *Apology* 38a, trans. Hugh Tredennick in *The Collected Dialogues of Plato*, ed. Edith Hamilton and Huntington Cairns (Princeton: Princeton University Press, 1963).

p. 157   "anything at all in the sciences": Descartes, *Meditations I*, 121.

p. 157   "[The *ātman*] dreams with its own light": *Bṛhadāraṇyaka Upaniṣad* 4.3.9 (Olivelle 59).

p. 158   "the person becomes his own light": ibid.

p. 158   On dreams in Indian culture and reality's "soft boundaries," see W. Doniger O'Flaherty, *Dreams, Illusion, and Other Realities* (Chicago: University of Chicago Press, 1984).

p. 158   "Wherever he may travel in his dream": *Bṛhadāraṇyaka Upaniṣad* 2.1.18 (Olivelle 25).

p. 158   "In that place there are no carriages": *Bṛhadāraṇyaka Upaniṣad* 4.3.10 (Olivelle 59). See also *Bṛhadāraṇyaka Upaniṣad* 4.3.13; *Bṛhadāraṇyaka Upaniṣad* 4.3.20; *Chāndogya Upaniṣad* 8.10.1

p. 158   Thomas Nagel considers Descartes proposed internalization in the second chapter of T. Nagel, *The Last Word* (New York: Oxford University Press, 1997).

p. 160   For the simile of deep, dreamless, sleep see, e.g., *Bṛhadāraṇyaka Upaniṣad* 4.3.19ff.

p. 160   "oblivious to everything": *Bṛhadāraṇyaka Upaniṣad* 4.3.21 (Olivelle 61).

p. 160   "When a man is in deep dreamless sleep": *Bṛhadāraṇyaka Upaniṣad* 2.1.19 (Olivelle 25).

p. 160   "Here a father is not a father": *Bṛhadāraṇyaka Upaniṣad* 4.3.22 (Olivelle 61).

p. 161   For a cross-cultural discussion on sleep see Y. Ariel and S. Biderman, "The Big Sleep," in Y. Ariel et al., eds., *Relativism and Beyond* (Leiden: Brill, 1998), 197–224.

p. 162   The use of spatial metaphors in designating dreams: *Bṛhadāraṇyaka Upaniṣad* 4.3.14.

p. 163   Taylor considers spatial orientation in *Sources of the Self*, 28.

p. 165   Kierkegaard's discussion of *Don Giovanni* is to be found in *Either/Or*, in the essay entitled "The Immediate Erotic Stages or the Musical Erotic," trans. Howard V. Hong and Edna H. Hong (Princeton: Princeton University Press,1987), 45–135. I have quoted from Alastair Hanny's (abridged) but richer and more satisfying translation; S. Kierkegaard, *Either/Or*, trans. Alastair Hanny (Harmondsworth: Penguin,1992), 59–136.

p. 165   "equally great": ibid., 64.

p. 166   "in bringing the idea": ibid., 70.

p. 166   "It must of course not be forgotten": ibid., 94.

p. 166   "power of nature": ibid., 99.

p. 166   B. Williams, "Don Giovanni as an Idea" in J. Rushtin, ed., *Don Giovanni* (Cambridge: Cambridge University Press, 1981), 81–91.

p. 168   T. Nagel, *The View from Nowhere* (New York: Oxford University Press, 1986).

p. 169   "Don Giovanni's own life": Kierkegaard 121.

p. 169   "the outward consequences": ibid., 122.

4. No-Self

p. 175   "The observer of the soul": F. Kafka, *The Blue Octavo Notebooks*, trans. E. Keiser and Eithne Wilkins (Cambridge: Exact Change, 1991), 30.

p. 176   "There is no such thing": ibid., 14.

p. 176   Nāgārjuna, dedication to *Mūlamadhyamakakārikā*, my transla-
            tion. B. K. Inada, *Nāgārjuna: A Translation of His Mūlamadhya-
            makakārikā* (Tokyo: Hokuseido, 1970) offers a pedantic transla-
            tion in a dual-language edition. For a more refreshing translation
            consider J. L. Garfield, *The Fundamental Wisdom of the Middle
            Way* (New York: Oxford University Press, 1995). The quotations
            in this chapter are from Garfield.

p. 177   T. W. Adorno's remark is from his 'Note on Kafka' in: *Prisms*
            trans. Samuel and Shierry Weber (Cambridge: MIT Press,
            1994), 246.

p. 178   See I. Kant, *Critique of Pure Reason*, trans. Norman Kemp Smith
            (New York: St. Martin's, 1965 [1929]). References are to either
            first or second edition (A and B, respectively) and then page
            numbers in the Kemp Smith translation.

p. 178   "Objects must conform to our knowledge": Bxvi (Kemp Smith
            22)

p. 178   "we can know *a priori* . . .' Bxviii (Kemp Smith 23).

p. 179   "I entitle transcendental all knowledge": B25 (Kemp Smith 59).

p. 179   Kant's distinction between "intuition" and "concept," see B74
            (Kemp Smith 94).

p. 179   "two pure forms of sensible intuition": B36 (Kemp Smith 67).

p. 179, n1 *"things in space and time* are given": B147 (Kemp Smith 162);
            "space and time are only forms": Bxxv (Kemp Smith 27).

p. 180   "pure concepts of human understanding": B91 (Kemp Smith
            103).

p. 180   "have no kind of application": B147–148 (Kemp Smith 162).

p. 181   For a discussion of the thing-in-itself as something aspatial see
            B308f (Kemp Smith 269f).

p. 181   "the object is to be taken": Bxxvii (Kemp Smith 28).

p. 181   "the greatest absurdity one could hit upon": Kant's letter to Herz,
            1772, quoted by S. Gardner, *Kant and the Critique of Pure Reason*
            (London: Routledge, 1999), 29.

p. 183   "pure apperception" and "transcendental unity": B132 (Kemp
            Smith 152).

p. 183   "It must be possible": B132 (Kemp Smith 152–153).

p. 184   "Without some empirical representation": B423 (Kemp Smith
            378).

p. 184, n4 "For otherwise I should have": B134 (Kemp Smith 154).

p. 185   "as something which actually exists . . .' B423 (Kemp Smith
            378).

p. 185   "I am conscious of myself": B157 (Kemp Smith 168).

p. 185   "we cannot even say": B404 (Kemp Smith 331).

p. 185   "We can assign no other basis": B404 (Kemp Smith 331).

p. 186   For Adorno's description of Kafka's writings as having served as "an information bureau": see T. W. Adorno, "Notes on Kafka," in Harold Bloom, ed., *Franz Kafka* (New York: Chelsea House, 1986), 95.

p. 187   "Don't misunderstand me": F. Kafka, *The Trial*, trans. Willa and Edwin Muir (New York: Schocken, 1992), 217.

p. 189   The references in this chapter to Maurice Blanchot are mainly to two articles in his book, M. Blanchot, *The Work of Fire*, trans. C. Mandell (Stanford: Stanford University Press, 1995). See "Reading Kafka," 1–11, and "Kafka and Literature," 12–26.

p. 191   "uncommonly manifold" and "can be put to the test": Kafka, *Blue Octavo*, 55.

p. 192   "But when shall we ever be done with": F. Nietzsche, *The Gay Science*, trans. Walter Kaufman (New York: Vintage, 1974), para. 109, 168–169.

p. 193   "you . . . [are] condemned not only in innocence": Kafka, *The Trial*, 50.

p. 193   "The court wants nothing from you": ibid., 222.

p. 193   "old dog's eared volumes": ibid., 51.

p. 193   For Kant's critical remarks on the *aqedah*, see I. Kant, *The Conflict of the Faculties*, trans. Mary J. Gregor (New York: Arabis, 1979), 115.

p. 194   "We can use": Kant, ibid.

p. 195   For Kafka's reflections on the 'aqedah see F. Kafka, *Parables and Paradoxes* (New York: Schocken, 1961), 41ff, *Blue Octavo*, 55f.

p. 196   "The Cruelty of death": Kafka, *Blue Octavo*, 53.; "The lamentation around the deathbed": ibid.; "Our salvation is death": ibid.

p. 197   "The transient world is not adequate": ibid., 55.

p. 198   "from which faith but not the pursuit of faith": M. Blanchot, "Reading Kafka" in *The Sirens' Song* (Sussex: Harvester, 1982), 25.

p. 198   "The cause of this is that there are fundamental rules": B353–354 (Kemp Smith 299).

p. 199   F. Kafka, "The Burrow," trans. Willa and Edwin Muir in *The Complete Short Stories of Franz Kafka* (London: Minerva, 1992), 325–359.

p. 199   "Poor homeless wanderers in the roads and woods": ibid., 327.

p. 199   "The Burrow has probably protected me": ibid., 335.

p. 200   "I seek out a good hiding place": ibid., 334.

p. 200   "No, I do not watch over my own sleep": ibid., 335.

p. 201   "And it is not only by external enemies": ibid., 326.

p. 201   "But all remained unchanged": ibid., 359.

p. 202   "longing for a prophesized day": F. Kafka, "The City Coat of Arms," trans. Willa and Edwin Muir in *The Complete Short Stories of Franz Kafka* (London: Minerva, 1992), 433–434.

p. 203   "The observer of the soul": Kafka, *Blue Octavo*, 30.

p. 205   "When this exists, that comes to be": *Majjhima Nikāya* 115.11, trans. B. Nānamoli and B. Bodhi (Boston: Wisdom,1995), 927.

p. 209   "Emptiness is the relinquishing of all views": Nāgārjuna: *Mūlamadhyamakakārikā*, Garfield 36.

p. 210   "it is increasingly recognized": M. Siderits, "Causation and Emptiness in Early Madhyamaka," *Journal of Indian Philosophy* 32:395 2004.

p. 211   For reading Nāgārjuna as an "anti-ontologist," see, e.g., R. King, "Śunyatā and Ajāti: Absolutism and the Philosophies of Nāgārjuna and Gaudapāda', *Journal of Indian Philosophy* 17(4): 385–405 1989. See also D. F. Burton, *Emptiness Appraised: A Critical Study of Nāgārjuna's Philosophy* (London: Curzon, 1999). For a linguistic interpretation of Nāgārjuna's view, see P. M. Williams, "Some Aspects of Language and Construction in the Madhyamaka," *Journal of Indian Philosophy*, 8(1): 1–46 1980.

p. 211   Robinson was the first of Nāgārjuna's modern interpreters that considered his philosophy as an attempt to execute a complete conceptual annihilation. See R. H. Robinson, "Some Logical Aspects of Nāgārjuna's System," *Philosophy East and West* 6:291–308 1957.

p. 212   For Mahākaccāna's words, see *Majjhima Nikāya* 1.111 202–204.

p. 212   For Nāgārjuna's attack on the notion of *ātman*, see his *Mūlamadhyamakakārikā*, chapter 18.

p. 213, n13 See D. Hume, *A Treatise of Human Nature*, book 1, part 4, chapter 2, ed. L. A. Selby-Bigge (Oxford: Clarendon, 1951), 191.

p. 214   For Nāgārjuna's discussion on the difference between seeing and the seer, see his *Mūlamadhyamakakārikā*, chapter 3.

p. 216   "let him deceive me as much as he can": R. Descartes, *Meditations II*, trans. John Cottingham (Cambridge: Cambridge University Press, 1986), 17.

p. 217   "There is a goal": Kafka, *Blue Octavo*, 23.

p. 217   "If I would make any proposition whatever": K. Bhattacharya, trans., *The Dialectical Method of Nāgārjuna: Vigrahavyāvartanī*

([Sanskrit and English translation] Delhi: Motilal Banarsidass, 1978), proposition 29, 113.

p. 218   For the simile of the imaginary person preventing someone from falling in love with an imaginary woman, see Nāgārjuna, ibid., proposition 27.

p. 219, n15   See B. K. Matilal, *Epistemology, Logic, and Grammar in Indian Philosophical Analysis* (New Delhi: Oxford University Press, 2005 [1971]), chapter 5.

p. 220   "Whatever comes into being dependent on other": Nāgārjuna, *Mūlamadhyamakakārikā*, 18:10, Garfield 49.

p. 222   "It is by showing that any given proposition": M. Siderits, *Personal Identity and Buddhist Philosophy: Empty Persons* (Aldershot: Ashgate, 2003), 187.

p. 222   For the various translations of *prapañca* see J. L. Garfield, trans., *The Fundamental Wisdom of the Middle Way: Nāgārjuna's Mūlamadhyamakakārikā* (New York: Oxford University Press, 1995), 3; K. K. Inada, trans., *Nāgārjuna: A Translation of His Mūlamadhyamakakārikā* (Tokyo: Hokuseido, 1970), 180; B. K. Matilal, *Perception: An Essay on Classical Indian Theories of Knowledge* (Oxford: Clarendon, 1986), 309; D. Burton, *Buddhism, Knowledge and Liberation: A Philosophical Study* (Aldershot: Ashgate, 2004), 80; D. Lusthaus, *Buddhist Phenomenology* (London: RoutledgeCurzon, 2002), 204.

p. 223   "we have already established in detail": Bhattacharya, *The Dialectical Method of Nāgārjuna: Vigrahavyāvartanī*; proposition 59, 129.

p. 224   For Matilal's explanation of *prapañca*, see B. K. Matilal, *Perception: An Essay on Classical Indian Theories of Knowledge* (Oxford: Clarendon, 1986), 309ff.

p. 225   "things like a cart, a pot, a cloth, etc.": Bhattacharya, *The Dialectical Method of Nāgārjuna—Vigrahavyāvartanī*, proposition 22, 108.

p. 225   "If dependent arising is denied": Nāgārjuna's *Mūlamadhyamakakārikā*, 24:36–37, Garfield, 72.

p. 226   "there is a reality that is not conceptually constructed": See M. Siderits, "Causation and Emptiness in Early Madhyamaka", 396.

p. 226   "our conventions and our conceptual framework.": J. L. Garfield, *Empty Words: Buddhist Philosophy and Cross-Cultural Interpretation* (New York: Oxford University Press, 2002), 25.

p. 227   'Whatever is dependently co-arisen": Nāgārjuna's *Mūlamadhyamakakārikā*, 24:18, Garfield, 69.

p. 228   "No Dharma was taught": ibid., 25:24, Garfield, 76 (with minor alterations). See also ibid., 18:12.

p. 231   "K. now perceived clearly that he was supposed": Kafka, *The Trial*, 228.

p. 231   "lean abruptly far forward": ibid.

p. 233   "The idea of the impersonal": Blanchot, *The Work of Fire*, 22.

p. 234   H. Melville, "Bartleby, The Scrivener" in *Billy Budd, Sailor and Selected Tales* (Oxford: Oxford University Press, 1997), 4–41.

p. 235   "His dinner is ready": ibid., 40.

p. 236   "The attorney would be relieved": G. Deleuze, "Bartleby; or, The Formula" in *Essays Critical and Clinical*, trans. D. W. Smith and M. A. Greco (Minneapolis: University of Minnesota Press, 1997), 70–71, 73–74.

p. 239   "Bartleby had been a subordinate clerk": Melville, "Bartleby, The Scrivener." 41.

5. *"It's All in the Mind"*

p. 241   G. Orwell, *Nineteen Eighty-Four* (London: Penguin, 1989 (1949); "You preferred to be a lunatic": ibid., 261.

p. 243   In this chapter I refer to Berkeley's two major works: *A Treatise Concerning the Principles of Human Knowledge* and *Three Dialogues Between Hylas and Philonous*. See Berkeley, *Philosophical Works*, with introduction and notes by M. R. Ayers (London: Dent, 1975). Following the norm, references to *Principles* is by means of section number, while the references *Dialogues* is by means of page number in the Luce and Jessop edition (*Complete Works of George Berkeley*, ed. A. A. Luce and T. E. Jessop). I also supply page numbers to the Ayers edition.

p. 243   "It were to be wish'd": the letter was published in *Gentleman's Magazine* 22:13. Quoted from M. A. Box, *The Suasive Art of David Hume* (Princeton: Princeton University Press, 1990), 34–35.

p. 243   "as one who maintained the most extravagant opinion": *Dialogues I* 172 (Ayers, 136).

p. 244   On Locke's representational realism see J. Locke, *An Essay Concerning Human Understanding*, ed. Peter H. Nidditch (Oxford: Clarendon, 1975), 4.2.1, 4.4.3. See also J. Bennett, *Learning from Six Philosophers: Descartes, Spinoza, Leibniz, Locke, Berkeley, Hume* (Oxford: Clarendon, 2001), 2:9ff.

p. 245   "I am not for changing things into ideas": *Dialogues III* 244 (Ayers, 193).

p. 245   "It is indeed an opinion strangely prevailing amongst men": *Principles* §4 (Ayers, 78).

p. 246   "and we have gained our point": *Principles* §8 (Ayers, 78).

p. 246   "if there were external bodies, it is impossible": *Principles* §20 (Ayers, 83).

p. 247   "It is your opinion": *Dialogues III* 246 (Ayers, 194).

p. 247   "An idea can be like nothing but an idea": *Principles* §8 (Ayers, 79).

p. 248   "It is absolutely impossible, and a plain contradiction": *Dialogues III* 244 (Ayers, 193).

p. 248   "[The ideas] cannot exist otherwise than in a mind perceiving them": *Principles* §3 (Ayers, 77).

p. 249   "look into [their] own thoughts": *Principles* §22 (Ayers, 83).

p. 249   "Ask the first man you meet": *Dialogues III* 234 (Ayers, 185).

p. 250   "Ask the gardener, why he thinks": ibid.

p. 250   "But, say you, surely there is nothing easier": *Principles* §23 (Ayers, 83).

p. 251   "[The ideas] are altogether passive and inert": *Dialogues III* 231 (Ayers, 183).

p. 252   "That ideas should exist in what doth not perceive": *Dialogues III* 233 (Ayers, 184).

p. 252   "It is granted we have neither an immediate evidence": *Dialogues III* 233 (Ayers, 184–185).

p. 253   "since I know myself not to be their author": *Dialogues II* 214 (Ayers, 170). See also *Principles* §29.

p. 253   "sensible things cannot exist otherwise than in a mind or spirit": *Dialogues II* 214 (Ayers, 168).

p. 254   "When I deny sensible things an existence": *Dialogues III* 230–231 (Ayers, 183).

p. 255, n3   C. Ram-Prasad, *Advaita Epistemology and Metaphysics* (London: RoutledgeCurzon, 2002), 39; J. L. Garfield, *Empty Words: Buddhist Philosophy and Cross-Cultural Interpretation* (New York: Oxford University Press, 2002), esp. chapter 8.

p. 255   A comprehensive summary of how scholars tackle the problem of Vasubandhu's identity can be found in S. Kaplan, "The Yogācāra Roots of Advaita Idealism? Noting a Similarity Between Vasubandhu and Gaudapāda," *Journal of Indian Philosophy* 20(2): 191–218 1992.

p. 256   Vasubandhu's tripartite division of consciousness is explained in his *Trisvabhāvakārikā*. For an annotated translation with the original Sanskrit see F. Tola and C. Dragonetti "The Trisvabhāvakārikā of Vasubandhu", *Journal of Indian Philosophy* 11(3): 225–266 1983.

p. 258   A characteristic example of an ontological interpretation to Vasubandhu's idealism is to be found in Paul Grifitths' *On Being Mindless: Buddhist Meditation and the Mind-Body Problem* (La Salle: Open Court, 1986).

p. 259   Prominent among those who suggested that Vasubandhu's philosophy is caught up in a net of internal contradictions is T. E. Wood in his book *Mind Only: A Philosophical and Doctrinal Analysis of the Vijñānavāda* (Honolulu: University of Hawaii Press, 1991). Matilal observed the "psychotic" element (hallucinations, delusions, and dreams—but not illusions) in Vasubandhu's examples. See B. K. Matilal, "A Critique of Buddhist Idealism" in L. Cousins et al., eds., *Buddhist Studies in Honour of I. B. Horner* (Dordrecht: Reidel, 1974), 139–169. Vasubandhu's epistemological arguments quoted in the following are drawn mostly from his short work (text and commentary) *Viṃśatikā Kārikā*. His exemplification by means of an ophthalmic disorder can be found in verses 1–4. Wood, *Mind Only*, 97–102.

p. 262   Wendy Doniger's views on ontology in India can be found in W. Doniger O'Flaherty, *Dreams Illusion and Other Realities* (Chicago: University of Chicago Press), 1984, 4ff.

p. 262, n8 "The ideas formed by the imagination:" *Dialogues III* 225–226 (Ayers, 178).

p. 264   For Vasubandhu's refutation of the exteriority of perceived objects see *Viṃśatikā Kārikā*, verses 16–17, Wood, *Mind Only*, 100.

p. 265, n9 See Vasubandhu's *Triṃsika* in Wood, *Mind Only*, 49–60 (Sanskrit and English translation). For Waldron's view see, W. S. Waldron, "How Innovative is the *ālayavijñāna?*, *Journal of Indian Philosophy*, 23(1): 32 1995. For Griffiths' remark, see P. Griffiths, *On Being Mindless: Buddhist Meditation and the Mind-Body Problem* (La Salle: Open Court, 1986), 93.

p. 266   Vasubandhu's arguments here and in the following pages refer to *Viṃśatikā Kārikā*, verses 18ff.

p. 270   See B. K. Matilal, "A Critique of Buddhist Idealism," 142.

p. 275   See Candrakīrti, *Madhyamakāvatāra*, trans. Robert F. Olson in his article, R. F. Olson, "Candrakirtī's Critique of Vijñānavada," *Philosophy East and West* 24:406 1974.

p. 275, n14 M. F. Burnyeat, "Idealism and Greek Philosophy: What Descartes Saw and Berkeley Missed" in G. Vesey, ed., *Idealism Past and Present* (Cambridge: Cambridge University Press, 1982), 19–50.

p. 278 In his *Principles of Human Knowledge* (§4–5) Berkeley demonstrates the connection between a belief in external objects and the doctrine of abstract ideas. In the introduction to the *Principles* (§6) he disparages the influence of this doctrine on the mind.

p. 278 "the plainest things in the world": *Principles* §97 (Ayers, 106). For Locke on abstract ideas see *An Essay Concerning Human Understanding* 3.3.6–7 and 2.11.

p. 278 For Berkeley's distinction between general and abstract ideas, see *Principles*, introduction §12.

p. 278, n15 See Bennett, *Learning from Six Philosophers*.

p. 279 "to abstract from one another": *Principles*, introduction §10 (Ayers, 68).

p. 279 "it is simpler to 'divide a thing from itself'": ibid., §5 (Ayers, 78)

p. 279 "[T]he mind, by leaving out of the particular colours": ibid., introduction, §8 (Ayers, 67).

p. 279 "the general idea of a triangle": ibid., introduction §14 (Ayers, 71). On the notion of an "abstract" idea of triangle, see ibid., introduction §13.

p. 279 "extends only to the conceiving": ibid., §5 (Ayers, 78).

p. 280 "innocent diversion and amusement": ibid., introduction §17 (Ayers, 72).

p. 280 "generality of men which are simple and illiterate": ibid., §17 (Ayers, 72).

p. 280 "a word becomes general by being made the sign": ibid., §11 (Ayers, 69).

p. 281 D. H. Lawrence, "The Future of the Novel" (1923) in *Selected Critical Writings* (Oxford: Oxford University Press, 1998), 145.

p. 282 "words to no manner or purpose": *Dialogues II* 223 (Ayers, 177). See also M. Atherton, "Berkeley's Anti-abstractionism" in E. Sosa, ed., *Essays on the Philosophy of George Berkeley* (Leiden: Reidel, 1987), 45–60.

p. 283 "If by *ideas* you mean immediate objects": *Dialogues III* 250–251 (Ayers, 198).

p. 284 "we first raised a dust": Berkeley, *Principles*, introduction §3 (Ayers, 66).

p. 285, n16 R. Rorty, "The Last Intellectual in Europe: Orwell on Cruelty" in *Contingency, Irony, and Solidarity* (Cambridge: Cambridge University Press, 1989), 169–188.

p. 288   "They can make you say anything": Orwell, *Nineteen Eighty-four*, 174.

p. 289   "Truisms are true, hold on to that!": ibid., 84.

p. 291   "The worst thing in the world": ibid., 296.

p. 291   "Have you ever seen a rat": ibid., 299.

p. 291   "There was one and only one way": ibid., 299–300.

p. 292   "what happens to you here is for ever": ibid., 268.

p. 292   "He gazed up at the enormous face": ibid., 311.

p. 293   "it was as if the shame of it": F. Kafka, *The Trial*, trans. Willa and Edwin Muir (New York: Schocken, 1992), 229.

p. 293   "It is but looking . . . I shall readily give up the cause": *Principles* §22 (Ayers, 83).

p. 296   "who have enough reason": R. Descartes, *Discourse on the Method II*, trans. Robert Stoothoff, in J. Cottingham et al., eds., *The Philosophical Writings of Descartes* (Cambridge: Cambridge University Press, 1985), 1:118.

p. 300   "The lamentation around the deathbed": F. Kafka, *The Blue Octavo Notebooks*, trans. E. Keiser and Eithne Wilkins (Cambridge: Exact Change, 1991), 53.

p. 301   "But this double character of our inner being": A. Schopenhauer, *The World as Will and Representation*, trans. E. F. J. Payne (New York: Dover, 1969), 1:278n.

p. 304   For the problem of self-knowledge in Buddhism see, e.g., Yao, Zhihua, *The Buddhist Theory of Self Cognition* (London: Routledge, 2005), p. 121ff; B.K. Matilal, *Perception: An Essay on Classical Indian Theories of Knowledge* (Oxford: Clarendon, 1986), 141–179.

p. 308   "By a grace of sense": T. S. Eliot, *Four Quartets* (London: Faber and Faber, 1948), 16.

INDEX

Abel, 30–36, 55, 57, 84
abhidharma, 318, 321
Abraham, 34, 37–38, 93, 105, 193–97, 231
abstract ideas, 277–85, 326
absurd, 181, 194–95, 215, 237, 263, 275
Adam, 31, 65, 81–82, 84–85, 95, 104, 112–13, 251
Adorno, Th., 177, 186–87
Advaita, 145, 318
After Babel (Steiner), 111
Agni, 63
Agnon, S. Y., 59, 237
akedah, 193–97, 231
ālayavijñāna, 324–25
Alice in Wonderland (Carrol), 216, 267, 285, 323
Amit, Y., 25
An Area of Darkness (Naipaul), 5
And the Ship Sails on (Fellini), 310–11
antirealism, 210, 222, 226, 257, 273, 310
Antistheses, 79

anxiety, 111, 114–17, 136, 140, 148, 150, 320, 322
Aquinas, T., 126
Archimedean point, 123–24, 139, 150, 175, 219, 289
Archimedes, 123
Aristotle, 21–23, 36, 41, 73, 79–80, 124, 126, 190, 211, 222, 326
arithmetic, 19, 222, 289
Assmann, J., 42
atheism, 54, 283
ātman, 60–61, 142–45, 147–55, 157, 159, 161–64, 167–69, 176, 204, 212–13, 301, 320, 322, 324; *see also* self, selfhood
aufhebung, 189
Augustine, 23, 49, 82–83, 92–96, 129–32, 159, 161
aum, 98
autpattika, 101
avidyā; *see* ignorance

Babel, 102–4, 107–14, 117–18, 190, 199, 201–2, 232, 318; *see also* tower of Babel

Babylon, *see* Babel
Bartleby the Scrivener (Melville),
    234–40, 292–93, 323
Beethoven, L., 93
Benjamin, W., 112–13, 116
Bennett, J., 125, 326
Bergman, I., 309–11
Berkeley, G., 182, 241, 243–55, 263–
    69, 274–86, 288, 290, 293–94,
    310, 323–26
bhakti, 52, 314
Bhartṛhari, 101
Bible, 9, 25, 28, 30–34, 36–38,
    41–45, 65–66, 81–84, 90, 96,
    102–18, 190, 193–94
Blanchot, M., 189, 192, 196, 198,
    233–34
Boswell, J., 276
Brāhamaṇas, 316
Brahmā, 64
brahman, 52, 60–61, 68, 142, 145,
    315
Brahmanism, 53, 62
Bṛhadāraṇyaka Upaniṣad, 60, 143,
    145, 151, 160
Buber, M., 52
Buddha, 53, 176–77, 204–9, 211–12,
    220, 223–24, 227–28, 230, 238,
    240, 272, 296, 321–22
Buddhism, 53–54, 62, 64–65, 100,
    102, 141, 164, 176–77, 204–34,
    238–40, 254–77, 285, 294–300,
    304, 321–26
Burnyeat, M., 326
Burton, D. F., 222

Cain, 30–36, 55, 57, 84
Calasso, R., 32
Camus, A., 237
Candrakīrti, 275
categories (Kant's), 180–81, 184–85

certainty, 86–87, 121–26, 131–35,
    137–40, 150, 156–57, 159, 164,
    175, 199–200, 218–19, 229, 289,
    319–20
Chaplin, C., 196, 286
Christianity 3, 23–24, 28, 30, 35, 49,
    53, 67, 76, 93, 129, 192, 323; *see
    also* religions, Western
Cittamātra, 255, 265
clarity and distinctness 121, 123, 133–
    35, 137, 168, 212, 216, 319–20
Coburn, T., 91
cogito, *see* I-think
Cohen, Meir Simcha of Dvinsk,
    33–34
common sense, 41, 206, 208, 244–
    45, 249, 263, 266–67, 275–76,
    281, 295–96
Conditioned (*paratantra*), 256–57,
    298–301, 307
Confessions (Augustine), 82, 92
Conrad, J., 127
consciousness, 47, 138, 159, 161,
    183–85, 191, 198, 212, 230, 237,
    255–58, 265–66, 272–73, 286,
    290, 294, 298–300, 305, 307–8,
    324–25
conventions, 100, 119, 124, 137,
    139, 169, 172–73, 210, 219,
    225–28, 234, 238, 267, 275–76,
    295–96, 322–23
Copernican revolution, 178, 181,
    203, 228, 230, 301
Copernicus, 120, 178
Coppola, F. F., 321
cosmology, 41, 58, 70–71, 73, 85, 87,
    144, 317
creation, 17, 30, 35, 36, 39, 41–42,
    47, 50, 58–60, 69–70, 83–85, 87,
    93, 102–4, 111–12, 116, 143–44,
    149–50, 167, 314

Da Ponte, L., 165, 170
deism, 39
Deleuze, G., 236–37
delusion, 203, 224, 229–30, 260–
    61, 266, 270, 294, 296, 299–
    300
demon (Descartes), 123, 139,
    150–51, 218–19, 274
dependent arising, 176–77, 205, 220,
    222, 225, 227–28
Derrida, J., 89, 108–14, 139, 228
Descartes, R., 35, 49, 119–27,
    129–41, 146–47, 150–51, 156–59,
    161–62, 164, 167–70, 173, 175,
    188, 203, 216, 218–19, 229, 242,
    244, 261–63, 274, 289, 296–97,
    319, 320
desire, 20, 22, 33–34, 84, 89, 111,
    147–49, 153, 166–69, 171–74,
    218, 232, 290, 298, 308, 318, 326
Dharma, 63–66, 227–28, 230, 317
dharmas, 210, 227, 321
Dignāga, 306
Discourse on the Method (Descartes),
    119, 124
Divodāsa, 63–66
Don Giovanni (Mozart), 165–74
Doniger, W., 71, 261
doubt, doubting, 84, 121–26, 132,
    135, 137–39, 141, 151, 156, 207,
    214, 229, 231, 244, 262–63, 284
Douglas, M., 38
dreams, 71, 78, 109, 122–23, 152,
    157–60, 162–64, 167, 202, 213,
    229, 261–63, 266, 268, 304, 317,
    324
Dumont, L., 129, 141

Ecclesiastes, 74, 110, 297
Eckhart, J. (Meister Eckhart), 45
Elijah, 37

Eliot, T.S., 75, 308
emptiness, 173, 177, 183, 188, 196–
    204, 209–11, 214, 216–32, 237,
    274, 293, 298, 301–5, 307, 322
Empty Persons (Siderits), 318
Enoch, 37
epistemology, 18, 35–36, 51, 56,
    80–81, 91, 123, 131, 133, 135,
    138, 152, 156, 180, 183, 188, 194,
    197, 239, 246, 248, 261, 264, 266,
    269, 273–74, 277, 283–84, 297,
    322, 325; see also knowledge
Esperanto, 112
Ethics (Spinoza), 50
Eve, 31, 65
excluded middle, see law of excluded
    middle
exteriority, 18, 22, 24–25, 27, 32,
    36, 38, 40–42, 44, 46–48, 71–72,
    74–77, 81, 84–85, 96, 102, 118,
    179, 182, 198, 202, 204, 208, 214,
    229–30, 242–43, 261–63, 267–68,
    272–73, 275–77, 282–84, 286–88,
    290, 292, 294, 314, 319

Fear and Trembling (Kierkegaard),
    193
Fellini, F., 310–11
Ferry, A., 128
fiction, 72, 123, 150–51, 218–19,
    225–28, 234, 272–74, 285, 289,
    292, 294, 320, 322
Forms (Platonic), 18–23, 36, 73,
    75–77, 80, 127, 130, 182, 289,
    313–14, 319
Four Quartets (Eliot), 75, 308
Frankfurt, H., 137
Freud, S., 162, 170, 176, 202, 307,
    325

Galileo, G., 120

Garfield, G. L., 222, 226, 323
Garuda, 64
Gay Science (Nietzsche), 192
Genesis, 103, 106
geometry, 19, 123, 289
Gnosticism, 49
God (in Western religions), 13–15,
  17, 21–54, 56, 59, 65–70, 72,
  76, 80–81, 83–84, 87, 90, 92–93,
  97, 103–10, 113, 116–17, 127,
  129–36, 138, 147, 159, 169, 174,
  181–82, 187, 192–94, 220–21,
  228, 238, 242, 253–54, 265–66,
  269, 274, 283, 286, 314–15, 317,
  319, 321, 325
gods (in Indian religions), 16–18,
  52–72, 94–99, 108, 142, 150,
  158–60, 315–16, 318
Golden Calf, 43–45, 63, 68
grammar, 87, 96, 101
Griffiths, P., 325
Gruenwald, I., 29

halacha, 14
hallucination, 224, 266, 269–70, 272,
  274, 296–97
Hasidism, 45, 51–52
Heart of Darkness (Conrad), 127,
  298
Hegel, G. W. F., 83, 126, 189
Heine, H., 23–24, 314
hell, 25, 171–72, 270–74, 281, 285,
  289–90, 292, 294, 326
Heller, E., 209
henotheism, 28
heresy, 36, 42
Hesiod, 317
Hinduism, 53–54, 62, 67, 88
history, 72–74, 287
holiness, 27–28, 47
Hume, D., 321–22

Ibn Ezra, A., 93–94
Ibsen, H., 151
idealism, 101, 243, 245–46, 249,
  255, 258, 262, 266–67, 272,
  275–77, 281, 283–86, 294, 324,
  326–27; see also immaterialism
ideas, 7, 18, 78–80, 100, 134–35,
  137, 165–67, 168, 180–82, 186,
  243–54, 258, 265–66, 269, 271,
  275, 277–88, 293, 313, 320, 324,
  326; see also abstract ideas
idolatry, 41–45, 68, 314
ignorance, 115, 193, 224, 295–98,
  327
illusion, 89, 145, 198, 200, 218, 244,
  259–61, 300
imagined (kalpita), 256–57, 298–300,
  307
immanence, 18, 25, 47–52, 67,
  69–71, 73, 102, 131, 173–74, 179,
  204, 229, 315
immaterialism (Berkeley), 243, 246,
  249, 255, 282; see also idealism
immortality, 56–58, 315
In the Penal Colony (Kafka), 192
Inada, B. K., 222
Individual, 40, 59, 77, 107, 126,
  128–29, 132, 139–41, 156, 161,
  166, 174, 204, 265, 286, 291,
  315
Indra, 63
insanity, 122, 138–40, 261, 274, 290,
  297, 323
interiority, inwardness, 18, 22, 27,
  36, 40, 46–49, 58, 61, 70–71,
  76–78, 81, 84, 96–97, 102, 114,
  124, 127, 129–31, 133, 135, 139,
  148–49, 158, 168, 172–73, 191,
  198–200, 202, 204, 207, 219,
  229–30, 239, 242–43, 251–52,
  256, 258, 262–63, 276, 282, 284–

86, 288–89, 291–94, 297–304,
    306–9, 315–16, 319, 324
internalization, 46, 59, 98–99, 129,
    134, 136, 142–43, 154, 158, 161,
    163, 168, 173, 282, 290, 316,
    327
intrinsic nature (*svabhāva*), 210, 219,
    223, 225, 227, 322
introspection 22, 46, 77, 123, 125,
    163–64, 173, 249, 253, 293–94,
    299, 307–8; *see also* self
inwardness, *see* interiority
Isaac, 193, 195
Isaiah, 25, 47
Islam, 24, 35, 53, 93; *see also* religions, Western
I-think, 124, 126–27, 131–35, 137–40, 150, 157, 159, 164, 167–70,
    173–75, 183–85, 188, 198, 289

Jacob, 109
Jaivali Pravāhaṇa, 142
Janaka, 151, 153, 156, 162–63
Job, 25, 39–40, 169, 174, 238–39
Johnson, S., 276
Judaism, 23–24, 26, 28, 29, 35,
    43–44, 93; *see also* religions,
    Western
Julius Caesar (Shakespeare), 241
justice, 33, 38–39, 270

Kabbalah, 45, 48, 50–51, 113
Kafka, F., 36, 65, 76, 117–18,
    175–78, 186–203, 209, 217, 222,
    227–34, 237, 242, 290, 293, 300,
    321, 326
Kant, I., 175, 177–86, 188, 192–99,
    202–3, 224, 228–30, 239, 242,
    263, 277, 285, 288, 297, 301, 303,
    314, 321
karma, 270, 326

Kierekegaard, S. 165–67, 169, 172,
    186, 193–95
King, R., 321
knowledge, 7, 14–5, 17–20, 22, 25,
    42, 45, 54, 60–61, 79–80, 83, 85,
    111, 121, 124–25, 130, 133, 135,
    137, 142–43, 146, 148, 152–53,
    157, 163–64, 168, 170, 173,
    178–83, 185–86, 191–92, 196,
    198, 203, 205, 210, 212, 215,
    222, 229, 239, 243–44, 246–47,
    252, 261, 264, 274, 278, 295–96,
    301–2, 306–8, 313–14, 316, 320,
    322; *see also* self-knowledge
Koheleth Rabbah, 111
Kṛṣṇa, 52

language, 42, 58, 75, 78–87, 89–92,
    94–110, 112–18, 164, 189–90,
    198, 211–12, 214–29, 233–34,
    236–38, 240, 246, 267, 280–85,
    294, 309, 311, 313, 318, 321, 323,
    327
law of excluded middle, 221–22
Lawrence, D.H., 281
Leviticus, 38
liberation, *see* mokṣa, nirvāṇa
linguistic turn, 83, 229, 322–23
Locke, J., 244–46, 251, 270, 277–78,
    280–81, 326
logos, 99
Lusthaus, D., 222

Madhyamaka, 208, 212, 276
madness, *see* insanity
magic, 30, 58, 64, 224, 319
Mahakāccāna, 211–12
Mahāyāna, 255, 270
Maimonides, M., 14–18, 297, 314,
    317
Mann, T., 237

mantra, 318–19
Marion, J-L., 49, 131
mathematics, 14, 86–87, 121, 123,
   180, 191, 209, 289–90, 319, 327
Matilal, B. T., 222, 224, 269–71,
   274, 322
matter, 243, 246, 248–50, 258–59
māyā, 320
Meditations on First Philosophy (Des-
   cartes), 124–25
Melville, H., 234, 236, 238, 292
Meno (Plato), 314, 319
Meshech Chochma (M. S. from
   Dvinsk), 33
metaphysics, 145, 180–81, 206, 209,
   221, 280, 315, 320
metapsychology, 164, 303–4, 308
midrash, 45, 105–6, 111
Mimamsa, 97–98, 100–1, 318
Mishneh Torah (Maimonides), 14
Mishra, K. N., 316
Mokṣa, 316, 327
Molière, 161
monotheism, 4, 16, 24, 26, 28–30,
   50, 67–70, 72, 75–77, 81, 135,
   177, 181, 314, 317
Montaigne, M., 161
Moses, 37–38, 43, 45, 90, 92, 317
Mosil, R., 237
Mozart, W. A. 165–74
Müller, M., 28
mysticism, mystical, 21, 45, 47–52,
   71, 113, 143, 210, 305, 314, 319

Nāgārjuna, 3, 100, 175–77, 189,
   204–5, 208–30, 232–34, 238,
   274–75, 281, 294–95, 301–2, 307,
   310–11, 321–23
Nagel, T., 158, 168
Naipul, V. S., 5–6
necessity, 17, 41, 76, 117–18, 125,

   139, 186, 194–95, 198, 213, 230,
   237, 243, 257, 270–71, 273, 280,
   285
negative theology, 176, 182, 220–21,
   314
Neher, A., 26
neoplatonism, 21, 25, 36, 48, 51, 53,
   95, 315
New Testament, 129
Nietzsche, F., 126, 192, 238
Nineteen Eighty Four (Orwell),
   241–43, 285–93, 326–27
Nirukta, 55
nirvāṇa, 3, 227–28, 321, 327
Noah's ark, 83–84, 311
noumenon, *see* thing-in-itself
Nyāya, 318

Oakeshott, M., 106–7
objectivity, 19, 21, 23, 27, 35, 38,
   40, 46–47, 73, 120–21, 131, 134,
   137–38, 145, 148, 151, 157, 159,
   164, 168, 173, 198, 207, 237, 241,
   272–73, 289–90, 303, 324
objects (of knowledge), 78–79, 81,
   101, 122, 127, 130, 132, 134–35,
   278–84, 186, 207, 210–11,
   224–25, 230, 244–47, 249, 251,
   255–59, 261, 263–64, 266–67,
   271, 276, 278–80, 282–84, 287,
   297–99, 305–7, 320, 323–24
Olivelle, P., 316
Only Yesterday (Agnon), 237
ontology, ontological, 3, 17–18, 23,
   28, 35–6, 42, 45, 48–49, 51–52,
   54, 58, 66–67, 71, 80–81, 84–85,
   91, 96, 130–31, 136–38, 149,
   151, 167, 207, 210–11, 215,
   218, 225–26, 258–60, 262, 264,
   273–74, 286–87, 298, 300, 315,
   318, 320, 325

orientalism, 4
orientation, 154–57, 159, 163, 296
Orwell, G., 214–42, 285–86, 288–90, 292–94, 298, 302, 326–27
other minds, 252–54, 264–65, 267–69

paganism, 23, 42
panfictionalism, 322
pantheism, 49, 51
paradox, 118, 137–38, 189–91, 230, 243
parapsychology, 266, 269, 272
Parmenides, 21
Pārvatī, 63
Pascal, B., 119, 135, 186
Paul, 25, 127–28
Peled, R., 318
Pensée (Pascal), 119
perfected (pariniṣpanna), 256–58, 298–300, 305, 307
permanence, 176, 204–7, 220, 222, 317, 321
Persona (Bergman), 309–10
Phaedrus (Plato), 89
Philo, 23
Philosophical Investigations (Wittgenstein), 82, 241
Plato, 18–23, 35–36, 49, 52–53, 69, 73, 75–77, 79–83, 89, 95, 120–21, 126–30, 132, 159, 181–82, 289, 314, 319, 326
Plotinus, 21, 53, 314–15
polytheism, 16, 67
postmodernism, 4, 60, 92, 186, 228
Prajāpati, 68
prajñā, 142
pramāṇas, 322
prapañca, see verbal expansion
prtītya-samutpāda, see dependent arising

psychologism, 132, 303
psychology, psychological, 17, 22, 44–46, 54, 71, 74, 77, 91, 131–32, 148–49, 163, 173, 212–14, 255, 258, 260, 270, 293, 302–3, 307, 314, 324–26
Purāṇas, 62–63
Puruṣa, 143–45, 149–52, 169, 320

Ram-Prasad, C., 324
rationality, 20, 55, 132, 139, 168
realism, 79–80, 100, 224, 226, 245–47, 251, 255–57, 261, 263–65, 274–76, 287–88, 294, 326
reason, 20, 36, 55, 124–25, 180, 198, 246
reasoning, 2, 10, 28–29, 55, 58–59, 97, 215, 224, 246, 258, 274, 296, 316
reducio ad absurdum, 215–17
reflection (Berkeley's), 252–53, 267, 293, 323
reflexivity, 22, 74, 130–31, 140, 146, 159, 161, 163–65, 168–70, 173, 244, 253, 264–65, 293, 301–2, 304–8, 319
relativism, 4, 92
religions, Western, 24, 26–30, 33, 35–36, 38, 40–42, 46–48, 72–73, 75, 77, 80, 93, 128–29, 181, 192
renunciation, 140–41, 204
representation, 44, 79, 99–101, 163, 179, 181, 183–86, 188–89, 198, 202, 211, 223, 225, 228, 244, 246–48, 257, 271, 273, 275, 282, 284, 287, 294, 297, 309, 320–21
revelation, 36–37, 43, 46–47, 76, 80–81, 169, 174, 194
Ṛg Veda, 16–18, 66, 94–95, 313, 316
Ricoeur, P., 41–42

rituals, 30, 38, 53, 55–60, 64, 87,
　94–99, 140–42, 150, 204, 286,
　313, 315–19; *see also* sacrifice
Rorschach test, 8
Rorty, R., 290, 326
Rudra, 95

Śabara, 97–98
śabda, 88
sacred, the, *see* holiness
sacrifice, 31–32, 55–57, 59, 64,
　94–98, 141, 150–51, 193–97, 231,
　315–16
sanctity, *see* holiness
Śaṅkara, 39–40, 145, 315, 320
Sanskrit, 90, 313, 319
Sarvāstivāda, 210, 212
Scholem, G., 50–51, 113
Schopenhauer, A., 301–2, 304–5,
　307–8, 327
scientific revolution, 120
scripture, 82, 87–89, 91–94, 128,
　131, 187
self nature, *see* intrinsic nature
self, selfhood, 22, 40, 61–62, 70,
　74, 77, 99, 100, 102, 119, 124,
　127–35, 138–43, 145–53, 157–65,
　167–68, 170, 172–73, 175–77,
　185, 188–89, 191, 194, 197, 200,
　202–8, 212–14, 216–19, 223,
　228–30, 237–39, 243–44, 252,
　275, 281, 284, 299, 301–2, 304–5,
　316, 319–21, 323–24
self-awareness, 46, 127, 132, 146–50,
　156, 158–59, 161, 163–64, 167,
　173, 198–99, 203, 213, 225,
　299–302, 304–11; *see also* self
　knowledge
self-consciousness (Kant), 183–85,
　191
self-existence, *see* intrinsic nature

self-knowledge, 18, 22, 61, 74, 124–
　25, 130, 146, 148, 164, 175–76,
　185, 199, 202–3, 301–2, 307–9;
　see also self awareness
Shakespeare, W., 161, 241, 301, 319
Siderits, M., 210, 222, 226–27, 318
Sifre Dvarim, 13
Śiva, 52, 62–66
skepticism, 194, 209, 218, 248, 263,
　282–83
sleep, 157, 159–64, 167, 191, 196,
　199–200, 202–3, 213, 229, 232,
　235, 238, 261, 304, 307
Socrates, 79, 129, 153, 156
space, 71, 119, 144, 154–55, 161–64,
　179–81, 191, 261–62, 304, 307,
　320–21
Spinoza, B., 49–50
Śrī, 64
Staal, F., 97, 318
Stalin, J., 242
Steiner, G., 33, 111–14, 116
Stock, B., 130–31
Stoics, 25, 49, 72
store consciousness, *see* ālayavijñāna
subject, 61, 68, 120–22, 124, 126–28,
　132, 138, 161, 163–64, 170, 172,
　174, 181, 183, 185, 188, 197–99,
　204, 207, 214, 218–19, 221,
　228–29, 238, 245–46, 257, 284,
　298–99, 301, 305, 307, 313, 320
subjectivity, 21, 23, 40, 46, 73, 77,
　121, 124, 128, 130–34, 137–38,
　140–41, 146–47, 151, 160–63,
　170, 172, 188, 203, 207, 210, 286,
　303
substance, 21, 23, 121, 124, 159,
　179, 183, 211–12, 214, 244, 248,
　250, 258, 283, 318
Sufism, 45
śūnya, see emptiness

Sūrya, 64
svabhāva, see intrinsic nature

tapas, 316
tarka, see reasoning
Tauber, Z., 314
Taylor, C., 127–32, 137, 163
telepathy, 266, 268–69, 274
The Burrow (Kafka), 199–202
The Conversation (Coppola), 321
The Great Wall of China (Kafka), 192,
    202
The Outsider (Camus), , 237
The Trial (Kafka), 76, 187, 193, 209,
    231, 293
Theogeny (Hesiod), 317
theology, 27, 47–49, 122, 176,
    182–83, 220–221, 314
theory of Forms, see Forms
thing-in-itself, 180–83, 185, 192,
    198, 321
time, 71, 162, 164, 179–81, 213–14,
    220, 261–62, 264, 304, 307–8,
    320–21
timira, 259
totalitarianism, 106, 242, 286
tower of Babel, 102–18, 190, 199,
    201–3, 232
tragedy, 32–34, 238
transcendence, 3, 14, 18–54, 56,
    58–59, 62, 65–69, 72–74, 76–77,
    81, 84–85, 87, 90, 92–93, 97, 99,
    102, 105, 108, 110, 113, 116–17,
    126–27, 129–31, 134–35, 137–38,
    140, 146–47, 151, 155–56,
    158–59, 162, 164, 168, 172–74,
    178–83, 192–93, 195–96, 198–99,
    201, 203, 224, 228–32, 237, 239,
    263, 270, 277, 281–82, 284–86,
    288, 290, 292, 294, 297, 302–3,
    308, 314, 317, 320

transcendental, 178–80, 183–86,
    188, 224
Treatise concerning the Principles of
    Human Knowledge (Berkeley), 243,
    278
Trotsky, L., 242
truth, 14–15, 17–20, 44, 49, 76–82,
    84, 86, 92, 100–2, 113, 120–21,
    123–24, 126, 128–31, 198, 206,
    217, 219, 222, 242–43, 247,
    272–74, 278, 283, 287–88, 295,
    304, 318
truth, correspondence theory of,
    78–84, 86, 96, 100–1, 112, 114,
    121, 132, 181, 191, 224, 226,
    246–48, 263–64, 268, 273, 287,
    309, 318

Upaniṣads, 9, 60–62, 68–70, 72,
    98, 119, 140–47, 149–51, 153,
    156–61, 163–65, 167–68, 173,
    176, 204–5, 212, 213, 229, 301,
    315, 316, 319–20, 322

Vāc, 94–99, 224
Vasubandhu, 3, 241, 254–77, 284–
    85, 289–90, 293–95, 297–301,
    303, 305–11, 323–26
Vayu, 63
Vedānta, 145, 316–18, 324
Vedas, 16–18, 55–59, 66, 87–88, 91,
    93–98, 100–1, 144–45 160, 224,
    313, 315–19
verbal expansion (prapañca), 176,
    220, 222–24, 226–29, 234, 238,
    285, 294
Vijñānvāda, 255
vijñāpti, 258, 261
Viṣṇu, 64, 66
voidness, see emptiness
Voltaire, 109

Westermann, K., 103
Williams, B., 166–67
Wittgenstein, L., 15, 82, 210, 241
Wood, T., 269–70, 314

Yājñavalkya, 144, 151–153, 155–63, 167, 173–74, 176, 202, 296, 304, 307–8

Yākṣa, 55
Yesod Mora (Ibn Ezra), 93
yoga, 3, 255
Yogācāra, 255–256, 275, 276, 296, 298, 306, 324–325

Zamenhof, L. L., 112